Student Solutions Manual

# BUSINESS STATISTICS: A FIRST COURSE

# Student Solutions Manual

# BUSINESS STATISTICS: A FIRST COURSE

*Fourth Edition*

David M. Levine
Timothy C. Krehbiel
Mark. L Berenson

Pin T. Ng
*Northern Arizona University*

PEARSON
Prentice Hall

Upper Saddle River, New Jersey 07458

**VP/Editorial Director:** Jeff Shelstad
**Executive Editor:** Mark Pfaltzgraff
**Supplement Coordinator:** Kathryn Madara
**Senior Editorial Assistant:** Jane Avery
**Manufacturing Manager:** Vincent Scelta
**Production Editor & Buyer:** Carol O'Rourke
**Printer/Binder:** Courier, Bookmart Press

---



PEARSON
Prentice Hall

10 9 8 7 6 5 4 3 2 1
ISBN 0-13-185173-X

# Table of Contents

# Preface

The ***Study Guide and Student's Solutions Manual*** consists of three major sections. The ***Objective*** section summarizes what is expected of a student after reading a chapter. The ***Overview and Key Concepts*** section provides an overview of the major topics covered in a chapter and lists the important key concepts. The overview and listing of the key concepts are meant not to replace but to supplement the textbook and to reinforce understanding. The ***Solutions to End of Section and Chapter Review Even Problems*** section provides extra detail in the problem solutions.

# CHAPTER 1

## OBJECTIVES

- To understand how statistics can be used in business
- To be able to identify sources of data
- To learn the different types of data used in business

## OVERVIEW AND KEY CONCEPTS

### The Growth and Development of Modern Statistics

Needs of government to collect data on its citizens

⇩

The development of the mathematics of probability theory

⇩

The advent of the computer

### Key Definitions

- **Population (universe):** The whole collection of things under consideration, e.g., all the students enrolled at a university.
- **Sample:** A portion of the population selected for analysis, e.g., all the freshmen at a university.
- **Parameter:** A summary measure computed to describe a characteristic of the population, e.g., the population average weight of all the students enrolled at a university.
- **Statistic:** A summary measure computed to describe a characteristic of the sample, e.g., the average weight of sample of freshmen at a university.

### Relationship between Population and Sample

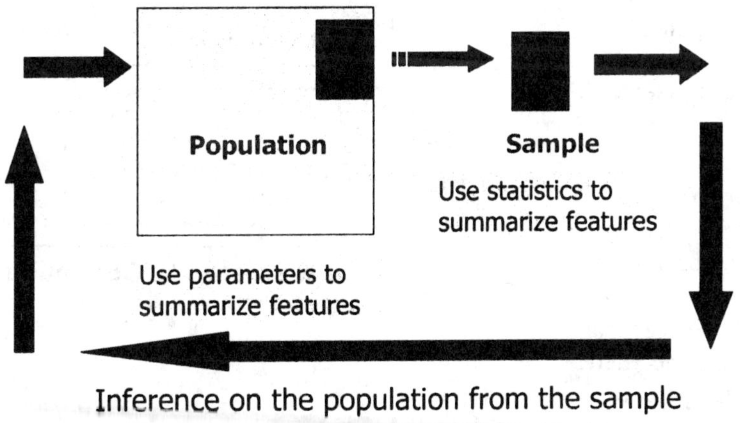

## The Difference between Descriptive Statistics and Inferential Statistics

- **Descriptive statistics:** Deal with collecting, presenting, summarizing, and analyzing data.
- **Inferential statistics:** Deal with drawing conclusions and/or making decisions concerning a population based only on sample data.

## The Primary Goal of the Text

To understand how the methods of statistics can be used in decision-making process. This understanding includes the following objectives:

- To properly present and describe business data and information
- To draw conclusions about large populations based solely on information collected from samples
- To make reliable forecasts about business trends
- To improve business processes

## The Different Types of Data Sources

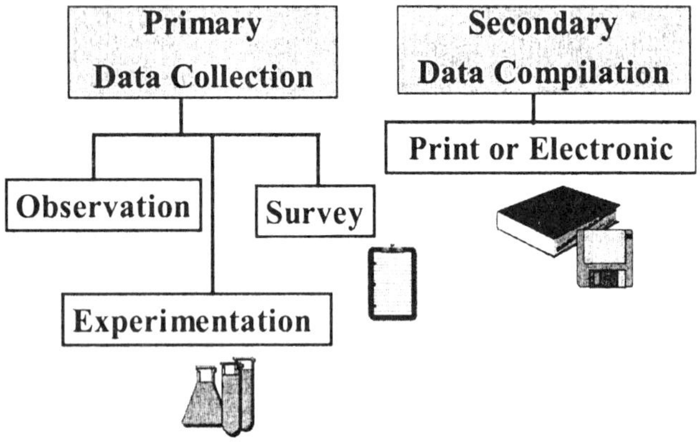


## The Different Types of Data

- **Qualitative (categorical) variable**: A nonnumeric variable, e.g., male or female.
- **Quantitative (numerical) variable:** A numeric variable, e.g., weight, exam score.
- **Discrete variable:** A variable with only certain values, there are usually gaps between values, e.g., the number of cars a company owns.
- **Continuous variable:** A variable that can have any value within a specified range, e.g., atmospheric temperature.

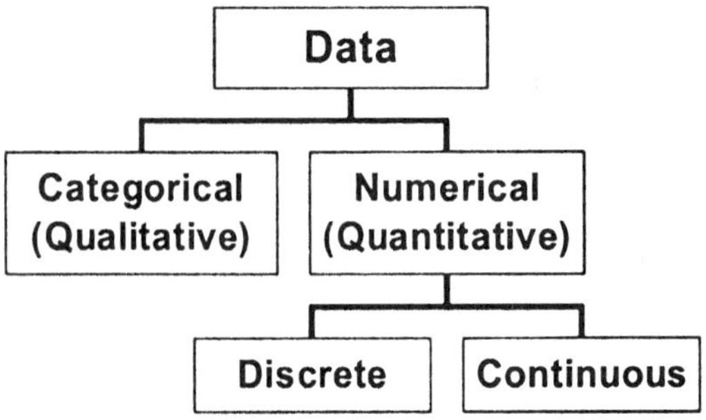

# SOLUTIONS TO END OF SECTION AND CHAPTER REVIEW EVEN PROBLEMS

1.2 The size of the soft drink yields three categorical or "qualitative" responses—small, medium, and large.

1.4 (a) numerical, discrete, ratio scale
(b) numerical, continuous, ratio scale
(c) categorical, nominal scale
(d) categorical, nominal scale

1.6 (a) categorical
(b) numerical, continuous
(c) numerical, discrete
(d) numerical, discrete

1.8 (a) numerical, continuous *
(b) numerical, discrete
(c) numerical, continuous *
(d) categorical
*Some researchers consider money as a discrete numerical variable because it can be "counted."

1.10 While it is theoretically true that ties cannot occur with continuous data, the grossness of the measuring instruments used often leads to the reporting of ties in practical applications. Hence two students may both score 90 on an exam—not because they possess identical ability but rather because the grossness of the scoring method used failed to detect a difference between them.

1.12 A population contains all the items of interest whereas a sample contains only a portion of the items in the population.

1.14 Descriptive statistical methods deal with the collection, presentation, summarization, and analysis of data whereas inferential statistical methods deal with decisions arising from the projection of sample information to the characteristics of a population.

1.16 Discrete random variables produce numerical responses that arise from a counting process. Continuous random variables produce numerical responses that arise from a measuring process.

Answers for 1.18 through 1.24 provided below are just some of the many different possible answers.

1.18 The story Billionaires 1992 at http://lib.stat.cmu.edu/DASL/Stories/Billionaires1992.html contains the data on wealth, age, and geographic location (Asia, Europe, Middle East, United States, and Other) of 233 individuals reported by the Fortune magazine. The data set provides an image of the world's billionaires.

1.20 Minitab could be used to obtain various summary statistics and to perform inferential statistical analysis.

1.22 Based on the article: "Do Debates Affect Presidential Contests?" dated October 5, 2004:
- (a) Categorical variable: The answer to the question "Do debates affect presidential contests?"
- (b) Numerical variable: The percentage of viewers who thought that Kerry won the debate.
- (c) The percentage of viewers who thought that Kerry won the debate is a discrete variable because it cannot be measured nor continuously subdivided

1.24
- (a) The answer to the question: "What is the sex of Owner 1?" is a categorical variable.
- (b) The answer to the question: "What was Owner 1's age as of December 31, 2002?" is a numerical variable.
- (c) Age measured in number of years is a discrete variable.

1.26
- (a) Population for the Goldman Sachs survey is all the U.S. households.
- (b) Population for Cyber Dialogue survey is all the people who have tried and quit online banking.
- (c) The response is categorical.
- (d) This is a statistic.

# CHAPTER 2

## OBJECTIVES

- To be able to develop tables and charts for numerical data
- To be able to develop tables and charts for categorical data
- To understand the principles of proper graphical presentation

## OVERVIEW AND KEY CONCEPTS

### Organizing Numerical Data

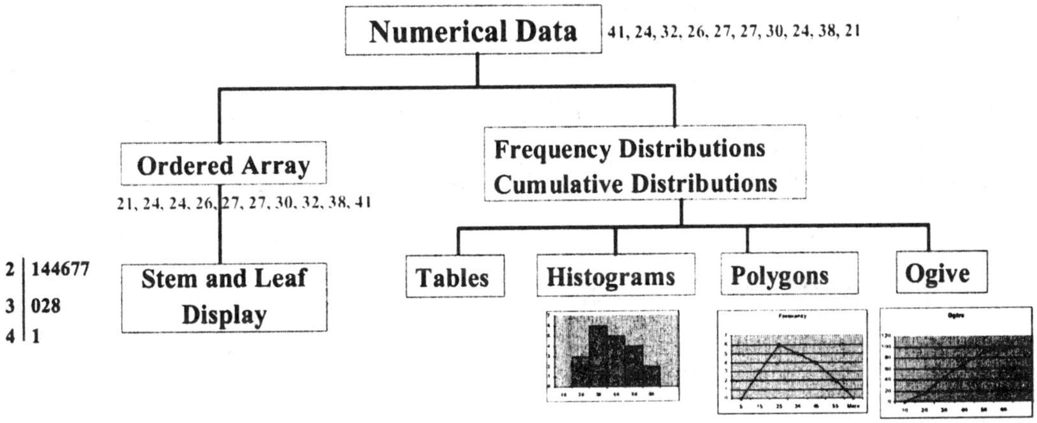


- **Ordered array:** Ordered sequence of raw data.
  - Ordered array makes it easier to pick out extremes, typical values, and concentrations of values.
- **Stem-and-leaf display:** Data are separated into leading digits (stems) and trailing digits (leaves).
  - Allows easy understanding of how the values distribute and cluster over the range of the observations in the data set.
- **Frequency distribution:** A summary table in which the data are arranged into numerically ordered class groupings or categories.
  - Makes the process of data analysis and interpretation much more manageable and meaningful
  - **Selecting the number of classes**: At least 5 but no more than 15 groupings
  - **Obtaining the class intervals:** $\text{width of interval} = \dfrac{\text{range}}{\text{number of desired class groupings}}$.
  - **Establishing the boundaries of the classes**: Non-overlapping classes must include the entire range of observations
  - **Class midpoint:** The point halfway between the boundaries of each class and is representative of the data within that class

- **Relative frequency distribution**: Formed by dividing the frequencies in each class of the frequency distribution by the total number of observations
    - Essential whenever one set of data is being compared with other sets of data if the number of observations in each set differs
- **Percentage distribution:** Formed by multiplying the relative frequencies by 100%
- **Cumulative distribution:** Formed from the frequency distribution, relative frequency distribution or percentage distribution by accumulating the frequencies, relative frequencies or percentages
    - It shows the number of observations below given values (lower boundaries)
- **Histogram:** Vertical bar chart in which the rectangular bars are constructed at the boundaries of each class
- **Percentage polygon:** Formed by having the midpoint of each class represent the data in that class and then connecting the sequence of midpoints at their respective class percentages
    - Useful when comparing two or more sets of data
- **Cumulative polygon (Ogive):** Formed by plotting cumulative percentages against the lower boundaries of the classes and connecting the cumulative percentages
    - It is useful when comparing two or more sets of data

## Graphing Bivariate Numerical Data

- **Scatter diagram (scatter plot):** Two-dimensional graph depicting how two numerical variables relate to each other
- **Time-series plot:** Two-dimensional graph that illustrates how a series of numerical data changes over time

## Table and Charts for Categorical Data

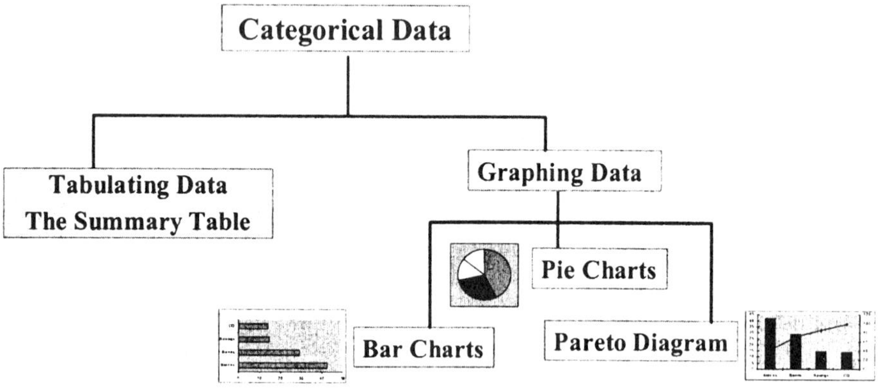


- **Summary table:** Similar to frequency distribution table for numerical data except there is no natural order of the classes
- **Bar chart:** Each category is depicted by a bar, the length of which represents the frequency or percentage of observations falling into a category
- **Pie chart:** The circle of $360^0$ is divided into slices according to the percentage in each category
- **Pareto diagram**: A special type of vertical bar chart in which the categorized responses are plotted in the descending rank order of their frequencies and combined with a cumulative polygon on the same scale
    - Useful when the number of classification increases. Enables the separation of the "vital few" from the "trivial many"

## Tabulating and Graphing Bivariate Categorical Data

- Contingency table (cross-classification table): Two-way table of cross-classification
- Side-by-side bar chart: Bar charts arranged side-by-side according to the different categories or the two categorical variables; useful when looking for patterns or relationship

## Principles of Graphical Excellence

- Well-designed presentation of data that provides substance, statistics and design
- Communicates complex ideas with clarity, precision and efficiency
- Gives the viewer the largest number of ideas in the shortest time with the least ink
- Almost always involves several dimensions
- Requires telling the truth about the data

## Common Errors in Presenting Data

- Using "chart junk"
- No relative basis in comparing data between groups
- Compressing the vertical axis
- No zero point on the vertical axis

# SOLUTIONS TO END OF SECTION AND CHAPTER REVIEW EVEN PROBLEMS

2.2 (a)

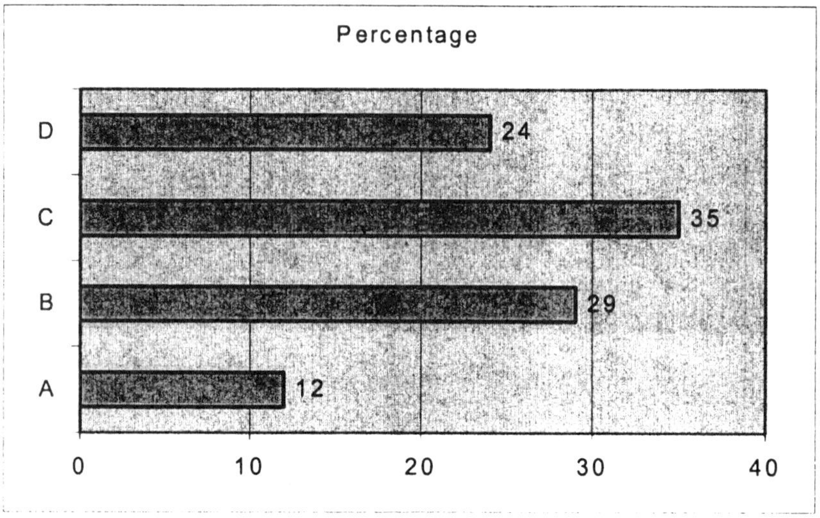


(b)

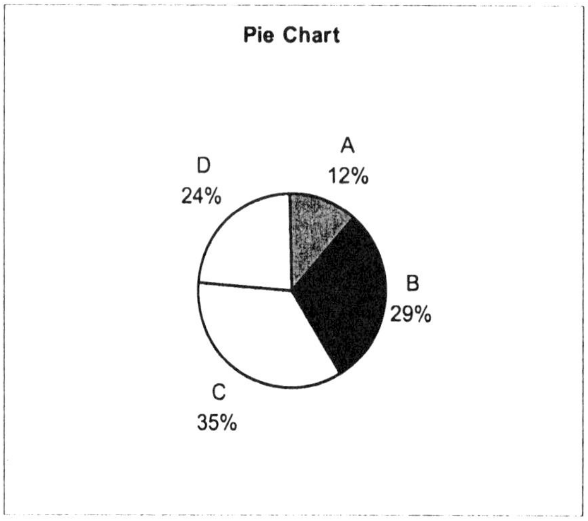

2.2 cont. (c)

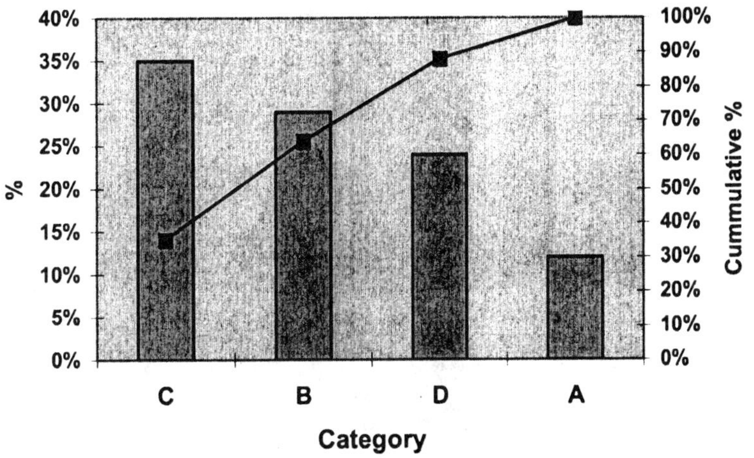
40%
35%
30%
25%
20%
15%
10%
5%
0%
%
100%
90%
80%
70%
60%
50%
40%
30%
20%
10%
0%
Cummulative %
C
B
D
A
Category

2.4 (a)

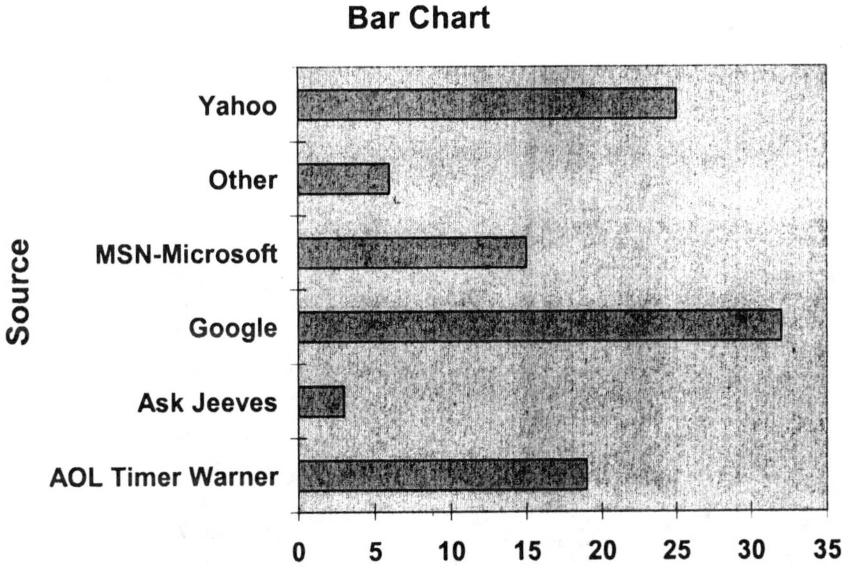
Bar Chart
Yahoo
Other
MSN-Microsoft
Google
Ask Jeeves
AOL Timer Warner
Source
0
5
10
15
20
25
30
35

2.4 (a)
cont.

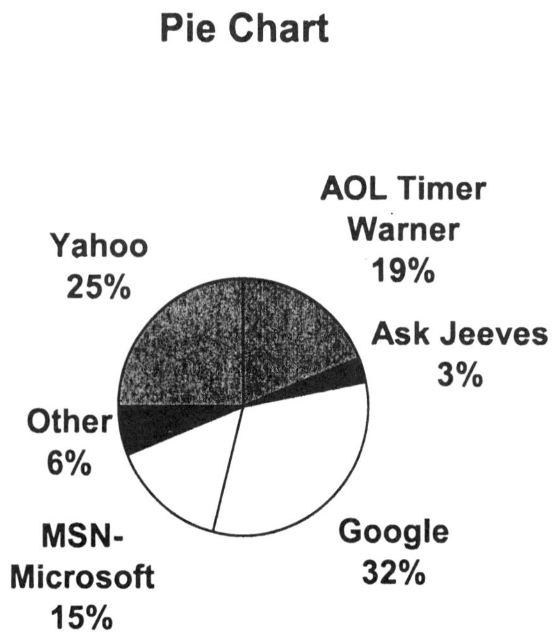


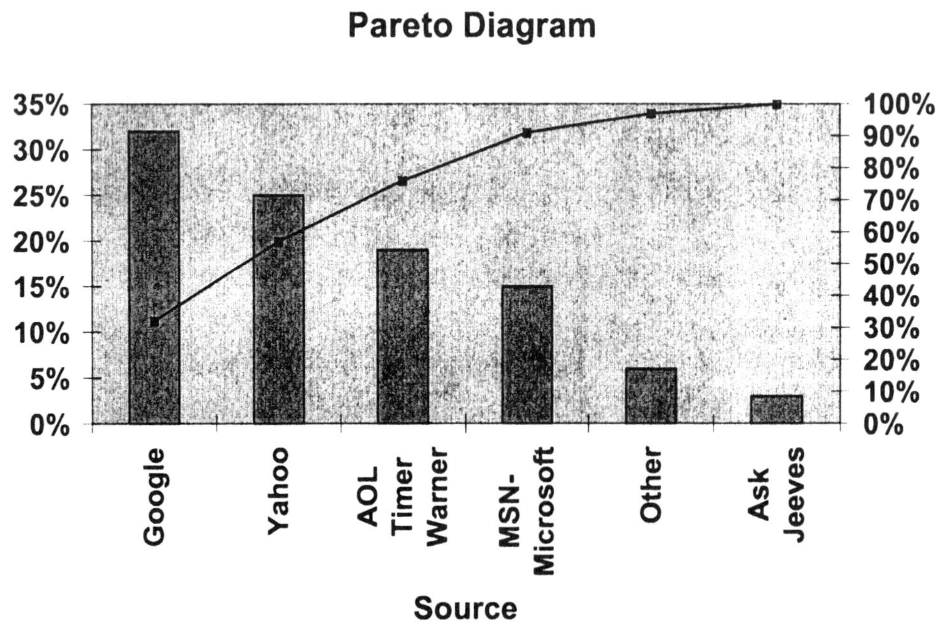


(b) The Pareto diagram is better than the pie chart to portray these data because it not only sorts the frequencies in descending order, it also provides the cumulative polygon on the same scale. From the Pareto diagram, it is obvious that "Google" has the largest market share at 32%.*

* Note: This is one of the many possible solutions for the question.

2.6 (a)

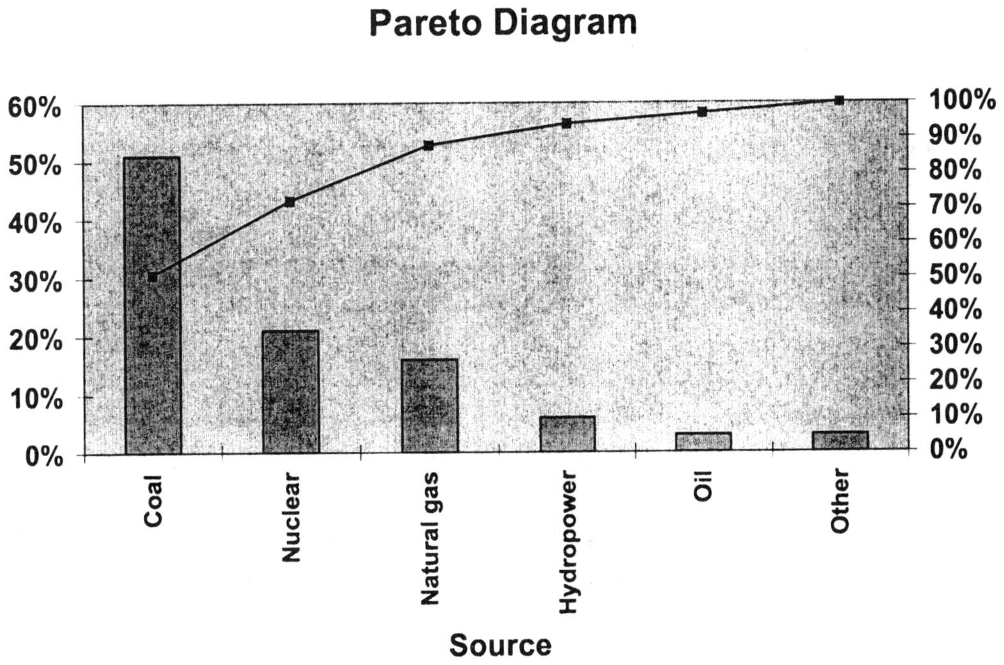


(b) Approximately 88% of the electricity is derived from coal, nuclear energy or natural gas.

(c)

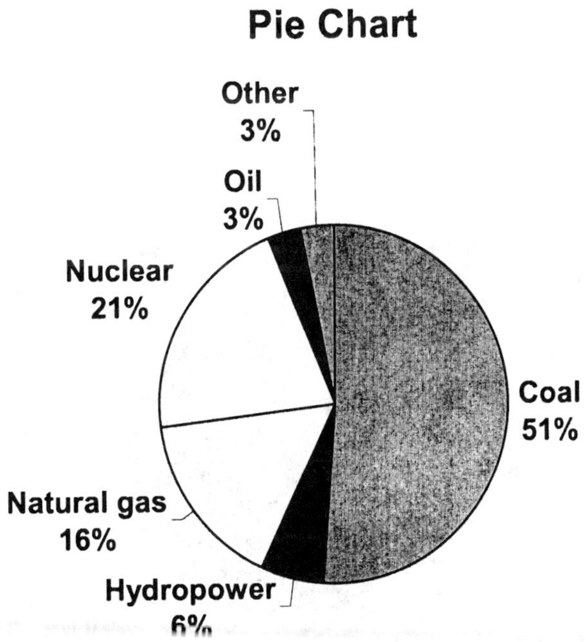

2.6 cont. (d) The Pareto diagram is better than the pie chart because it not only sorts the frequencies in descending order, it also provides the cumulative polygon on the same scale. From the Pareto diagram, it is obvious that almost 90% of the electricity is derived from coal, nuclear energy or natural gas.*

* Note: This is one of the many possible solutions for the question.

2.8 (a)

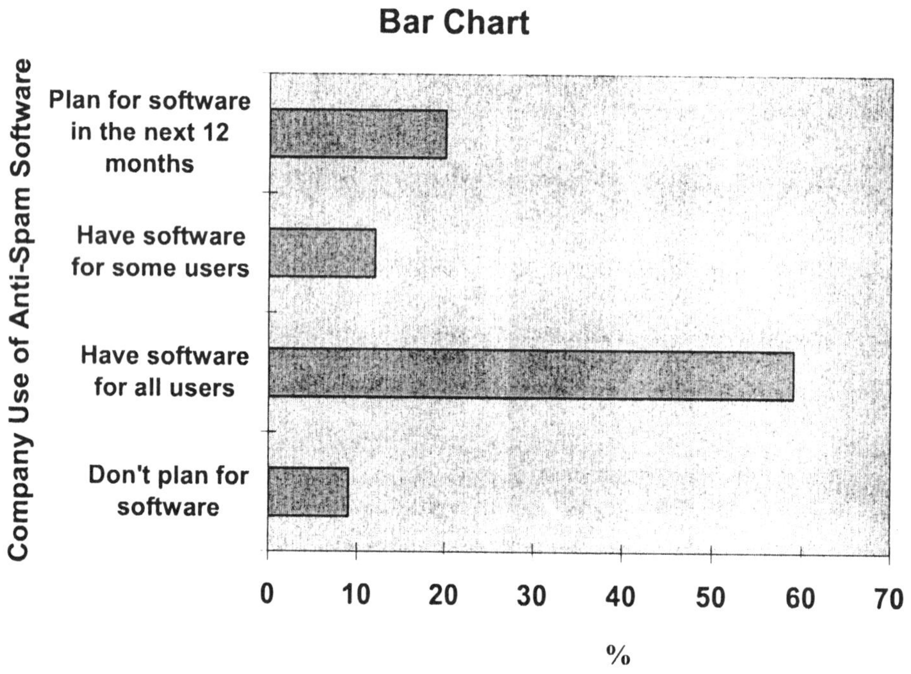


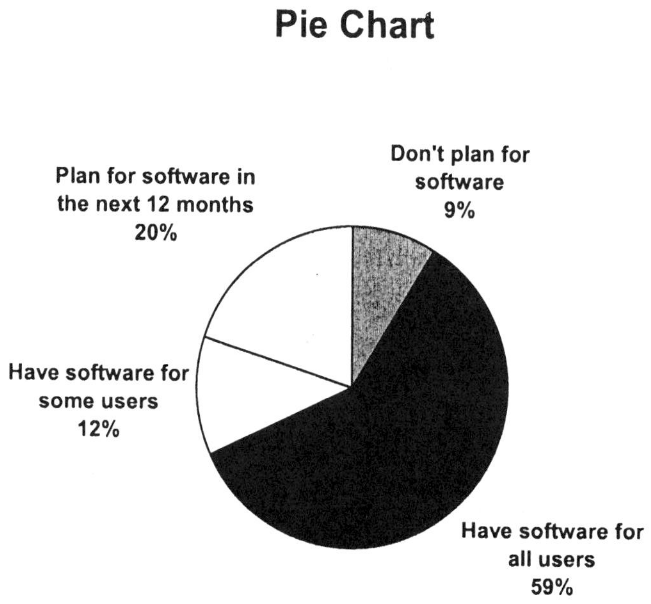

2.8 cont. (b) The bar chart is more suitable if the purpose is to compare the categories. The pie chart is more suitable if the main objective is to investigate the portion of the whole that is in a particular category.*

* Note: This is one of the many possible solutions for the question.

2.10 (a)

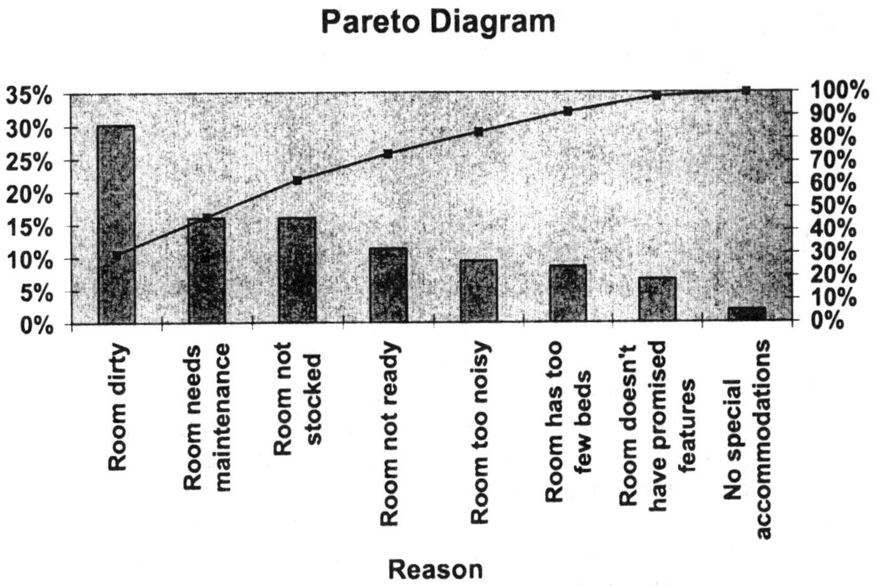


(b) The most frequent complain is about "room being dirty" followed by "room needs maintenance" and "room not stocked". The remaining complaints are the "trivial many" reasons.

2.12 Stem-and-leaf of Finance Scores

| | |
|---|---|
| 5 | 34 |
| 6 | 9 |
| 7 | 4 |
| 8 | 0 |
| 9 | 38 |
| | $n = 7$ |

2.14 Ordered array: 50 74 74 76 81 89 92

2.16 (a) Ordered array: $15 $15 $18 $18 $20 $20 $20 $20 $20 $21 $22 $22 $25 $25 $25 $25 $25 $26 $28 $29 $30 $30 $30

(b) **PHStat output:**

**Stem-and-Leaf Display**
**for Bounced-Check Fee**
**Stem unit: 10**

| | |
|---|---|
| 1 | 5 5 8 8 |
| 2 | 0 0 0 0 0 1 2 2 5 5 5 5 5 6 8 9 |
| 3 | 0 0 0 |

2.16 cont. (c) The stem-and-leaf display provides more information because it not only orders observations from the smallest to the largest into stems and leaves, it also conveys information on how the values distribute and cluster over the range of the observations in the data set.

(d) The bounced checked fees seem to be concentrated around $22 which is the center of the 20-row and also the median of the 23 observations.

2.18 (a) Ordered array for chicken: 7, 9, 15, 16, 16, 18, 22, 25, 27, 33, 39

Ordered array for burger: 19, 31, 34, 35, 39, 39, 43

(b) **PHStat output:**

**Stem-and-Leaf Display for Burger**

**Stem unit: 10**

| | |
|---|---|
| 1 | 9 |
| 2 | |
| 3 | 1 4 5 9 9 |
| 4 | 3 |

**Stem-and-Leaf Display for Chicken**

**Stem unit: 10**

| | |
|---|---|
| 0 | 7 9 |
| 1 | 5 6 6 8 |
| 2 | 2 5 7 |
| 3 | 3 9 |

(c) The stem-and-leaf display provides more information because it not only orders observations from the smallest to the largest into stems and leaves, it also conveys information on how the values distribute and cluster over the range of the observations in the data set.

(d) There seems to be higher fat content for burgers because 6 observations in the sample of 7 have fat content higher than 30 as compared to only 2 observations in the sample of 11 chicken items. Also, there is only 1 observation with a fat content lower than 20 for burgers as compared to 6 observations in the sample of 11 chicken items.

2.20 (a) The class boundaries of the 9 classes can be "10 to less than 20", "20 to less than 30", "30 to less than 40", "40 to less than 50", "50 to less than 60", "60 to less than 70", "70 to less than 80", "80 to less than 90", and "90 to less than 100".

(b) The class-interval width is $= \dfrac{97.8-11.6}{9} = 9.58 \cong 10$.

(c) The nine class midpoints are: 15, 25, 35, 45, 55, 65, 75, 85, and 95.

2.22 (a)

| Electricity Costs | Frequency | Percentage |
|---|---|---|
| $80 up to $99 | 4 | 8% |
| $100 up to $119 | 7 | 14 |
| $120 up to $139 | 9 | 18 |
| $140 up to $159 | 13 | 26 |
| $160 up to $179 | 9 | 18 |
| $180 up to $199 | 5 | 10 |
| $200 up to $219 | 3 | 6 |

2.22 (b)
cont.

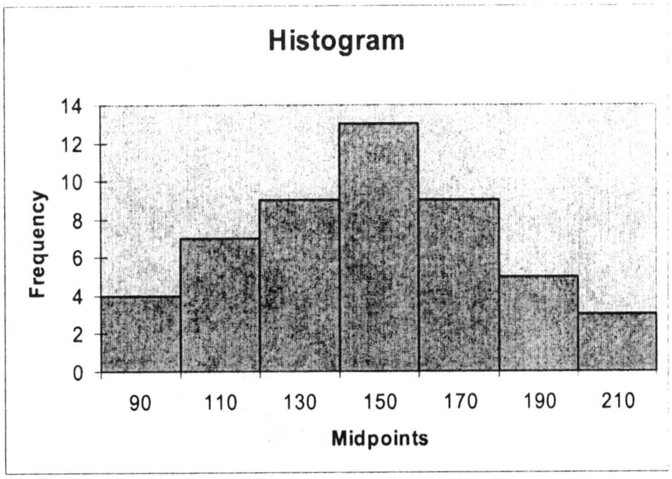


Monthly Electricity Costs

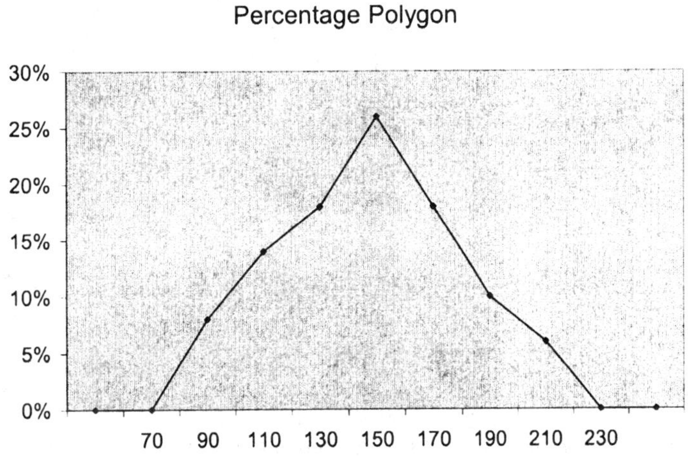


Monthly Electricity Costs

2.22 cont. (c)

| *Electricity Costs* | *Frequency* | *Percentage* | *Cumulative %* |
|---|---|---|---|
| $99 | 4 | 8% | 8% |
| $119 | 7 | 14% | 22% |
| $139 | 9 | 18% | 40% |
| $159 | 13 | 26% | 66% |
| $179 | 9 | 18% | 84% |
| $199 | 5 | 10% | 94% |
| $219 | 3 | 6% | 100% |

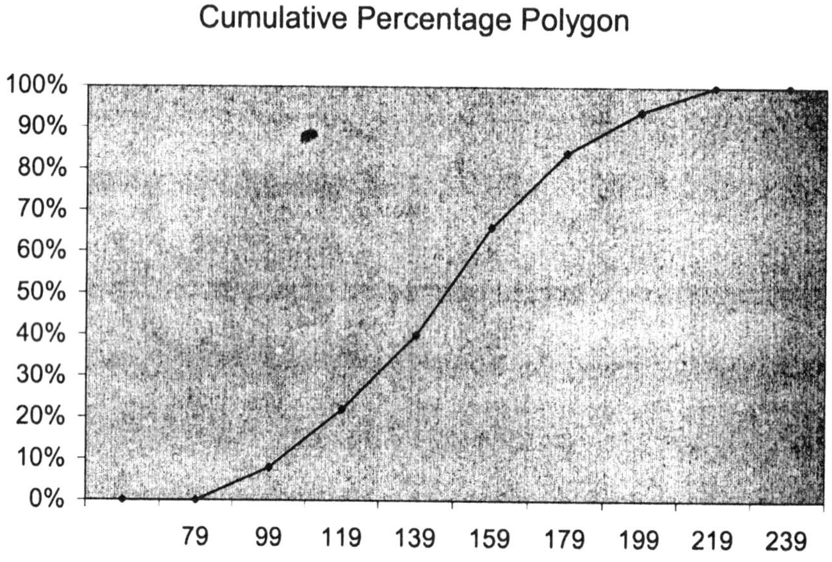


(d) Monthly electricity costs are most concentrated between $140 and $160 a month, with better than one-fourth of the costs falling in that interval.

2.24 (a)

| *Width* | *Frequency* | *Percentage* |
|---|---|---|
| 8.310 -- 8.329 | 3 | 6.12% |
| 8.330 -- 8.349 | 2 | 4.08% |
| 8.350 -- 8.369 | 1 | 2.04% |
| 8.370 -- 8.389 | 4 | 8.16% |
| 8.390 -- 8.409 | 4 | 8.16% |
| 8.410 -- 8.429 | 15 | 30.61% |
| 8.430 -- 8.449 | 7 | 14.29% |
| 8.450 -- 8.469 | 5 | 10.20% |
| 8.470 -- 8.489 | 5 | 10.20% |
| 8.490 -- 8.509 | 3 | 6.12% |

2.24 cont. (b)

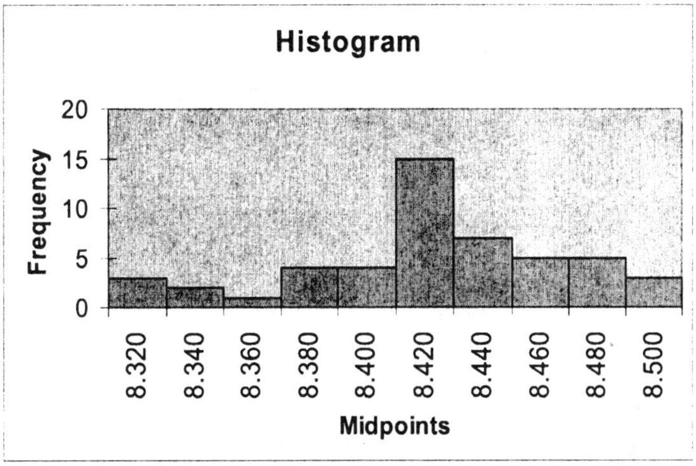
Histogram
Frequency
20
15
10
5
0
8.320
8.340
8.360
8.380
8.400
8.420
8.440
8.460
8.480
8.500
Midpoints

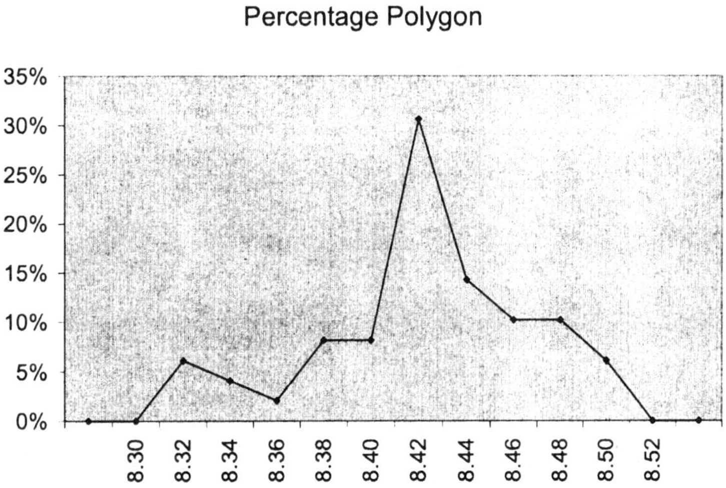
Percentage Polygon
35%
30%
25%
20%
15%
10%
5%
0%
8.30
8.32
8.34
8.36
8.38
8.40
8.42
8.44
8.46
8.48
8.50
8.52

(c)

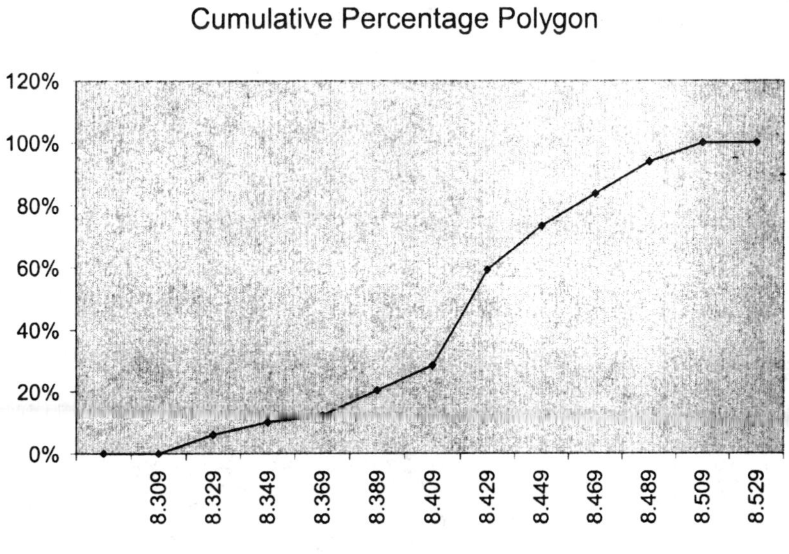
Cumulative Percentage Polygon
120%
100%
80%
60%
40%
20%
0%
8.309
8.329
8.349
8.369
8.389
8.409
8.429
8.449
8.469
8.489
8.509
8.529

2.24 cont. (d) All the troughs will meet the company's requirements of between 8.31 and 8.61 inches wide.

2.26 (a)

| *Bulb Life (hrs)* | *Frequency Manufacturer A* | *Bulb Life (hrs)* | *Frequency Manufacturer B* |
|---|---|---|---|
| 650 -- 749 | 3 | 750 -- 849 | 2 |
| 750 -- 849 | 5 | 850 -- 949 | 8 |
| 850 -- 949 | 20 | 950 -- 1049 | 16 |
| 950 -- 1049 | 9 | 1050 -- 1149 | 9 |
| 1050 -- 1149 | 3 | 1150 -- 1249 | 5 |

| Bulb Life (hrs) | Percentage, Mfgr A | Percentage, Mfgr B |
|---|---|---|
| 650 – 749 | 7.5% | 0.0% |
| 750 – 849 | 12.5 | 5.0 |
| 850 – 949 | 50.0 | 20.0 |
| 950 – 1049 | 22.5 | 40.0 |
| 1050 – 1149 | 7.5 | 22.5 |
| 1150 – 1249 | 0.0 | 12.5 |

(b)

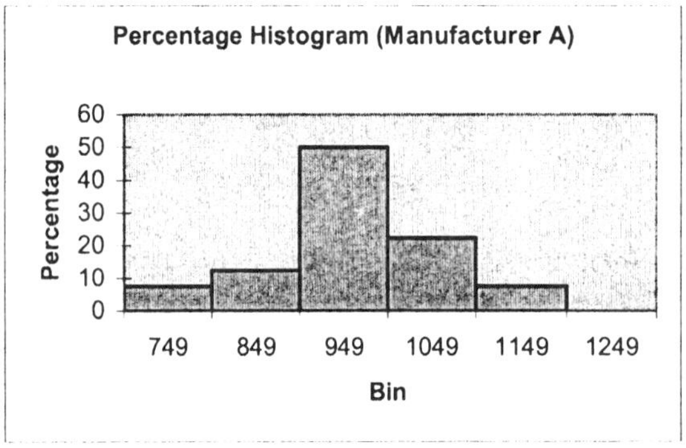


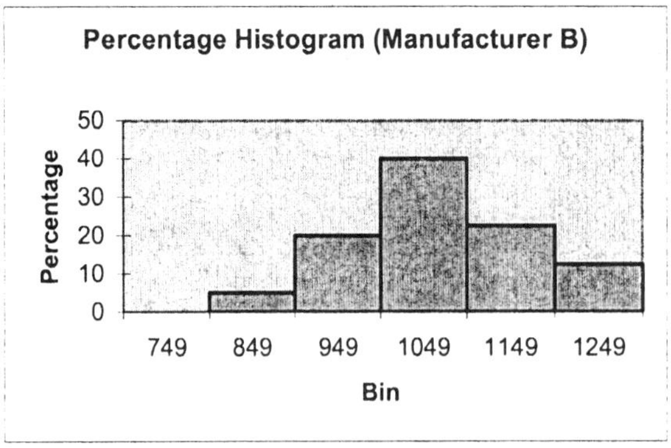

2.26 cont. (b)

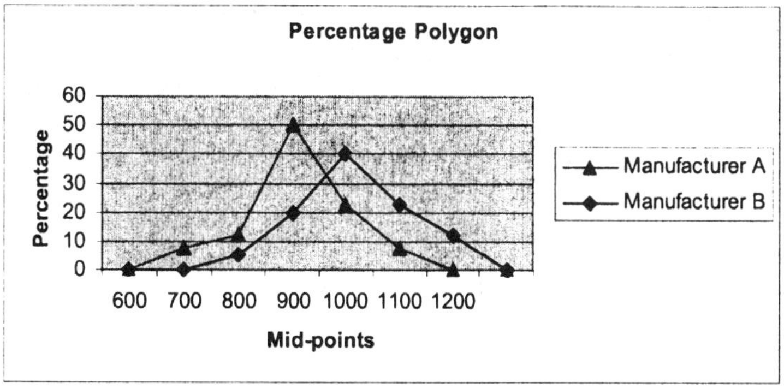


(c)

| Bulb Life (hrs) | Frequency Less Than, Mfgr A | Frequency Less Than, Mfgr B |
|---|---|---|
| 650 – 749 | 3 | 0 |
| 750 – 849 | 8 | 2 |
| 850 – 949 | 28 | 10 |
| 950 – 1049 | 37 | 26 |
| 1050 – 1149 | 40 | 35 |
| 1150 – 1249 | 40 | 40 |

| Bulb Life (hrs) | Percentage Less Than, Mfgr A | Percentage Less Than, Mfgr B |
|---|---|---|
| 650 – 749 | 7.5% | 0.0% |
| 750 – 849 | 20.0 | 5.0 |
| 850 – 949 | 70.0 | 25.0 |
| 950 – 1049 | 92.5 | 65.0 |
| 1050 – 1149 | 100.0 | 87.5 |
| 1150 – 1249 | 100.0 | 100.0 |

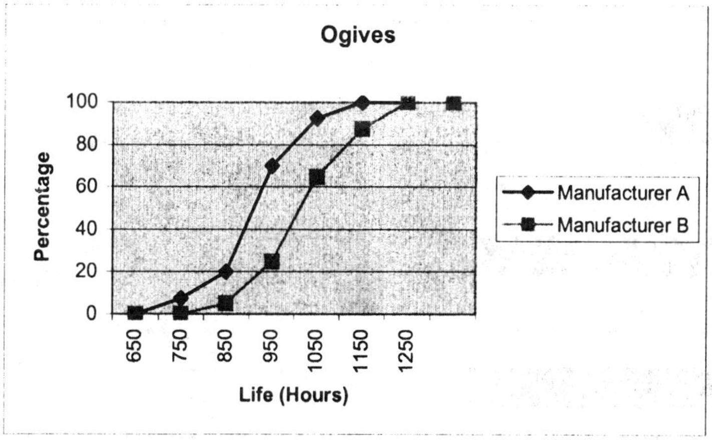

2.26 cont. (d) Manufacturer B produces bulbs with longer lives than Manufacturer A. The cumulative percentage for Manufacturer B shows 65% of their bulbs lasted 1049 hours or less contrasted with 70% of Manufacturer A's bulbs which lasted 949 hours or less. None of Manufacturer A's bulbs lasted more than 1149 hours, but 12.5% of Manufacturer B's bulbs lasted between 1150 and 1249 hours. At the same time, 7.5% of Manufacturer A's bulbs lasted less than 750 hours, while all of Manufacturer B's bulbs lasted at least 750 hours.

2.28 (a) Table frequencies for all student responses

Student Major Categories

| Gender | A | C | M | Totals |
|---|---|---|---|---|
| Male | 14 | 9 | 2 | 25 |
| Female | 6 | 6 | 3 | 15 |
| Totals | 20 | 15 | 5 | 40 |

(b) Table percentages based on overall student responses

Student Major Categories

| Gender | A | C | M | Totals |
|---|---|---|---|---|
| Male | 35.0% | 22.5% | 5.0% | 62.5% |
| Female | 15.0% | 15.0% | 7.5% | 37.5% |
| Totals | 50.0% | 37.5% | 12.5% | 100.0% |

Table based on row percentages

Student Major Categories

| Gender | A | C | M | Totals |
|---|---|---|---|---|
| Male | 56.0% | 36.0% | 8.0% | 100.0% |
| Female | 40.0% | 40.0% | 20.0% | 100.0% |
| Totals | 50.0% | 37.5% | 12.5% | 100.0% |

Table based on column percentages

Student Major Categories

| Gender | A | C | M | Totals |
|---|---|---|---|---|
| Male | 70.0% | 60.0% | 40.0% | 62.5% |
| Female | 30.0% | 40.0% | 60.0% | 37.5% |
| Totals | 100.0% | 100.0% | 100.0% | 100.0% |

(c)

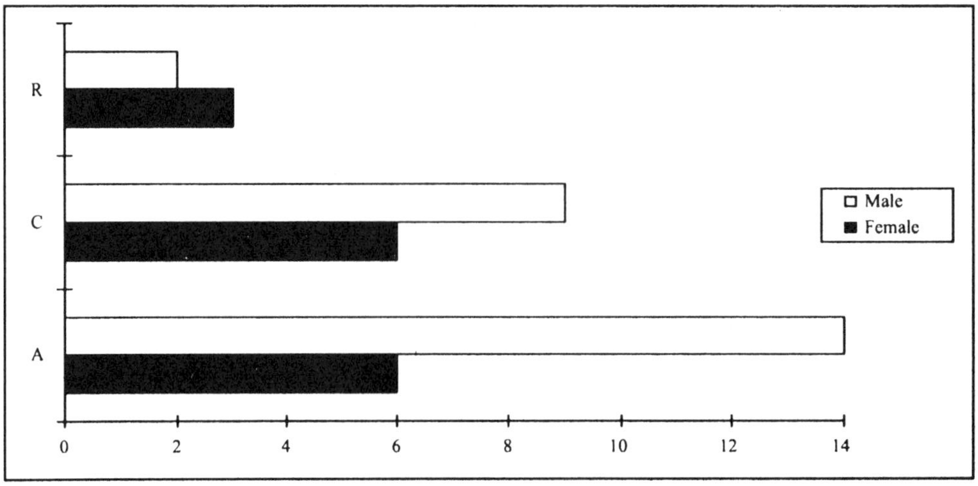

2.30 (a) **Contingency Table**

| Quality | No Particles | Particles | Totals |
|---|---|---|---|
| | Condition of Die | | |
| Good | 320 | 14 | 334 |
| Bad | 80 | 36 | 116 |
| Totals | 400 | 50 | 450 |

**Table of Total Percentages**

| Quality | No Particles | Particles | Totals |
|---|---|---|---|
| | Condition of Die | | |
| Good | 71% | 3% | 74% |
| Bad | 18% | 8% | 26% |
| Totals | 89% | 11% | 100% |

**Table of Row Percentages**

| Quality | No Particles | Particles | Totals |
|---|---|---|---|
| | Condition of Die | | |
| Good | 96% | 4% | 100% |
| Bad | 69% | 31% | 100% |
| Totals | 89% | 11% | 100% |

**Table of Column Percentages**

| Quality | No Particles | Particles | Totals |
|---|---|---|---|
| | Condition of Die | | |
| Good | 80% | 28% | 74% |
| Bad | 20% | 72% | 26% |
| Totals | 100% | 100% | 100% |

(b)

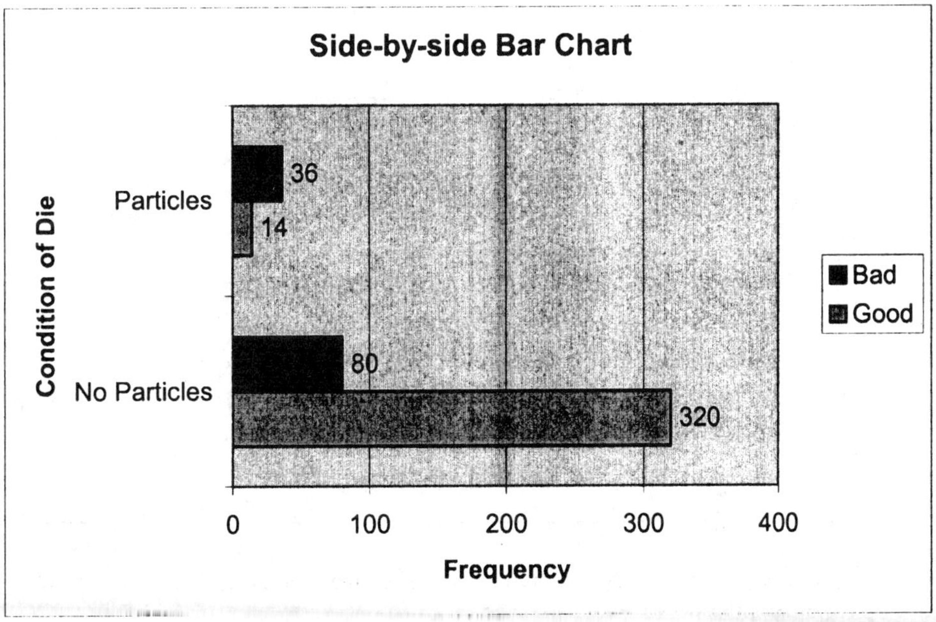


(c) The data suggests that there is some association between condition of the die and the quality of wafer because more good wafers are produced when no particles are found in the die and more bad wafers are produced when there are particles found in the die.

2.32 (a) Table of total percentages

| | Gender | | |
|---|---|---|---|
| Enjoy Shopping for Clothing | Male | Female | Total |
| Yes | 27% | 45% | 72% |
| No | 21% | 7% | 28% |
| Total | 48% | 52% | 100% |

Table of row percentages

| | Gender | | |
|---|---|---|---|
| Enjoy Shopping for Clothing | Male | Female | Total |
| Yes | 38% | 62% | 100% |
| No | 74% | 26% | 100% |
| Total | 48% | 52% | 100% |

Table of column percentages

| | Gender | | |
|---|---|---|---|
| Enjoy Shopping for Clothing | Male | Female | Total |
| Yes | 57% | 86% | 72% |
| No | 43% | 14% | 28% |
| Total | 100% | 100% | 100% |

(b)

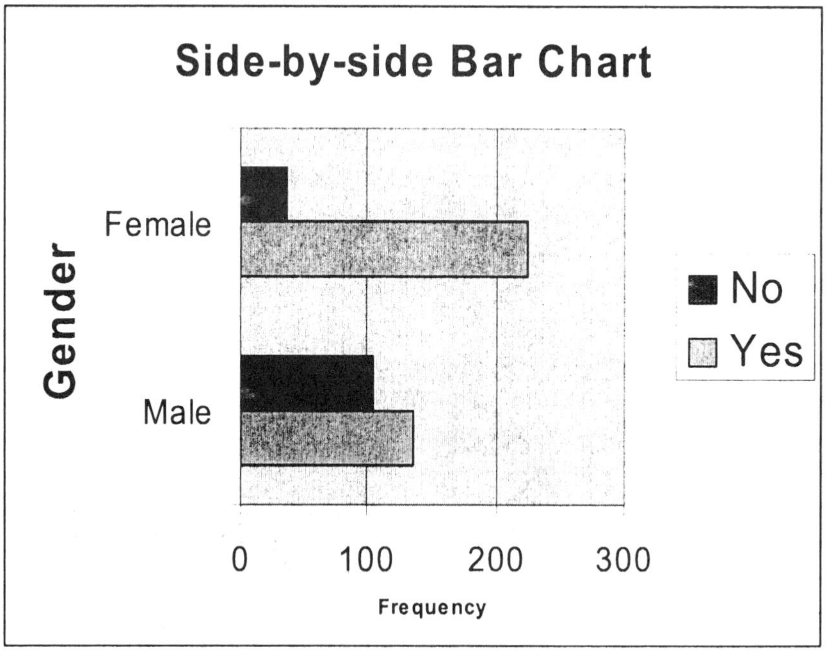


(c) The percentage of shoppers who enjoy shopping for clothing is higher among females than males.

2.34 (a)

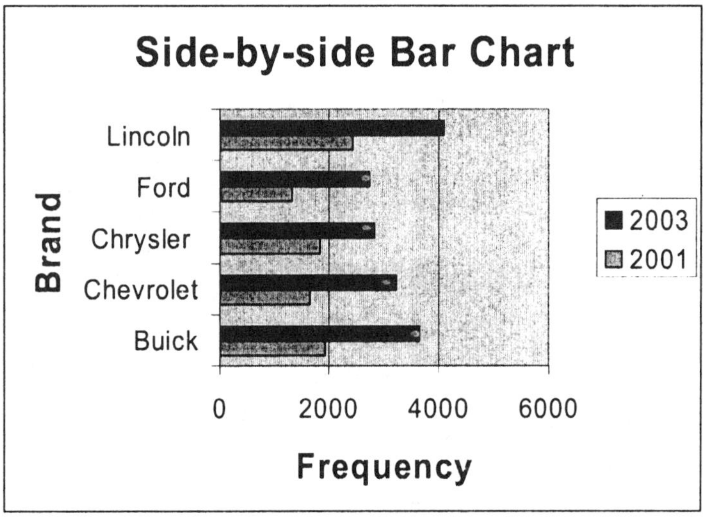


(b) All five brands increased the amount of rebates from 2001 to 2003 with Ford more than doubling, Chevrolet and Buick almost doubling the amount of rebates.

2.36 (a)

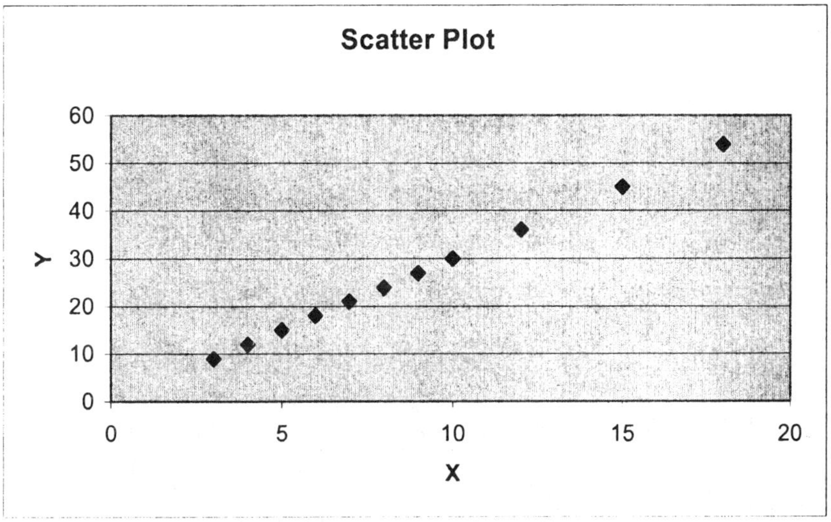


(b) Yes, there appears to be a positive linear relationship between $X$ and $Y$.

2.38 (a)

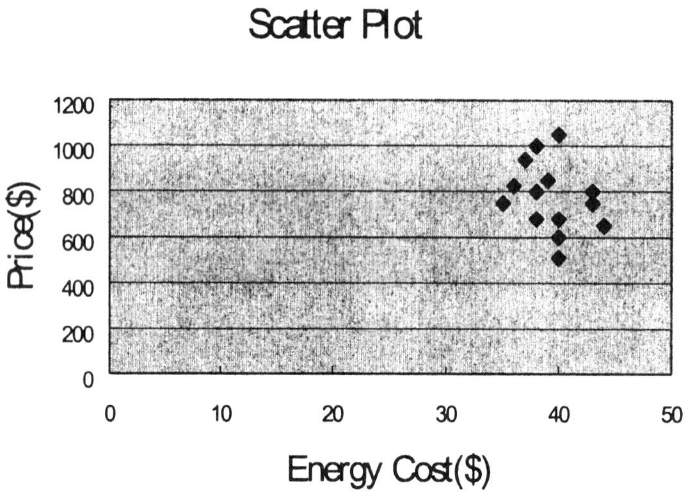


(b) There does not appear to be any relationship between price and energy cost.
(c) The data do not seem to indicate that higher-priced refrigerators have greater energy efficiency.

2.40 (a)

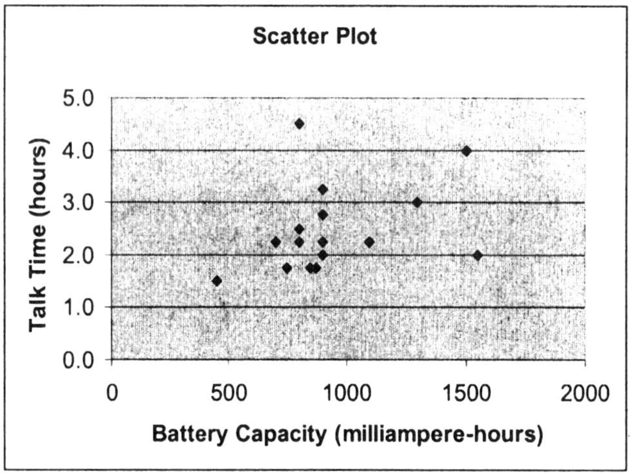


(b) There does not appear to be any relationship between the battery capacity and the digital-mode talk time.
(c) No, the data do not support the expectation that higher battery capacity is associated with higher talk time.

2.42 (a)

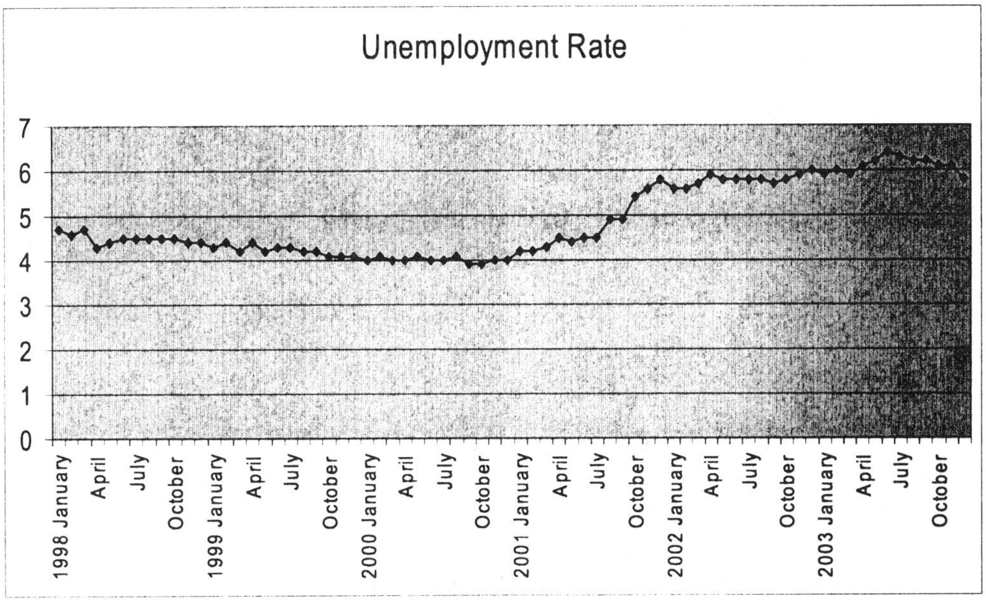


(b) The unemployment rate followed a downward trend from January of 1998 to September of 2000 and changed to an upward trend from there onwards.

2.44 (a)

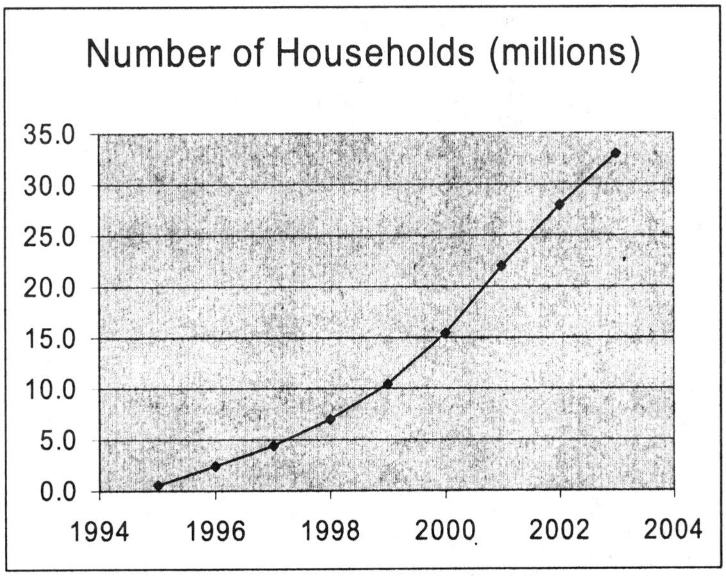


(b) There is an upward trend in the number of households using online banking and/or online bill payment.

(c) The number of U.S. households actively using online banking and/or online bill payment in 2004 will be around 36 millions.

2.50 (a) The size of the policeman for Washington is not only taller but also bigger in overall size. This has a tendency to distort the actual difference in the size of the police forces. A simple bar chart would do a much better job.

2.54 (a)

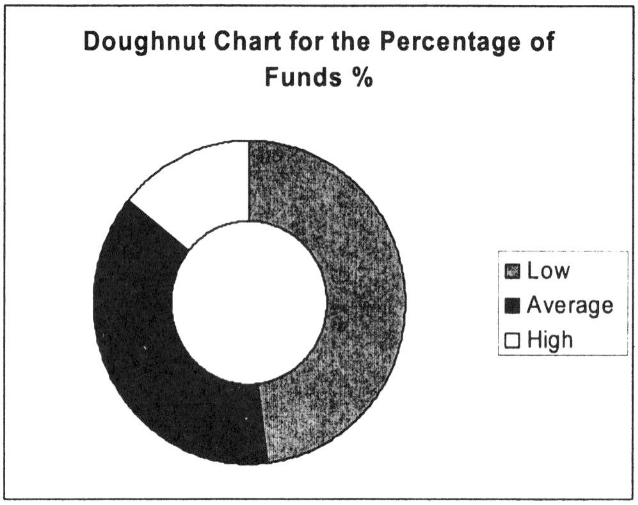
Doughnut Chart for the Percentage of Funds %
Low
Average
High

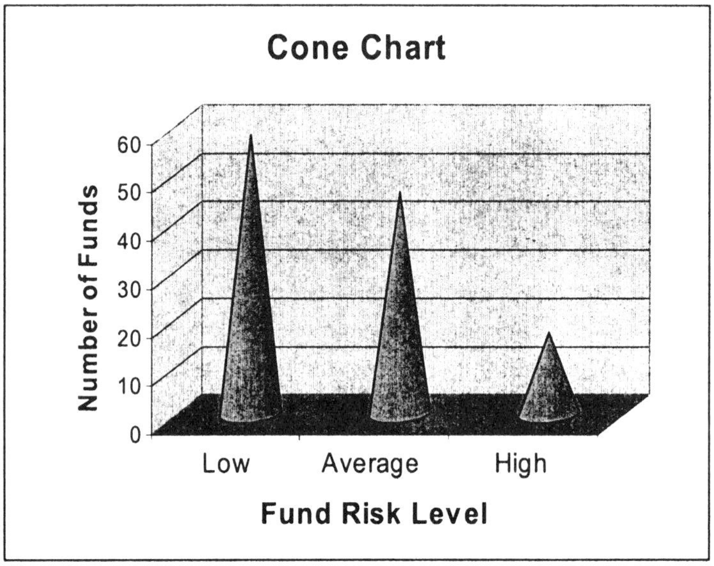
Cone Chart
Number of Funds
60
50
40
30
20
10
0
Low
Average
High
Fund Risk Level

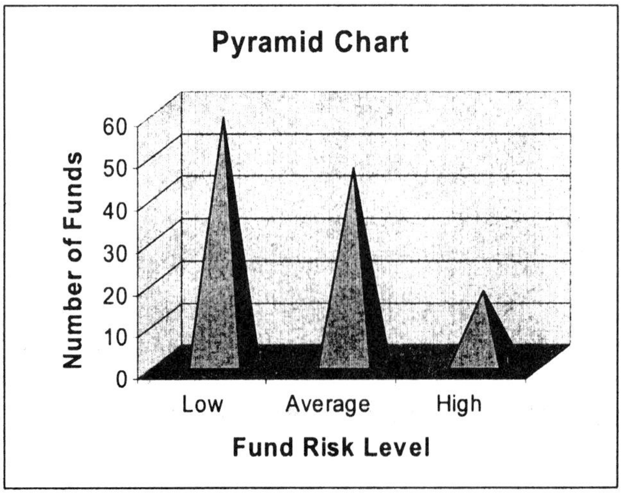
Pyramid Chart
Number of Funds
60
50
40
30
20
10
0
Low
Average
High
Fund Risk Level

2.54 cont. (b) The bar chart, the pie chart and the Pareto diagram should be preferred over the doughnut chart, the cone chart and the pyramid chart since the former set is simpler and easier to interpret.

2.56 A summary table allows one to determine the frequency or percentage of occurrences in each category.

2.58 The bar chart for categorical data is plotted with the categories on the vertical axis and the frequencies or percentages on the horizontal axis. In addition, there is a separation between categories. The histogram is plotted with the class grouping on the horizontal axis and the frequencies or percentages on the vertical axis. This allows one to more easily determine the distribution of the data. In addition, there are no gaps between classes in the histogram.

2.60 Because the categories are arranged according to frequency or importance, it allows the user to focus attention on the categories that have the greatest frequency or importance.

2.62 (a)

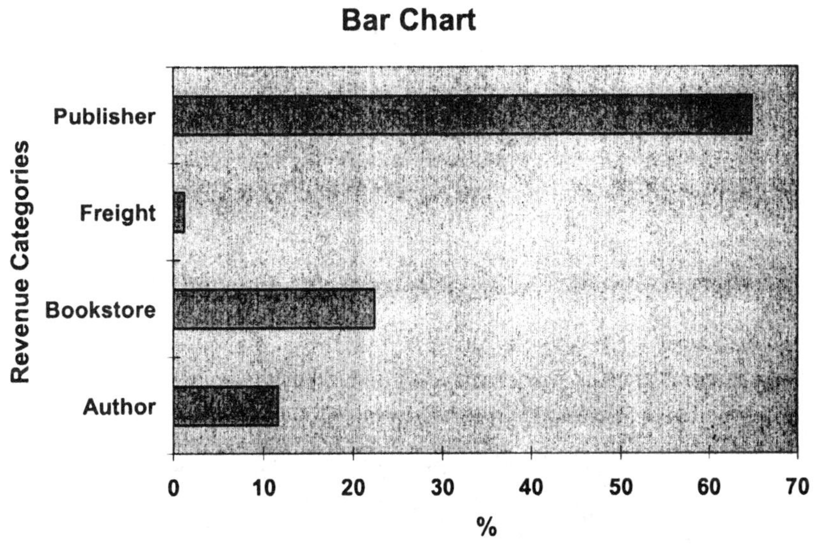

2.62 cont. (a)

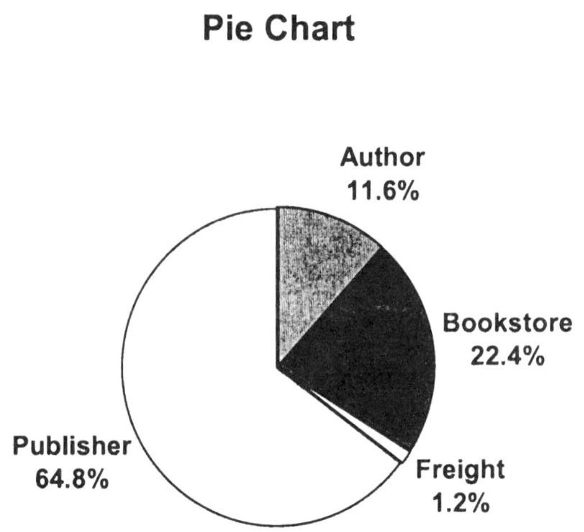
Pie Chart
Author
11.6%
Bookstore
22.4%
Freight
1.2%
Publisher
64.8%

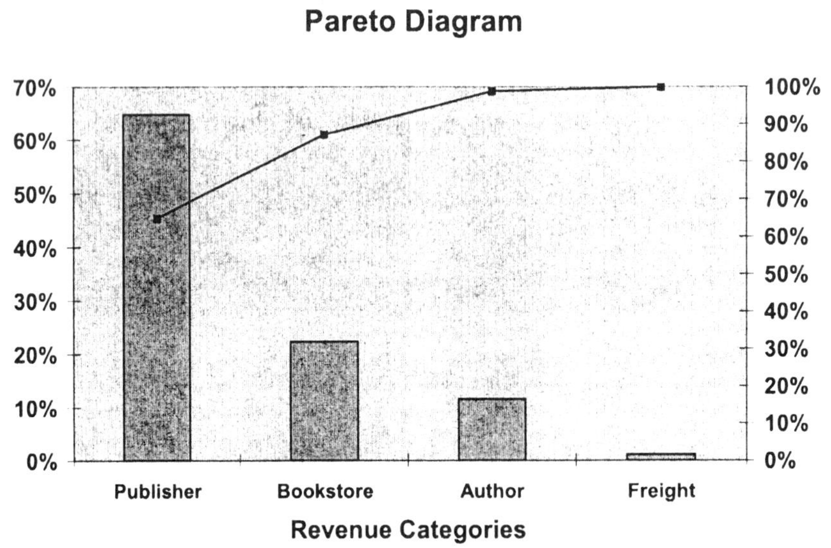
Pareto Diagram
70%
60%
50%
40%
30%
20%
10%
0%
100%
90%
80%
70%
60%
50%
40%
30%
20%
10%
0%
Publisher
Bookstore
Author
Freight
Revenue Categories

2.62 cont. (b)

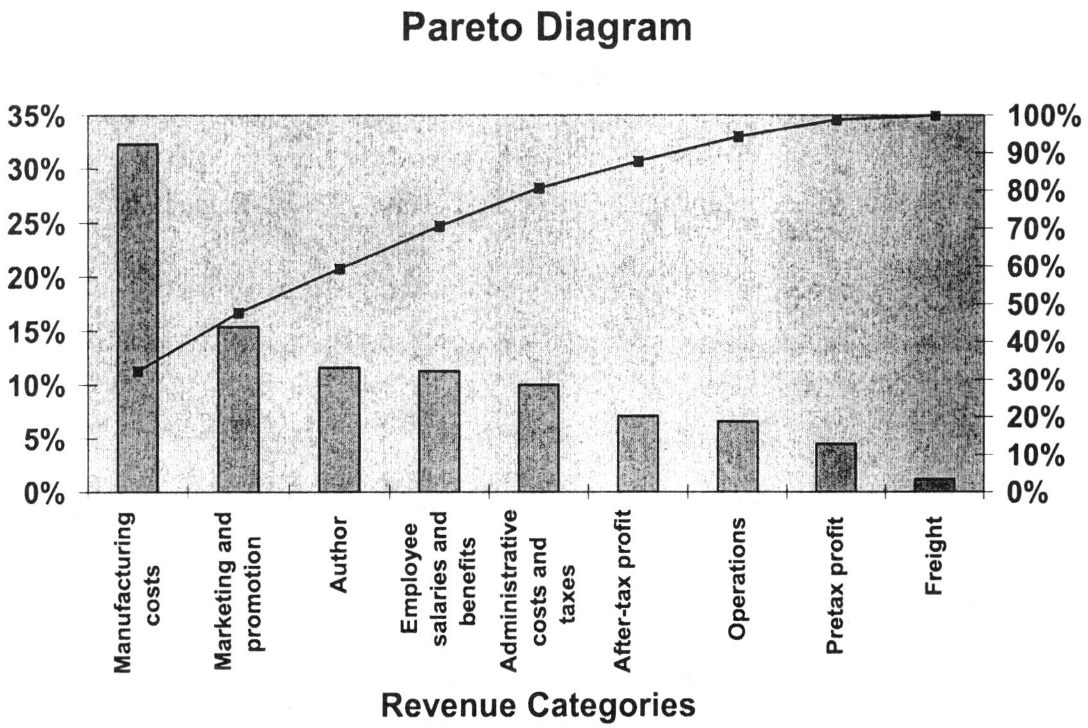


(c) The publisher gets the largest portion (64.8%) of the revenue. About half (32.2%) of the revenue received by the publisher is used for manufacturing costs. Bookstore marketing and promotion account for the next larger share of the revenue at 15.4%. Author, bookstore employee salaries and benefits, and publisher administrative costs and taxes each accounts for around 10% of the revenue while the publisher after-tax profit, bookstore operations, bookstore pretax profit and freight constitute the "trivial few" allocations of the revenue.

2.64 (a)

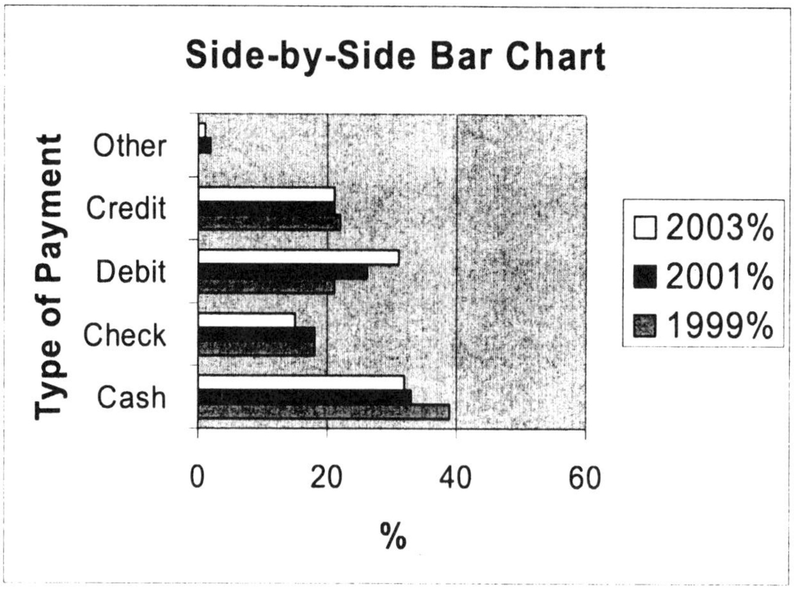


(b) From 1999 to 2003, payment by cash and check had declined while payment by debit and other type of payment had increased. The percentage of payment by credit had remained more or less constant.

2.66 (a)

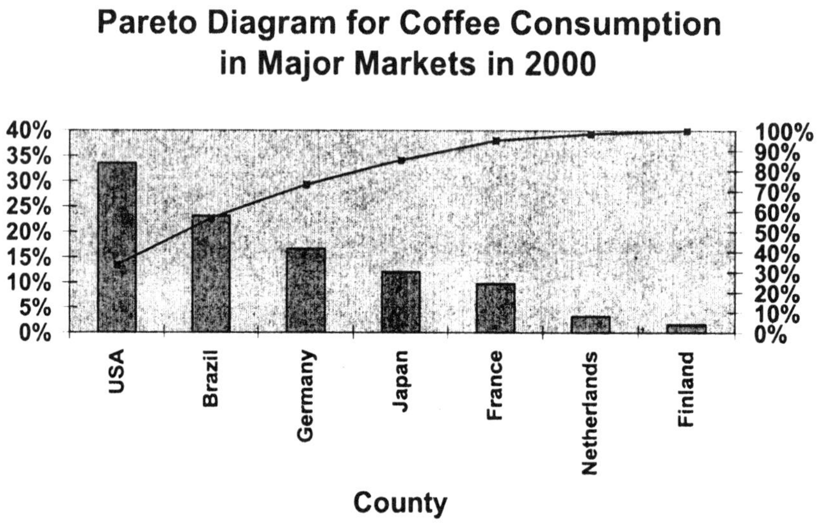


The Pareto diagram is most appropriate because it not only sorts the frequencies in descending order, it also provides the cumulative polygon on the same scale. From the Pareto diagram, it is obvious that USA and Brazil make up more than half of the coffee consumption in major markets in 2000.

2.66 cont. (b)

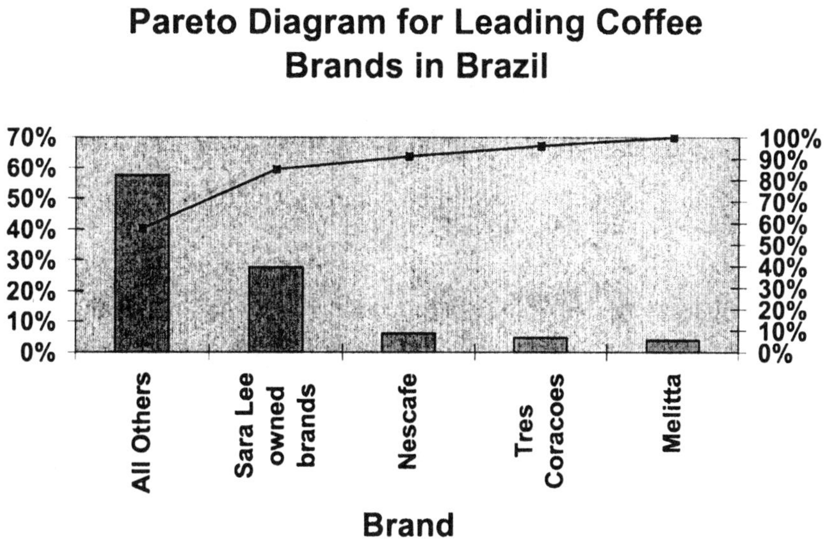


The Pareto diagram is most appropriate because it not only sorts the frequencies in descending order, it also provides the cumulative polygon on the same scale. From the Pareto diagram, it is obvious that no single major corporation dominates the coffee market in Brazil. The corporation that owns the largest share of the market, Sara Lee owned brands, captures only less than 30% of the market share.

2.68 (a)

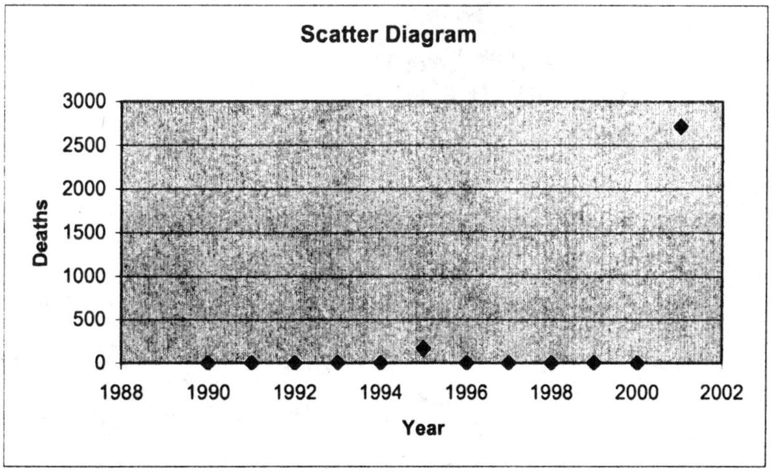


There is no particular pattern to the deaths due to terrorism on U.S. soil between 1990 and 2001. There are exceptionally high death counts in 1995 and 2001 due to the Okalahoma City and New York City bombings.

2.68 (b)
cont.

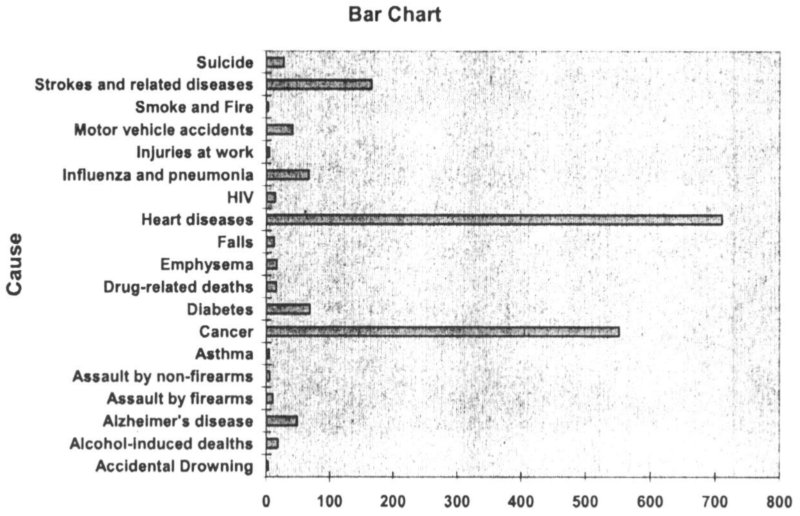
Bar Chart
Suicide
Strokes and related diseases
Smoke and Fire
Motor vehicle accidents
Injuries at work
Influenza and pneumonia
HIV
Heart diseases
Falls
Emphysema
Drug-related deaths
Diabetes
Cancer
Asthma
Assault by non-firearms
Assault by firearms
Alzheimer's disease
Alcohol-induced dealths
Accidental Drowning
Cause
0
100
200
300
400
500
600
700
800

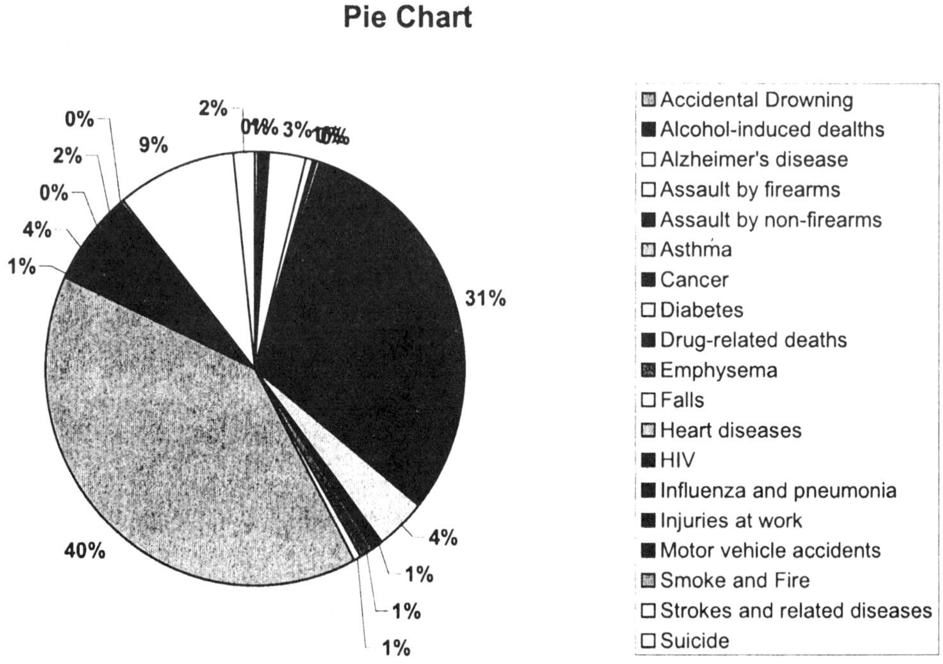
Pie Chart
0%
2%
0%
4%
1%
9%
2%
3%
31%
4%
1%
1%
1%
40%
Accidental Drowning
Alcohol-induced dealths
Alzheimer's disease
Assault by firearms
Assault by non-firearms
Asthma
Cancer
Diabetes
Drug-related deaths
Emphysema
Falls
Heart diseases
HIV
Influenza and pneumonia
Injuries at work
Motor vehicle accidents
Smoke and Fire
Strokes and related diseases
Suicide

2.68 cont. (b)

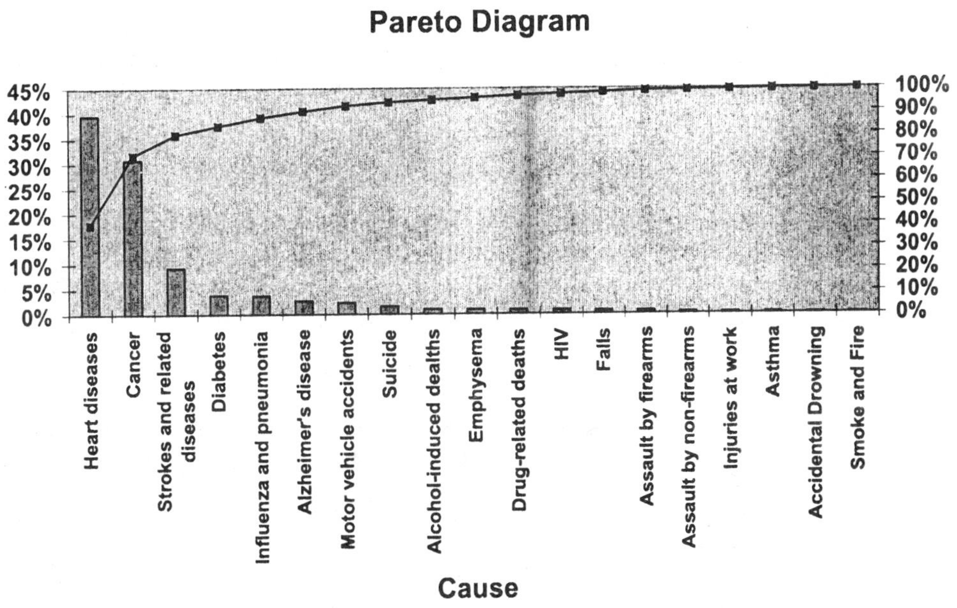


(c) The Pareto diagram is best to portray these data because it not only sorts the frequencies in descending order, it also provides the cumulative polygon on the same scale. The labels in the pie chart are unreadable because there are too many categories in the causes of death.

(d) The major causes of death in the U.S. in 2000 are heart diseases followed by cancer. These two accounted for more than 70% of the total deaths.

2.70 (a) Table of row percentages

| | Gender | | |
|---|---|---|---|
| Dessert Ordered | Male | Female | Total |
| Yes | 71% | 29% | 100% |
| No | 48% | 52% | 100% |
| Total | 53% | 47% | 100% |

| | Beef Entrée | | |
|---|---|---|---|
| Dessert Ordered | Yes | No | Total |
| Yes | 52% | 48% | 100% |
| No | 25% | 75% | 100% |
| Total | 31% | 69% | 100% |

Table of column percentages

| | Gender | | |
|---|---|---|---|
| Dessert Ordered | Male | Female | Total |
| Yes | 30% | 14% | 23% |
| No | 70% | 86% | 77% |
| Total | 100% | 100% | 100% |

| | Beef Entrée | | |
|---|---|---|---|
| Dessert Ordered | Yes | No | Total |
| Yes | 38% | 16% | 23% |
| No | 62% | 84% | 77% |
| Total | 100% | 100% | 100% |

Table of total percentages

| | Gender | | |
|---|---|---|---|
| Dessert Ordered | Male | Female | Total |
| Yes | 16% | 7% | 23% |
| No | 37% | 40% | 77% |
| Total | 53% | 47% | 100% |

| | Beef Entrée | | |
|---|---|---|---|
| Dessert Ordered | Yes | No | Total |
| Yes | 12% | 11% | 23% |
| No | 19% | 58% | 77% |
| Total | 31% | 69% | 100% |

2.70 cont. (b) If the owner is interested in finding out the percentage of joint occurrence of gender and ordering of dessert or the percentage of joint occurrence of ordering a beef entrée and a dessert among all patrons, the table of total percentages is most informative. If the owner is interested in the effect of gender on ordering of dessert or the effect of ordering a beef entrée on the ordering of dessert, the table of column percentages will be most informative. Since dessert will usually be ordered after the main entree and the owner has no direct control over the gender of patrons, the table of row percentages is not very useful here.

(c) 30% of the men sampled ordered desserts compared to 14% of the women. Men are more than twice as likely to order desserts as women. Almost 38% of the patrons ordering a beef entree ordered dessert compared to less than 16% of patrons ordering all other entrees. Patrons ordering beef are better than 2.3 times as likely to order dessert as patrons ordering any other entree.

2.72 (a)

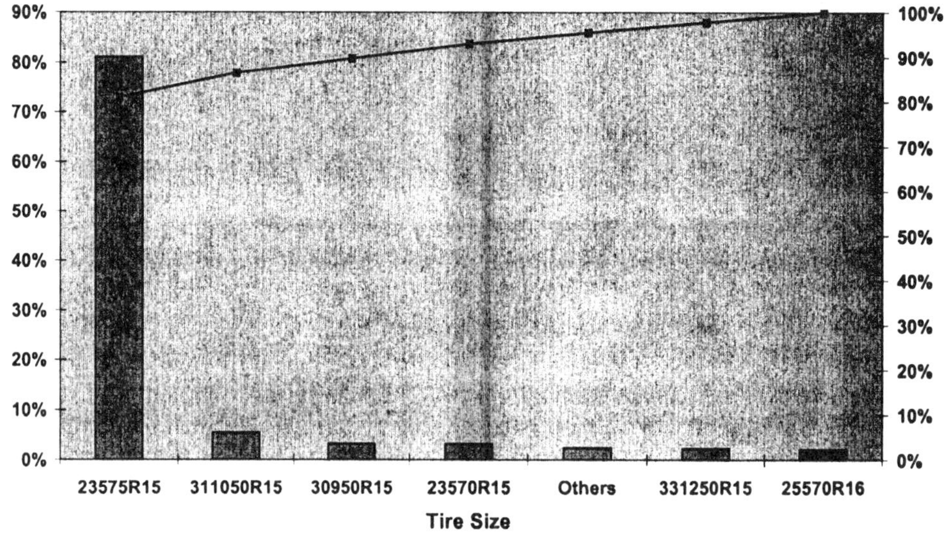


23575R15 accounts for over 80% of the warranty claims.

2.72 cont. (b)

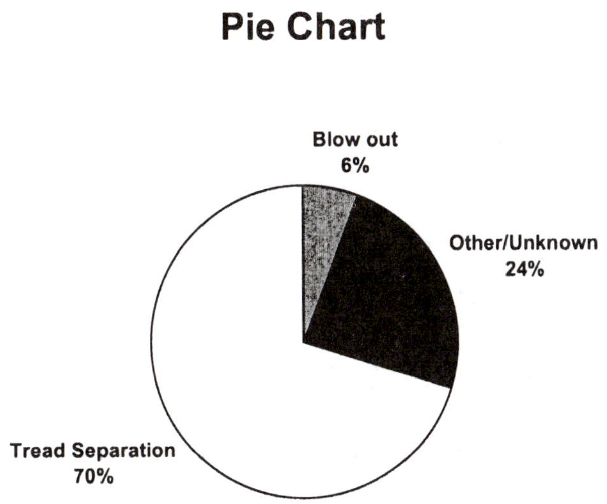


Tread separation accounts for the majority (70%) of the warranty claims.

(c)

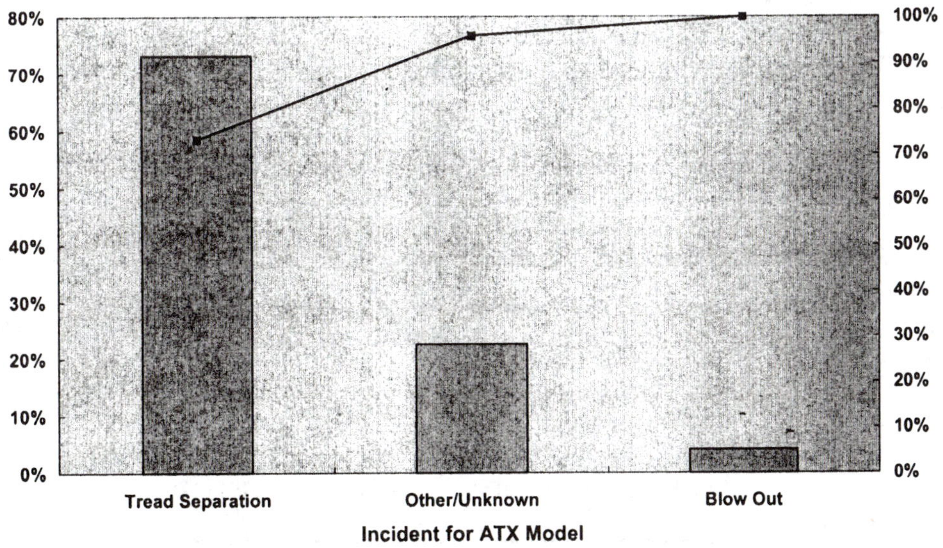


Tread separation accounts for more than 70% of the warranty claims among the ATX model.

2.72 (d)
cont.

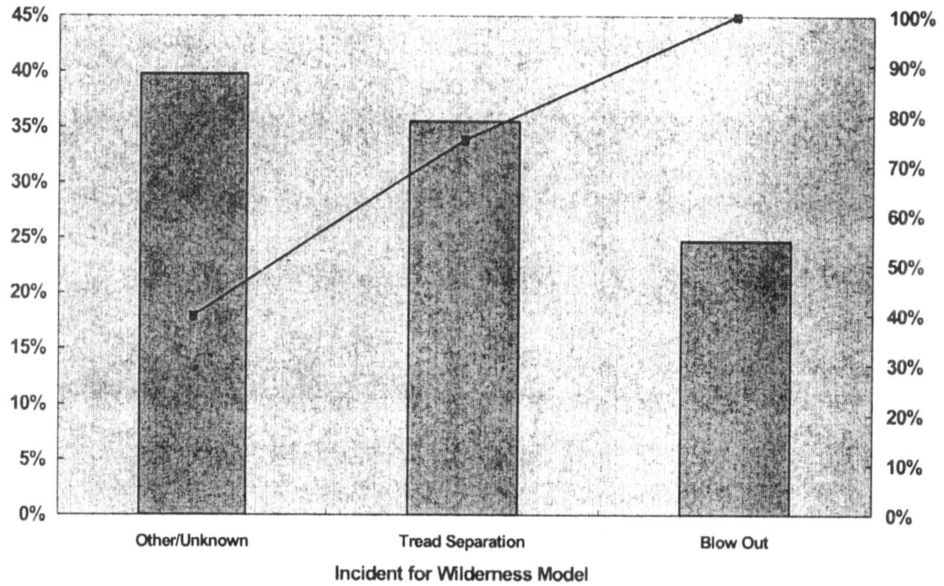


The number of claims is quite evenly distributed among the three incidents. The incident of "other/unknown" accounts for almost 40% of the claims, the incident of "tread separation" accounts for about 35% of the claims while the incident of "blow out" accounts for about 25% of the claims.

2.74 (a), (c)

| *Cost* | *Frequency* | *Percentage* | *Cumulative Percentage* |
|---|---|---|---|
| Less than 0.75 | 4 | 11.11% | 11.11% |
| 0.75 but less than 1 | 16 | 44.44% | 55.56% |
| 1 but less than 1.25 | 3 | 8.33% | 63.89% |
| 1.25 but less than 1.5 | 8 | 22.22% | 86.11% |
| 1.5 but less than 1.75 | 4 | 11.11% | 97.22% |
| 1.75 but less than 2 | 1 | 2.78% | 100.00% |

| *Calories* | *Frequency* | *Percentage* | *Cumulative Percentage* |
|---|---|---|---|
| 280 but less than 310 | 5 | 13.89% | 13.89% |
| 310 but less than 340 | 9 | 25.00% | 38.89% |
| 340 but less than 370 | 10 | 27.78% | 66.67% |
| 370 but less than 400 | 8 | 22.22% | 88.89% |
| 400 but less than 430 | 4 | 11.11% | 100.00% |

| *Fat* | *Frequency* | *Percentage* | *Cumulative Percentage* |
|---|---|---|---|
| Less than 5 | 1 | 2.78% | 2.78% |
| 5 but less than 10 | 4 | 11.11% | 13.89% |
| 10 but less than 15 | 13 | 36.11% | 50.00% |
| 15 but less than 20 | 9 | 25.00% | 75.00% |
| 20 but less than 25 | 7 | 19.44% | 94.44% |
| 25 but less than 30 | 2 | 5.56% | 100.00% |

2.74 (b)
cont.

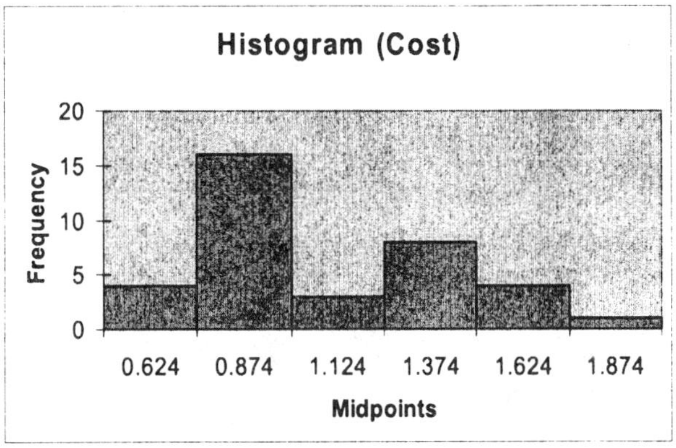
Histogram (Cost)
Frequency
20
15
10
5
0
0.624
0.874
1.124
1.374
1.624
1.874
Midpoints

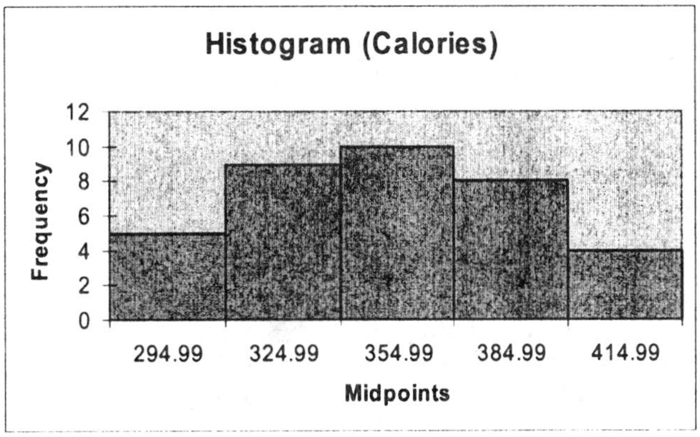
Histogram (Calories)
Frequency
12
10
8
6
4
2
0
294.99
324.99
354.99
384.99
414.99
Midpoints

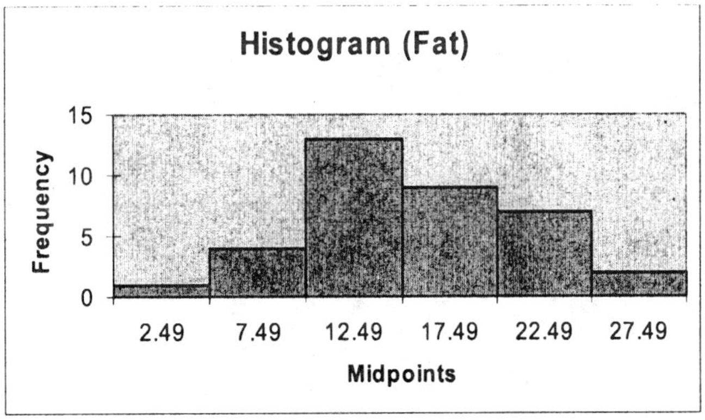
Histogram (Fat)
Frequency
15
10
5
0
2.49
7.49
12.49
17.49
22.49
27.49
Midpoints

2.74 (b)
cont.

Percentage Polygon for Cost

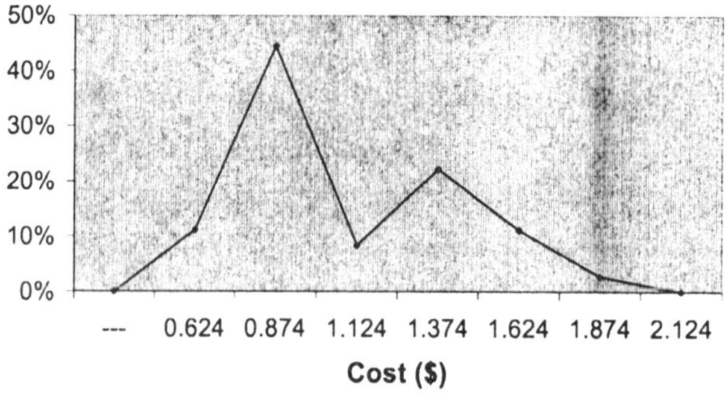


Percentage Polygon for Calories

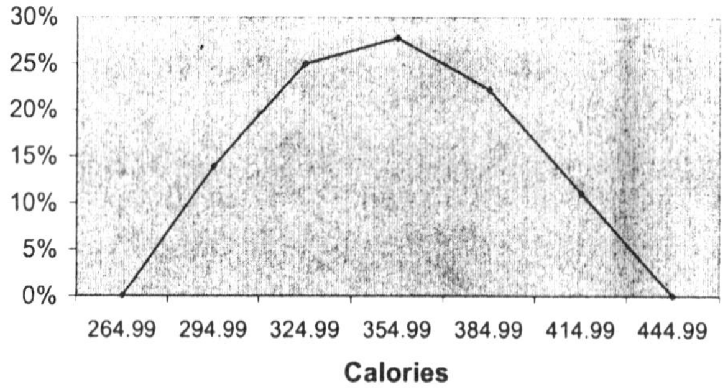


Percentage Polygon for Fat

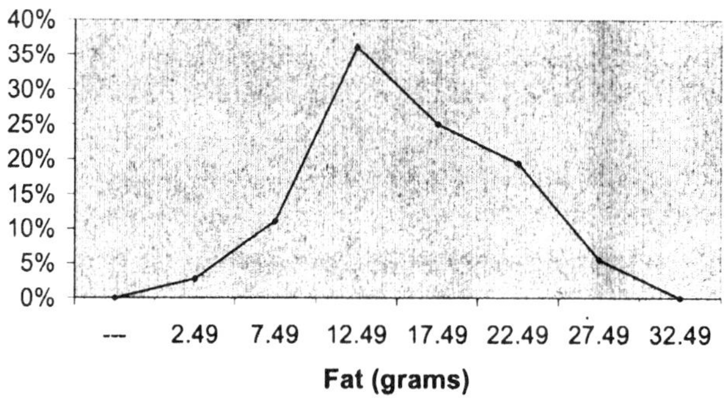

2.74 (c)
cont.

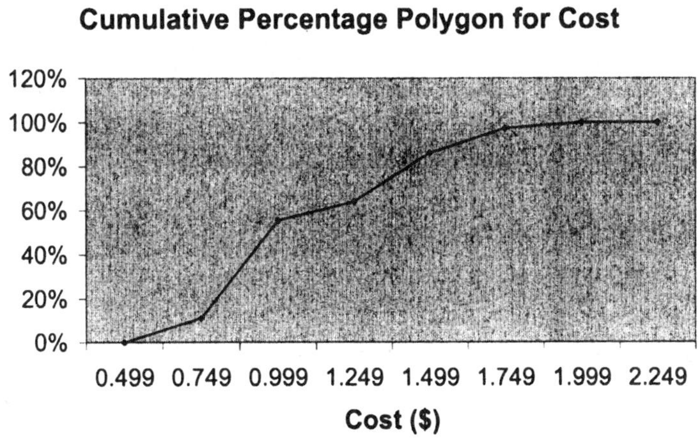
Cumulative Percentage Polygon for Cost
120%
100%
80%
60%
40%
20%
0%
0.499 0.749 0.999 1.249 1.499 1.749 1.999 2.249
Cost ($)

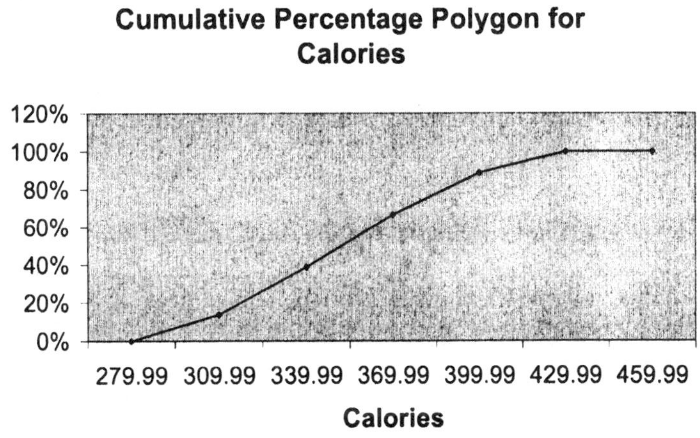
Cumulative Percentage Polygon for Calories
120%
100%
80%
60%
40%
20%
0%
279.99 309.99 339.99 369.99 399.99 429.99 459.99
Calories

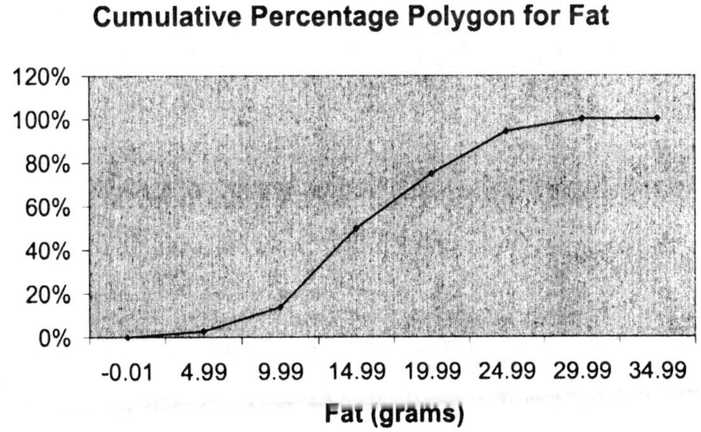
Cumulative Percentage Polygon for Fat
120%
100%
80%
60%
40%
20%
0%
-0.01 4.99 9.99 14.99 19.99 24.99 29.99 34.99
Fat (grams)

2.74 (d)
cont.

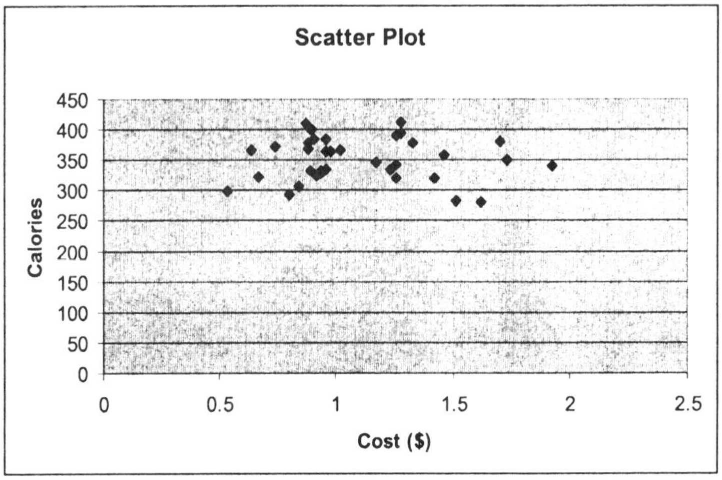
Scatter Plot
Calories
450
400
350
300
250
200
150
100
50
0
0
0.5
1
1.5
2
2.5
Cost ($)

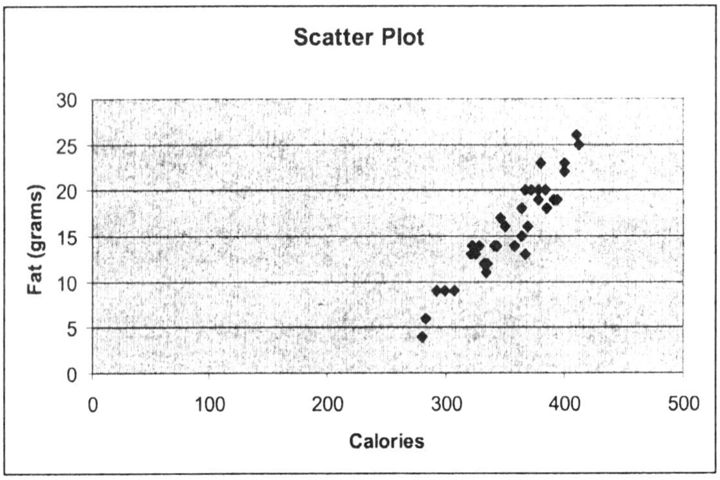
Scatter Plot
Fat (grams)
30
25
20
15
10
5
0
0
100
200
300
400
500
Calories

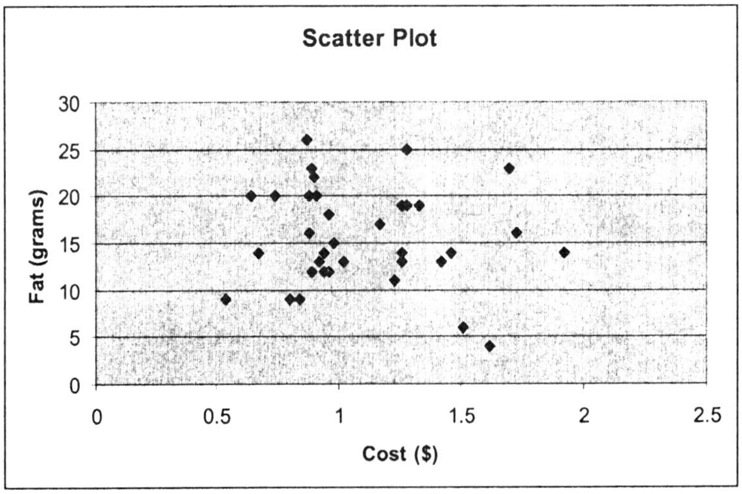
Scatter Plot
Fat (grams)
30
25
20
15
10
5
0
0
0.5
1
1.5
2
2.5
Cost ($)

2.74 cont. (e) The typical cost for a slice of pizza is between $.75 and $1.00 since that is the most frequently occurring interval and better than 50% of the sample is less than or equal to $1.00. The typical caloric content for a slice of pizza is between 310 and 400 calories since better than 80% of the sample falls in that range. More than 73% of the pizzas have between 10 to 20 grams of fat. Based on the results of the pair-wise scatter diagrams, calories and fat seem to be related. Other variables do not show any particular pattern in the scatter plot. But the graph of calories and fat has a positive slope because it rises from left to right, showing that as one variable increases, the other tends to also increase. The data points are tightly distributed within the cloud of points, indicating that the relationship between calories and fat content is strong.

2.76 (a)

**Frequencies (Boston)**

| *Weight (Boston)* | *Frequency* | *Percentage* |
|---|---|---|
| 3015 but less than 3050 | 2 | 0.54% |
| 3050 but less than 3085 | 44 | 11.96% |
| 3085 but less than 3120 | 122 | 33.15% |
| 3120 but less than 3155 | 131 | 35.60% |
| 3155 but less than 3190 | 58 | 15.76% |
| 3190 but less than 3225 | 7 | 1.90% |
| 3225 but less than 3260 | 3 | 0.82% |
| 3260 but less than 3295 | 1 | 0.27% |

(b)

**Frequencies (Vermont)**

| *Weight (Vermont)* | *Frequency* | *Percentage* |
|---|---|---|
| 3550 but less than 3600 | 4 | 1.21% |
| 3600 but less than 3650 | 31 | 9.39% |
| 3650 but less than 3700 | 115 | 34.85% |
| 3700 but less than 3750 | 131 | 39.70% |
| 3750 but less than 3800 | 36 | 10.91% |
| 3800 but less than 3850 | 12 | 3.64% |
| 3850 but less than 3900 | 1 | 0.30% |

2.76 (c)
cont.

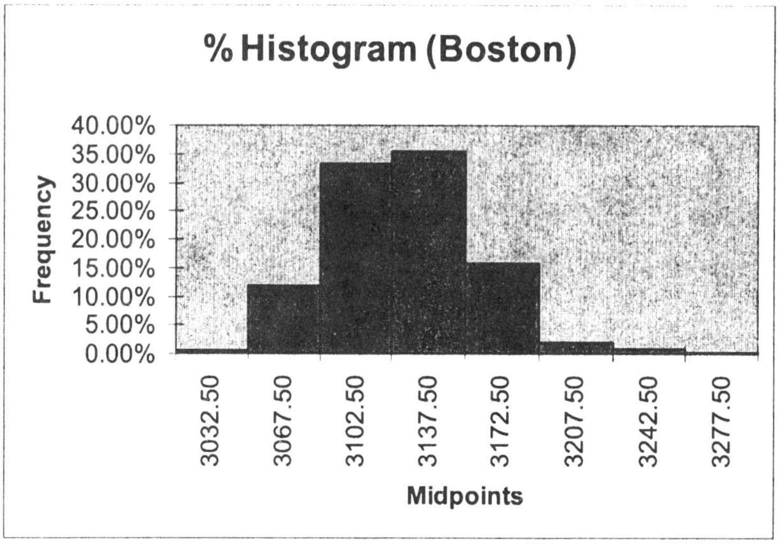


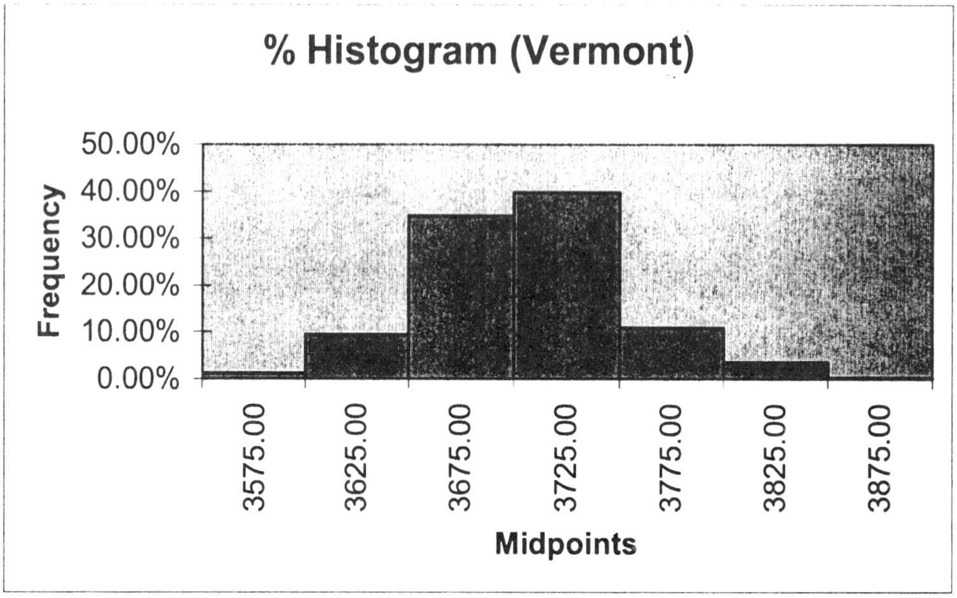


(d) 0.54% of the "Boston" shingles pallets are underweight while 0.27% are overweight. 1.21% of the "Vermont" shingles pallets are underweight while 3.94% are overweight.

2.78 (a), (c)

| Calories | Frequency | Percentage | Percentage Less Than |
|---|---|---|---|
| 50 up to 100 | 3 | 12% | 12% |
| 100 up to 150 | 3 | 12 | 24 |
| 150 up to 200 | 9 | 36 | 60 |
| 200 up to 250 | 6 | 24 | 84 |
| 250 up to 300 | 3 | 12 | 96 |
| 300 up to 350 | 0 | 0 | 96 |
| 350 up to 400 | 1 | 4 | 100 |
| **Protein** | **Frequency** | **Percentage** | **Percentage Less Than** |
| 16 up to 20 | 1 | 4 | 4 |
| 20 up to 24 | 5 | 20 | 24 |
| 24 up to 28 | 8 | 32 | 56 |
| 28 up to 32 | 9 | 36 | 92 |
| 32 up to 36 | 2 | 8 | 100 |
| **Calories from Fat** | **Frequency** | **Percentage of Percentage** | **Percentage Less Than** |
| 0% up to 10% | 3 | 12 | 12 |
| 10% up to 20% | 4 | 16 | 28 |
| 20% up to 30% | 2 | 8 | 36 |
| 30% up to 40% | 5 | 20 | 56 |
| 40% up to 50% | 3 | 12 | 68 |
| 50% up to 60% | 5 | 20 | 88 |
| 60% up to 70% | 2 | 8 | 96 |
| 70% up to 80% | 1 | 4 | 100 |
| **Calories from Saturated Fat** | **Frequency** | **Percentage of Percentage** | **Percentage Less Than** |
| 0% up to 5% | 6 | 24 | 24 |
| 5% up to 10% | 2 | 8 | 32 |
| 10% up to 15% | 5 | 20 | 52 |
| 15% up to 20% | 5 | 20 | 72 |
| 20% up to 25% | 5 | 20 | 92 |
| 25% up to 30% | 2 | 8 | 100 |
| **Cholesterol** | **Frequency** | **Percentage** | **Percentage Less Than** |
| 0 up to 50 | 2 | 8 | 8% |
| 50 up to 100 | 17 | 68 | 76 |
| 100 up to 150 | 4 | 16 | 92 |
| 150 up to 200 | 1 | 4 | 96 |
| 200 up to 250 | 0 | 0 | 96 |
| 250 up to 300 | 0 | 0 | 96 |
| 300 up to 350 | 0 | 0 | 96 |
| 350 up to 400 | 0 | 0 | 96 |
| 400 up to 450 | 0 | 0 | 96 |
| 450 up to 500 | 1 | 4 | 100 |

2.78 (b)
cont.

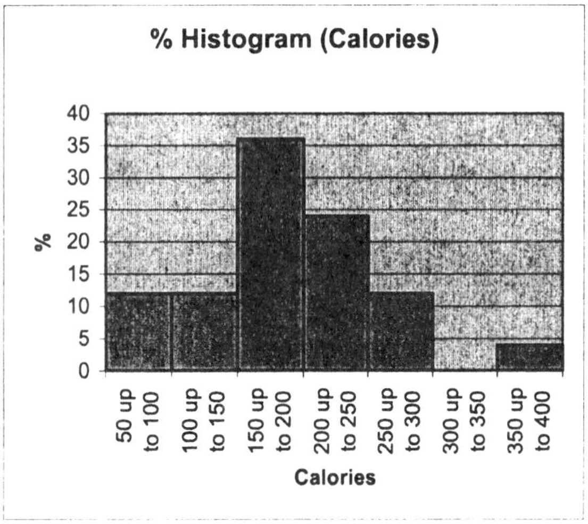
% Histogram (Calories)
%
40
35
30
25
20
15
10
5
0
50 up to 100
100 up to 150
150 up to 200
200 up to 250
250 up to 300
300 up to 350
350 up to 400
Calories

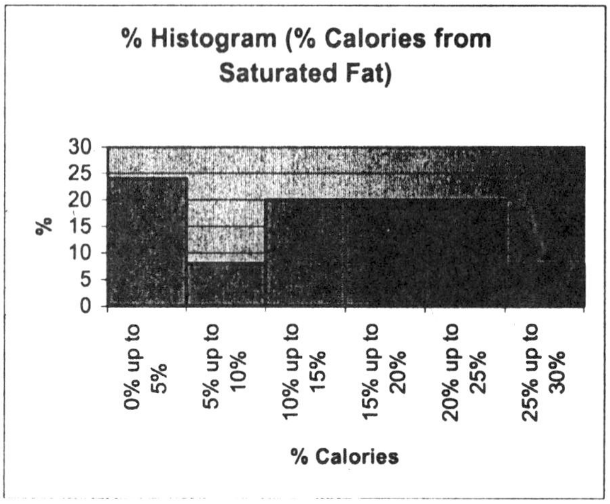
% Histogram (% Calories from Saturated Fat)
%
30
25
20
15
10
5
0
0% up to 5%
5% up to 10%
10% up to 15%
15% up to 20%
20% up to 25%
25% up to 30%
% Calories

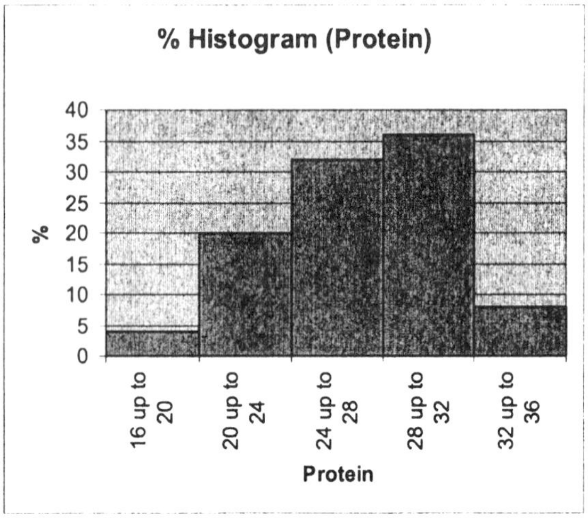
% Histogram (Protein)
%
40
35
30
25
20
15
10
5
0
16 up to 20
20 up to 24
24 up to 28
28 up to 32
32 up to 36
Protein

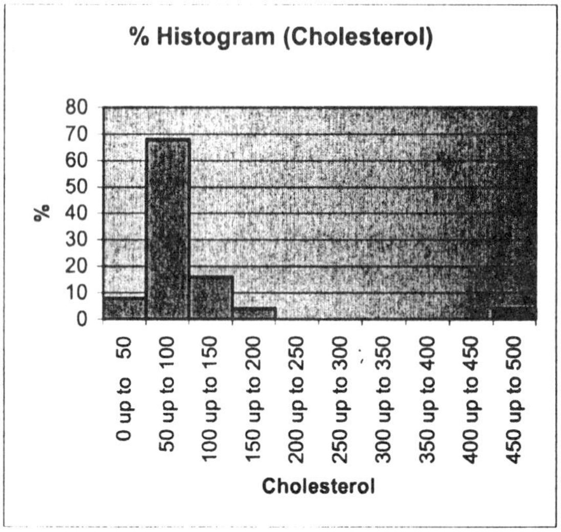
% Histogram (Cholesterol)
%
80
70
60
50
40
30
20
10
0
0 up to 50
50 up to 100
100 up to 150
150 up to 200
200 up to 250
250 up to 300
300 up to 350
350 up to 400
400 up to 450
450 up to 500
Cholesterol

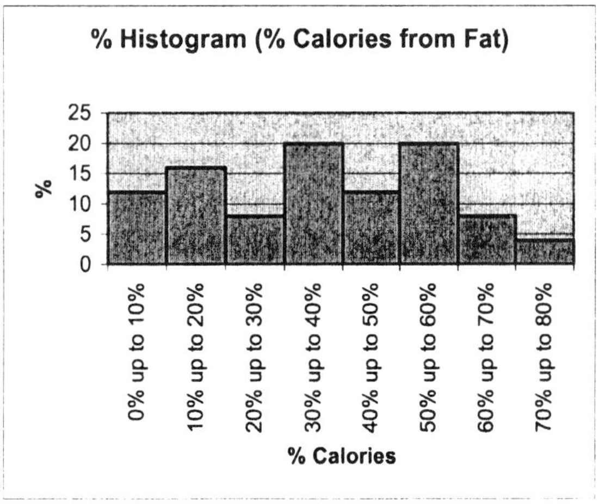
% Histogram (% Calories from Fat)
%
25
20
15
10
5
0
0% up to 10%
10% up to 20%
20% up to 30%
30% up to 40%
40% up to 50%
50% up to 60%
60% up to 70%
70% up to 80%
% Calories

2.78 (b)
cont.

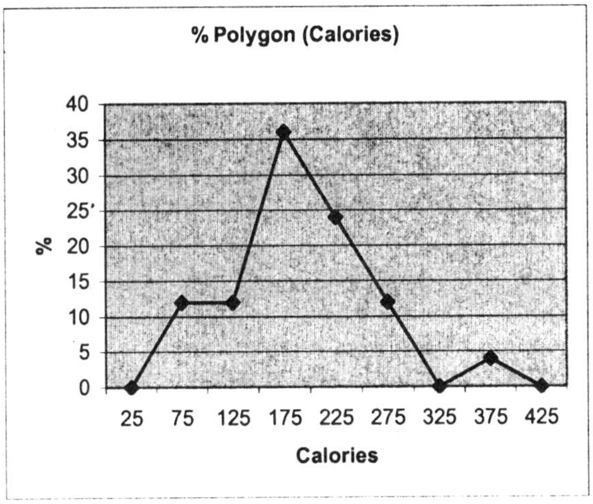
% Polygon (Calories)
40
35
30
25
20
15
10
5
0
%
25 75 125 175 225 275 325 375 425
Calories

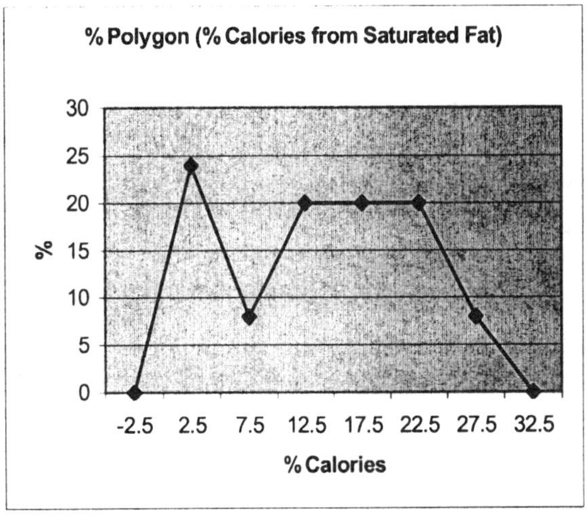
% Polygon (% Calories from Saturated Fat)
30
25
20
15
10
5
0
%
-2.5 2.5 7.5 12.5 17.5 22.5 27.5 32.5
% Calories

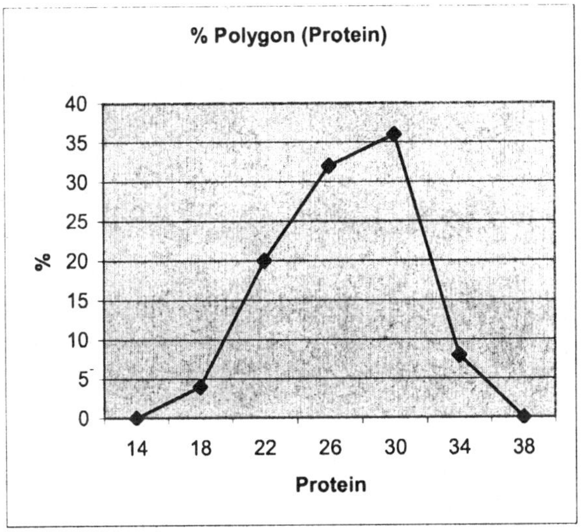
% Polygon (Protein)
40
35
30
25
20
15
10
5
0
%
14 18 22 26 30 34 38
Protein

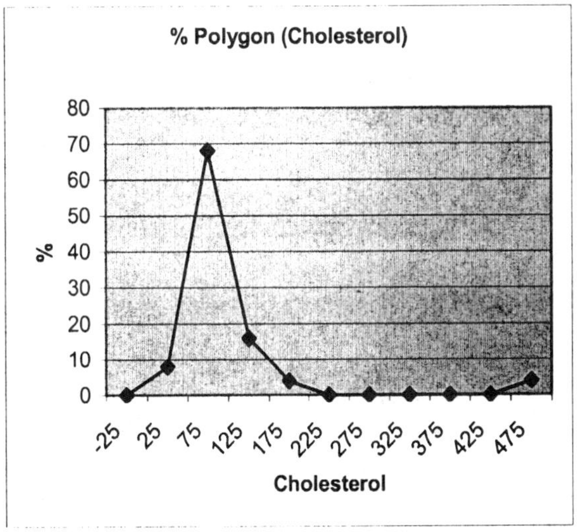
% Polygon (Cholesterol)
80
70
60
50
40
30
20
10
0
%
-25 25 75 125 175 225 275 325 375 425 475
Cholesterol

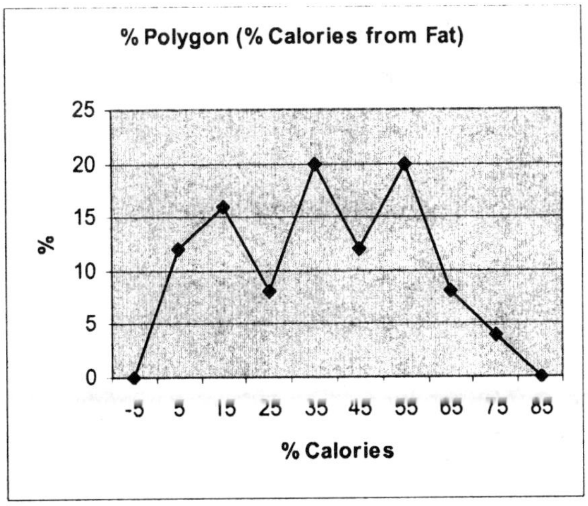
% Polygon (% Calories from Fat)
25
20
15
10
5
0
%
-5 5 15 25 35 45 55 65 75 85
% Calories

2.78 (c)
cont.

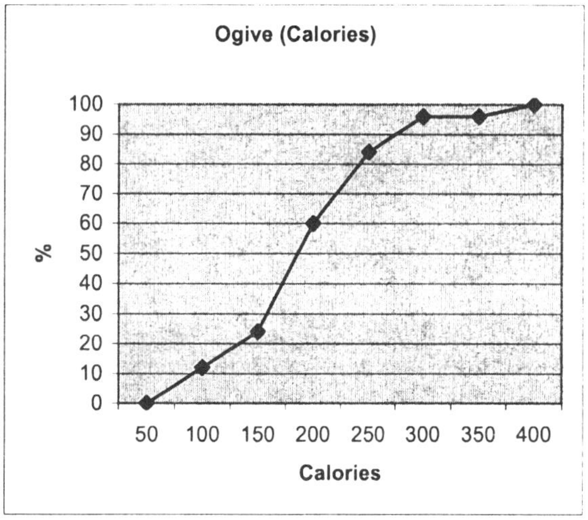
Ogive (Calories)
%
100
90
80
70
60
50
40
30
20
10
0
50 100 150 200 250 300 350 400
Calories

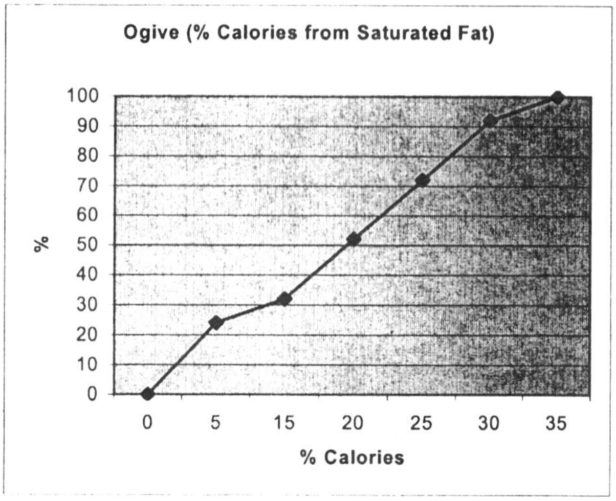
Ogive (% Calories from Saturated Fat)
%
100
90
80
70
60
50
40
30
20
10
0
0 5 15 20 25 30 35
% Calories

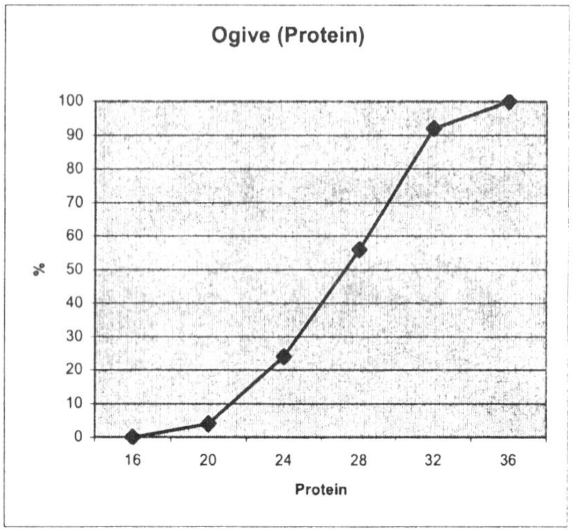
Ogive (Protein)
%
100
90
80
70
60
50
40
30
20
10
0
16 20 24 28 32 36
Protein

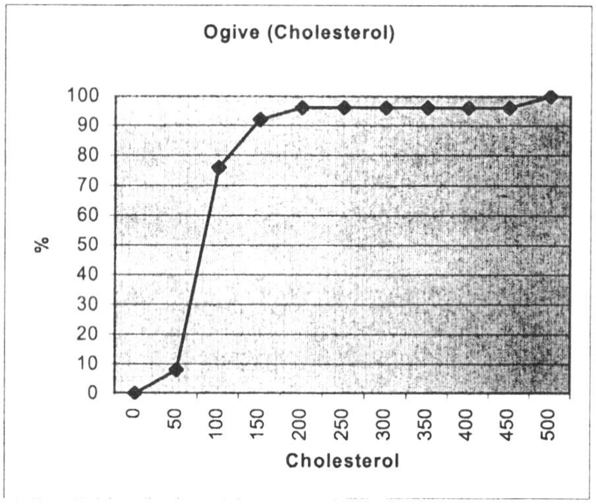
Ogive (Cholesterol)
%
100
90
80
70
60
50
40
30
20
10
0
0 50 100 150 200 250 300 350 400 450 500
Cholesterol

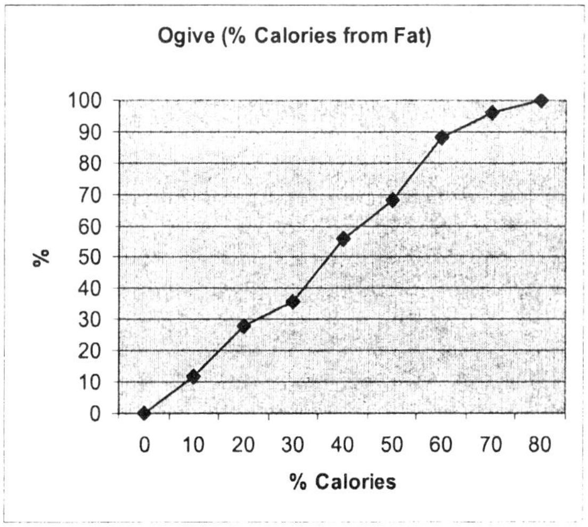
Ogive (% Calories from Fat)
%
100
90
80
70
60
50
40
30
20
10
0
0 10 20 30 40 50 60 70 80
% Calories

2.78 cont. (d) The sampled fresh red meats, poultry, and fish vary from 98 to 397 calories per serving with the highest concentration between 150 to 200 calories. One protein source, spareribs with 397 calories, was over 100 calories beyond the next highest caloric food. The protein content of the sampled foods varies from 16 to 33 grams with 68% of the data values falling between 24 and 32 grams. Spareribs and fried liver are both very different from other foods sampled, the former on calories and the latter on cholesterol content.

2.80 (a)

| Count of Drive Type | Fuel Type | | | |
|---|---|---|---|---|
| Drive Type | Diesel | Premium | Regular | Grand Total |
| AWD | 0 | 5 | 2 | 7 |
| Front | 1 | 18 | 63 | 82 |
| Front, AWD | 0 | 0 | 1 | 1 |
| Permanent 4WD | 0 | 3 | 0 | 3 |
| Rear | 0 | 11 | 17 | 28 |
| Grand Total | 1 | 37 | 83 | 121 |

(b)

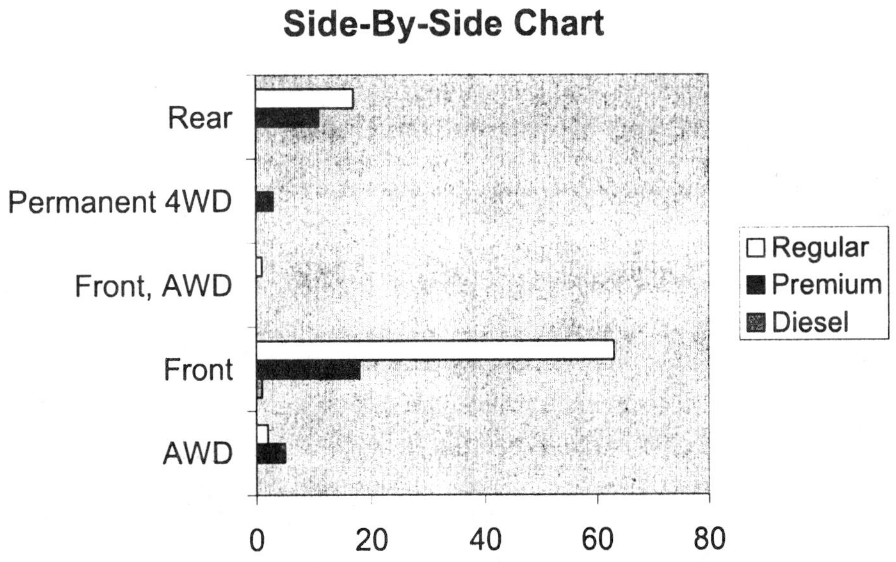


(c) Based on the results of (a) and (b), the percentage of front-wheels drive cars that use regular gasoline appears to be higher than that for rear-wheel drive cars.

2.82 (a), (c)

| *Average Ticket$* | *Frequency* | *Percentage* | *Cumulative %* |
|---|---|---|---|
| More than 6 and up to 12 | 3 | 10.00% | 10.00% |
| More than 12 and up to 18 | 12 | 40.00% | 50.00% |
| More than 18 and up to 24 | 11 | 36.67% | 86.67% |
| More than 24 and up to 30 | 3 | 10.00% | 96.67% |
| More than 30 and up to 36 | 0 | 0.00% | 96.67% |
| More than 36 and up to 42 | 1 | 3.33% | 100.00% |

| *Fan Cost Index* | *Frequency* | *Percentage* | *Cumulative %* |
|---|---|---|---|
| More than 80 and up to 105 | 2 | 6.67% | 6.67% |
| More than 105 and up to 130 | 7 | 23.33% | 30.00% |
| More than 130 and up to 155 | 10 | 33.33% | 63.33% |
| More than 155 and up to 180 | 9 | 30.00% | 93.33% |
| More than 180 and up to 205 | 1 | 3.33% | 96.67% |
| More than 205 and up to 230 | 1 | 3.33% | 100.00% |

| *Regular season game receipts ($millions)* | *Frequency* | *Percentage* | *Cumulative %* |
|---|---|---|---|
| More than 5 and up to 20 | 5 | 16.67% | 16.67% |
| More than 20 and up to 35 | 7 | 23.33% | 40.00% |
| More than 35 and up to 50 | 5 | 16.67% | 56.67% |
| More than 50 and up to 65 | 6 | 20.00% | 76.67% |
| More than 65 and up to 80 | 5 | 16.67% | 93.33% |
| More than 80 and up to 95 | 1 | 3.33% | 96.67% |
| More than 95 and up to 110 | 1 | 3.33% | 100.00% |

| *Local TV, radio and cable ($millions)* | *Frequency* | *Percentage* | *Cumulative %* |
|---|---|---|---|
| More than 0 and up to 10 | 7 | 23.33% | 23.33% |
| More than 10 and up to 20 | 13 | 43.33% | 66.67% |
| More than 20 and up to 30 | 5 | 16.67% | 83.33% |
| More than 30 and up to 40 | 3 | 10.00% | 93.33% |
| More than 40 and up to 50 | 1 | 3.33% | 96.67% |
| More than 50 and up to 60 | 1 | 3.33% | 100.00% |

| *Other Local Operating Revenue* | *Frequency* | *Percentage* | *Cumulative %* |
|---|---|---|---|
| More than 0 and up to 10 | 6 | 20.00% | 20.00% |
| More than 10 and up to 20 | 3 | 10.00% | 30.00% |
| More than 20 and up to 30 | 8 | 26.67% | 56.67% |
| More than 30 and up to 40 | 8 | 26.67% | 83.33% |
| More than 40 and up to 50 | 3 | 10.00% | 93.33% |
| More than 50 and up to 60 | 1 | 3.33% | 96.67% |
| More than 60 and up to 70 | 1 | 3.33% | 100.00% |

2.82 cont. (a), (c)

| *Player compensation and benefits* | *Frequency* | *Percentage* | *Cumulative %* |
|---|---|---|---|
| More than 30 and up to 45 | 5 | 16.67% | 16.67% |
| More than 45 and up to 60 | 8 | 26.67% | 43.33% |
| More than 60 and up to 75 | 4 | 13.33% | 56.67% |
| More than 75 and up to 90 | 5 | 16.67% | 73.33% |
| More than 90 and up to 105 | 5 | 16.67% | 90.00% |
| More than 105 and up to 120 | 3 | 10.00% | 100.00% |

| *National and other local Expenses* | *Frequency* | *Percentage* | *Cumulative %* |
|---|---|---|---|
| More than 30 and up to 40 | 4 | 13.33% | 13.33% |
| More than 40 and up to 50 | 10 | 33.33% | 46.67% |
| More than 50 and up to 60 | 9 | 30.00% | 76.67% |
| More than 60 and up to 70 | 2 | 6.67% | 83.33% |
| More than 70 and up to 80 | 3 | 10.00% | 93.33% |
| More than 80 and up to 90 | 2 | 6.67% | 100.00% |

| *Income from Baseball Operations* | *Frequency* | *Percentage* | *Cumulative %* |
|---|---|---|---|
| More than -60 and up to -45 | 2 | 6.67% | 6.67% |
| More than -45 and up to -30 | 2 | 6.67% | 13.33% |
| More than -45 and up to –15 | 8 | 26.67% | 40.00% |
| More than -15 and up to 0 | 8 | 26.67% | 66.67% |
| More than 0 and up to 15 | 7 | 23.33% | 90.00% |
| More than 15 and up to 30 | 1 | 3.33% | 93.33% |
| More than 30 and up to 45 | 2 | 6.67% | 100.00% |

(b), (c)

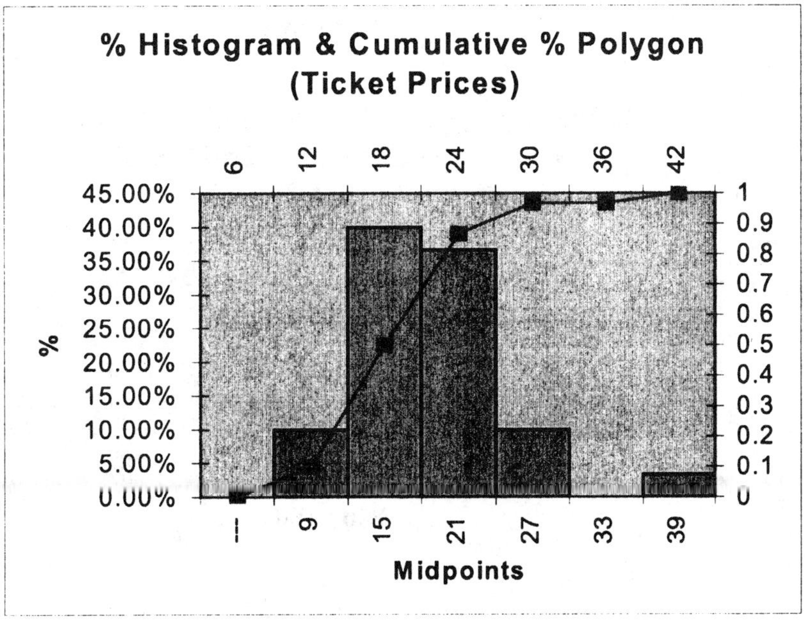

2.82 cont. (b), (c)

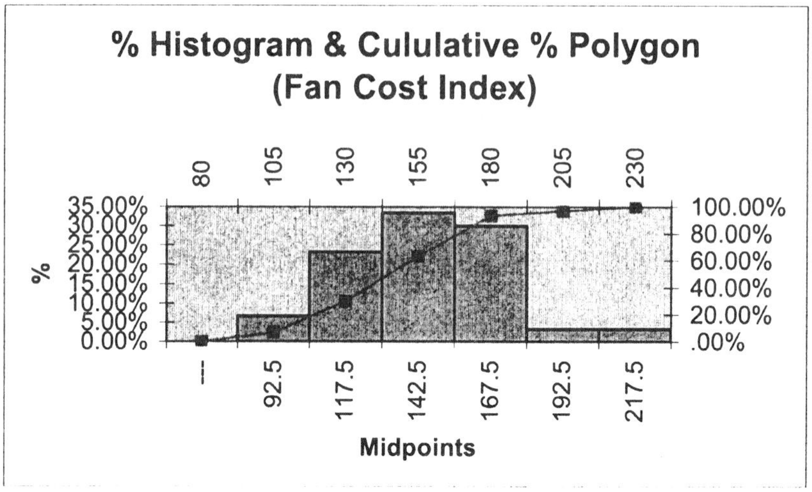
% Histogram & Cululative % Polygon
(Fan Cost Index)
80 105 130 155 180 205 230
35.00% 30.00% 25.00% 20.00% 15.00% 10.00% 5.00% 0.00%
%
100.00% 80.00% 60.00% 40.00% 20.00% .00%
--- 92.5 117.5 142.5 167.5 192.5 217.5
Midpoints

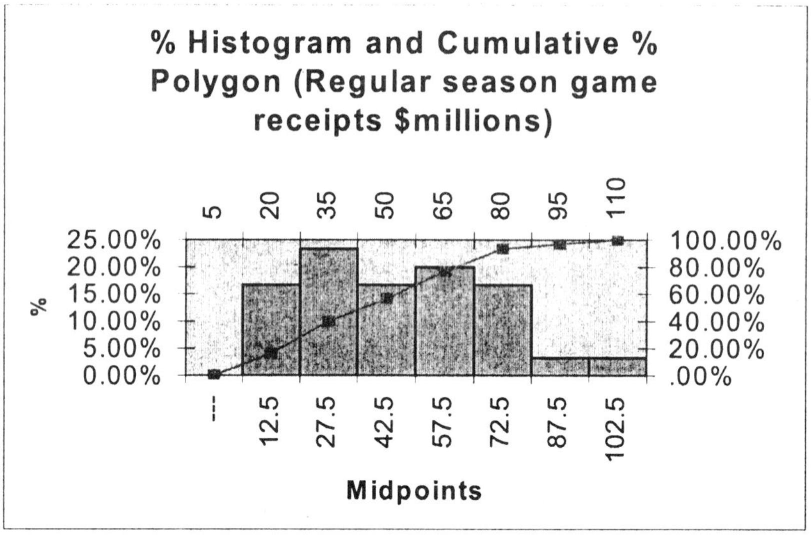
% Histogram and Cumulative % Polygon (Regular season game receipts $millions)
5 20 35 50 65 80 95 110
25.00% 20.00% 15.00% 10.00% 5.00% 0.00%
%
100.00% 80.00% 60.00% 40.00% 20.00% .00%
--- 12.5 27.5 42.5 57.5 72.5 87.5 102.5
Midpoints

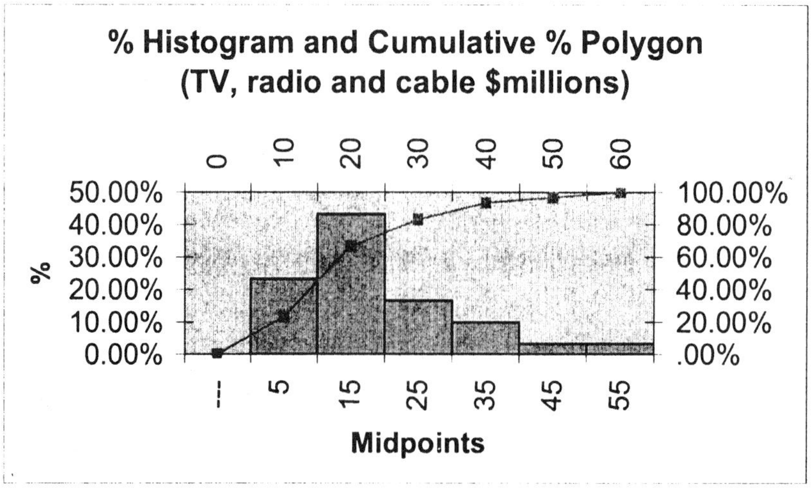
% Histogram and Cumulative % Polygon
(TV, radio and cable $millions)
0 10 20 30 40 50 60
50.00% 40.00% 30.00% 20.00% 10.00% 0.00%
%
100.00% 80.00% 60.00% 40.00% 20.00% .00%
--- 5 15 25 35 45 55
Midpoints

2.82 cont. (b), (c)

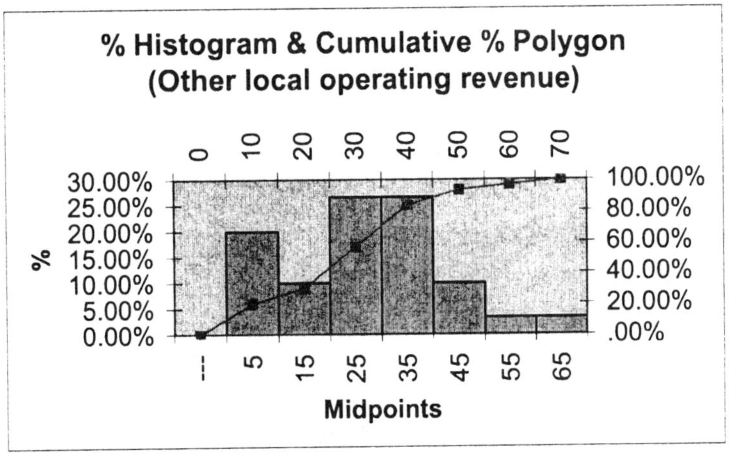
% Histogram & Cumulative % Polygon
(Other local operating revenue)
0 10 20 30 40 50 60 70
30.00% 25.00% 20.00% 15.00% 10.00% 5.00% 0.00%
%
100.00% 80.00% 60.00% 40.00% 20.00% .00%
--- 5 15 25 35 45 55 65
Midpoints

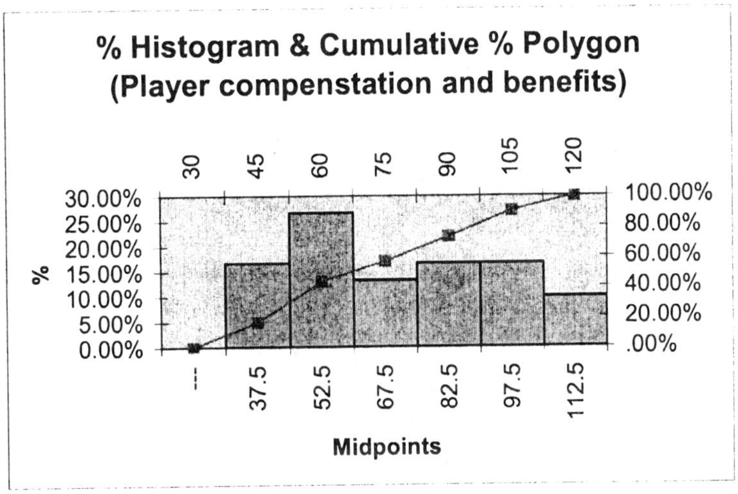
% Histogram & Cumulative % Polygon
(Player compenstation and benefits)
30 45 60 75 90 105 120
30.00% 25.00% 20.00% 15.00% 10.00% 5.00% 0.00%
%
100.00% 80.00% 60.00% 40.00% 20.00% .00%
--- 37.5 52.5 67.5 82.5 97.5 112.5
Midpoints

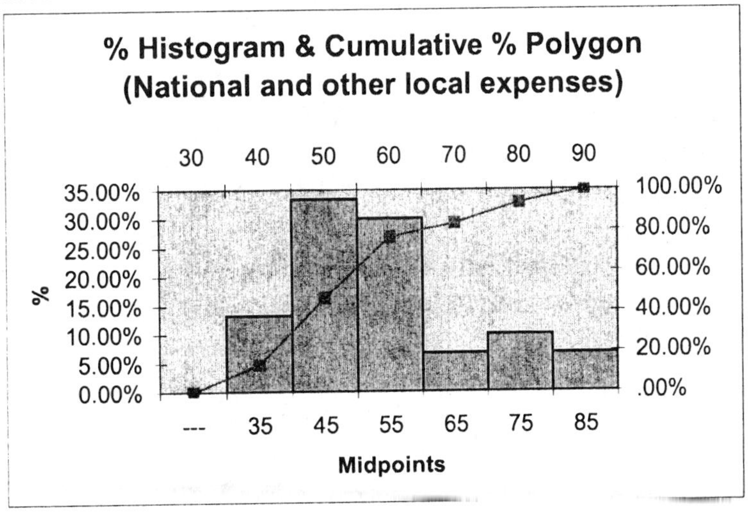
% Histogram & Cumulative % Polygon
(National and other local expenses)
30 40 50 60 70 80 90
35.00% 30.00% 25.00% 20.00% 15.00% 10.00% 5.00% 0.00%
%
100.00% 80.00% 60.00% 40.00% 20.00% .00%
--- 35 45 55 65 75 85
Midpoints

2.82 cont. (b), (c)

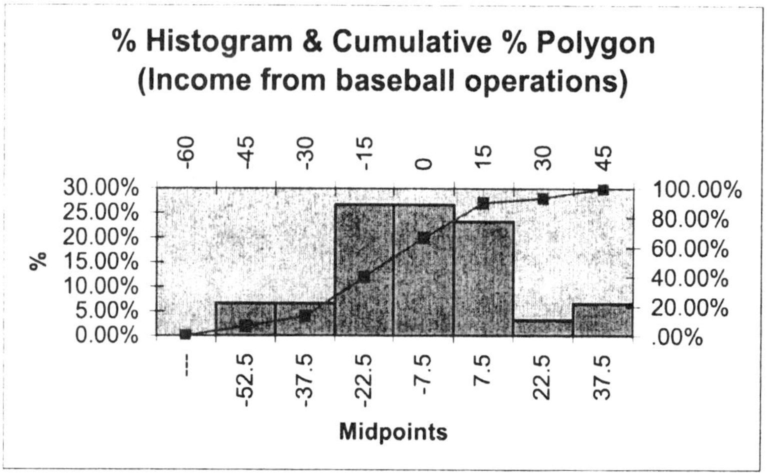
% Histogram & Cumulative % Polygon
(Income from baseball operations)
-60
-45
-30
-15
0
15
30
45
30.00%
25.00%
20.00%
15.00%
10.00%
5.00%
0.00%
%
100.00%
80.00%
60.00%
40.00%
20.00%
.00%
---
-52.5
-37.5
-22.5
-7.5
7.5
22.5
37.5
Midpoints

(b)

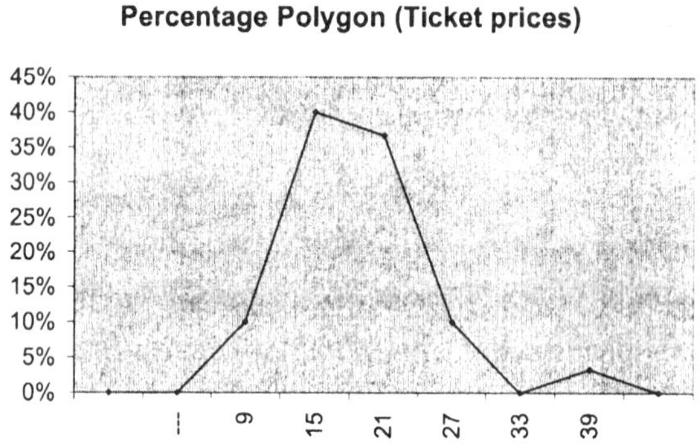
Percentage Polygon (Ticket prices)
45%
40%
35%
30%
25%
20%
15%
10%
5%
0%
---
9
15
21
27
33
39

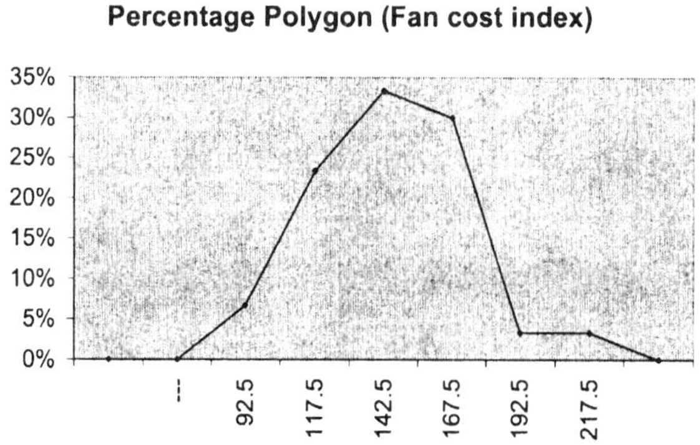
Percentage Polygon (Fan cost index)
35%
30%
25%
20%
15%
10%
5%
0%
---
92.5
117.5
142.5
167.5
192.5
217.5

2.82 (b)
cont.

**Percentage Polygon (Regular season game receipts)**

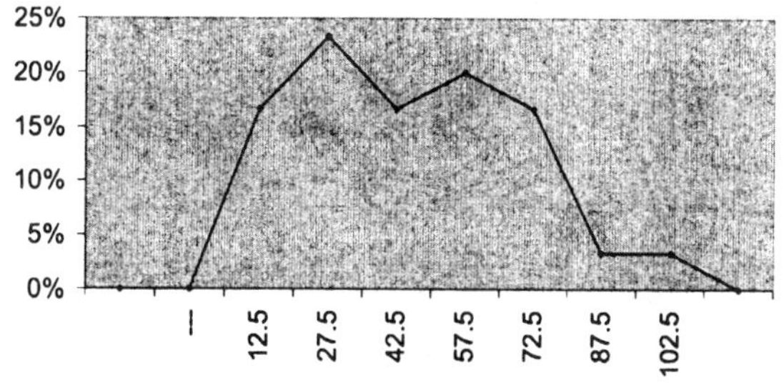


**Percentage Polygon (Local TV, radio and cable ($millions))**

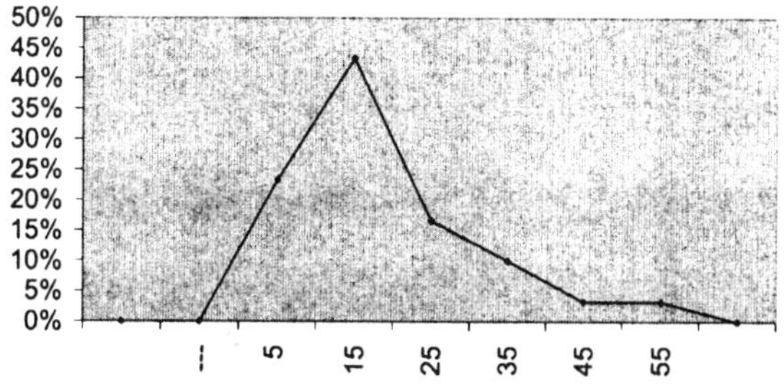


**Percentage Polygon (Other Local Operating Revenue)**

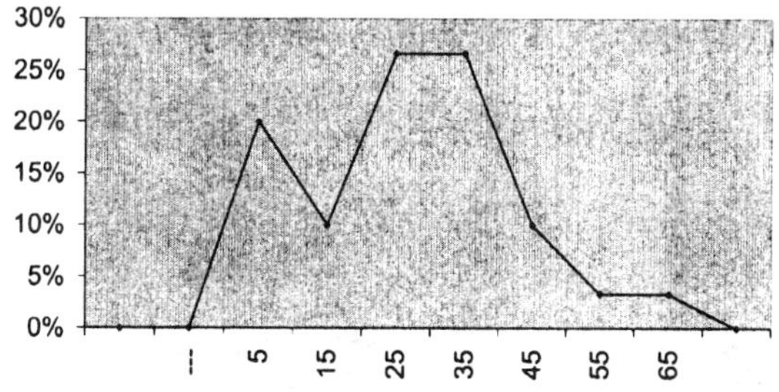


**Percentage Polygon (Player compensation and benefits)**

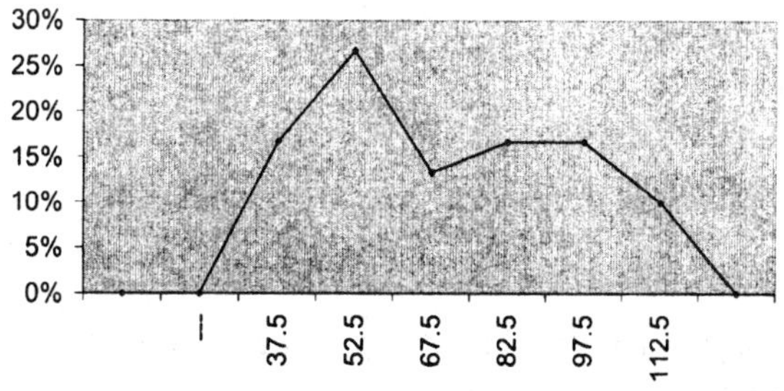

2.82 (b)
cont.

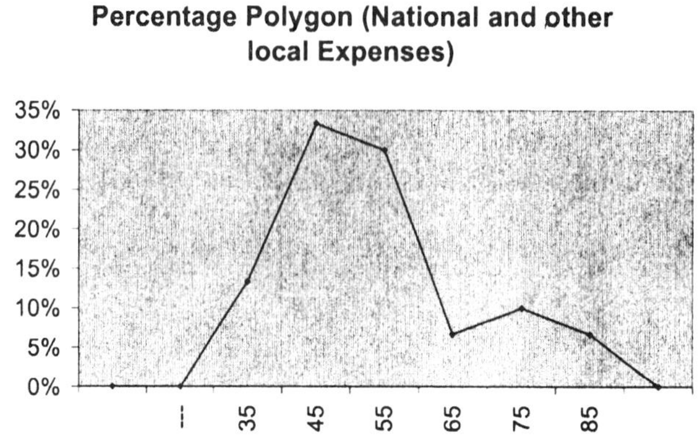


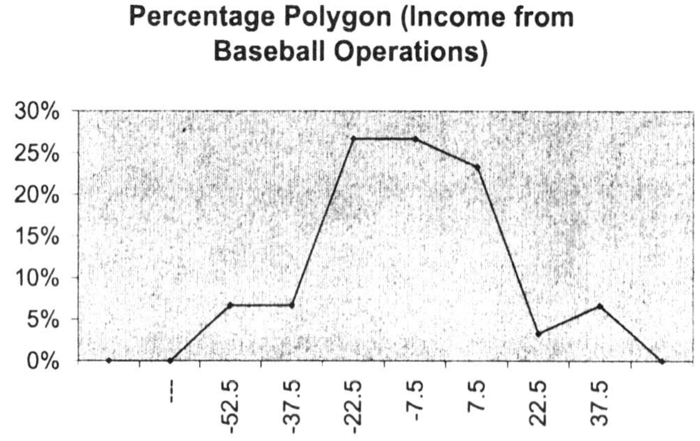


(d)

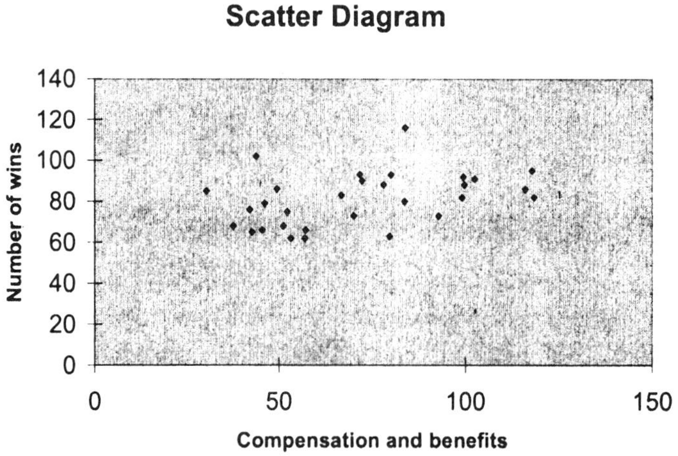


There appears to be a positive linear relationship between number of wins and player compensation and benefits.

2.84 (a)

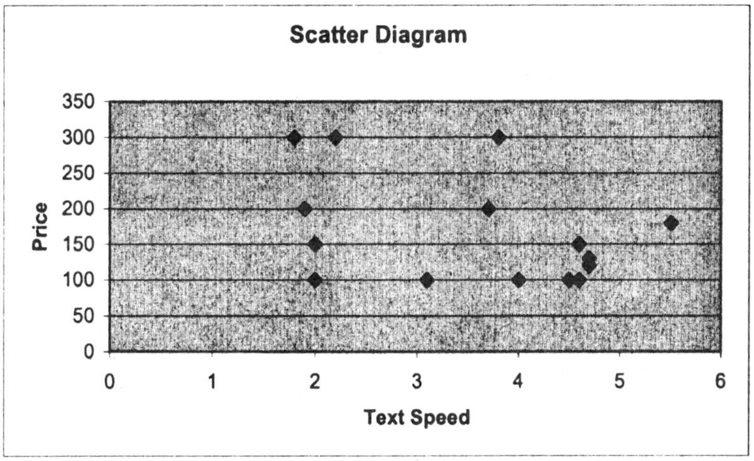
Scatter Diagram
Price
350
300
250
200
150
100
50
0
0 1 2 3 4 5 6
Text Speed

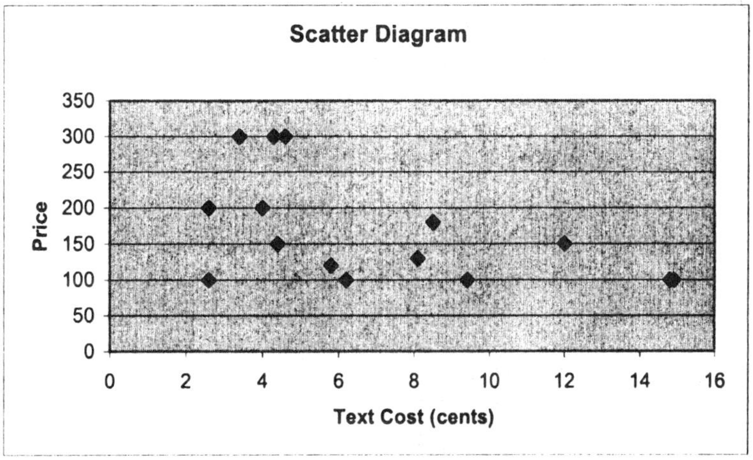
Scatter Diagram
Price
350
300
250
200
150
100
50
0
0 2 4 6 8 10 12 14 16
Text Cost (cents)

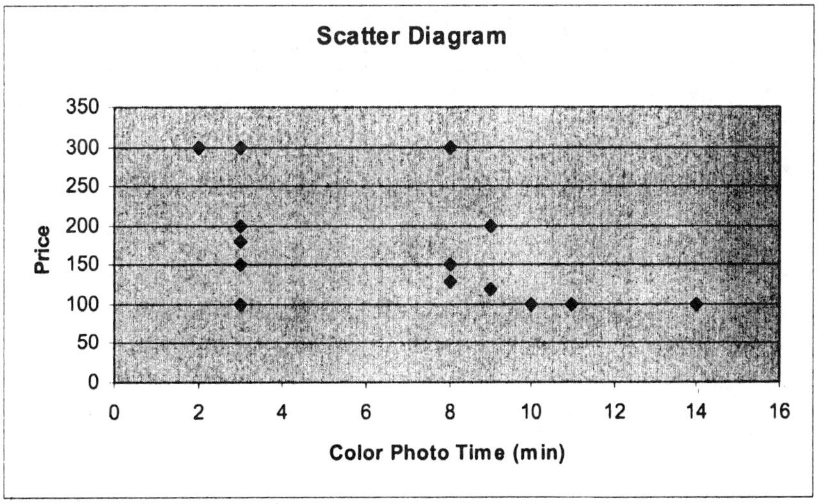
Scatter Diagram
Price
350
300
250
200
150
100
50
0
0 2 4 6 8 10 12 14 16
Color Photo Time (min)

2.84 cont. (a)

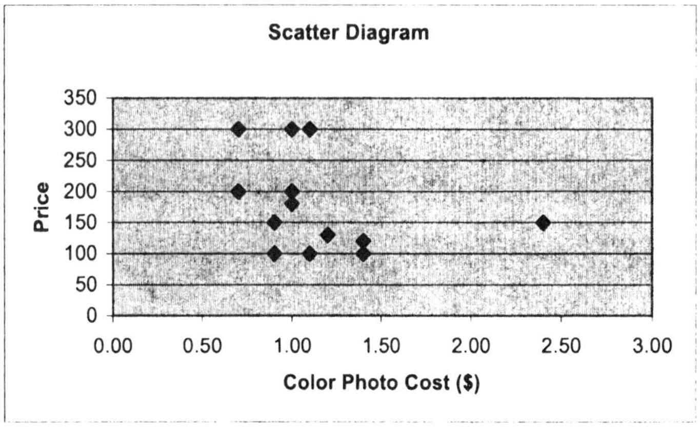


(b) The only variable that appears to be useful in predicting printer price is text cost. There appears to be a negative relationship between price and text cost. The higher the text cost, the lower the printer cost.

2.90 (a)

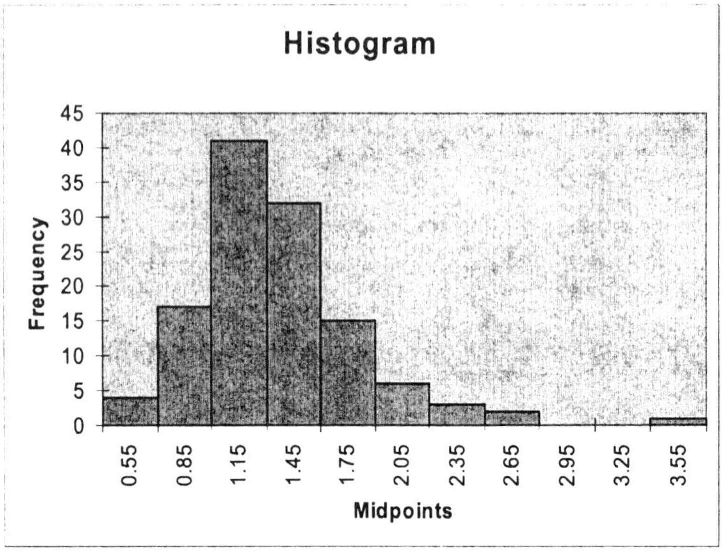

2.90 cont. (b)

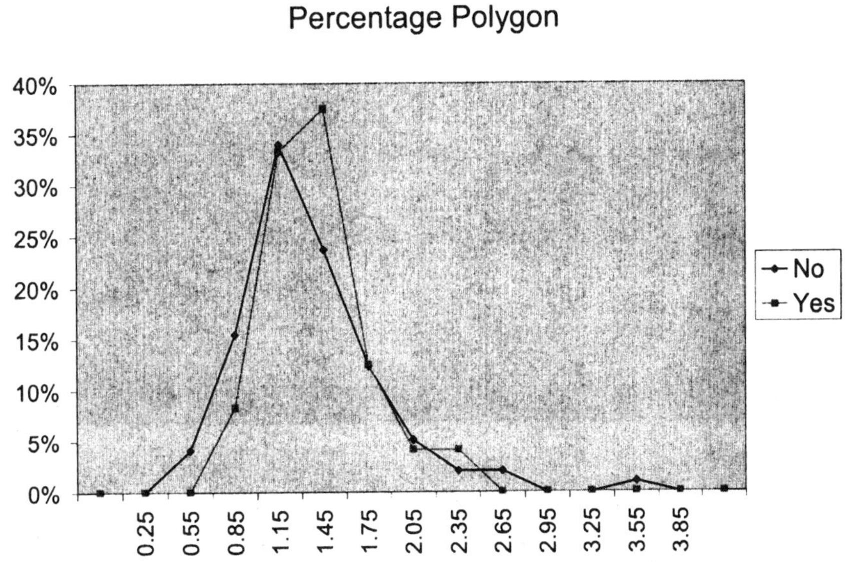


(c) The expense ratio of the 121 mutual funds is skewed to the right with an outlier higher than 3.4%. Majority (105 out of 121) of the expense ratios fall between 0.7% and 1.9%. The expense ratios of both types of mutual funds are skewed to the right. In general, the mutual funds with fees have slightly higher expense ratios than those that do not have fees.

2.92 (a)

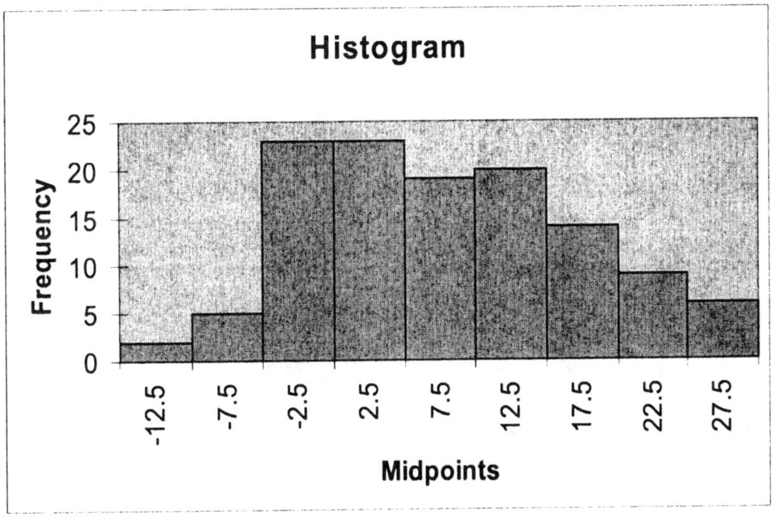

2.92 (b)
cont.

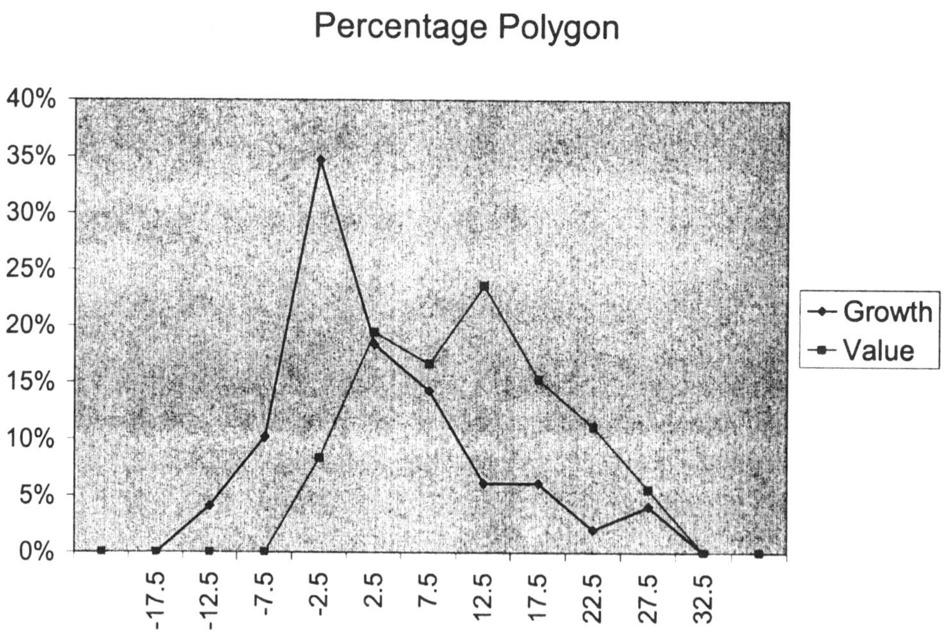


(c) In general, growth mutual funds have lower 3-year annualized return than value mutual funds. The 3-year return of growth mutual funds is right skewed while that of value mutual funds is rather symmetric. More growth mutual funds have a negative return than value mutual funds.

# CHAPTER 3

## OBJECTIVES

- To be able to describe the properties of central tendency, variation, and shape in numerical data
- To be able to calculate descriptive summary measures from population
- To be able to develop and interpret a box-and-whisker plot
- To be able to describe the covariance and the coefficient of correlation

## OVERVIEW AND KEY CONCEPTS

### Measures of Central Tendency

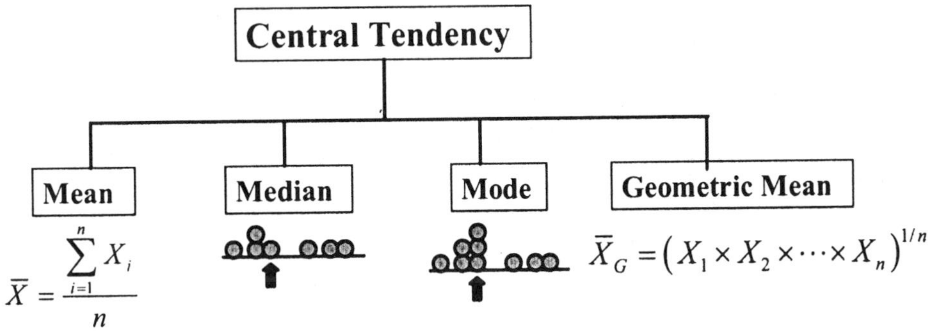


- **Arithmetic mean:** The sum of all the observations in a set of data divided by the total number of observations.
  - $\bar{X} = \dfrac{\sum_{i=1}^{n} X_i}{n}$
  - The arithmetic mean is the most common measure of central tendency.
  - It is very sensitive to extreme values, called outliers.
- **Median:** The value such that 50% of the observations are smaller and 50% of the observations are larger.
  - Median = $\dfrac{n+1}{2}$ ranked observation.
  - If $n$ is odd, the median is the middle ranked observation.
  - If $n$ is even, the median is the average of the two middle ranked observations.
  - The median is not affected by extreme values.

- **Mode:** The value that occurs most often in a set of data.
  - It is not affected by extreme values.
  - There may be several modes or there may be no mode in a set of data.
  - It can be used for either numerical or categorical data.
- **Geometric mean:** The n^th^ root of the product of $n$ values.
  - $\bar{X}_G = (X_1 \times X_2 \times \cdots \times X_n)^{1/n}$
  - It is useful in the measure of rate of change of a variable over time.
  - The geometric mean rate of return can be used to measure the status of an investment over time. $\bar{R}_G = [(1+R_1)\times(1+R_2)\times\cdots\times(1+R_n)]^{1/n} - 1$
- **Quartiles:** The most widely used measures of noncentral location.
  - The ordered data is split into four equal portions.
  - The first quartile ($Q_1$) is the value for which 25% of the observations are smaller and 75% are larger.

    $Q_1 = \dfrac{n+1}{4}$ ordered observation.
  - The third quartile ($Q_3$) is the value for which 75% of the observations are smaller and 25% are larger.

    $Q_3 = \dfrac{3(n+1)}{4}$ ordered observation.
  - The median is the second quartile.

    $Q_2 = \dfrac{(n+1)}{2}$ ordered observation.

## Measures of Variation

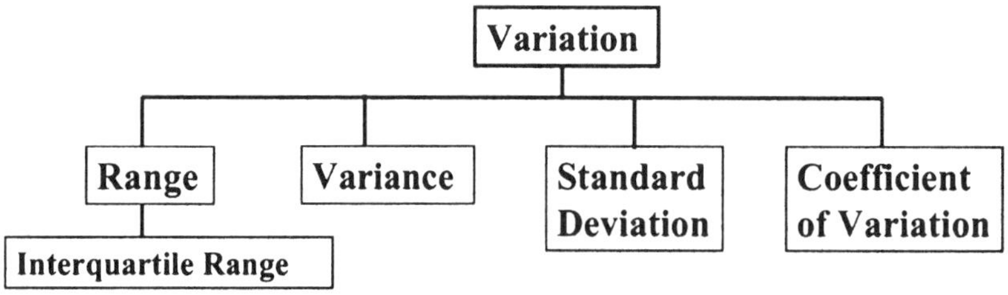


- **Range:** The largest value minus the smallest value.
  - The range ignores how the data are distributed.
  - It is very sensitive to extreme values.
- **Interquartile range (mid-spread):** The 3^rd^ quartile minus the 1^st^ quartile.
  - It is not affected by extreme values.
  - It measures the spread of the middle 50% of the observations.

- **Sample variance:** The sum of the squared differences around the arithmetic mean divided by the sample size minus 1.
  - $S^2 = \dfrac{\sum_{i=1}^{n}(X_i - \bar{X})^2}{n-1}$
  - Sample variance measures the average scatter around the mean.
- **Sample standard deviation:** The square root of the sample variance.
  - $S = \sqrt{\dfrac{\sum_{i=1}^{n}(X_i - \bar{X})^2}{n-1}}$
  - Sample standard deviation has the same units of measurement as the original data.
- **Coefficient of Variation:** The standard deviation divided by the arithmetic mean, multiplied by 100%.
  - $CV = \left(\dfrac{S}{\bar{X}}\right)100\%$
  - It is a relative measure of variation.
  - It is used in comparing two or more sets of data measured in different units.

## Shape of a Distribution

- The shape describes how data is distributed.
- Measures of shapes can be symmetric or skewed.

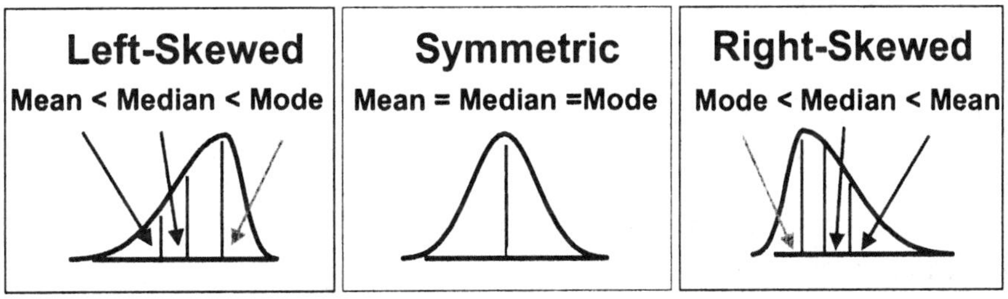


## Exploratory Data Analysis

- A five-number summary consists of $X_{\text{smallest}}$, $Q_1$, Median, $Q_3$, $X_{\text{largest}}$.
- **Box-and-whisker plot:** Provides a graphical representation of the data based on the five-number summary.

## Distribution Shape and Box-and-Whisker Plot

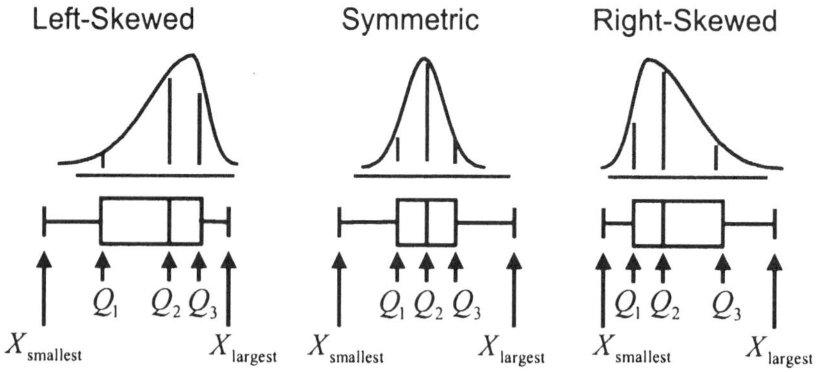


- In right-skewed distributions, the distance from the median to $X_{largest}$ is greater than the distance from $X_{smallest}$ to the median.
- In right-skewed distribution, the distance from $Q_3$ to $X_{largest}$ is greater than the distance from $X_{smallest}$ to $Q_1$.
- In left-skewed distributions, the distance from the median to $X_{largest}$ is smaller than the distance from $X_{smallest}$ to the median.
- In left-skewed distribution, the distance from $Q_3$ to $X_{largest}$ is smaller than the distance from $X_{smallest}$ to $Q_1$.

## Obtaining Descriptive Summary Measures from a Population

- **Population mean:** $\mu = \frac{\sum_{i=1}^{N} X_i}{N}$
- **Population variance:** $\sigma^2 = \frac{\sum_{i=1}^{N} (X_i - \mu)^2}{N}$
- **Population standard deviation:** $\sigma = \sqrt{\frac{\sum_{i=1}^{N} (X_i - \mu)^2}{N}}$
- **The empirical rule:** In bell-shaped distributions, roughly 68% of the observations are contained within a distance of $\pm 1$ standard deviation around the mean, approximately 95% of the observations are contained within a distance of $\pm 2$ standard deviation around the mean and approximately 99.7% are contained within a distance of $\pm 3$ standard deviation around the mean.

- **The Bienaymé-Chebyshev rule:** Regardless of how skewed a set of data is distributed, the percentage of observations that are contained within distances of $k$ standard deviations around the mean must be at least $\left(1-\frac{1}{k^2}\right)100\%$
  - At least 75% of the observations must be contained within distances of $\pm 2$ standard deviation around the mean.
  - At least 88.89% of the observations must be contained within distances of $\pm 3$ standard deviation around the mean.
  - At least 93.75% of the observations must be contained within distances of $\pm 4$ standard deviation around the mean.

## Covariance and Correlation Coefficient as a Measure of Strength between Two Numerical Variables

- **The sample covariance:** $\operatorname{cov}(X,Y)=\frac{\sum_{i=1}^{n}(X_i-\bar{X})(Y_i-\bar{Y})}{n-1}$
  - Measures the strength of a linear relationship between 2 numerical variables $X$ and $Y$.
  - Can have any value.
  - Unsuitable for determining the relative strength of the relationship.
- **The sample coefficient of correlation:** $r=\frac{\sum_{i=1}^{n}(X_i-\bar{X})(Y_i-\bar{Y})}{\sqrt{\sum_{i=1}^{n}(X_i-\bar{X})^2\sum_{i=1}^{n}(Y_i-\bar{Y})^2}}$
  - Measures the strength of a linear relationship between 2 numerical variables $X$ and $Y$.
  - Is unit free.
  - Suitable for determining the relative strength of the relationship.
  - The values are between $-1$ and 1.
  - The closer $r$ is to $-1$, the stronger the negative linear relationship.
  - The closer $r$ is to $+1$, the stronger the positive linear relationship.
  - If $r$ is close to 0, little or no linear relationship exists.

# SOLUTIONS TO END OF SECTION AND CHAPTER REVIEW EVEN PROBLEMS

3.2 (a) Mean = 7 Median = 7 Mode = 7

(b) Range = 9 Variance = 10.8 Interquartile range = 5
Standard deviation = 3.286 Coefficient of variation = (3.286/7)•100% = 46.94%

(c) Z scores: 0, -0.913, 0.609, 0, -1.217, 1.522
None of the Z scores is larger than 3.0 or smaller than -3.0. There is no outlier.

(d) Since the mean equals the median, the distribution is symmetrical.

3.4 (a) Mean = 2 Median = 7 Mode = 7

(b) Range = 17 Variance = 62 Interquartile range = 14.5
Standard deviation = 7.874 Coefficient of variation = (7.874/2)•100% = 393.7%

(c) Since the mean is less than the median, the distribution is left-skewed.

3.6 (a)

| | Grade X | Grade Y |
|---|---|---|
| Mean | 575 | 575.4 |
| Median | 575 | 575 |
| Standard deviation | 6.4 | 2.1 |

(b) If quality is measured by the average inner diameter, Grade X tires provide slightly better quality because X's mean and median are both equal to the expected value, 575 mm. If, however, quality is measured by consistency, Grade Y provides better quality because, even though Y's mean is only slightly larger than the mean for Grade X, Y's standard deviation is much smaller. The range in values for Grade Y is 5 mm compared to the range in values for Grade X which is 16 mm.

(c)

| | Grade X | Grade Y, Altered |
|---|---|---|
| Mean | 575 | 577.4 |
| Median | 575 | 575 |
| Standard deviation | 6.4 | 6.1 |

In the event the fifth Y tire measures 588 mm rather than 578 mm, Y's average inner diameter becomes 577.4 mm, which is larger than X's average inner diameter, and Y's standard deviation swells from 2.07 mm to 6.11 mm. In this case, X's tires are providing better quality in terms of the average inner diameter with only slightly more variation among the tires than Y's.

3.8 (a) The distribution of the price of homes sold will most likely be skewed to the right due to the presence of some extremely expensive homes.

(b) The article reports the median home price and not the mean home price because it is a better measure of central tendency in the presence of some extremely expensive homes that will drive the mean home price upward.

3.10 Excel output:

| Product | Calories | Fat | Calories Z Score | Fat Z Score |
|---|---|---|---|---|
| Dunkin' Donuts Iced Mocha Swirl latte (whole milk) | 240 | 8 | -1.24 | -1.07 |
| Starbucks Coffee Frappuccino blended coffee | 260 | 3.5 | -1.06 | -1.69 |
| Dunkin' Donuts Coffee Coolatta (cream) | 350 | 22 | -0.27 | 0.86 |
| Starbucks Iced Coffee Mocha Expresso (whole milk and whipped cream) | 350 | 20 | -0.27 | 0.58 |
| Starbucks Mocha Frappuccino blended coffee (whipped cream) | 420 | 16 | 0.35 | 0.03 |
| Starbucks Chocolate Brownie Frappuccino blended coffee (whipped cream) | 510 | 22 | 1.15 | 0.86 |
| Starbucks Chocolate Frappuccino Blended Crème (whipped cream) | 530 | 19 | 1.33 | 0.44 |

(a) Calories: mean = 380 median = 350 1st quartile = 260 3rd quartile = 510
Fat: mean = 15.8 median = 19 1st quartile = 8 3rd quartile = 22

(b) Calories: variance = 12800 standard deviation = 113.1 range = 290
interquartile range = 250 CV = 29.77%
None of the Z scores are less than -3 or greater than 3. There is no outlier in calories.
Fat: variance = 52.82 standard deviation = 7.3 range = 18.5
Interquartile range = 14 CV = 46.04%
None of the Z scores are less than -3 or greater than 3. There is no outlier in fat.

(c) Calories are slightly right-skewed while fat is slightly left-skewed.

(d) The mean calories is 380 while the middle ranked calorie is 350. The average scatter of calories around the mean is 113.14. 50% of the calories are scattered over 250 while the difference between the highest and the lowest calories is 290.
The mean fat is 15.79 grams while the middle ranked fat is 19 grams. The average scatter of fat around the mean is 7.27 grams. 50% of the fat is scattered over 14 grams while the difference between the highest and the lowest fat is 18.5 grams.

3.12 Excel output:

| Price($) | Price Z Score |
|---|---|
| 340 | -0.1121 |
| 450 | 1.4576 |
| 450 | 1.4576 |
| 280 | -0.9684 |
| 220 | -1.8246 |
| 340 | -0.1121 |
| 290 | -0.8257 |
| 370 | 0.3160 |
| 400 | 0.7441 |
| 310 | -0.5402 |
| 340 | -0.1121 |
| 430 | 1.1722 |
| 270 | -1.1111 |
| 380 | 0.4587 |

(a) mean = \$348 median = \$340 1st quartile = \$290 3rd quartile = \$400

3.12 cont.
(b) variance = 4910 standard deviation = $70 range = $230
interquartile range = $110 CV = 20.14%
None of the Z scores are less than -3 or greater than 3. There is no outlier in the price.
(c) The price of 3-megapixel cameras is rather symmetrical.
(d) The mean price is $348 while the middle ranked price is $340. The average scatter of price around the mean is $70. 50% of the price is scattered over $110 while the difference between the highest and the lowest price is $230.

3.14 (a) Mean = 473.5 Median = 451 There is no mode.
The median seems to be a better descriptive measure of the data, since it is closer to the observed values than is the mean. Also the outlier of 1049 affects the mean.
(b) Range = 785 Variance = 44,422.44 Standard deviation = 210.77
(c) From the manufacturer's viewpoint, the worst measure would be to compute the percentage of batteries that last over 400 hours (8/13 = .61). The median (451) and the mean (473.5) are both over 400, and would be better measures for the manufacturer to use in advertisements.
(d) (a), (b)

| | Original Data | Altered Data |
|---|---|---|
| Mean | 473.5 | 550.4 |
| Median | 451 | 492 |
| Mode | none | none |
| Range | 785 | 1,078 |
| Variance | 44,422.44 | 99,435.26 |
| Standard deviation | 210.77 | 315.33 |

(c) From the manufacturer's viewpoint, the worst measure remains the percentage of batteries that last over 400 hours (9/13 = .69). The median (492) and the mean (550.38) are both well over 400, and would be better measures for the manufacturer to use in advertisements.
The shape of the distribution of the original data is right-skewed, since the mean is larger than the median.
The shape of the distribution of the altered data set is right-skewed as well, since its mean is also larger than its median.

3.16 (a) Mean = 7.114 Median = 6.68 $Q_1 = 5.64$ $Q_3 = 8.73$
(b) Variance = 4.336 Standard deviation = 2.082 Range = 6.67
Interquartile range = 3.09 Coefficient of variation = 29.27%
There is no outlier since none of the observations are greater than 3 standard deviations away from the mean.
(c) Since the mean is greater than the median, the distribution is right-skewed.
(d) The mean and median are both well over 5 minutes and the distribution is right-skewed, meaning that there are more unusually high observations than low. Further, 13 of the 15 bank customers sampled (or 86.7%) had wait times in excess of 5 minutes. So, the customer is more likely to experience a wait time in excess of 5 minutes. The manager overstated the bank's service record in responding that the customer would "almost certainly" not wait longer than 5 minutes for service.

3.18 (a)

| Year | DJIA | SP500 | Russell2000 | Wilshire5000 |
|---|---|---|---|---|
| 2003 | 25.30 | 26.40 | 45.40 | 29.40 |
| 2002 | -15.01 | -22.10 | -21.58 | -20.90 |
| 2001 | -5.44 | -11.90 | -1.03 | -10.97 |
| 2000 | -6.20 | -9.10 | -3.02 | -10.89 |
| **Geometric mean** | - 1.42% | -5.77% | 2.28% | -5.07% |

(b) The rate of return of SP500 is the worst at -5.77% followed by Wilshire 5000 at -5.07% and DJIA -1.42%. Russell 2000 is the only stock among the four that has a positive rate of return at 2.28% over the four-year period.

(c) In general, investments in the metal market achieved a higher rate of return than investments in the certificate of deposit market from 2000 to 2003. Investments in the stock market had the worse rate of return.

3.20 (a)

| Year | Platinum | Gold | Silver |
|---|---|---|---|
| **2003** | 34.2 | 19.5 | 24.0 |
| **2002** | 24.5 | 24.5 | 5.5 |
| **2001** | -21.3 | 1.2 | -3.0 |
| **2000** | -23.3 | 1.8 | -5.9 |
| **Geometric Mean** | 0.21% | 11.27% | 4.53% |

(b) All three metals achieved positive rate of returns over the four-year period with gold yielding the highest rate of return at 11.27%, followed by silver at 4.53% and platinum at 0.21%.

(c) In general, investments in the metal market achieved a higher rate of return than investments in the certificate of deposit market from 2000 to 2003. Investments in the stock market had the worse rate of return.

3.22 (a) Population Mean = 6

(b) $\sigma^2 = 2.8$ $\qquad \sigma = 1.67$

3.24 (a) 68% (b) 95% (c) not calculable 75% 88.89%

(d) $\mu - 4\sigma$ to $\mu + 4\sigma$ or -2.8 to 19.2

3.26 (a) mean = 12999.2158, variance = 14959700.52, std. dev. = 3867.7772

(b) 64.71%, 98.04% and 100% of these states have average per capita energy consumption within 1, 2 and 3 standard deviation of the mean, respectively.

(c) This is consistent with the 68%, 95% and 99.7% according to the empirical rule.

(d) (a) mean = 12857.7402, variance = 14238110.67, std. dev. = 3773.3421

(b) 66%, 98% and 100% of these states have average per capita energy consumption within 1, 2 and 3 standard deviation of the mean, respectively.

(c) This is consistent with the 68%, 95% and 99.7% according to the empirical rule.

3.28 (a) Five-number summary: 3 4 7 9 12
(b)

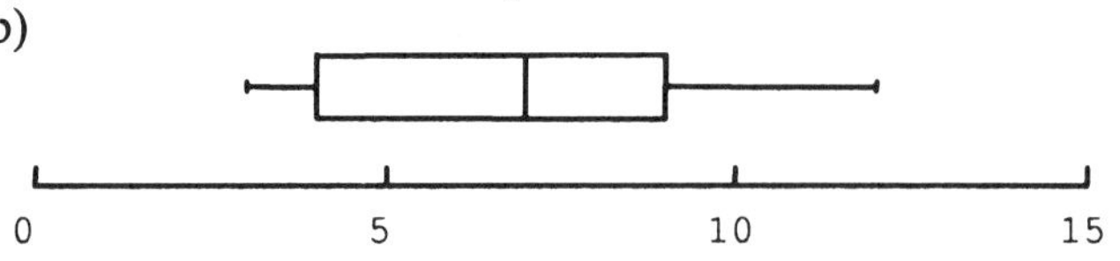


The distribution is almost symmetrical.
(c) The data set is almost symmetrical since the median line almost divides the box in half but the whiskers show right skewness.

3.30 (a) Five-number summary: – 8 – 6.5 7 8 9
(b)

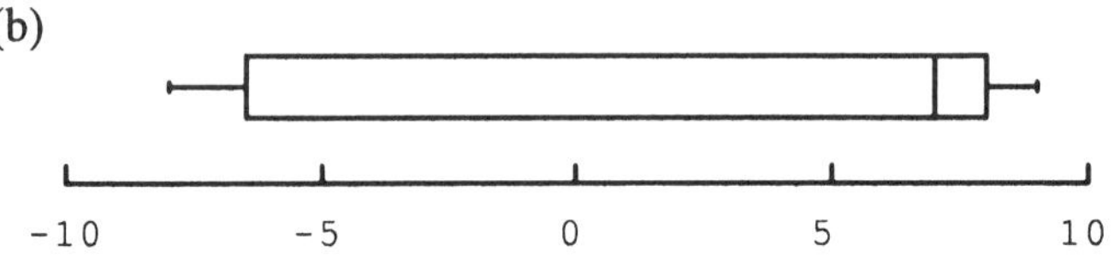


The distribution is left-skewed.
(c) The box-and-whisker plot shows a longer left box from $Q_1$ to $Q_2$ than from $Q_2$ to $Q_3$, visually confirming our conclusion that the data are left-skewed.

3.32 (a) Five-number summary: 308 593 895.5 1425 1720
(b) PHStat output:

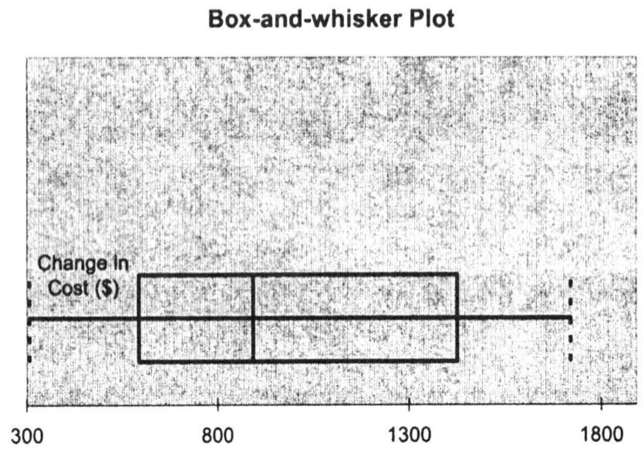


The distribution is skewed slightly to the right.

3.34 (a) **Bounced check fee:** Five-number summary: 15 20 22 26 30
**Monthly service fee:** Five-number summary: 0 5 7 10 12
(b)

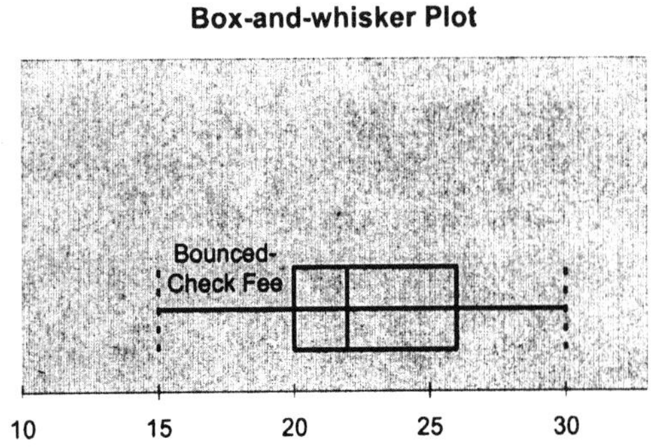


The distribution of bounced-check fee is skewed slightly to the right

3.34 (b)
cont.

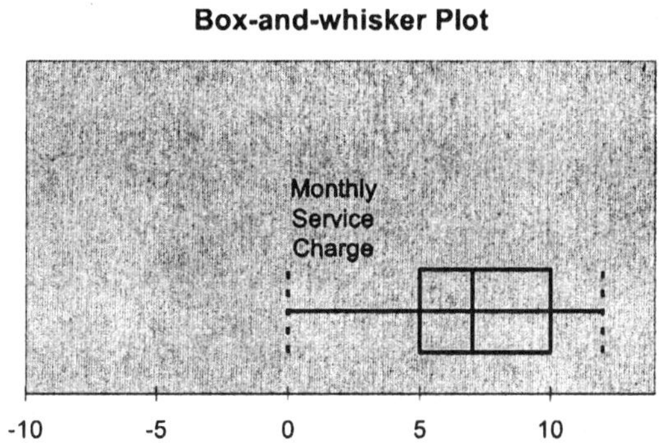


The distribution of monthly service charge is skewed to the left.

(c) The central tendency of the bounced-check fee is substantially higher than that of monthly service fee. While the distribution of the bounced-check fee is quite symmetrical, the distribution of monthly service fee is skewed more to the left with a few banks charging very low or no monthly service fee.

3.36 (a) **Commercial district**: Five-number summary: 0.38 3.2 4.5 5.55 6.46
**Residential area:** Five-number summary: 3.82 5.64 6.68 8.73 10.49

(b) **Commercial district:**

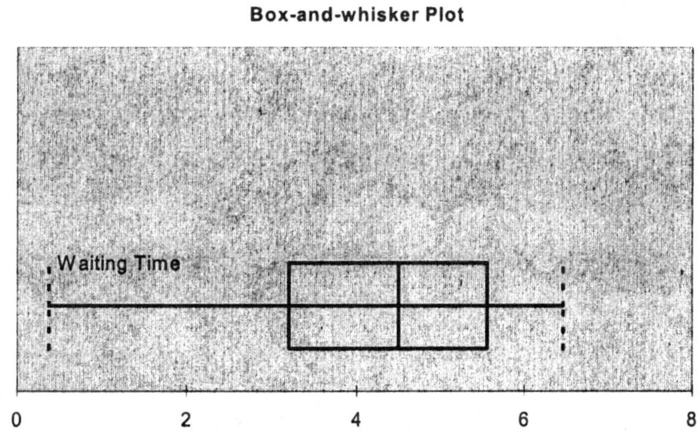


The distribution is skewed to the left.

3.36 cont. (b) **Residential area:**

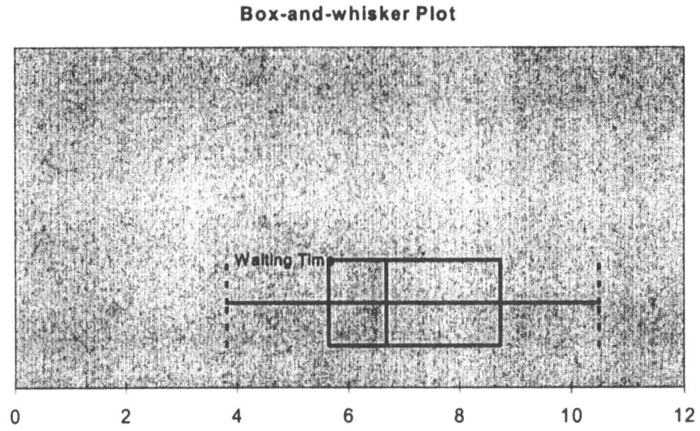


The distribution is skewed slightly to the right.

(c) The central tendency of the waiting times for the bank branch located in the commercial district of a city is lower than that of the branch located in the residential area. There are a few longer than normal waiting times for the branch located in the residential area whereas there are a few exceptionally short waiting times for the branch located in the commercial area.

3.38 (a)

| Pair of Investments | Relationship |
|---|---|
| U.S. stocks and the International Large Cap stocks | strong positive linear relationship |
| U.S. stocks and Emerging market stocks | strong positive linear relationship |
| U.S. stocks and International Small Cap stocks | moderate positive linear relationship |
| U.S. stocks and Emerging market debt stocks | moderate positive linear relationship |
| U.S. stocks and International Bonds | very weak positive linear |

(b) In general, there is a positive linear relationship between the return on investment of U.S. stocks and international stocks, U.S. bonds and international bonds, U.S. stocks and Emerging market debt, and a very weak negative linear relationship, if any, between the return on investment of U.S. bonds and international stocks.

3.40 (a) $$\text{cov}(X,Y)=\frac{\sum_{i=1}^{n}(X_i-\bar{X})(Y_i-\bar{Y})}{n-1}=\frac{3550}{6}=591.6667$$

(b) $$r=\frac{\text{cov}(X,Y)}{S_X S_Y}=\frac{591.6667}{(113.1371)(7.2678)}=0.7196$$

(c) The correlation coefficient is more valuable for expressing the relationship between calories and fat because it does not depend on the units used to measure calories and fat.

(d) There is a rather strong positive linear relationship between calories and fat.

3.42 (a) $\text{cov}(X,Y) = \frac{\sum_{i=1}^{n}(X_i - \bar{X})(Y_i - \bar{Y})}{n-1} = \frac{-6065.2421}{18} = -336.9579$

(b) $r = \frac{\text{cov}(X,Y)}{S_X S_Y} = \frac{-336.9579}{(105.3617)(7.9670)} = -0.4014$

(c) The coefficient of correlation between turnover rate and security violations indicates that there is a moderate negative linear relationship between the two.

3.44 We should look for ways to describe the typical value, the variation, and the distribution of the data within a range.

3.46 The arithmetic mean is a simple average of all the values, but is subject to the effect of extreme values. The median is the middle ranked value, but varies more from sample to sample than the arithmetic mean, although it is less susceptible to extreme values. The mode is the most common value, but is extremely variable from sample to sample.

3.48 Variation is the amount of dispersion, or "spread," in the data.

3.50 The range is a simple measure, but only measures the difference between the extremes. The interquartile range measures the range of the center fifty percent of the data. The standard deviation measures variation around the mean while the variance measures the squared variation around the mean, and these are the only measures that take into account each observation. The coefficient of variation measures the variation around the mean relative to the mean.

3.52 The Chebyshev rule applies to any type of distribution while the empirical rule applies only to data sets that are approximately bell-shaped. The empirical rule is more accurate than Chebyshev rule in approximating the concentration of data around the mean.

3.54 The covariance measures the strength of the linear relationship between two numerical variables while the coefficient of correlation measures the relative strength of the linear relationship. The value of the covariance depends very much on the units used to measure the two numerical variables while the value of the coefficient of correlation is totally free from the units used.

3.56 (a) mean = 43.89 median = 45 1$^{st}$ quartile = 18 3$^{rd}$ quartile = 63

(b) range = 76 interquartile range = 45 variance = 639.2564
standard deviation = 25.28 coefficient of variation = 57.61%

3.56 (c) cont.

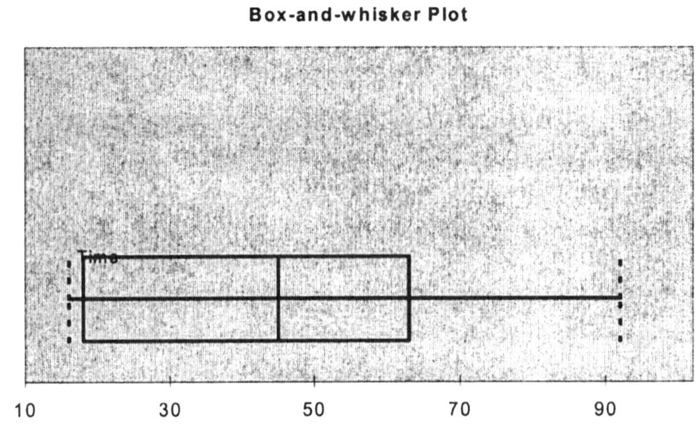


The distribution is skewed to the right because there are a few policies that require an exceptionally long period to be approved. However, if one compares the mean with the median, one can conclude that the distribution is skewed to the left because the mean is smaller than the median.

(d) The mean approval process takes 43.89 days with 50% of the policies being approved in less than 45 days. 50% of the applications are approved between 18 and 63 days. About 67% of the applications are approved between 18.6 to 69.2 days.

3.58 (a) mean = 8.421, median = 8.42, range = 0.186 and standard deviation = 0.0461. On average, the width is 8.421 inches. The width of the middle ranked observation is 8.42. The difference between the largest and smallest width is 0.186 and majority of the widths fall between 0.0461 inches around the mean of 8.421 inches.

(b) Minimum = 8.312, 1st quartile = 8.404, median = 8.42, 3rd quartile = 8.459 and maximum = 8.498

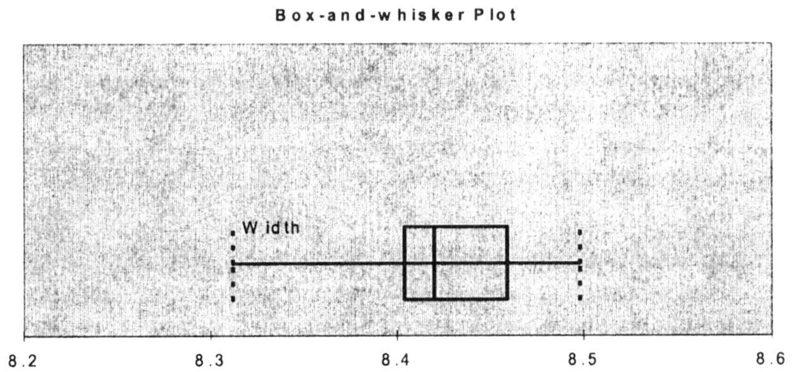


(c) Even though the median is equal to the mean, the distribution is not symmetrical but skewed to the left.

(d) All the troughs fall within the limit of 8.31 and 8.61 inches.

3.60 (a), (b)

| | *Time* | |
|---|---|---|
| | Office I | Office II |
| Mean | 2.214 | 2.012 |
| Median | 1.54 | 1.505 |
| Standard Deviation | 1.7180 | 1.8917 |
| Sample Variance | 2.9517 | 3.5786 |
| Range | 5.8 | 7.47 |
| First Quartile | 0.93 | 0.6 |
| Third Quartile | 3.93 | 3.75 |
| Interquartile Range | 3 | 3.15 |
| Coefficient of Variation | 77.60% | 94.04% |

(c)

**Box-and-whisker Plot**

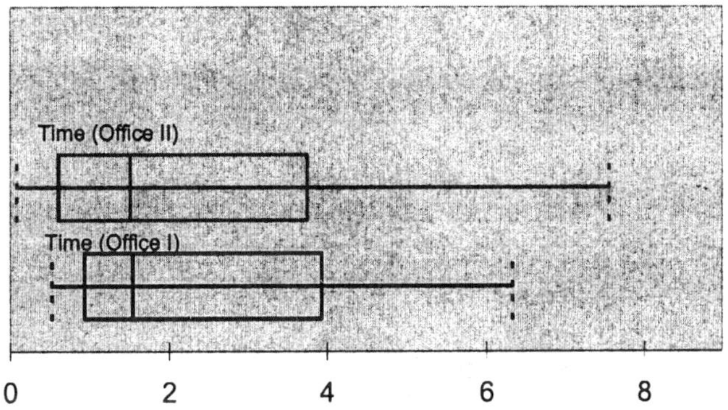


Times to clear problems at both central offices are right-skewed.

(d) Times to clear problems for Office I are less dispersed about the mean than times to clear problems for Office II, even though the mean for Office I times is higher (2.214) than that for Office II (2.012).

3.62 (a), (b)

| | Cost (per ounce) | Calories | Fiber (grams) | Sugar (grams) |
|---|---|---|---|---|
| Minimum | 0.100000 | 50.000000 | 5.000000 | 0.000000 |
| First Quartile | 0.130000 | 135.000000 | 5.000000 | 6.000000 |
| Median | 0.170000 | 190.000000 | 6.000000 | 11.000000 |
| Third Quartile | 0.200000 | 200.000000 | 8.000000 | 17.500000 |
| Maximum | 0.270000 | 210.000000 | 13.000000 | 23.000000 |
| Mean | 0.170606 | 165.757576 | 6.909091 | 11.393939 |
| Standard Deviation | 0.046900 | 51.782617 | 2.402650 | 6.651783 |
| Sample Variance | 0.002200 | 2681.439394 | 5.772727 | 44.246212 |
| Range | 0.170000 | 160.000000 | 8.000000 | 23.000000 |
| Interquartile range | 0.070000 | 65.000000 | 3.000000 | 11.500000 |
| Coefficient of Variations | 27.4903% | 31.2400% | 34.7752% | 58.3800% |

3.62 (c)
cont.

Box-and-whisker Plot (Cost per ounce)

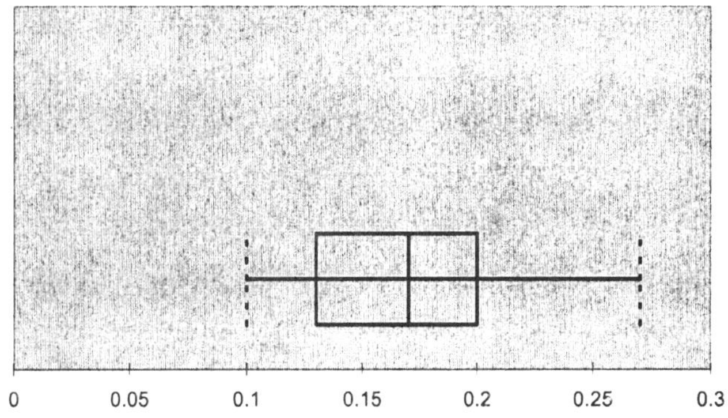


Box-and-whisker Plot (Calories)

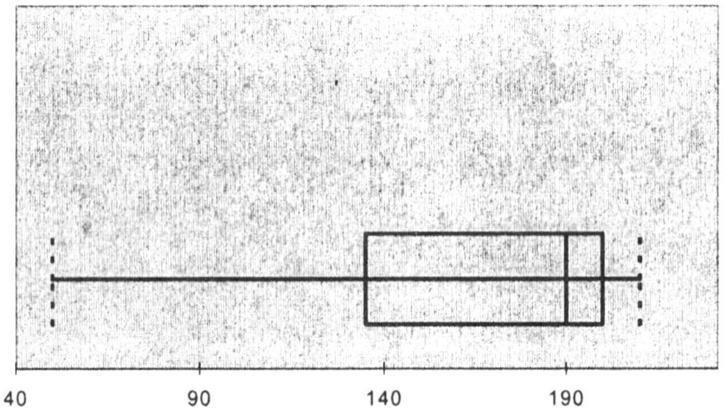


Box-and-whisker Plot (Fiber)

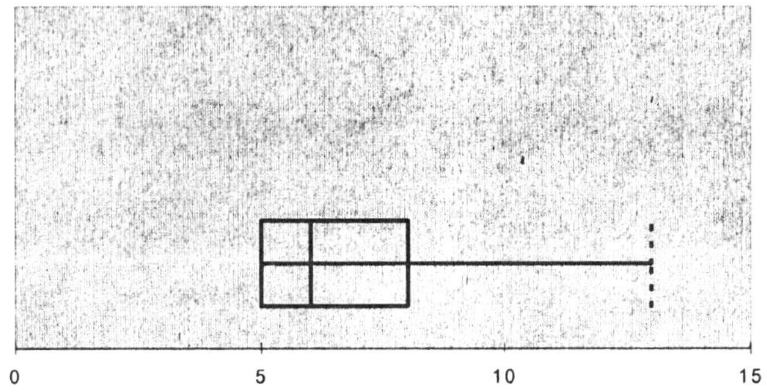


Box-and-whisker Plot (Sugar)

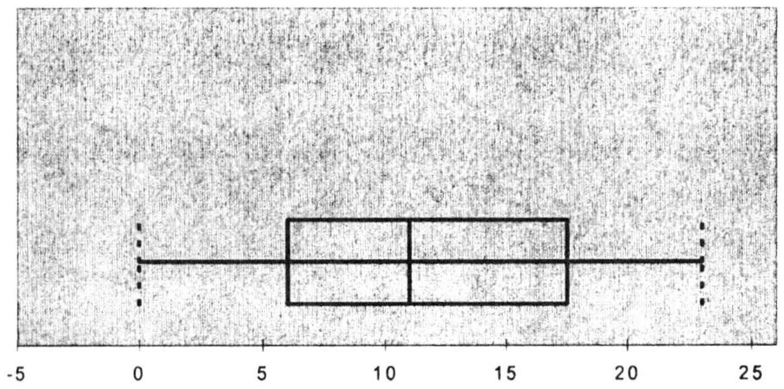

3.62 (c) cont. The distribution for fiber content is skewed to the right while the distribution for calories is skewed to the left. The distributions for cost per ounce and sugar content are quite symmetrical.

(d) Cost: The mean cost is about 17 cents per ounce; most cereals cluster around this cost with a few high priced cereals. The average scatter around the mean is about 5 cents per ounce.
Calories: The mean calories is about 166 and a middle value of 190, with an average scatter around the mean of about 52. Since the data are left skewed most of the calories are clustered at the high end with a few lower calorie cereals.

3.64 (a) With promotion: mean = 20748.93, standard deviation = 8109.50
Without promotion: mean = 13935.70, standard deviation = 4437.92

(b) With promotion: minimum = 10470, 1st quartile = 14905, median = 19775, 3rd quartile = 24456, maximum = 40605
Without promotion: minimum = 9555, 1st quartile = 11779, median = 12952, 3rd quartile = 14367, maximum = 28834

(c)

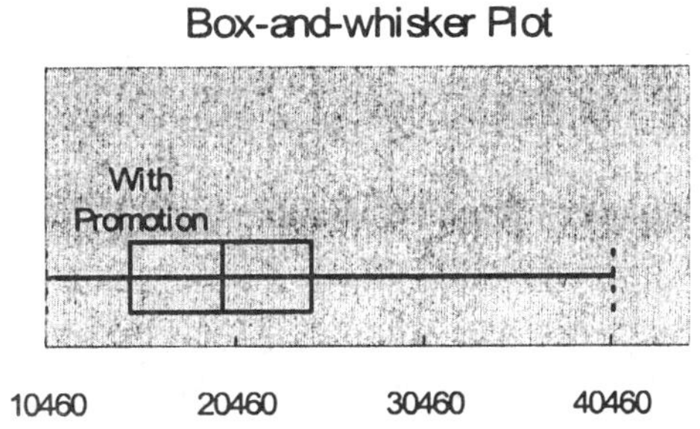


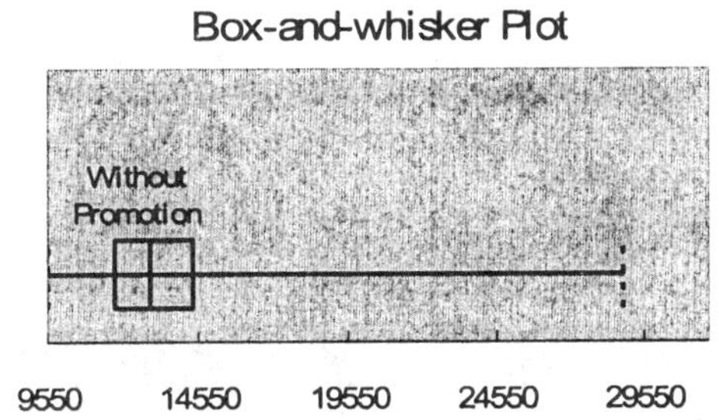


(d) The mean attendance is 6813 more when there is a promotion than when there is not, and the variation in attendance when there is a promotion is larger than when there is no promotion. There are many factors that can cause variation in the paid attendance. Some of them are weather condition, time and day of the game, home or visiting team, etc.

3.66 (a) Excel output:

Five-number Summary

| | Boston | Vermont |
|---|---|---|
| Minimum | 0.04 | 0.02 |
| First Quartile | 0.17 | 0.13 |
| Median | 0.23 | 0.2 |
| Third Quartile | 0.32 | 0.28 |
| Maximum | 0.98 | 0.83 |

3.66 cont. (b)

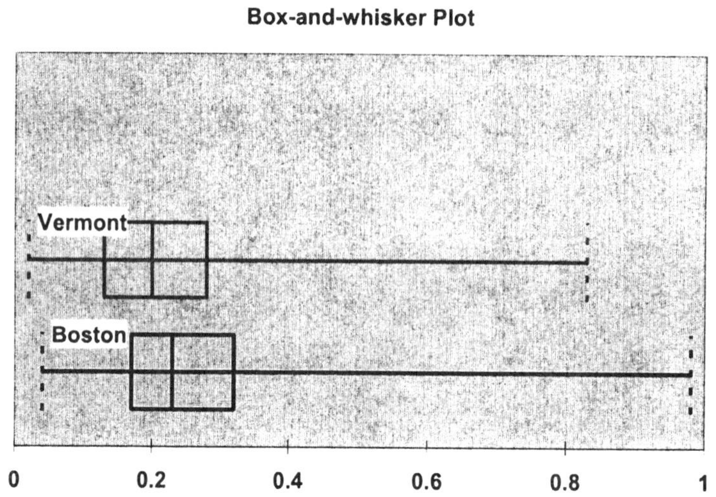


Both distributions are right skewed.

(c) Majority (75%) of the Boston and Vermont shingles are able to achieve a granule loss of 0.8 grams or less. However, the highest amount of granule loss of the Boston and Vermont shingles are 0.98 grams and 0.83 grams, respectively, which are above the 0.8 grams threshold.

3.68 (a), (b) Excel output:

| | Average Ticket$ | Fan Cost Index | Regular season gate receipts ($millions) | Local TV, radio and cable ($millions) | Other Local Operating Revenue | Player compensation and benefits | National and other local Expenses | Income from Baseball Operations |
|---|---|---|---|---|---|---|---|---|
| Minimum | 6.61 | 84.89 | 6.4 | 0.5 | 2.8 | 30.5 | 35 | -52.9 |
| First Quartile | 15.2 | 124.25 | 30.2 | 10.9 | 13.9 | 49.4 | 46.9 | -18.5 |
| Median | 17.83 | 143.475 | 47.55 | 16.35 | 29.05 | 70.8 | 50.5 | -8.35 |
| Third Quartile | 20.84 | 160.76 | 62.1 | 23.6 | 37 | 92.8 | 58.5 | 1.9 |
| Maximum | 39.68 | 228.73 | 98 | 56.8 | 61.5 | 118.5 | 84.2 | 40.9 |
| Mean | 18.1333 | 144.5737 | 46.1367 | 19.0467 | 27.5933 | 71.3567 | 54.6467 | -8.3733 |
| Variance | 35.9797 | 843.4552 | 512.5445 | 151.0184 | 234.6186 | 663.8405 | 176.4081 | 428.1531 |
| Standard Dev | 5.9983 | 29.0423 | 22.6394 | 12.2890 | 15.3173 | 25.7651 | 13.2819 | 20.6919 |
| Range | 33.07 | 143.84 | 91.60 | 56.30 | 58.70 | 88.00 | 49.20 | 93.80 |
| Interquartile Range | 5.64 | 36.51 | 31.90 | 12.70 | 23.10 | 43.40 | 11.60 | 20.40 |
| Coefficient of Variation | 33.08% | 20.09% | 49.07% | 64.52% | 55.51% | 36.11% | 24.30% | -247.12% |

3.68 (c) cont.

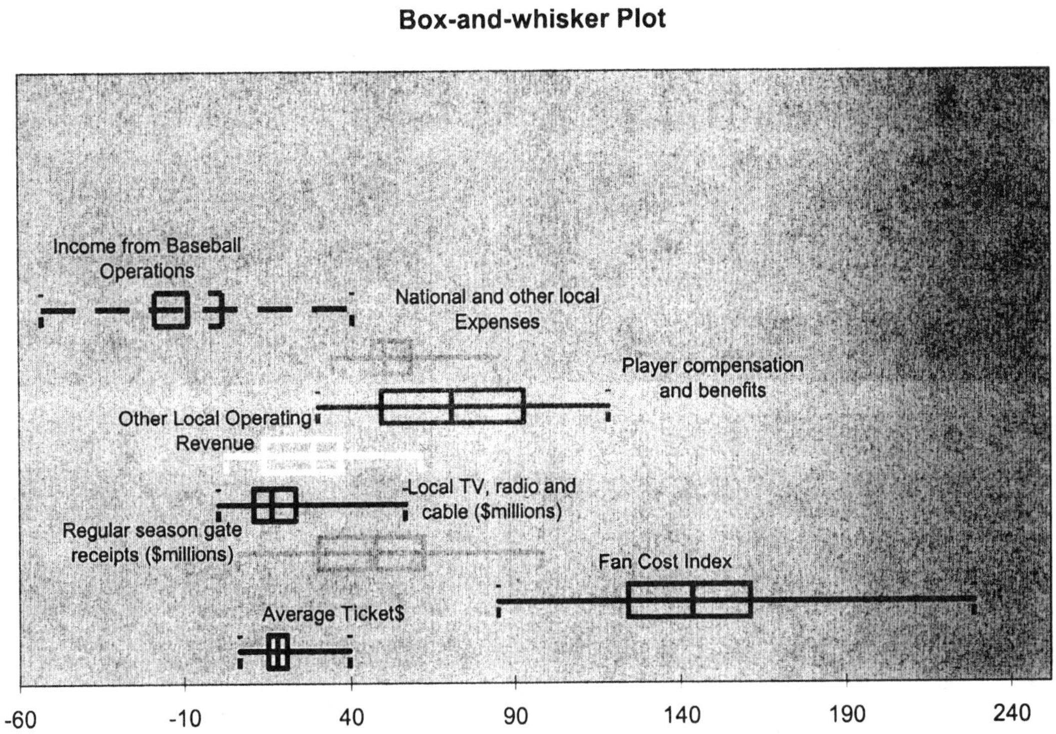


Average ticket prices, local TV, radio and cable receipts, national and other local expenses are skewed to the right; fan cost index is slightly skewed to the right; all other variables are pretty symmetrical.

(d) $r = 0.3985$. There is a moderate positive linear relationship between the number of wins and player compensation and benefits.

3.70 (a) Price and text speed: $r = -0.3842$
Price and text cost: $r = -0.5123$
Price and color photo time: $r = -0.5443$
Price and color photo cost: $r = -0.2614$

(b) Color photo time has the strongest relationship with price of the four variables, although it is still only a moderate relationship, so it would be the most helpful in predicting price. As the price increases the color photo time tends to decrease. All four variables have a negative (inverse) relationship with price.

3.72 **For not SUV:**

(a), (b)

| | MPG | Length | Width | Cargo Volume | Turning Circle | Weight |
|---|---|---|---|---|---|---|
| Minimum | 17 | 155 | 65 | 5 | 33 | 2150 |
| First Quartile | 19 | 178 | 68 | 13 | 38 | 3095 |
| Median | 21 | 189 | 71 | 15 | 40 | 3427.5 |
| Third Quartile | 23 | 198 | 73 | 19 | 41 | 3750 |
| Maximum | 41 | 215 | 79 | 75.5 | 45 | 4315 |
| Mean | 22.1556 | 187.9778 | 71.0000 | 22.3944 | 39.7000 | 3391.7222 |
| Variance | 18.7396 | 161.4377 | 9.8652 | 323.7837 | 6.3247 | 232210.7647 |
| Std. Dev | 4.3289 | 12.7058 | 3.1409 | 17.9940 | 2.5149 | 481.8825 |
| Range | 24 | 60 | 14 | 70.5 | 12 | 2165 |
| Interquartile Range | 4 | 20 | 5 | 6 | 3 | 655 |
| Coefficient Variation | 19.54% | 6.76% | 4.42% | 80.35% | 6.33% | 14.21% |

(c)

**Not SUV Box-and-whisker Plot**

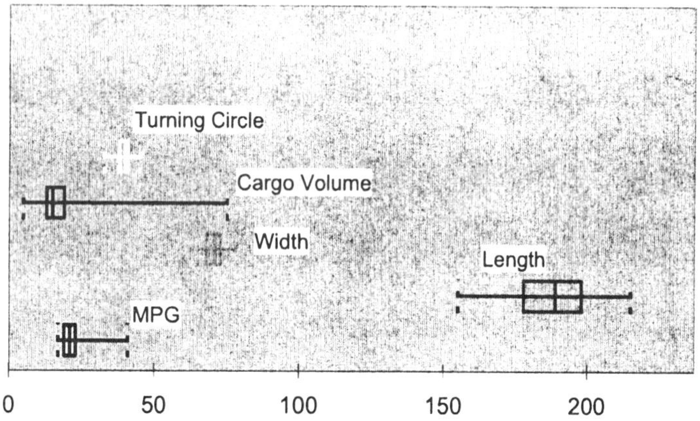


**Not SUV Box-and-whisker Plot**

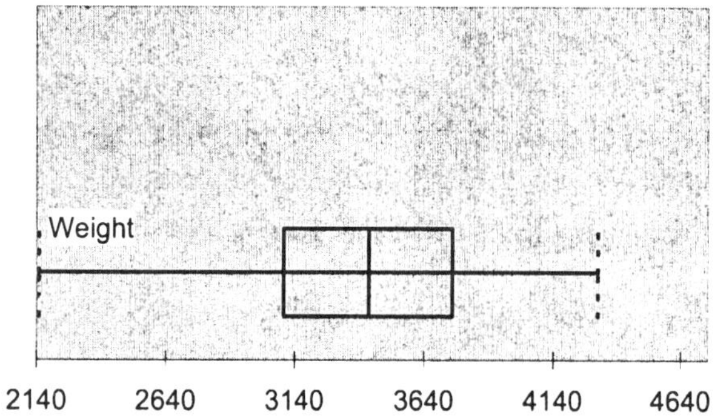


Miles per gallon and luggage capacity (cargo volume) are skewed to the right; length and weight are skewed to the left; width is slightly skewed to the right and turning circle requirement is quite symmetrical.

3.72 **For SUV**
cont. (a), (b)

| | MPG | Length | Width | Cargo Volume | Turning Circle | Weight |
|---|---|---|---|---|---|---|
| Minimum | 10 | 163 | 67 | 28 | 37 | 3055 |
| First Quartile | 15 | 175 | 70 | 34.5 | 39 | 3590 |
| Median | 16 | 183 | 72 | 37.5 | 40 | 4135 |
| Third Quartile | 18 | 190 | 74 | 45.5 | 41 | 4715 |
| Maximum | 22 | 227 | 80 | 84 | 52 | 7270 |
| Mean | 16.4839 | 184.9032 | 72.3226 | 42.3548 | 40.5806 | 4267.4194 |
| Variance | 7.2581 | 209.5570 | 11.0925 | 183.7532 | 11.3183 | 783086.4516 |
| Std. Dev | 2.6941 | 14.4761 | 3.3305 | 13.5556 | 3.3643 | 884.9217 |
| Range | 12 | 64 | 13 | 56 | 15 | 4215 |
| Interquartile Range | 3 | 15 | 4 | 11 | 2 | 1125 |
| Coefficient Variation | 16.34% | 7.83% | 4.61% | 32.00% | 8.29% | 20.74% |

(c)

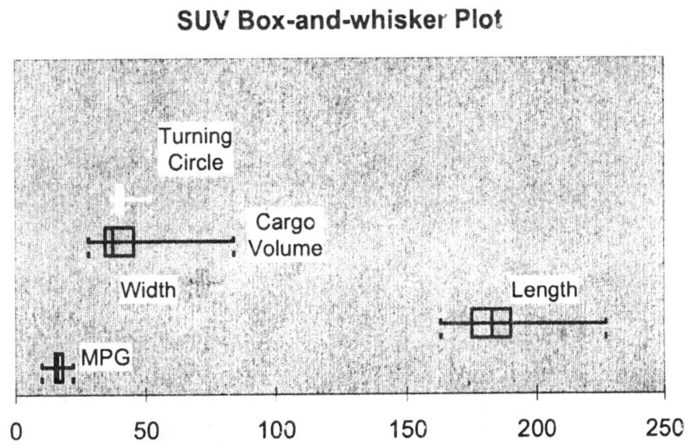


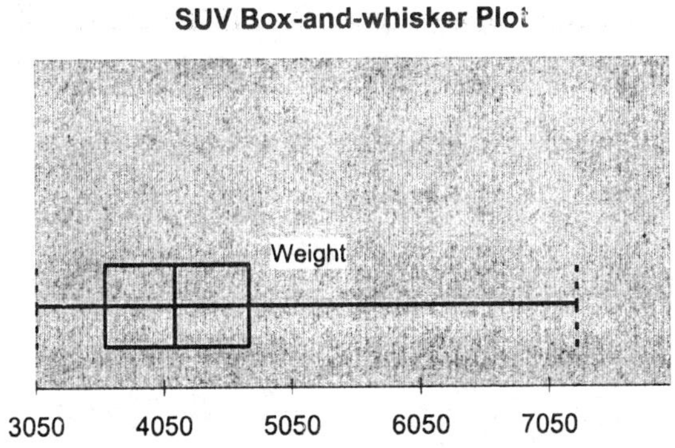


All variables are skewed to the right except miles per gallon is only slightly skewed to the right.

3.74 Answers will vary.

3.76 Answers will vary.

3.78 (a), (b) Excel and PHStat output:

**With fees:**

| | *Expense ratio* | *Return 2003* | *3Yr-Return* | *5-Yr-Return* |
|---|---|---|---|---|
| Mean | 1.3704 | 42.6875 | 8.3542 | 13.3667 |
| Median | 1.3300 | 41.3500 | 5.0500 | 14.4000 |
| Standard Deviation | 0.3355 | 10.9817 | 10.6477 | 5.5605 |
| Sample Variance | 0.1126 | 120.5977 | 113.3730 | 30.9188 |
| Range | 1.4900 | 37.1000 | 35.7000 | 18.9000 |
| First Quartile | 1.1500 | 33.8000 | -0.6000 | 9.2000 |
| Third Quartile | 1.5500 | 51.5000 | 16.8000 | 18.7000 |
| Interquartile Range | 0.4000 | 17.7000 | 17.4000 | 9.5000 |
| Coefficient of variation | 24.48% | 25.73% | 127.45% | 41.60% |

**Without fees:**

| | *Expense ratio* | *Return 2003* | *3Yr-Return* | *5-Yr-Return* |
|---|---|---|---|---|
| Mean | 1.3408 | 42.6052 | 7.5969 | 12.4134 |
| Median | 1.2600 | 40.8000 | 7.7000 | 13.9000 |
| Standard Deviation | 0.4702 | 13.5483 | 9.5416 | 6.5031 |
| Sample Variance | 0.2211 | 183.5565 | 91.0428 | 42.2897 |
| Range | 3.0500 | 63.1000 | 38.4000 | 27.9000 |
| First Quartile | 1.0100 | 32.7500 | 0.1000 | 6.9500 |
| Third Quartile | 1.5600 | 49.9000 | 14.6500 | 16.5000 |
| Interquartile Range | 0.5500 | 17.1500 | 14.5500 | 9.5500 |
| Coefficient of Variation | 35.07% | 31.80% | 125.60% | 52.39% |

3.78 cont. (c) **With fees:**

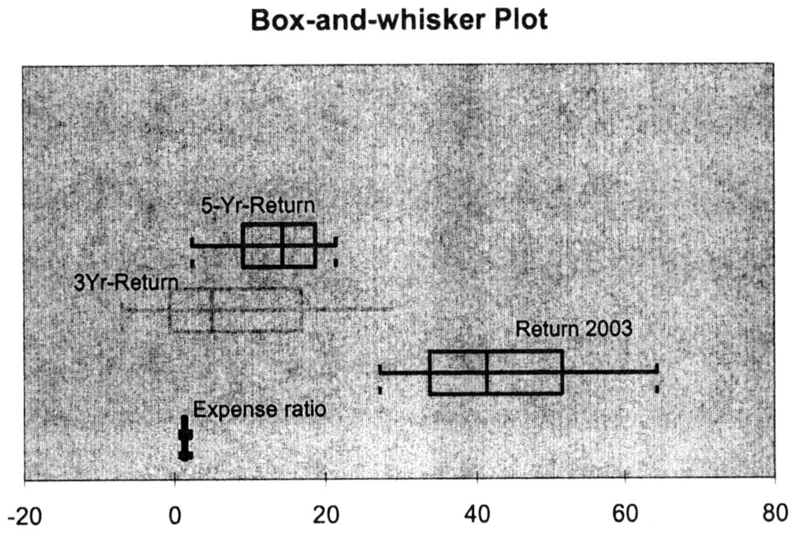


**Without fees:**

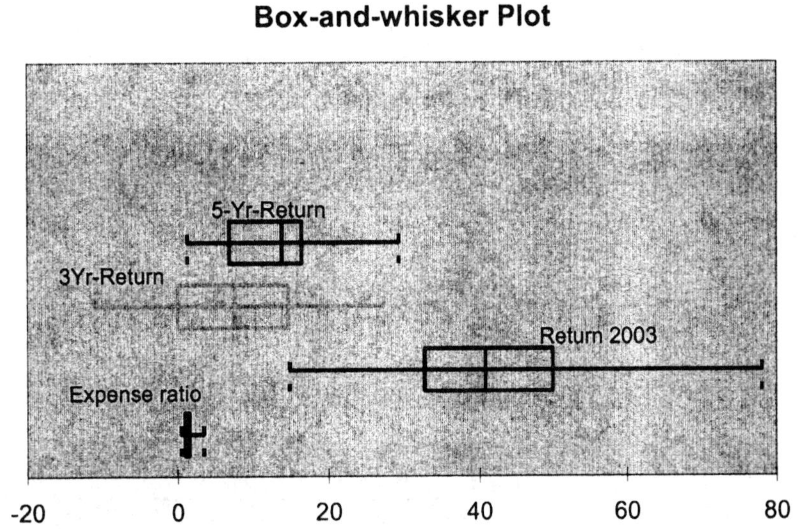


The 2003 return of both groups of mutual funds, three-year return of mutual funds with fees, five-year return of mutual funds with no fees, and the expense ratio of mutual funds with no fees are skewed to the right while the five-year return of mutual funds with fees is skewed slightly to the left.

(d) In general, mutual funds that do not have fees have a wider spread in the four variables than those that have fees. The median values of the four variables in the two groups are very similar with the exception of the three-year return, of which mutual funds without fees have a slightly higher median return than those that do have fees.

3.80 (a), (b)

**Large Cap:**

| | *Expense ratio* | *Return 2003* | *3Yr-Return* | *5-Yr-Return* |
|---|---|---|---|---|
| Mean | 1.2317 | 32.7738 | 1.3429 | 7.0976 |
| Median | 1.0800 | 32.4000 | 0.3500 | 6.9500 |
| Standard Deviation | 0.5354 | 9.1786 | 6.3157 | 3.9975 |
| Sample Variance | 0.2867 | 84.2469 | 39.8884 | 15.9802 |
| Range | 3.0500 | 38.6000 | 25.9000 | 15.5000 |
| First Quartile | 0.9600 | 27.2000 | -3.5000 | 3.4000 |
| Third Quartile | 1.4000 | 38.6000 | 6.4000 | 9.5000 |
| Interquartile Range | 0.4400 | 11.4000 | 9.9000 | 6.1000 |
| Coefficient of Variation | 43.47% | 28.01% | 470.32% | 56.32% |

**Mid Cap:**

| | *Expense ratio* | *Return 2003* | *3Yr-Return* | *5-Yr-Return* |
|---|---|---|---|---|
| Mean | 1.3521 | 46.1947 | 6.2105 | 15.0158 |
| Median | 1.2500 | 46.1000 | 5.7000 | 15.0000 |
| Standard Deviation | 0.4876 | 13.0622 | 8.9771 | 4.5786 |
| Sample Variance | 0.2378 | 170.6205 | 80.5888 | 20.9636 |
| Range | 2.0900 | 48.4000 | 32.3000 | 18.1000 |
| First Quartile | 1.1100 | 34.7000 | -0.9000 | 13.0000 |
| Third Quartile | 1.6500 | 54.9000 | 13.2000 | 18.8000 |
| Interquartile Range | 0.5400 | 20.2000 | 14.1000 | 5.8000 |
| Coefficient of Variation | 36.06% | 28.28% | 144.55% | 30.49% |

**Small Cap:**

| | *Expense ratio* | *Return 2003* | *3Yr-Return* | *5-Yr-Return* |
|---|---|---|---|---|
| Mean | 1.4255 | 48.3833 | 12.7167 | 15.6917 |
| Median | 1.4000 | 46.7500 | 14.2500 | 15.5500 |
| Standard Deviation | 0.3413 | 11.3215 | 9.2273 | 5.5233 |
| Sample Variance | 0.1165 | 128.1773 | 85.1431 | 30.5069 |
| Range | 1.7800 | 43.9000 | 39.9000 | 27.2000 |
| First Quartile | 1.2000 | 38.3000 | 5.3000 | 14.2000 |
| Third Quartile | 1.6000 | 59.3000 | 19.8000 | 19.0000 |
| Interquartile Range | 0.4000 | 21.0000 | 14.5000 | 4.8000 |
| Coefficient of Variation | 23.94% | 23.40% | 72.56% | 35.20% |

3.80 (c) **Large Cap:**
cont.

Box-and-whisker Plot

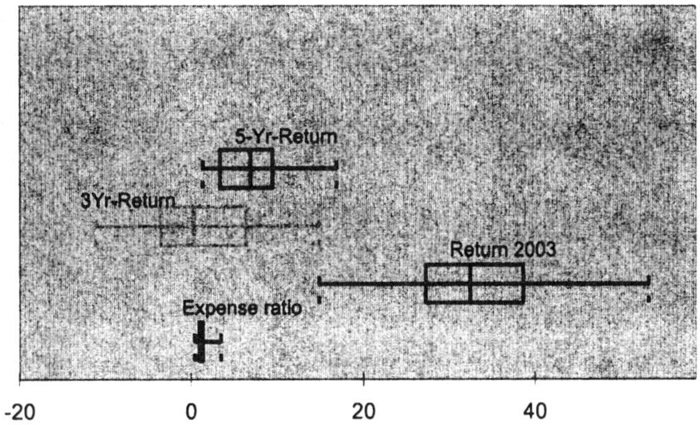


**Mid Cap:**

Box-and-whisker Plot

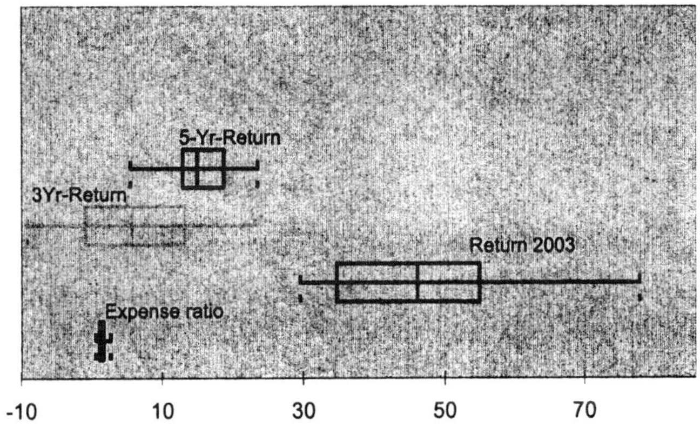


**Small Cap:**

Box-and-whisker Plot

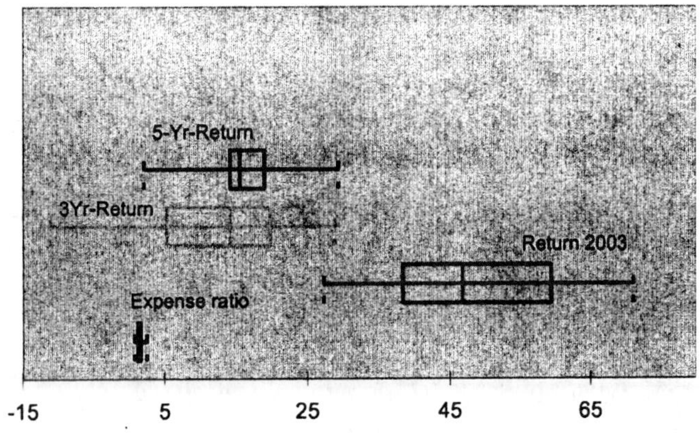

3.80 cont. (c) The 2003 return and expense ratio of mid cap mutual funds, five-year return and expense ratio of large cap mutual funds, and the expense ratio of small cap mutual funds are right-skewed. The three-year return of small cap mutual funds is skewed to the left.

(d) In general, the four variables of large cap and small cap mutual funds are quite comparable and are higher than those of mid cap mutual funds. The spread of the three-year return and five-year return of small cap mutual funds is higher compared to the mid cap and large cap mutual funds while the spread of the expense ratio of the large cap mutual funds is larger than that of the mid cap and small cap mutual funds.

# CHAPTER 4

## OBJECTIVES

- To understand the basic probability concepts
- To understand conditional probability
- To use Bayes theorem to revise probability in the light of new information
- To use rules for counting the number of possible events

## OVERVIEW AND KEY CONCEPTS

### Some Basic Probability Concepts

- **A priori probability:** The probability is based on prior knowledge of the process involved.
- **Empirical probability:** The probability is based on observed data.
- **Subjective probability:** Chance of occurrence assigned to an event by particular individual.
- **Sample space:** Collection of all possible outcomes, e.g., the set of all six faces of a die.
- **Simple event:** Outcome from a sample space with one characteristic, e.g., a red card from a deck of cards.
- **Joint event:** Involves two or more characteristics simultaneously, e.g., an Ace that is also a Red Card from a deck of cards.
- **Impossible event:** Event that will never happen, e.g., a club and diamond on a single card.
- **Complement event:** The complement of event *A*, denoted as $A'$, includes all events that are not part of event *A*, e.g., If event *A* is the queen of diamonds, then the complement of event *A* is all the cards in a deck that are not the queen of diamonds.
- **Mutually exclusive events:** Two events are mutually exclusive if they cannot occur together. E.g., If event *A* is the queen of diamonds and event *B* is the queen of clubs, then both event *A* and event *B* cannot occur together on one card. An event and its complement are always mutually exclusive.
- **Collectively exhaustive events:** A set of events is collectively exhaustive if one of the events must occur. The set of collectively exhaustive events covers the whole sample space. E.g., Event *A*: all the aces, event *B*: all the black cards, event *C*: all the diamonds, event *D*: all the hearts. Then events *A*, *B*, *C*, and *D* are collectively exhaustive and so are events *B*, *C*, and *D*. An event and its complement are always collectively exhaustive.
- **Rules of probability:** (1) Its value is between 0 and 1; (2) the sum of probabilities of all collectively exhaustive and mutually exclusive events is 1.
- **The addition rule:** $P(A \text{ or } B) = P(A) + P(B) - P(A \text{ and } B)$
  - For two mutually exclusive events: $P(A \text{ and } B) = 0$
- **The multiplication rule:** $P(A \text{ and } B) = P(A \mid B)P(B) = P(B \mid A)P(A)$
- **Conditional probability:** $P(A \mid B) = \dfrac{P(A \text{ and } B)}{P(B)}$; $P(B \mid A) = \dfrac{P(A \text{ and } B)}{P(A)}$
- **Statistically independent events:** Two events are statistically independent if $P(A \mid B) = P(A)$, $P(B \mid A) = P(B)$ or $P(A \text{ and } B) = P(A)P(B)$. That is, any information about a given event does not affect the probability of the other event.

- **Bayes theorem:** $P(B_i \mid A) = \dfrac{P(A \mid B_i)P(B_i)}{P(A \mid B_1)P(B_1) + \cdots + P(A \mid B_k)P(B_k)} = \dfrac{P(B_i \text{ and } A)}{P(A)}$
  - **E.g.** We know that 50% of borrowers repaid their loans. Out of those who repaid, 40% had a college degree. Ten percent of those who defaulted had a college degree. What is the probability that a randomly selected borrower who has a college degree will repay the loan?
    **Solution:** Let *R* represent those who repaid and *C* represent those who have a college degree. $P(R) = 0.50$, $P(C \mid R) = 0.4$, $P(C \mid R') = 0.10$.
    $$P(R \mid C) = \frac{P(C \mid R)P(R)}{P(C \mid R)P(R) + P(C \mid R')P(R')} = \frac{(.4)(.5)}{(.4)(.5) + (.1)(.5)} = \frac{.2}{.25} = .8$$
  - Bayes theorem is used if $P(A \mid B)$ is needed when $P(B \mid A)$ is given or vice-versa.

## Viewing and Computing Marginal (Simple) Probability and Joint Probability Using a Contingency Table

| | Event | | |
|---|---|---|---|
| Event | $B_1$ | $B_2$ | Total |
| $A_1$ | $P(A_1 \text{ and } B_1)$ | $P(A_1 \text{ and } B_2)$ | $P(A_1)$ |
| $A_2$ | $P(A_2 \text{ and } B_1)$ | $P(A_2 \text{ and } B_2)$ | $P(A_2)$ |
| Total | $P(B_1)$ | $P(B_2)$ | 1 |

Joint Probability

Marginal (Simple) Probability

## Viewing and Computing Compound Probability Using a Contingency Table

$P(A_1 \text{ or } B_1) = P(A_1) + P(B_1) - P(A_1 \text{ and } B_1)$

| | Event | | |
|---|---|---|---|
| Event | $B_1$ | $B_2$ | Total |
| $A_1$ | $P(A_1 \text{ and } B_1)$ | $P(A_1 \text{ and } B_2)$ | [redacted] |
| $A_2$ | $P(A_2 \text{ and } B_1)$ | $P(A_2 \text{ and } B_2)$ | $P(A_2)$ |
| Total | $P(B_1)$ | $P(B_2)$ | 1 |

**For Mutually Exclusive Events: P(A or B) = P(A) + P(B)**

## Viewing and Computing Conditional Probability Using a Contingency Table

First setup the contingency table.

| Type | Color: Red | Color: Black | Total |
|---|---|---|---|
| Ace | 2 | 2 | 4 |
| Non-Ace | 24 | 24 | 48 |
| Total | 26 | 26 | 52 |

Revised Sample Space

To find $P(\text{Ace}|\text{Red})$, we only need to focus on the revised sample space of $P(\text{Red}) = 26/52$.
Out of this, 2/52 belongs to Ace and Red.
Hence, $P(\text{Ace}|\text{Red})$ is the ratio of 2/52 to 26/52 or 2/26.

Likewise, $P(\text{Red} \mid \text{Ace}) = \dfrac{P(\text{Ace and Red})}{P(\text{Ace})} = \dfrac{2/52}{4/52} = \dfrac{2}{4}$

## Applying Bayes theorem Using a Contingency Table

- **E.g.** We know that 50% of borrowers repaid their loans. Out of those who repaid, 40% had a college degree. Ten percent of those who defaulted had a college degree. What is the probability that a randomly selected borrower who has a college degree will repay the loan?
  **Solution:** Let $R$ represents those who repaid and $C$ represents those who have a college degree. We know that $P(R) = 0.50$, $P(C \mid R) = 0.4$, $P(C \mid R') = 0.10$.

| | Repay | $\overline{\text{Repay}}$ | Total |
|---|---|---|---|
| College | .2 | .05 | .25 |
| $\overline{\text{College}}$ | .3 | .45 | .75 |
| Total | .5 | .5 | 1.0 |

First we fill in the marginal probabilities of $P(R) = 0.5$ and $P(R') = 0.5$ in the contingency table. Then we make use of the conditional probability $P(C \mid R) = 0.4$. It says that if $R$ has already occurred, the probability of $C$ is 0.4. Since $R$ has already occurred, we are restricted to the revised sample space of $P(R) = 0.5$. Forty percent or 0.4 of this $P(R) = 0.5$ belongs to $P(C \text{ and } R)$. Hence, the $0.4(0.5) = 0.2$ for $P(C \text{ and } R)$ in the contingency table. Likewise, given that $R'$ has already occurred, the probability of $C$ is 0.10. Hence, $P(C \text{ and } R')$ is 10% of $P(R') = 0.5$, which is 0.05. Utilizing the fact that the joint probabilities add up vertically and horizontally to their respective marginal probabilities, the contingency table is completed.
We want the probability of $R$ given $C$. Now we are restricted to the revised sample space of $P(C) = 0.25$ since we know that $C$ has already occurred. Out of this 0.25, 0.2 belongs to $P(C \text{ and } R)$. Hence, $P(R \mid C) = \dfrac{0.2}{0.25} = 0.8$

## Counting Rules

- If any one of the $k$ different mutually exclusive and collectively exhaustive events can occur on each of the $n$ trials, the number of possible outcomes is equal to $k^n$
- If there are $k_1$ events on the first trial, $k_2$ events on the second trials, …, and $k_n$ events on the $n$th trial, then the number of possible outcomes is $(k_1)(k_2)\cdots(k_n)$
- The number of ways that all $n$ objects can be arranged in order is $n! = n(n-1)\cdots(1)$
  - $n!$ is called *n factorial*
  - $0! = 1$
- **Permutation**: The number of ways of arranging $X$ objects selected from $n$ objects in order is $\frac{n!}{(n-X)!}$
- **Combination**: The number of ways of selecting $X$ objects out of $n$ objects, irrespective or order, is $\binom{n}{X} = \frac{n!}{X!(n-X)!}$

# SOLUTIONS TO END OF SECTION AND CHAPTER REVIEW EVEN PROBLEMS

4.2 (a) Simple events include selecting a red ball. (b) Selecting a white ball

4.4 (a) 60/100 = 3/5 = 0.6 (b) 10/100 = 1/10 = 0.1

(c) 35/100 = 7/20 = 0.35 (d) $\frac{60}{100}+\frac{65}{100}-\frac{35}{100}=\frac{90}{100}=\frac{9}{10}=0.9$

4.6 (a) Mutually exclusive, not collectively exhaustive. "Registered voters in the United States were asked whether they registered as Republicans, Democrats, or none of the above." will be mutually exclusive and collectively exhaustive.

(b) Mutually exclusive, not collectively exhaustive. "Respondents were classified by country of manufacture of car owned into the categories American, European, Japanese, or none of the above." will be mutually exclusive and collectively exhaustive.

(c) Mutually exclusive, not collectively exhaustive. "People were asked, "Do you currently live in (i) an apartment, (ii) a house or (iii) none of the above?" will be mutually exclusive and collectively exhaustive.

(d) Mutually exclusive, collectively exhaustive

4.8 (a) "Is a homeowner."

(b) "A homeowner who drives to work."

(c) "Does not drive to work."

(d) A person can drive to work and is also a homeowner.

4.10 (a) "A wafer is good."

(b) "A wafer is good and no particle was found on the die."

(c) "bad wafer."

(d) A wafer can be a "good wafer" and was produced by a die "with particles".

4.12

| | | Company Size | | |
|---|---|---|---|---|
| | | Large | Small-to-midsized | |
| Stock | Yes | 40 | 43 | 83 |
| Options | No | 149 | 137 | 286 |
| | | 189 | .180 | 369 |

(a) $P$(offered stock options) = 83/369 = 0.2249

(b) $P$(small-to-midsized and did not offer stock options) = 137/369 = 0.3713

(c) $P$(small-to-midsized or offered stock options) = (180 + 83 – 43)/369 = 0.5962

(d) The probability of "small-to-midsized or offered stock options" includes the probability of "small-to-midsized and offered stock options", the probability of "small-to-midsized but did not offer stock options" and the probability of "large and offered stock options".

4.14

| Enjoy Clothes Shopping | Male | Female | Total |
|---|---|---|---|
| Yes | 136 | 224 | 360 |
| No | 104 | 36 | 140 |
| Total | 240 | 260 | 500 |

(a) *P*(enjoys clothes shopping) = 360/500 = 18/25 = 0.72

(b) *P*(female *and* enjoys clothes shopping) = 224/500 = 56/125 = 0.448

(c) *P*(female *or* enjoys clothes shopping) = 396/500 = 99/125 = 0.792

(d) *P*(male *or* female) = 500/500 = 1.00

4.16 (a) $P(A \mid B) = 10/30 = 1/3 = 0.33$

(b) $P(A \mid B') = 20/60 = 1/3 = 0.33$

(c) $P(A' \mid B') = 40/60 = 2/3 = 0.67$

(d) Since $P(A \mid B) = P(A) = 1/3$, events *A* and *B* are statistically independent.

4.18 $$P(A \mid B) = \frac{P(A \text{ and } B)}{P(B)} = \frac{0.4}{0.8} = \frac{1}{2} = 0.5$$

4.20 Since $P(A \text{ and } B) = .20$ and $P(A)\,P(B) = 0.12$, events *A* and *B* are not statistically independent.

4.22 (a) *P*(had particles | bad) = 36/116 = 0.3103

(b) *P*(had particles | good) = 14/334 = 0.0419

(c) *P*(no particles | good ) = 320/334 = 0.9581

*P*(no particles) = 400/450 = 0.8889

Since *P*(no particles | good ) ≠ *P*(no particles), "a good wafer" and "a die with no particle" are not statistically independent.

4.24 (a) *P*(claimed bias | white ) = 29/56 = 0.5179

(b) *P*(while | claim bias) = 29/155 = 0.1871

(c) The conditional events are reversed.

(d) Since *P*(white | claim bias) = 0.1871 is not equal to *P*(white) = 0.1210, being white and claiming bias are not statistically independent.

4.26 (a) *P*(needs warranty repair | manufacturer based in U.S.) = 0.025/0.6 = 0.0417

(b) *P*(needs warranty repair | manufacturer not based in U.S.) = 0.015/0.4 = 0.0375

(c) Since *P*(needs warranty repair | manufacturer based in U.S.) = 0.0417 and *P*(needs warranty repair) = 0.04, the two events are not statistically independent.

4.28 (a) $$P(\text{both queens}) = \frac{4}{52}\cdot\frac{3}{51} = \frac{12}{2{,}652} = \frac{1}{221} = 0.0045$$

(b) $$P(\text{10 followed by 5 or 6}) = \frac{4}{52}\cdot\frac{8}{51} = \frac{32}{2{,}652} = \frac{8}{663} = 0.012$$

(c) $$P(\text{both queens}) = \frac{4}{52}\cdot\frac{4}{52} = \frac{16}{2{,}704} = \frac{1}{169} = 0.0059$$

(d) $$P(\text{blackjack}) = \frac{16}{52}\cdot\frac{4}{51} + \frac{4}{52}\cdot\frac{16}{51} = \frac{128}{2{,}652} = \frac{32}{663} = 0.0483$$

4.30

$$P(B \mid A) = \frac{P(A \mid B) \cdot P(B)}{P(A \mid B) \cdot P(B) + P(A \mid B') \cdot P(B')}$$

$$= \frac{0.8 \cdot 0.05}{0.8 \cdot 0.05 + 0.4 \cdot 0.95} = \frac{0.04}{0.42} = 0.095$$

4.32 (a) $D$ = has disease $T$ = tests positive

$$P(D \mid T) = \frac{P(T \mid D) \cdot P(D)}{P(T \mid D) \cdot P(D) + P(T \mid D') \cdot P(D')}$$

$$= \frac{0.9 \cdot 0.03}{0.9 \cdot 0.03 + 0.01 \cdot 0.97} = \frac{0.027}{0.0367} = 0.736$$

(b)

$$P(D' \mid T') = \frac{P(T' \mid D') \cdot P(D')}{P(T' \mid D') \cdot P(D') + P(T' \mid D) \cdot P(D)}$$

$$= \frac{0.99 \cdot 0.97}{0.99 \cdot 0.97 + 0.10 \cdot 0.03} = \frac{0.9603}{0.9633} = 0.997$$

4.34 (a) $B$ = Base Construction Co. enters a bid
$O$ = Olive Construction Co. wins the contract

$$P(B' \mid O) = \frac{P(O \mid B') \cdot P(B')}{P(O \mid B') \cdot P(B') + P(O \mid B) \cdot P(B)}$$

$$= \frac{0.5 \cdot 0.3}{0.5 \cdot 0.3 + 0.25 \cdot 0.7} = \frac{0.15}{0.325} = 0.4615$$

(b) $P(O) = 0.175 + 0.15 = 0.325$

4.36 (a) $P$(huge success | favorable review) = 0.099/0.459 = 0.2157
$P$(moderate success | favorable review) = 0.14/0.459 = 0.3050
$P$(break even | favorable review) = 0.16/0.459 = 0.3486
$P$(loser | favorable review) = 0.06/0.459 = 0.1307

(b) $P$(favorable review) = 0.99(0.1) + 0.7(0.2) + 0.4(0.4) + 0.2(0.3) = 0.459

4.38 $3^{10} = 59049$

4.40 (a) $2^7 = 128$ (b) $6^7 = 279936$
(c) There are two mutually exclusive and collectively exhaustive outcomes in (a) and six in (b).

4.42 $(8)(4)(3)(3) = 288$

4.44 $5! = (5)(4)(3)(2)(1) = 120$. Not all these orders are equally likely because the players are different in each team.

4.46 $n! = 6! = 720$

4.48 $\frac{n!}{X!(n-X)!} = \frac{8!}{2!(6!)} = \frac{(8)(7)}{2} = 28$

4.50 $\frac{n!}{X!(n-X)!} = \frac{100!}{2!(98!)} = \frac{(100)(99)}{2} = 4950$

4.54 With a priori probability, the probability of success is based on prior knowledge of the process involved. With empirical probability, outcomes are based on observed data. Subjective probability refers to the chance of occurrence assigned to an event by a particular individual.

4.56 The addition rule is used by adding the probability of A and the probability of B and then subtracting the joint probability of A and B.

4.58 If events A and B are statistically independent, the conditional probability of event A given B is equal to the probability of A.

4.60 Bayes theorem uses conditional probabilities to revise the probability of an event in the light of new information.

4.62
(a) *P*(nonconforming bottle) = 0.01 + 0.025 = 0.035
(b) *P*(machine I *and* conforming bottle) = 0.49
(c) *P*(machine I *or* conforming bottle) = 0.5 + 0.965 – 0.49 = 0.5 + 0.475 = 0.975
(d) *P*(nonconforming | machine I) = 0.02
(e) *P*(machine I | nonconforming) = 0.01/0.035 = 0.2857
(f) The conditions are switched. Part (d) answers $P(A|B)$ and part (e) answers $P(B|A)$.

4.64
(a) A simple event can be "a firm that has a transactional public web site" and a joint event can be "a firm that has a transactional public web site and has sales greater than $10 billion".
(b) *P*(transactional public web site) = 170/490 = 0.3469
(c) *P*(transactional public web site and sales in excess of $10 billion) = 71/490 = 0.1449
(d) Since *P*(transactional public web site) × *P*(sales in excess of $10 billion) ≠ *P*(transactional public web site and sales in excess of $10 billion), the two events, "sales in excess of ten billion dollars" and "has a transactional publicWeb site" are not independent.

4.66 R = read the advertisement, O = place an order
*P*(R) = 0.15 *P*(O | R) = 0.15
(a) *P*(R and O) = *P*(O | R) P(R) = 0.0225
(b) (175000)(0.0225) = 3937.5 ≅ 3938 can be expected to read the advertisement and place an order.
(c) *P*(R) = 0.20. *P*(R and O) = *P*(O | R) P(R) = (0.15)(0.20) = 0.03
(d) (175000)(0.03) = 5250 can be expected to read the advertisement and place an order.

4.68 (a) $P(B \mid A) = (0.158)(0.24)/((0.158)(0.24)+(0.056)(0.76)) = 0.4712$

(b) Since the probability that a fatality involved a rollover given that the fatality involved an SUV, van or pickup is 0.4712, which is almost twice the probability that a fatality involved a rollover with any vehicle type at 0.24, SUV's, vans or pickups are generally more prone to rollover accidents.

# CHAPTER 5

## OBJECTIVES

- To understand the properties of a probability distribution
- To be able to compute the expected value and variance of a probability distribution
- To understand how to compute probabilities from binomial, and Poisson distributions
- To know when and how to use the binomial, and Poisson distributions to solve business problems

## OVERVIEW AND KEY CONCEPTS

### Some Basic Concepts of Discrete Probability Distribution

- **Random variable:** Outcomes of an experiment expressed numerically, e.g., Toss a die twice and count the number of times the number four appears (0, 1 or 2 times).
- **Discrete random variable:** A random variable that can have only certain distinct values. It is usually obtained by counting. E.g., Toss a coin five times and count the number of tails (0, 1, 2, 3, 4 or 5 tails).
- **Discrete probability distribution:** A mutually exclusive listing of all possible numerical outcomes for a discrete random variable such that a particular probability of occurrence is associated with each outcome.

### Concepts of Expectation for a Discrete Random Variable

- **Expected value of a discrete random variable:** A weighted average over all possible outcomes.
  - The weights being the probabilities associated with each of the outcomes.
  - $\mu = E(X) = \sum_{i=1}^{N} X_i P(X_i)$
- **Variance of a discrete random variable:** The weighted average of the squared differences between each possible outcome and its mean
  - The weights being the probabilities of each of the respective outcomes.
  - $\sigma^2 = \sum_{i=1}^{N} [X_i - E(X)]^2 P(X_i)$
- **Standard deviation of a discrete random variable:** The square root of the variance.
  - $\sigma = \sqrt{\sum_{i=1}^{N} [X_i - E(X)]^2 P(X_i)}$

## The Binomial Distribution

- **Properties of the binomial distribution:**
  - The sample has n observations.
  - Each observation is classified into one of the two mutually exclusive and collectively exhaustive categories, usually called *success* and *failure*.
  - The probability of getting a *success* is *p* while the probability of a *failure* is (1-*p*).
  - The outcome (i.e., *success* or *failure*) of any observation is independent of the outcome of any other observation. This can be achieved by selecting each observation randomly either from an *infinite population without replacement* or from a *finite population with replacement.*
- **The binomial probability distribution function:**
  - $P(X)=\frac{n!}{X!(n-X)!}p^{X}(1-p)^{n-X}$

  where

  $P(X)$: probability of $X$ successes given $n$ and $p$

  $X$: number of "successes" in the sample $(X=0,1,\cdots,n)$

  $p$: the probability of "success"

  $(1-p)$: the probability of "failure"

  $n$: sample size
- **The mean and variance of a binomial distribution:**
  - $\mu=E(X)=np$
  - $\sigma^2=np(1-p)$
  - $\sigma=\sqrt{np(1-p)}$
- **Applications:** Useful in evaluating the probability of *X* successes in a sample of size *n* drawn with replacement from a finite population or without replacement from an infinite population.

## The Poisson Distribution

- **Properties of the Poisson distribution:**
  1. The area of opportunity, in which the number of times a particular event occurs is of interest, is defined by time, length, surface area, etc.
  2. The probability that an event occurs in a given area of opportunity is the same for all of the areas of opportunity.
  3. The number of events that occur in one area of opportunity is independent of the number of events that occur in other areas of opportunity.
  4. The probability that two or more events will occur in an area of opportunity approaches zero as the area of opportunity becomes smaller.

- **The Poisson probability distribution function:**
  - $P(X) = \frac{e^{-\lambda}\lambda^X}{X!}$

    where

    $P(X)$: probability of $X$ "successes" given $\lambda$

    $X$: number of "successes" per unit

    $\lambda$: expected (average) number of "successes"

    $e$: 2.71828 (base of natural logs)
- **The mean and variance of a Poisson Distribution**
  - $\mu = E(X) = \lambda$
  - $\sigma^2 = \lambda$
  - $\sigma = \sqrt{\lambda}$
- **Applications:** Useful in modeling the number of successes in a given continuous interval of time, length, surface area, etc.

# SOLUTIONS TO END OF SECTION AND CHAPTER REVIEW EVEN PROBLEMS

5.2 (a)

Distribution C

| $X$ | $P(X)$ | $X*P(X)$ |
|---|---|---|
| 0 | 0.20 | 0.00 |
| 1 | 0.20 | 0.20 |
| 2 | 0.20 | 0.40 |
| 3 | 0.20 | 0.60 |
| 4 | 0.20 | 0.80 |
| | 1.00 | 2.00 |

$\mu = 2.00$

Distribution D

| $X$ | $P(X)$ | $X*P(X)$ |
|---|---|---|
| 0 | 0.10 | 0.00 |
| 1 | 0.20 | 0.20 |
| 2 | 0.40 | 0.80 |
| 3 | 0.20 | 0.60 |
| 4 | 0.10 | 0.40 |
| | 1.00 | 2.00 |

$\mu = 2.00$

(b) Distribution C

| $X$ | $(X-\mu)^2$ | $P(X)$ | $(X-\mu)^2*P(X)$ |
|---|---|---|---|
| 0 | $(-2)^2$ | 0.20 | 0.80 |
| 1 | $(-1)^2$ | 0.20 | 0.20 |
| 2 | $(0)^2$ | 0.20 | 0.00 |
| 3 | $(1)^2$ | 0.20 | 0.20 |
| 4 | $(2)^2$ | 0.20 | 0.80 |
| | | $\sigma^2=$ | 2.00 |

$$\sigma = \sqrt{\Sigma(X-\mu)^2 \cdot P(X)} = \sqrt{2.00} = 1.414$$

Distribution D

| $X$ | $(X-\mu)^2$ | $P(X)$ | $(X-\mu)^2*P(X)$ |
|---|---|---|---|
| 0 | $(-2)^2$ | 0.10 | 0.40 |
| 1 | $(-1)^2$ | 0.20 | 0.20 |
| 2 | $(0)^2$ | 0.40 | 0.00 |
| 3 | $(1)^2$ | 0.20 | 0.20 |
| 4 | $(2)^2$ | 0.10 | 0.40 |
| | | $\sigma^2=$ | 1.20 |

$$\sigma = \sqrt{\Sigma(X-\mu)^2 \cdot P(X)} = \sqrt{1.20} = 1.095$$

(c) Distribution C is uniform and symmetric; D is unimodal and symmetric. Means are the same but variances are different.

5.4 (a)-(b)

| $X$ | $P(x)$ | $X*P(X)$ | $(X-\mu_X)^2$ | $(X-\mu_X)^2*P(X)$ |
|---|---|---|---|---|
| 0 | 0.10 | 0.00 | 4 | 0.40 |
| 1 | 0.20 | 0.20 | 1 | 0.20 |
| 2 | 0.45 | 0.90 | 0 | 0.00 |
| 3 | 0.15 | 0.45 | 1 | 0.15 |
| 4 | 0.05 | 0.20 | 4 | 0.20 |
| 5 | 0.05 | 0.25 | 9 | 0.45 |
| | (a) Mean = | 2.00 | Variance = | 1.40 |
| | | | (b) Stdev = | 1.18321596 |

5.6 (a)

| $X$ | $P(X)$ |
|---|---|
| $ − 1 | 21/36 |
| $ + 1 | 15/36 |

(b)

| $X$ | $P(X)$ |
|---|---|
| $ − 1 | 21/36 |
| $ + 1 | 15/36 |

(c)

| $X$ | $P(X)$ |
|---|---|
| $ − 1 | 30/36 |
| $ + 4 | 6/36 |

(d) $ − 0.167 for each method of play

5.8 (a) 0.5997 (c) 0.0439
(b) 0.0016 (d) 0.4018

5.10 Given $p = .6$ and $n = 5$,
(a) $P(X = 5) = 0.0778$
(b) $P(X \geq 3) = 0.6826$
(c) $P(X < 2) = 0.0870$
(d) (a) $P(X = 5) = 0.3277$
(b) $P(X \geq 3) = 0.9421$
(c) $P(X < 2) = 0.0067$

5.12 Given $p = 0.90$ and $n = 3$,

(a) $P(X = 3) = \frac{n!}{X!(n-X)!}p^X(1-p)^{n-X} = \frac{3!}{3!0!}(.9)^3(.1)^0 = 0.729$

(b) $P(X = 0) = \frac{n!}{X!(n-X)!}p^X(1-p)^{n-X} = \frac{3!}{0!3!}(.9)^0(.1)^3 = 0.001$

(c) $P(X \geq 2) = P(X = 2) + P(X = 3) = \frac{3!}{2!1!}(.9)^2(.1)^1 + \frac{3!}{3!0!}(.9)^3(.1)^0 = 0.972$

(d) $E(X) = np = 3(.9) = 2.7$

$\sigma = \sqrt{np(1-p)} = \sqrt{3(.9)(.1)} = 0.5196$

5.14 (a) $P(X = 0) = 1.0 \times 10^{-10}$ (b) $P(X = 1) = 9.0 \times 10^{-9}$
(c) $P(X \leq 2) = 3.74 \times 10^{-7}$ (d) $P(X \geq 3) = 1.0$

5.16 (a) Since the 68% and 24% figures are obtained from the survey results conducted by the networks, they are best classified as empirical classical probability.
(b) $P(X < 5) = 1.4 \times 10^{-5} = 0.000014$ (c) $P(X \geq 10) = 0.9721$
(d) $P(X = 20) = 0.000447$

5.18 (a) Using the equation, if $\lambda = 2.5$, $P(X = 2) = \frac{e^{-2.5} \cdot (2.5)^2}{2!} = 0.2565$
(b) If $\lambda = 8.0$, $P(X = 8) = 0.1396$
(c) If $\lambda = 0.5$, $P(X = 1) = 0.3033$
(d) If $\lambda = 3.7$, $P(X = 0) = 0.0247$

5.20 PHStat output for (a) – (d)

| **Poisson Probabilities Table** | | | | | | |
|---|---|---|---|---|---|---|
| | **X** | **P(X)** | **P(<=X)** | **P(<X)** | **P(>X)** | **P(>=X)** |
| | **0** | **0.006738** | **0.006738** | **0.000000** | **0.993262** | **1.000000** |
| | **1** | **0.033690** | **0.040428** | **0.006738** | **0.959572** | **0.993262** |
| | **2** | **0.084224** | **0.124652** | **0.040428** | **0.875348** | **0.959572** |
| | **3** | **0.140374** | **0.265026** | **0.124652** | **0.734974** | **0.875348** |
| | **4** | **0.175467** | **0.440493** | **0.265026** | **0.559507** | **0.734974** |
| | **5** | **0.175467** | **0.615961** | **0.440493** | **0.384039** | **0.559507** |
| | **6** | **0.146223** | **0.762183** | **0.615961** | **0.237817** | **0.384039** |
| | **7** | **0.104445** | **0.866628** | **0.762183** | **0.133372** | **0.237817** |
| | **8** | **0.065278** | **0.931906** | **0.866628** | **0.068094** | **0.133372** |
| | **9** | **0.036266** | **0.968172** | **0.931906** | **0.031828** | **0.068094** |
| | **10** | **0.018133** | **0.986305** | **0.968172** | **0.013695** | **0.031828** |
| | **11** | **0.008242** | **0.994547** | **0.986305** | **0.005453** | **0.013695** |
| | **12** | **0.003434** | **0.997981** | **0.994547** | **0.002019** | **0.005453** |
| | **13** | **0.001321** | **0.999302** | **0.997981** | **0.000698** | **0.002019** |
| | **14** | **0.000472** | **0.999774** | **0.999302** | **0.000226** | **0.000698** |
| | **15** | **0.000157** | **0.999931** | **0.999774** | **0.000069** | **0.000226** |
| | **16** | **0.000049** | **0.999980** | **0.999931** | **0.000020** | **0.000069** |
| | **17** | **0.000014** | **0.999995** | **0.999980** | **0.000005** | **0.000020** |
| | **18** | **0.000004** | **0.999999** | **0.999995** | **0.000001** | **0.000005** |
| | **19** | **0.000001** | **1.000000** | **0.999999** | **0.000000** | **0.000001** |
| | **20** | **0.000000** | **1.000000** | **1.000000** | **0.000000** | **0.000000** |

Given $\lambda$=5.0,

(a) $P(X = 1) = 0.0337$

(b) $P(X < 1) = 0.0067$

(c) $P(X > 1) = 0.9596$

(d) $P(X \leq 1) = 0.0404$

5.22 (a) – (c) Portion of PHStat output

| Data | | | | | |
|---|---|---|---|---|---|
| Average/Expected number of successes: | | | 6 | | |
| Poisson Probabilities Table | | | | | |
| | X | P(X) | P(<=X) | P(<X) | P(>X) | P(>=X) |
| | 0 | 0.002479 | 0.002479 | 0.000000 | 0.997521 | 1.000000 |
| | 1 | 0.014873 | 0.017351 | 0.002479 | 0.982649 | 0.997521 |
| | 2 | 0.044618 | 0.061969 | 0.017351 | 0.938031 | 0.982649 |
| | 3 | 0.089235 | 0.151204 | 0.061969 | 0.848796 | 0.938031 |
| | 4 | 0.133853 | 0.285057 | 0.151204 | 0.714943 | 0.848796 |
| | 5 | (b) 0.160623 | 0.445680 | (a) 0.285057 | 0.554320 | [redacted] |
| | 6 | 0.160623 | 0.606303 | 0.445680 | 0.393697 | 0.554320 |
| | 7 | 0.137677 | 0.743980 | 0.606303 | 0.256020 | 0.393697 |
| | 8 | 0.103258 | 0.847237 | 0.743980 | 0.152763 | 0.256020 |
| | 9 | 0.068838 | 0.916076 | 0.847237 | 0.083924 | 0.152763 |
| | 10 | 0.041303 | 0.957379 | 0.916076 | 0.042621 | 0.083924 |
| | 11 | 0.022529 | 0.979908 | 0.957379 | 0.020092 | 0.042621 |
| | 12 | 0.011264 | 0.991173 | 0.979908 | 0.008827 | 0.020092 |
| | 13 | 0.005199 | 0.996372 | 0.991173 | 0.003628 | 0.008827 |
| | 14 | 0.002228 | 0.998600 | 0.996372 | 0.001400 | 0.003628 |
| | 15 | 0.000891 | 0.999491 | 0.998600 | 0.000509 | 0.001400 |
| | 16 | 0.000334 | 0.999825 | 0.999491 | 0.000175 | 0.000509 |
| | 17 | 0.000118 | 0.999943 | 0.999825 | 0.000057 | 0.000175 |

(a) $P(X<5) = P(X=0) + P(X=1) + P(X=2) + P(X=3) + P(X=4)$

$$= \frac{e^{-6}(6)^0}{0!} + \frac{e^{-6}(6)^1}{1!} + \frac{e^{-6}(6)^2}{2!} + \frac{e^{-6}(6)^3}{3!} + \frac{e^{-6}(6)^4}{4!}$$

$$= 0.002479 + 0.014873 + 0.044618 + 0.089235 + 0.133853 = 0.2851$$

(b) $P(X=5) = \dfrac{e^{-6}(6)^5}{5!} = 0.1606$

(c) $P(X \geq 5) = 1 - P(X<5) = 1 - 0.2851 = 0.7149$

(d) $P(X=4 \text{ or } X=5) = P(X=4) + P(X=5) = \dfrac{e^{-6}(6)^4}{4!} + \dfrac{e^{-6}(6)^5}{5!} = 0.2945$

5.24 Given $\lambda = 3.21$,

(a) $P(X=0) = 0.0404$ (b) $P(X \geq 1) = 0.9596$

(c) $P(X \geq 2) = 0.8301$

(d) Because Delta has a higher mean rate of mishandled bags per 1000 passengers than Jet Blue, its probability of mishandling at least a certain number of bags is higher than that of Jet Blue.

5.26 (a) If $\lambda = 0.2$, $P(X \geq 2) = 1 - [P(X=0) + P(X=1)] = 1 - [0.8187 + 0.1637]$ $= 0.0176$

(b) If there are 0.2 flaws per foot on the average, then there are 0.2•(12) or 2.4 flaws on the average in a 12-foot roll.
If $\lambda = 2.4$, $P(X \geq 1) = 1 - P(X=0) = 1 - 0.0907 = 0.9093$

(c) If there are 0.2 flaws per foot on the average, then there are 0.2•(50) or 10 flaws on the average in a 50-foot roll.
If $\lambda = 10$, $P(5 \leq X \leq 15) = 0.9220$

5.28 (a) $\lambda = 5.09$, $P(X = 0) = 0.0062$ (b) $\lambda = 5.09$, $P(X \leq 2) = 0.1173$

(c) Because Kia had a higher mean rate of problems per car, the probability of a randomly selected Kia having no more than 2 problems is lower than that of a randomly chosen Lexus. Likewise, the probability of a randomly selected Kia having zero problems is lower than that of a randomly chosen Lexus

5.30 (a) $\lambda = 1.53$, $P(X = 0) = 0.2165$ (b) $\lambda = 1.53$, $P(X \leq 2) = 0.8013$

(c) . Because Kia had a lower mean rate of problems per car in 2004 compared to 2003, the probability of a randomly selected Kia having zero problems and the probability of no more than 2 problems are both higher than their values in 2003.

5.32 The expected value is the average of a probability distribution. It is the value that can be expected to occur on the average, in the long run.

5.34 The four properties of a situation that must be present in order to use the Poisson distribution are (i) you are interested in counting the number of times a particular event occurs in a given area of opportunity (defined by time, length, surface area, and so forth), (ii) the probability that an event occurs in a given area of opportunity is the same for all of the areas of opportunity, (iii) the number of events that occur in one area of opportunity is independent of the number of events that occur in other areas of opportunity and (iv) the probability that two or more events will occur in an area of opportunity approaches zero as the area of opportunity becomes smaller.

5.36 (a) 0.74

(b) 0.74

$p = 0.74$, $n = 5$

(c) $P(X = 4) = 0.3898$ (d) $P(X = 0) = 0.0012$

(e) Stock prices tend to rise in the years when the economy is expanding and fall in the years of recession or contraction. Hence, the probability that the price will rise in one year is not independent from year to year.

5.38 (a) If $p = 0.50$ and $n = 10$, $P(X \geq 8) = 0.0547$

(b) If $p = 0.70$ and $n = 10$, $P(X \geq 8) = 0.3829$

(c) If $p = 0.90$ and $n = 10$, $P(X \geq 8) = 0.9298$

(d) If the indicator is a random event, the probability that it will make a correct prediction in 8 or more times out of 10 is 5.47%. If one is willing to accept the argument that the amount of campaign expenditures spent during an election year exerts some multiplying impact on the stock market, the probability that the Dow Jones Industrial Average will increase in a U.S. Presidential election year is likely to be near 0.90 based on the result of (a)-(c).

5.40 (a)-(d) Portion of the PHStat output:

| | | | | |
|---|---|---|---|---|
| Binomial Probabilities | | | | |
| Data | | | | |
| Sample size | 10 | | | |
| Probability of success | 0.33 | | | |
| Statistics | | | | |
| Mean | (d) 3.3 | | | |
| Variance | 2.211 | | | |
| Standard deviation | (d) 1.486943 | | | |
| Binomial Probabilities Table | | | | |
| | X | P(X) | P(<=X) | P(>=X) |
| | 0 | (a) 0.018228 | 0.018228 | 1 |
| | 1 | (b) 0.089782 | 0.10801 | 0.981772 |
| | 2 | 0.198993 | 0.307003 | (c) 0.89199 |
| | 10 | 1.53E-05 | 1 | 1.53E-05 |

(d) Because the probability that a single Priority Mail shipment will fail to deliver on-time is higher than that of a single first-class shipment, the probability of zero items taking more than 3 days and the probability of exactly one taking more than 3 days are lower for Priority Mail shipments compared to first-class shipments whereas the probability of two or more that will take more than 3 days is higher for Priority Mail shipments compared to first-class shipments.

5.42 (a)-(d) Portion of the PHStat output:

| | | | | | |
|---|---|---|---|---|---|
| Binomial Probabilities | | | | | |
| Data | | | | | |
| Sample size | 10 | | | | |
| Probability of success | 0.74 | | | | |
| Statistics | | | | | |
| Mean | 7.4 | | | | |
| Variance | 1.924 | | | | |
| Standard deviation | 1.387083 | | | | |
| Binomial Probabilities Table | | | | | |
| | X | P(X) | P(<X) | P(>X) | P(>=X) |
| | 0 | (a) 1.41E-06 | 0 | 0.999999 | 1 |
| | 5 | 0.066439 | 0.023915 | (c) 0.909646 | 0.976085 |
| | 8 | 0.273535 | 0.50422 | 0.222245 | (d) 0.49578 |
| | 10 | (b) 0.04924 | 0.95076 | 0 | 0.04924 |

5.44 (a) – (e) Portion of the PHStat output: $p = 1628/3700 = 0.44$

| Binomial Probabilities | | | | | | |
|---|---|---|---|---|---|---|
| Data | | | | | | |
| Sample size | 10 | | | | | |
| Probability of success | 0.44 | | | | | |
| Statistics | | | | | | |
| Mean | (f) 4.4 | | | | | |
| Variance | 2.464 | | | | | |
| Standard deviation | 1.569713 | | | | | |
| Binomial Probabilities Table | | | | | | |
| | X | P(X) | P(<=X) | P(<X) | P(>X) | P(>=X) |
| | 0 | 0.003033 | 0.003033 | 0 | 0.996967 | 1 |
| | 5 | (b) 0.228878 | 0.759297 | (d) 0.530419 | 0.240703 | (c),(e) 0.469581 |
| | 6 | 0.149861 | 0.909157 | 0.759297 | 0.090843 | 0.240703 |
| | 7 | 0.067284 | 0.976442 | 0.909157 | 0.023558 | 0.090843 |
| | 8 | 0.019825 | 0.996267 | 0.976442 | 0.003733 | 0.023558 |
| | 9 | 0.003461 | 0.999728 | 0.996267 | 0.000272 | 0.003733 |
| | 10 | (a) 0.000272 | 1 | 0.999728 | 0 | 0.000272 |

(f) On average 4.4 people will refuse to participate out of every 10 people. You would have to survey about 227 ($\approx 100 / 0.44$) people to get 100 responses

5.46 If $p = 0.88$ and $n = 20$,

(a) $\mu = 17.6$ (b) $\sigma = 1.453$

(c) $P(X = 20) = 0.0776$ (d) $P(X \geq 18) = 0.5631$

(e) $P(X \geq 15) = 0.9740$

5.48 (a) If $p = 0.50$ and $n = 34$, $P(X \geq 29) = 1.92791\text{E-}05$

(b) If $p = 0.70$ and $n = 34$, $P(X \geq 29) = 0.0334$

(c) If $p = 0.90$ and $n = 34$, $P(X \geq 29) = 0.8815$

(d) Based on the results in (a)-(c), the probability that the Standard & Poor's 500 index will increase if there is an early gain in the first five trading days of the year is very likely to be close to 0.90 because that yields a probability of 88.15% that at least 29 of the 34 years the Standard & Poor's 500 index will increase the entire year.

5.50 (a) The assumptions needed are (i) the probability that a golfer loses a golf ball in a given interval in a game is constant, (ii) the probability that a golfer loses more than one golf ball in this interval is 0, (iii) the probability that a golfer loses a golf ball is independent from interval to interval.

$\lambda = 4.5$

(b) $P(X = 0) = 0.0111$

(c) $P(X \leq 5) = 0.70293$

(d) $P(X \geq 6) = 0.29707$

# CHAPTER 6

## OBJECTIVES

- To know how to compute probabilities from the normal distribution
- To be able to use the normal probability plot to determine whether a set of data is approximately normally distributed

## OVERVIEW AND KEY CONCEPTS

### Some Basic Concepts of Continuous Probability Density Function

- **Continuous random variable:** A variable that can take an infinite number of values within a specific range, e.g. Weight, height, daily changes in closing prices of stocks, and time between arrivals of planes landing on a runway.
- **Continuous probability density function:** A mathematical expression that represents the continuous phenomenon of a continuous random variable, and can be used to calculate the probability that the random variable occurs within certain ranges or intervals.
- The probability that a continuous random variable is equal to a *particular value* is 0. This distinguishes continuous phenomena, which are measured, from discrete phenomena, which are counted. For example, the probability that a task can be completed in between 20 and 30 seconds can be measured. With a more precise measuring instrument, we can compute the probability that the task can be completed between a very small interval such as 19.99 to 20.01. However, the probability that the task can be completed in *exactly* 21 seconds is 0.
- Obtaining probabilities or computing expected values and standard deviations for continuous random variables involves mathematical expressions that require knowledge of integral calculus. In this book, these are achieved via special probability tables or computer statistical software like Minitab or PHStat.

### The Normal Distribution

- **Properties of the normal distribution:**
  - Bell-shaped (and thus symmetrical) in its appearance.
  - Its measures of central tendency (mean, median, and mode) are all identical.
  - Its "middle spread" (interquartile range) is equal to 1.33 standard deviations.
  - Its associated random variable has an infinite range $(-\infty < X < +\infty)$.

- **The normal probability density function:**
    - $f(X) = \frac{1}{\sqrt{2\pi\sigma^2}} e^{-\frac{1}{2\sigma^2}(X-\mu)^2}$ where

      $f(X)$: density of random variable $X$

      $\pi = 3.14159$; $e = 2.71828$

      $\mu$: population mean

      $\sigma$: population standard deviation

      $X$: value of random variable $(-\infty < X < \infty)$
    - A particular combination of $\mu$ and $\sigma$ will yield a particular normal probability distribution.
- **Standardization or normalization of a normal continuous random variable:** By standardizing (normalizing) a normal random variable, we need only one table to tabulate the probabilities of the whole family of normal distributions.
- **The transformation (standardization) formula:** $Z = \frac{X-\mu}{\sigma}$
    - The standardized normal distribution is one whose random variable $Z$ always has a mean 0 and a standard deviation 1.
- **Finding range probability of a normal random variable:**
    1. Standardize the value of $X$ into $Z$.
    2. Lookup the cumulative probabilities from the cumulative standardized normal distribution table.

    **E.g.,** For $\mu = 5$ and $\sigma = 10$, $P(2.9 < X < 7.1) = ?$

$$Z = \frac{X-\mu}{\sigma} = \frac{2.9-5}{10} = -.21 \qquad Z = \frac{X-\mu}{\sigma} = \frac{7.1-5}{10} = .21$$

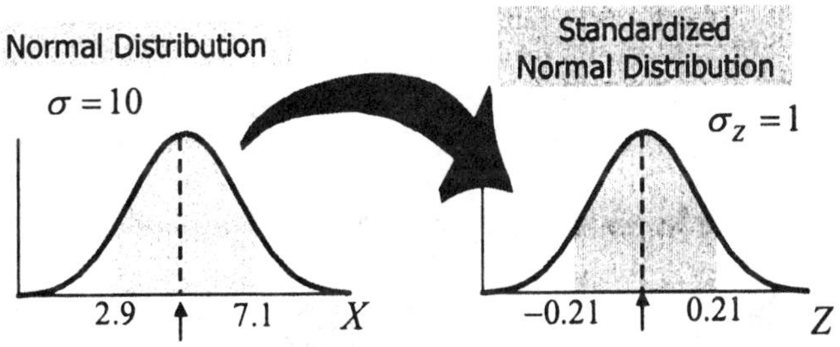


Cumulative Standardized Normal Distribution Table (Portion)

| Z | .00 | .01 | .02 |
|---|---|---|---|
| 0.0 | .5000 | .5040 | .5080 |
| 0.1 | .5398 | .5438 | .5478 |
| 0.2 | .5793 | **.5832** | .5871 |
| 0.3 | .6179 | .6217 | .6255 |

$\mu_Z = 0 \quad \sigma_Z = 1$

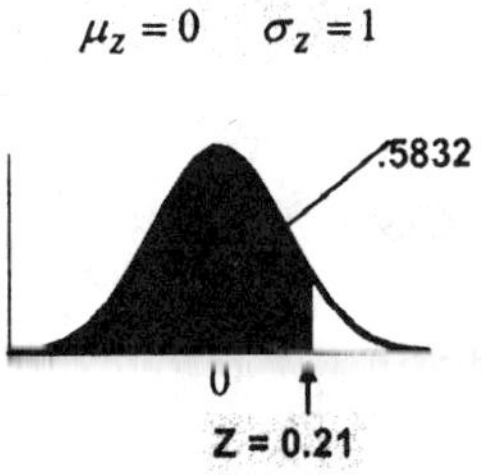


Cumulative Standardized Normal Distribution Table (Portion)

| Z | .00 | .01 | .02 |
|---|---|---|---|
| -03 | .3821 | .3783 | .3745 |
| -02 | .4207 | **.4168** | .4129 |
| -0.1 | .4602 | .4562 | .4522 |
| 0.0 | .5000 | .4960 | .4920 |

$\mu_Z = 0 \quad \sigma_Z = 1$

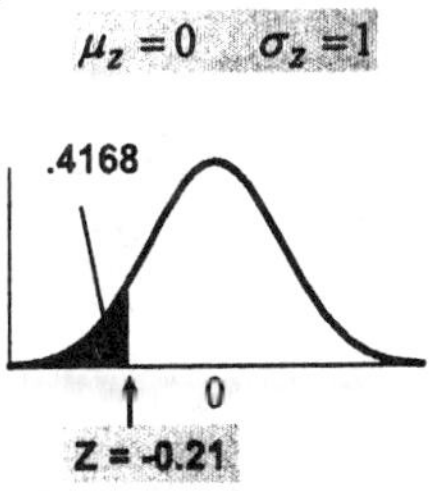


$$P(2.9 < X < 7.1) = P(-0.21 < Z < 0.21) = 0.5832 - 0.4168 = 0.1664$$

**E.g.,** For $\mu = 5$ and $\sigma = 10$, $P(X \geq 8) = ?$

$$Z = \frac{X - \mu}{\sigma} = \frac{8-5}{10} = .30$$

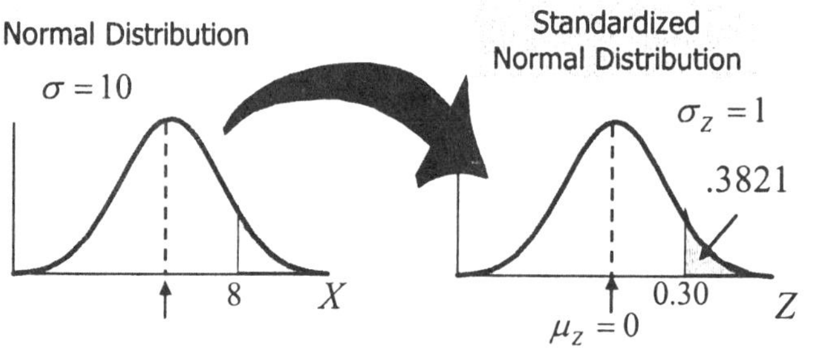


Cumulative Standardized Normal Distribution Table (Portion)

| Z | .00 | .01 | .02 |
|---|---|---|---|
| 0.0 | .5000 | .5040 | .5080 |
| 0.1 | .5398 | .5438 | .5478 |
| 0.2 | .5793 | .5832 | .5871 |
| 0.3 | **.6179** | .6217 | .6255 |

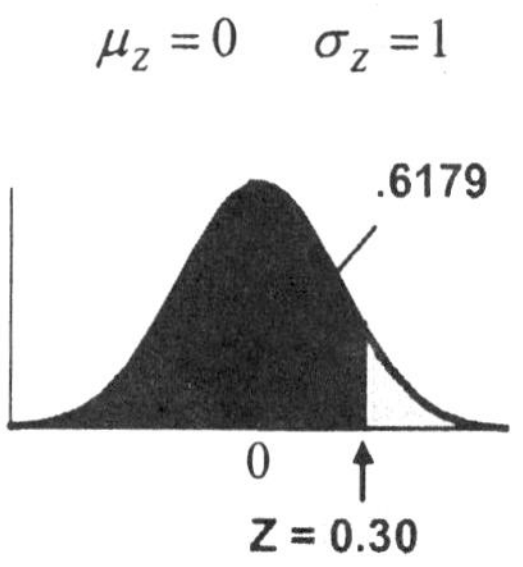


$$P(X \geq 8) = P(Z \geq 0.30) = 1 - 0.6179 = 0.3821$$

- **Recovering *X* values for known probabilities:**
  1. Lookup the *Z* value from the cumulative standardized normal distribution table.
  2. Recover the value of *X* using the formula $X = \mu + Z\sigma$

  **E.g.,** For $\mu = 5$ and $\sigma = 10$, $P(X \leq A) = 0.6179$, what is the value of *A*?

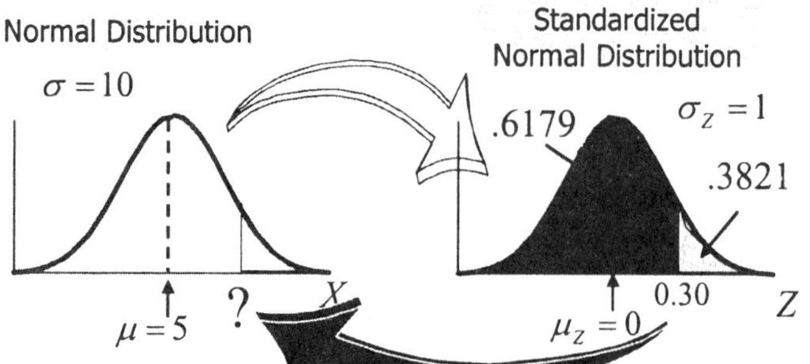


$$P(X \leq A) = P\left(Z \leq \frac{A-5}{10}\right) = 0.6179, \ \frac{A-5}{10} = 0.30, \ A = 5 + 0.30(10) = 8$$

- **Applications:** Many continuous random phenomena are either normally distributed or can be approximated by a normal distribution. Hence, it is important to know how to assess whether a distribution is normally distributed.

## Evaluating the Normality Assumption

- For small and moderate-sized data sets, construct a stem-and-leaf display and box-and-whisker plot. For large data sets, construct the frequency distribution and plot the histogram or polygon.
- Obtain the mean, median, and mode, and note the similarities or differences among these measures of central tendency.
- Obtain the interquartile range and standard deviation. Note how well the interquartile range can be approximated by 1.33 times the standard deviation.
- Obtain the range and note how well it can be approximated by 6 times the standard deviation.
- Determine whether approximately 2/3 of the observations lie between the mean $\pm$ 1 standard deviation. Determine whether approximately 4/5 of the observations lie between the mean $\pm$ 1.28 standard deviations. Determine whether approximately 19/20 of the observations lie between the mean $\pm$ 2 standard deviations.
- Construct a normal probability plot and evaluate the likelihood that the variable of interest is at least approximately normally distributed by inspecting the plot for evidence of linearity (i.e., a straight line).

## The Normal Probability Plot

- **The normal probability plot:** A two-dimensional plot of the observed data values on the vertical axis with their corresponding quantile values from a standardized normal distribution on the horizontal axis.

Left-Skewed

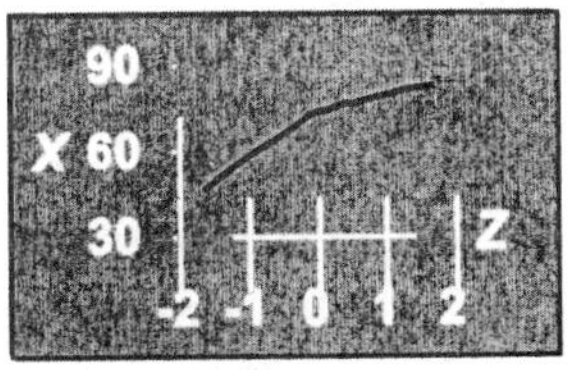


Right-Skewed

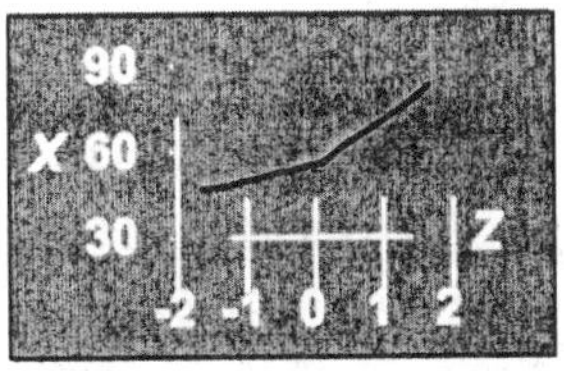


Rectangular

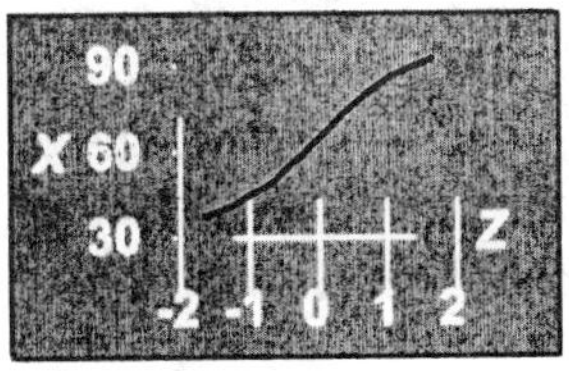


U-Shaped

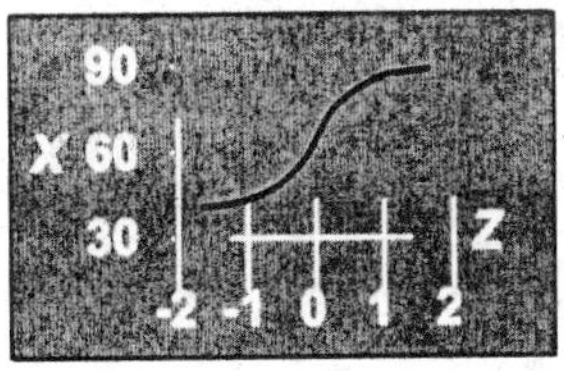

## SOLUTIONS TO END OF SECTION AND CHAPTER REVIEW EVEN PROBLEMS

6.2 (a) $P(-1.57 < Z < 1.84) = 0.9671 - 0.0582 = 0.9089$
(b) $P(Z < -1.57) + P(Z > 1.84) = 0.0582 + 0.0329 = 0.0911$
(c) If $P(Z > A) = 0.025$, $P(Z < A) = 0.975$. $A = +1.96$.
(d) If $P(-A < Z < A) = 0.6826$, $P(Z < A) = 0.8413$. So 68.26% of the area is captured between $-A = -1.00$ and $A = +1.00$.

6.4 (a) $P(Z > 1.08) = 1 - 0.8599 = 0.1401$
(b) $P(Z < -0.21) = 0.4168$
(c) $P(-1.96 < Z < -0.21) = 0.4168 - 0.0250 = 0.3918$
(d) $P(Z > A) = 0.1587$, $P(Z < A) = 0.8413$. $A = +1.00$.

6.6 (a) $P(X > 43) = P(Z > -1.75) = 1 - 0.0401 = 0.9599$
(b) $P(X < 42) = P(Z < -2.00) = 0.0228$
(c) $P(X < A) = 0.05$,

$$Z = -1.645 = \frac{A-50}{4} \qquad A = 50 - 1.645(4) = 43.42$$

(d) $P(X_{lower} < X < X_{upper}) = 0.60$
$P(Z < -0.84) = 0.20$ and $P(Z < 0.84) = 0.80$

$$Z = -0.84 = \frac{X_{lower} - 50}{4} \qquad Z = +0.84 = \frac{X_{upper} - 50}{4}$$

$X_{lower} = 50 - 0.84(4) = 46.64$ and $X_{upper} = 50 + 0.84(4) = 53.36$

6.8 (a) $P(34 < X < 50) = P(-1.33 < Z < 0) = 0.4082$
(b) $P(X < 30) + P(X > 60) = P(Z < -1.67) + P(Z > 0.83)$
$= 0.0475 + (1.0 - 0.7967) = 0.2508$
(c) $P(X > \text{A}) = 0.80$ $\qquad P(Z < -0.84) \cong 0.20 \qquad Z = -0.84 = \dfrac{A-50}{12}$

$A = 50 - 0.84(12) = 39.92$ thousand miles or 39,920 miles
(d) The smaller standard deviation makes the $Z$-values larger.
 (a) $P(34 < X < 50) = P(-1.60 < Z < 0) = 0.4452$
 (b) $P(X < 30) + P(X > 60) = P(Z < -2.00) + P(Z > 1.00)$
 $= 0.0228 + (1.0 - 0.8413) = 0.1815$
 (c) $A = 50 - 0.84(10) = 41.6$ thousand miles or 41,600 miles

6.10 (a) $P(X < 91) = P(Z < 2.25) = 0.9878$
(b) $P(65 < X < 89) = P(-1.00 < Z < 2.00) = 0.9772 - 0.1587 = 0.8185$
(c) $P(X > A) = 0.05$ $\qquad P(Z < 1.645) = 0.9500$

$$Z = 1.645 = \frac{A-73}{8} \qquad A = 73 + 1.645(8) = 86.16\%$$

6.10 cont. (d) Option 1: $P(X > A) = 0.10$ $P(Z < 1.28) \cong 0.9000$

$$Z = \frac{81-73}{8} = 1.00$$

Since your score of 81% on this exam represents a Z-score of 1.00, which is below the minimum Z-score of 1.28, you will not earn an "A" grade on the exam under this grading option.

Option 2: $Z = \frac{68-62}{3} = 2.00$

Since your score of 68% on this exam represents a Z-score of 2.00, which is well above the minimum Z-score of 1.28, you will earn an "A" grade on the exam under this grading option. You should prefer Option 2.

6.12 (a) $P(X < 1.7) = P(Z < 2.0) = 0.9772$
(b) $P(X < 1.25) = P(Z < -1.0) = 0.1587$
(c) $P(X < 1.0) = P(Z < -2.6667) = 0.0038$
(d) $P(X > 1.0) = P(Z > -2.6667) = 0.9962$

6.14 With 39 observations, the smallest of the standard normal quantile values covers an area under the normal curve of 0.025. The corresponding Z-value is – 1.96. The largest of the standard normal quantile values covers an area under the normal curve of 0.975 and its corresponding Z-value is +1.96.

6.16 (a) $\text{mean} = \frac{\sum_{i=1}^{n} X_i}{n} = \frac{2491.55}{25} = 99.662$, median = 95.78,

range = max – min = 167.43 – 62.88 = 104.55,

$$S_X = \sqrt{\frac{\sum_{i=1}^{n}(X-\bar{X})^2}{n-1}} = \sqrt{\frac{14861.7724}{24}} = 24.8845,$$

$6 \bullet S_X = 6 \bullet 24.8845 = 149.3072$,

interquartile range = $Q_3 - Q_1 = 120.675 - 77.57 = 43.105$,

$1.33 \bullet S_X = 1.33 \bullet 24.8845 = 33.0964$

The mean is greater than the median; the range is smaller than 6 times the standard deviation and the interquartile range is larger than 1.33 times the standard deviation. The data do not appear to follow a normal distribution.

6.16 cont. (b)

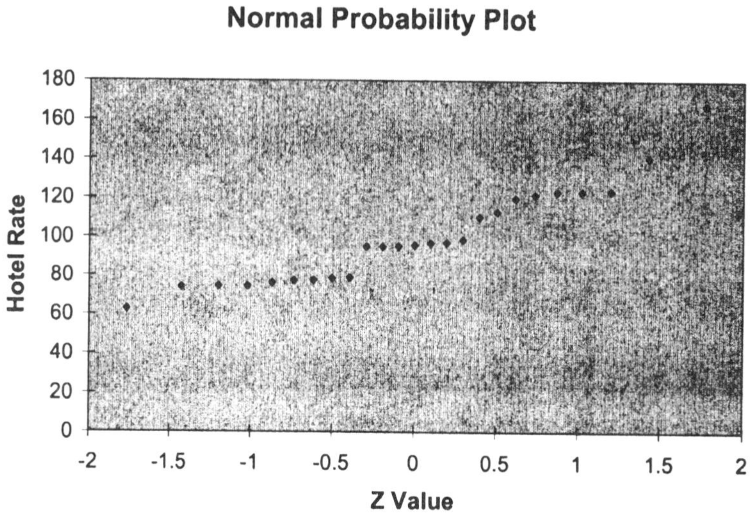


The normal probability plot suggests that the data are skewed to the right.

6.18 (a) Plant A: $\bar{X} = 9.382$ $S = 3.998$

Five-number summary 4.42 7.29 8.515 11.42 21.62

Interquartile range = 4.13 $1.33\,S = 5.317$

Range = 17.2 $6\,S = 23.986$

Between $\bar{X} \pm 1S_X = 80\%$

Between $\bar{X} \pm 1.28S_X = 90\%$

Between $\bar{X} \pm 2S_X = 95\%$

The median is smaller than the mean. The interquartile range is smaller than 1.33 times the standard deviation and the range is much smaller than 6 times the standard deviation.

The distribution is right-skewed since the mean is greater than the median.

Note: The quartiles are obtained using PHStat without any interpolation.

Plant B: $\bar{X} = 11.354$ $S = 5.126$

Five-number summary 2.33 6.25 11.96 14.25 25.75

Interquartile range = 8 $1.33\,S = 6.818$

Range = 23.42 $6\,S = 30.757$

Between $\bar{X} \pm 1S_X = 75\%$

Between $\bar{X} \pm 1.28S_X = 95\%$

Between $\bar{X} \pm 2S_X = 95\%$

The median is slightly larger than the mean. The interquartile range is larger than 1.33 times the standard deviation and the range is smaller than 6 times the standard deviation.

Although the results are inconsistent due to an extreme value in the sample, since the mean is less than the median, we can say that the data for Plant B is left-skewed.

6.18 cont. (a) Note: The quartiles are obtained using PHStat without any interpolation.

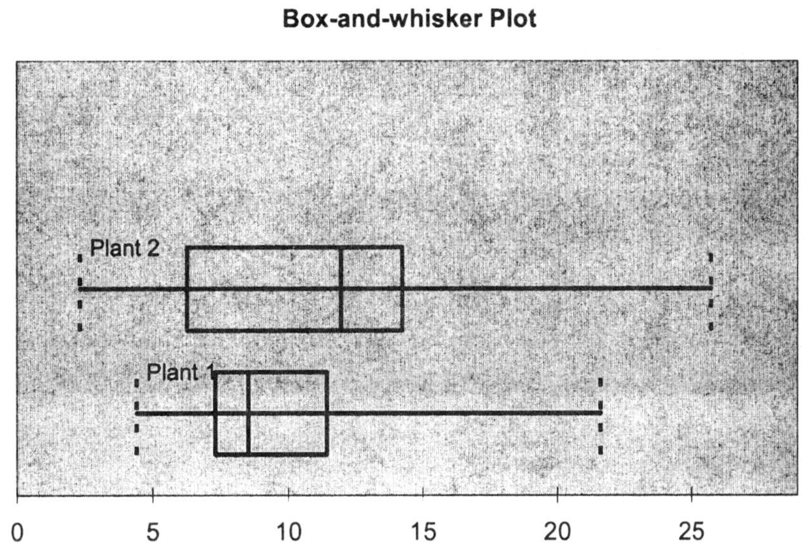


(b)

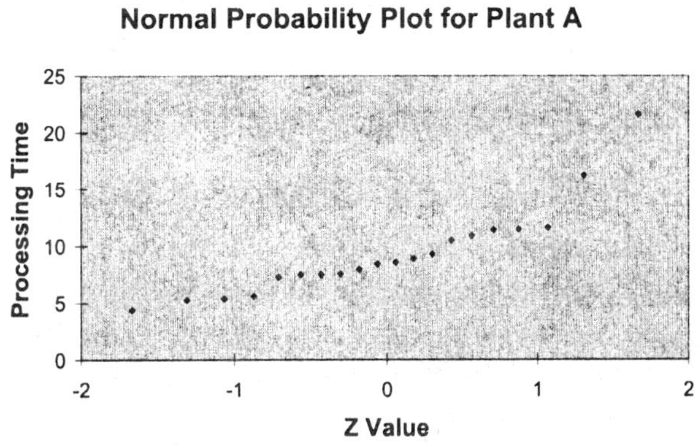


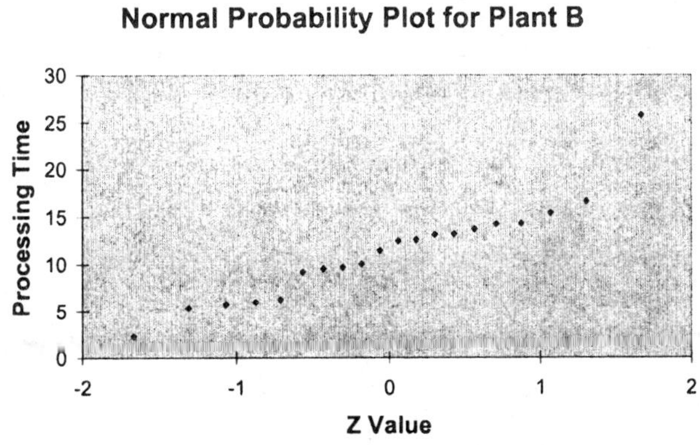

6.20 (a) $\bar{X} = -0.00023$ median = 0

Interquartile range = 0.0025 $S_X = 0.0017$ Range = 0.008

1.33 ( $S_X$ ) = 0.0023 6 ( $S_X$ ) = 0.0102

Between $\bar{X} \pm 1S_X = 61\%$ Between $\bar{X} \pm 1.28S_X = 72\%$

Between $\bar{X} \pm 2S_X = 98\%$

Since the interquartile range is quite close to 1.33 ( $S_X$ ) and the range is also quite close to 6 ( $S_X$ ), the data appear to be approximately normally distributed.

(b)

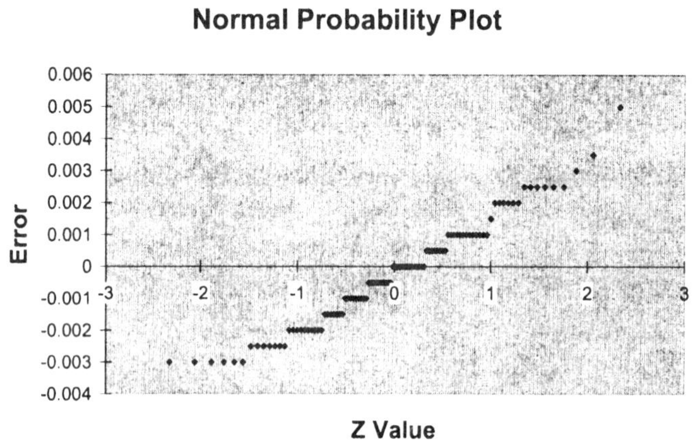


The normal probability plot suggests that the data appear to be approximately normally distributed.

6.22 (a) Five-number summary: 82 127 148.5 168 213 mean = 147.06
range = 131 interquartile range = 41 standard deviation = 31.69
The mean is very close to the median. The five-number summary suggests that the distribution is quite symmetrical around the median. The interquartile range is very close to 1.33 times the standard deviation. The range is about $50 below 6 times the standard deviation. In general, the distribution of the data appears to closely resemble a normal distribution.
Note: The quartiles are obtained using PHStat without any interpolation.

6.22 (b)
cont.

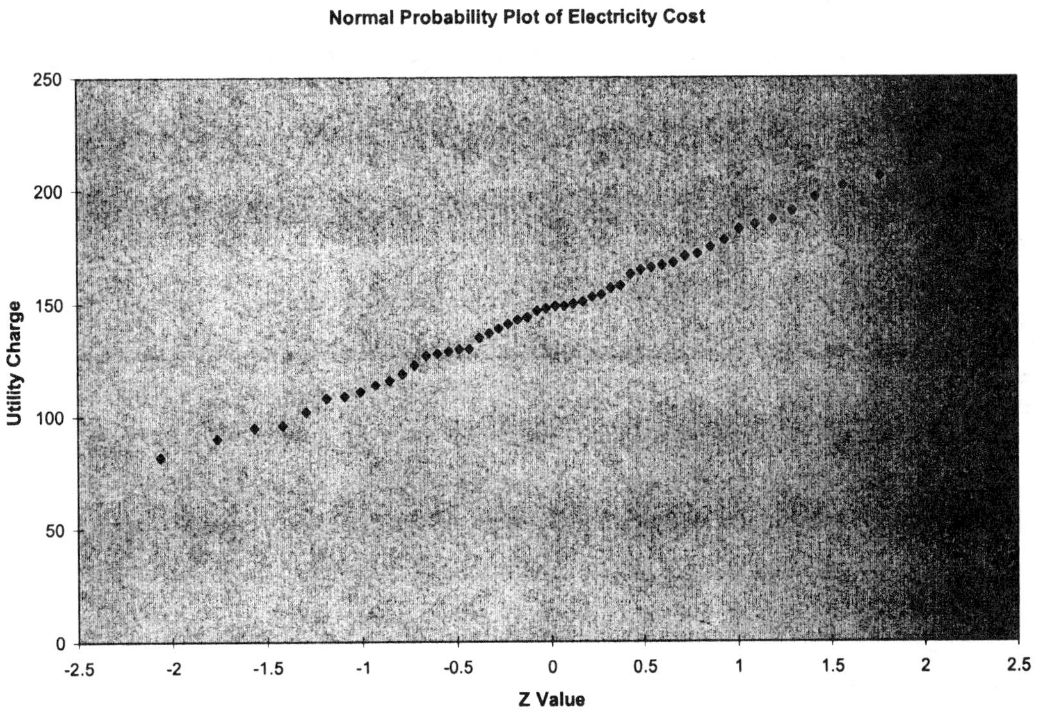


The normal probability plot confirms that the data appear to be approximately normally distributed.

6.24 Using Table E.2, first find the cumulative area up to the largest value, and then subtract the cumulative area up to the smallest value.

6.26 If the distribution is normal, the plot of the Z values on the horizontal axis and the original values on the vertical axis will be a straight line.

6.28 (a) $P(1.90 < X < 2.00) = P(-2.00 < Z < 0) = 0.4772$

(b) $P(1.90 < X < 2.10) = P(-2.00 < Z < 2.00) = 0.9772 - 0.0228 = 0.9544$

(c) $P(X < 1.90) + P(X > 2.10) = 1 - P(1.90 < X < 2.10) = 0.0456$

(d) $P(X > A) = P(Z > -2.33) = 0.99$ $A = 2.00 - 2.33(0.05) = 1.8835$

(e) $P(A < X < B) = P(-2.58 < Z < 2.58) = 0.99$

$A = 2.00 - 2.58(0.05) = 1.8710$ $B = 2.00 + 2.58(0.05) = 2.1290$

6.30 (a) $P(4.70 < X < 5.00) = P(0 < Z < 0.75) = 0.2734$

(b) $P(5.00 < X < 5.50) = P(0.75 < Z < 2.00) = 0.9772 - 0.7734 = 0.2038$

(c) $P(X > A) = P(Z > -0.74) = 0.77$ $A = 4.70 - 0.74(0.40) = 4.404$ ounces

(d) $P(A < X < B) = P(-1.28 < Z < 1.28) = 0.80$

$A = 4.70 - 1.28(0.40) = 4.188$ ounces

$B = 4.70 + 1.28(0.40) = 5.212$ ounces

6.32 (a) $P(X > 0) = P(Z > -0.6047) = 0.7273$
(b) $P(X > 10) = P(Z > 0.5581) = 0.2884$
(c) $P(X > 20) = P(Z > 1.7209) = 0.0426$
(d) $P(X < -10) = P(Z < -1.7674) = 0.0386$
(e) The common stocks have higher mean annual returns than the long-term government bonds. But they also have higher volatility as reflected by their larger standard deviation. This is the usual trade-off between high return and high volatility in an investment instrument.

*Note*: The above answers are obtained using PHStat. They may be slightly different when Table E.2 is used.

6.34 (a) $P(X < 1) = P(Z < 1) = 0.8413$
(b) $P(0.5 < X < 1.5) = P(-1.5 < Z < 3.5) = 0.9330$
(c) $P(0.5 < X) = P(-1.5 < Z) = 0.9332$
(d) $P(A < X) = 0.99$ $\quad \frac{A - 0.8}{0.2} = -2.3263$ $\quad A = 0.3347$
(e) $P(A < X < B) = 0.95$ $\quad \frac{A - 0.8}{0.2} = -1.960$ $\quad A = 0.4080$

$\frac{B - 0.8}{0.2} = 1.96$ $\quad B = 1.1920$

# CHAPTER 7

## OBJECTIVES

- To understand the concept of the sampling distribution
- To be able to compute probabilities related to the sample mean and sample proportion
- To understand and be able to apply the central limit theorem
- To be able to distinguish between different survey sampling methods

## OVERVIEW AND KEY CONCEPTS

### Some Basic Concepts on Sampling Distribution

- **Why do we study sampling distribution?**
  - Sample statistics are used to estimate population parameters, but different samples yield different estimates. The solution is to develop a theoretical basis based on sampling distribution.
- **What is a sampling distribution?**
  - A sampling distribution is a theoretical probability distribution of a sample statistic. A sample statistic (e.g., sample mean, sample proportion) is a random variable because a different sample will yield a different value for the statistic, and, hence, a different estimate for the parameter of interest. The sampling distribution is the probability distribution of the sample statistic as a result of taking all possible samples of the same size from the population.

### Sampling Distribution of the Sample Mean

- **Population mean of the sample mean**
  - $\mu_{\bar{X}} = \mu$
  - This is the unbiased property of the sample mean.
- **Standard error (population standard deviation) of the sample mean**
  - $\sigma_{\bar{X}} = \dfrac{\sigma}{\sqrt{n}}$
  - Standard error of the sample mean is smaller than the standard deviation of the population.
  - The larger the sample size, the smaller the standard error.
- **The central limit theorem:** As the sample size (i.e., the number of the observations in a sample) gets *large enough*, the sampling distribution of the mean can be approximated by the normal distribution regardless of the distribution of the individual values in the population.
- **The distribution of the sample mean**
  - If the population is normally distributed, the sampling distribution of the mean is normally distributed regardless of the sample size.
  - If the population distribution is fairly symmetrical, the sampling distribution of the mean is approximately normal if sample size is at least 15.
  - For most population distributions, regardless of the shape, the sampling distribution of the mean is approximately normally distributed if the sample size is at least 30.

- **Finite population correction (Note: the finite population correction factor is covered in section 7.6 on the CD-ROM)**
  - Use the finite population correction factor to modify the standard error if sample size $n$ is large relative to the population size $N$, i.e. $n/N > 0.05$.
  - Standard error with finite population correction factor: $\sigma_{\bar{X}} = \frac{\sigma}{\sqrt{n}}\sqrt{\frac{N-n}{N-1}}$

## Finding Range Probability of the Sample Mean

1. Standardize the value of the sample mean using $Z = \frac{\bar{X} - \mu_{\bar{X}}}{\sigma_{\bar{X}}} = \frac{\bar{X} - \mu}{\frac{\sigma}{\sqrt{n}}}$.
2. Look up the cumulative probabilities from the cumulative standardized normal distribution table.

E.g., for $\mu = 8$, $\sigma = 2$, $n = 25$ and $X$ normally distributed. $P(7.8 < \bar{X} < 8.2) = ?$

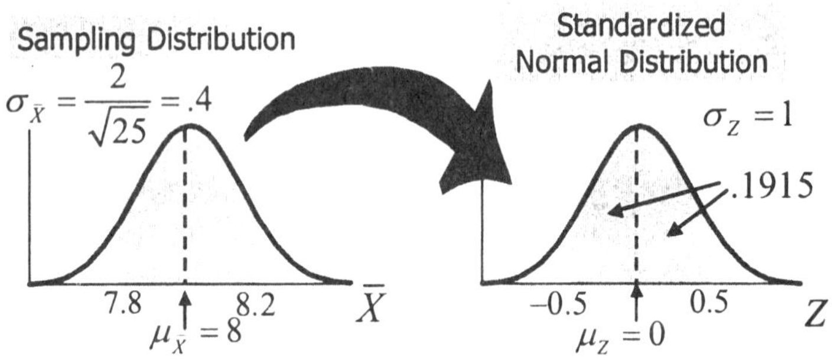


$$P(7.8 < \bar{X} < 8.2) = P\left(\frac{7.8-8}{2/\sqrt{25}} < \frac{\bar{X} - \mu_{\bar{X}}}{\sigma_{\bar{X}}} < \frac{8.2-8}{2/\sqrt{25}}\right) = P(-.5 < Z < .5) = .3830$$

## Sampling Distribution of the Sample Proportion

- **Sample proportion:** $p = \frac{X}{n} = \frac{\text{number of items having the characteristic of interest}}{\text{sample size}}$
- **Population mean of the sample proportion**
  - $\mu_p = \pi$ where $\pi$ is the population proportion.
- **Standard error of the sample proportion**
  - $\sigma_p = \sqrt{\frac{\pi(1-\pi)}{n}}$
- **The distribution of the sample proportion**
  - When $n\pi$ and $n(1-\pi)$ are each at least 5, the sampling distribution of the sample proportion can be approximated by the normal distribution with mean $\mu_p$ and standard deviation $\sigma_p$.

- **Finite population correction (Note: the finite population correction factor is covered in section 7.6 on the CD-ROM)**
    - Use the finite population correction factor to modify the standard error if sample size $n$ is large relative to the population size $N$, i.e. $n/N > 0.05$.
    - Standard error with finite population correction factor: $\sigma_p = \sqrt{\frac{\pi(1-\pi)}{n}}\sqrt{\frac{N-n}{N-1}}$

## Finding Range Probability of the Sample Proportion

1. Standardize the value of the sample proportion using $Z = \frac{p-\mu_p}{\sigma_p} = \frac{p-\pi}{\sqrt{\frac{\pi(1-\pi)}{n}}}$.
2. Lookup the cumulative probabilities from the cumulative standardized normal distribution table.

**E.g.,** for $n = 200$, $\pi = 0.4$. $P(p < 0.43) = ?$

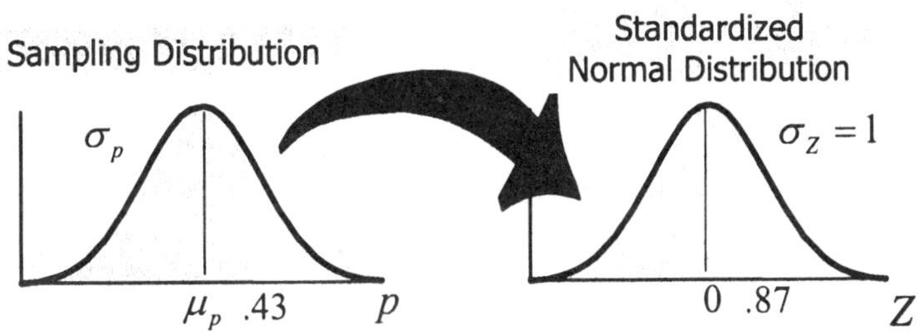


$$P(p < .43) = P\left(\frac{p-\mu_p}{\sigma_p} < \frac{.43-.4}{\sqrt{\frac{.4(1-.4)}{200}}}\right) = P(Z < .87) = .8078$$

## Reasons for Drawing Sample

- Less time consuming than a census
- Less costly to administer than a census
- Less cumbersome and more practical to administer than a census of the targeted population

## The Different Methods of Sample Selection

- **A nonprobability sample:** Items or individuals are chosen without regard to their probability of occurrence.
- **A probability sample:** The subjects of the sample are chosen on the basis of known probability.
- **A simple random sample:** Every individual or item from the frame has an equal chance of being selected. Selection may be with replacement or without replacement.
- **A systematic sample:** Decide on a sample size, n; divide frame of N individuals into groups of k individuals, k = N/n; randomly select one individual from the first group; select every $k^{th}$ individual thereafter.

- **A stratified sample:** The population is divided into two or more groups according to some common characteristic, e.g., whether an employee is full-time or part-time; simple random sample is selected from each group; the two or more samples are combined into one.
- **A cluster sample:** The population is divided into several "clusters", e.g., counties or election districts, in which each is representative of the population; a simple random sample is selected from each cluster; the samples are combined into one.

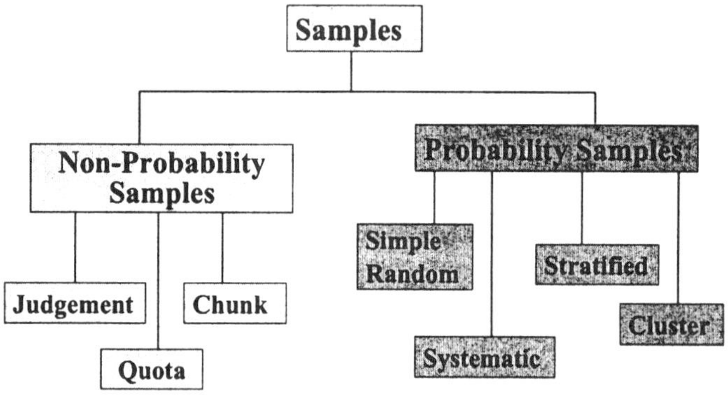


## Evaluating Survey Worthiness

- What is the purpose of the survey?
- Is the survey based on a probability sample?
- **Coverage error:** Certain groups of subjects are excluded from the frame and have no chance of being selected in the sample.
- **Nonresponse error:** Failure to collect data on all subjects in the sample.
- **Measurement error:** Inaccuracies in the recorded responses that occur because of a weakness in question wording, an interviewer's effect on the respondent, or the effort made by the respondent.
- **Sampling error:** The chance differences from sample to sample based on the probability of particular individuals or items being selected in the particular samples. Sampling error always exists in a survey.

# SOLUTIONS TO END OF SECTION AND CHAPTER REVIEW EVEN PROBLEMS

7.2 (a) $P(\overline{X} < 47) = P(Z < -6.00) =$ virtually zero

(b) $P(47 < \overline{X} < 49.5) = P(-6.00 < Z < -1.00) = 0.1587 - 0.00 = 0.1587$

(c) $P(\overline{X} > 51.1) = P(Z > 2.20) = 1.0 - 0.9861 = 0.0139$

(d) $P(\overline{X} > A) = P(Z > 0.39) = 0.35$ $\quad \overline{X} = 50 + 0.39(0.5) = 50.195$

7.4 (a) Sampling Distribution of the Mean for $n = 2$ (without replacement)

| Sample Number | Outcomes | Sample Means $\overline{X}_i$ |
|---|---|---|
| 1 | 1, 3 | $\overline{X}_1 = 2$ |
| 2 | 1, 6 | $\overline{X}_2 = 3.5$ |
| 3 | 1, 7 | $\overline{X}_3 = 4$ |
| 4 | 1, 9 | $\overline{X}_4 = 5$ |
| 5 | 1, 10 | $\overline{X}_5 = 5.5$ |
| 6 | 3, 6 | $\overline{X}_6 = 4.5$ |
| 7 | 3, 7 | $\overline{X}_7 = 5$ |
| 8 | 3, 9 | $\overline{X}_8 = 6$ |
| 9 | 3, 10 | $\overline{X}_9 = 6.5$ |
| 10 | 6, 7 | $\overline{X}_{10} = 6.5$ |
| 11 | 6, 9 | $\overline{X}_{11} = 7.5$ |
| 12 | 6, 10 | $\overline{X}_{12} = 8$ |
| 13 | 7, 9 | $\overline{X}_{13} = 8$ |
| 14 | 7, 10 | $\overline{X}_{14} = 8.5$ |
| 15 | 9, 10 | $\overline{X}_{15} = 9.5$ |

Mean of All Possible Sample Means:

$$\mu_{\overline{X}} = \frac{90}{15} = 6$$

Mean of All Population Elements:

$$\mu = \frac{1+3+6+7+9+10}{6} = 6$$

Both means are equal to 6. This property is called unbiasedness.

7.4 cont. (b) Sampling Distribution of the Mean for $n = 3$ (without replacement)

| Sample Number | Outcomes | Sample Means $\bar{X}_i$ |
|---|---|---|
| 1 | 1, 3, 6 | $\bar{X}_1 = 3\ 1/3$ |
| 2 | 1, 3, 7 | $\bar{X}_2 = 3\ 2/3$ |
| 3 | 1, 3, 9 | $\bar{X}_3 = 4\ 1/3$ |
| 4 | 1, 3, 10 | $\bar{X}_4 = 4\ 2/3$ |
| 5 | 1, 6, 7 | $\bar{X}_5 = 4\ 2/3$ |
| 6 | 1, 6, 9 | $\bar{X}_6 = 5\ 1/3$ |
| 7 | 1, 6, 10 | $\bar{X}_7 = 5\ 2/3$ |
| 8 | 3, 6, 7 | $\bar{X}_8 = 5\ 1/3$ |
| 9 | 3, 6, 9 | $\bar{X}_9 = 6$ |
| 10 | 3, 6, 10 | $\bar{X}_{10} = 6\ 1/3$ |
| 11 | 6, 7, 9 | $\bar{X}_{11} = 7\ 1/3$ |
| 12 | 6, 7, 10 | $\bar{X}_{12} = 7\ 2/3$ |
| 13 | 6, 9, 10 | $\bar{X}_{13} = 8\ 1/3$ |
| 14 | 7, 9, 10 | $\bar{X}_{14} = 8\ 2/3$ |
| 15 | 1, 7, 9 | $\bar{X}_{15} = 5\ 2/3$ |
| 16 | 1, 7, 10 | $\bar{X}_{16} = 6$ |
| 17 | 1, 9, 10 | $\bar{X}_{17} = 6\ 2/3$ |
| 18 | 3, 7, 9 | $\bar{X}_{18} = 6\ 1/3$ |
| 19 | 3, 7, 10 | $\bar{X}_{19} = 6\ 2/3$ |
| 20 | 3, 9, 10 | $\bar{X}_{20} = 7\ 1/3$ |

$$\mu_{\bar{X}} = \frac{120}{20} = 6$$

This is equal to $\mu$, the population mean.

(c) The distribution for $n = 3$ has less variability. The larger sample size has resulted in sample means being closer to $\mu$.

7.4 cont. (d) (a) Sampling Distribution of the Mean for $n = 2$ (with replacement)

| Sample Number | Outcomes | Sample Means $\bar{X}_i$ |
|---|---|---|
| 1 | 1, 1 | $\bar{X}_1 = 1$ |
| 2 | 1, 3 | $\bar{X}_2 = 2$ |
| 3 | 1, 6 | $\bar{X}_3 = 3.5$ |
| 4 | 1, 7 | $\bar{X}_4 = 4$ |
| 5 | 1, 9 | $\bar{X}_5 = 5$ |
| 6 | 1, 10 | $\bar{X}_6 = 5.5$ |
| 7 | 3, 1 | $\bar{X}_7 = 2$ |
| 8 | 3, 3 | $\bar{X}_8 = 3$ |
| 9 | 3, 6 | $\bar{X}_9 = 4.5$ |
| 10 | 3, 7 | $\bar{X}_{10} = 5$ |
| 11 | 3, 9 | $\bar{X}_{11} = 6$ |
| 12 | 3, 10 | $\bar{X}_{12} = 6.5$ |
| 13 | 6, 1 | $\bar{X}_{13} = 3.5$ |
| 14 | 6, 3 | $\bar{X}_{14} = 4.5$ |
| 15 | 6, 6 | $\bar{X}_{15} = 6$ |
| 16 | 6, 7 | $\bar{X}_{16} = 6.5$ |
| 17 | 6, 9 | $\bar{X}_{17} = 7.5$ |
| 18 | 6, 10 | $\bar{X}_{18} = 8$ |
| 19 | 7, 1 | $\bar{X}_{19} = 4$ |
| 20 | 7, 3 | $\bar{X}_{20} = 5$ |
| 21 | 7, 6 | $\bar{X}_{21} = 6.5$ |
| 22 | 7, 7 | $\bar{X}_{22} = 7$ |
| 23 | 7, 9 | $\bar{X}_{23} = 8$ |
| 24 | 7, 10 | $\bar{X}_{24} = 8.5$ |
| 25 | 9, 1 | $\bar{X}_{25} = 5$ |
| 26 | 9, 3 | $\bar{X}_{26} = 6$ |
| 27 | 9, 6 | $\bar{X}_{27} = 7.5$ |
| 28 | 9, 7 | $\bar{X}_{28} = 8$ |
| 29 | 9, 9 | $\bar{X}_{29} = 9$ |
| 30 | 9, 10 | $\bar{X}_{30} = 9.5$ |
| 31 | 10, 1 | $\bar{X}_{31} = 5.5$ |
| 32 | 10, 3 | $\bar{X}_{32} = 6.5$ |

| | | |
|---|---|---|
| 33 | 10, 6 | $\bar{X}_{33} = 8$ |
| 34 | 10, 7 | $\bar{X}_{34} = 8.5$ |
| 35 | 10, 9 | $\bar{X}_{35} = 9.5$ |
| 36 | 10, 10 | $\bar{X}_{36} = 10$ |

7.4 cont. (d) (a) Mean of All Possible Sample Means: $\mu_{\bar{X}} = \frac{216}{36} = 6$ Mean of All Population Elements: $\mu = \frac{1+3+6+7+7+12}{6} = 6$

Both means are equal to 6. This property is called unbiasedness.

(b) Repeat the same process for the sampling distribution of the mean for $n = 3$ (with replacement). There will be $6^3 = 216$ different samples.

$\mu_{\bar{X}} = 6$ This is equal to $\mu$, the population mean.

(c) The distribution for $n = 3$ has less variability. The larger sample size has resulted in more sample means being close to $\mu$.

7.6 (a) For samples of size 2, the sampling distribution of $\bar{X}$ will resemble the right-skewed population distribution.

(b) When the sample size is 100, the sampling distribution of $\bar{X}$ will be very close to a normal distribution as a result of the central limit theorem.

(c) $P(\bar{X} < 250{,}000) = P(Z < -1.1111) = 0.1333$

7.8 (a) $P(\bar{X} > 3) = P(Z > -1.00) = 1 - 0.1587 = 0.8413$

(b) $P(\bar{X} < A) = P(Z < 1.04) = 0.85$ $\bar{X} = 3.10 + 1.04(0.1) = 3.204$

(c) To be able to use the standard normal distribution as an approximation for the area under the curve, we must assume that the population is symmetrically distributed such that the central limit theorem will likely hold for samples of $n = 16$.

(d) $P(\bar{X} < A) = P(Z < 1.04) = 0.85$ $\bar{X} = 3.10 + 1.04(0.05) = 3.152$

7.10 (a) $P(\bar{X} < 2.75) = P(Z < 2.7386) = 0.9969$

(b) $P(2.7 < \bar{X} < 2.9) = P(2.1909 < Z < 4.3818) = 0.0142$

(c) $P(A < \bar{X} < B) = P(-1.2816 < Z < 1.2816) = 0.80$

$A = 2.5 - 1.2816\ (0.0913) = 2.3830$ $B = 2.5 + 1.2816\ (0.0913) = 2.6170$

(d) $P(\bar{X} < A) = P(Z < 1.2816) = 0.90$ $A = 2.5 + 1.2816\ (0.0913) = 2.6170$

*Note*: The above answers are obtained using PHStat. They may be slightly different when Table E.2 is used.

7.12 (a) $p = 15/50 = 0.30$ (b) $\sigma_p = \sqrt{\frac{0.40(0.60)}{50}} = 0.0693$

7.14 (a) $\mu_p = \pi = 0.501$, $\sigma_p = \sqrt{\frac{\pi(1-\pi)}{n}} = \sqrt{\frac{0.501(1-0.501)}{100}} = 0.05$

$P(p > 0.55) = P(Z > 0.98) = 1 - 0.8365 = 0.1635$

(b) $\mu_p = \pi = 0.60$, $\sigma_p = \sqrt{\frac{\pi(1-\pi)}{n}} = \sqrt{\frac{0.6(1-0.6)}{100}} = 0.04899$

$P(p > 0.55) = P(Z > -1.021) = 1 - 0.1539 = 0.8461$

(c) $\mu_p = \pi = 0.49$, $\sigma_p = \sqrt{\frac{\pi(1-\pi)}{n}} = \sqrt{\frac{0.49(1-0.49)}{100}} = 0.05$

$P(p > 0.55) = P(Z > 1.20) = 1 - 0.8849 = 0.1151$

(d) Increasing the sample size by a factor of 4 decreases the standard error by a factor of 2.

(a) $P(p > 0.55) = P(Z > 1.96) = 1 - 0.9750 = 0.0250$

(b) $P(p > 0.55) = P(Z > -2.04) = 1 - 0.0207 = 0.9793$

(c) $P(p > 0.55) = P(Z > 2.40) = 1 - 0.9918 = 0.0082$

7.16 (a) $P(p < 0.15) = P(Z < 0) = 0.50$

(b) $P(0.13 < p < 0.17) = P(-0.7921 < Z < 0.7921) = 0.5717$

(c) $P(0.10 < p < 0.20) = P(-1.9803 < Z < 1.9803) = 0.9523$

(d) (a) $P(p < 0.15) = P(Z < 0) = 0.50$

(b) $P(0.13 < p < 0.17) = P(-0.5601 < Z < 0.5601) = 0.4246$

(c) $P(0.10 < p < 0.20) = P(-1.4003 < Z < 1.4003) = 0.8386$

7.18 (a) $P(0.75 < p < 0.80) = P(-0.6721 < Z < 1.0082) = 0.5926$

(b) $P(A < p < B) = P(-1.6449 < Z < 1.6449) = 0.90$

$A = 0.77 - 1.6449(0.0298) = 0.7211$

$B = 0.77 + 1.6449(0.0298) = 0.8189$

(c) $P(A < p < B) = P(-1.960 < Z < 1.960) = 0.95$

$A = 0.77 - 1.960(0.0298) = 0.7117$

$B = 0.77 + 1.96(0.0298) = 0.8283$

7.20 (a) $P(0.25 < p < 0.30) = P(-1.7630 < Z < 0.4408) = 0.6314$

(b) $P(p > .35) = P(Z > 2.6446) = 0.0041$

If the true population proportion is indeed 29%, the proportion of the samples with 35% or more who do not intend to work for pay at all is 0.41%, a very unlikely occurrence. Hence, the population estimate of 29% is very likely to be unrealistic and an under estimation.

(c) $P(p > .35) = P(Z > 1.3223) = 0.0930$

If the true population proportion is indeed 29%, the proportion of the samples with 35% or more who do not intend to work for pay at all is 9.3%, still a very unlikely occurrence. Hence, the population estimate of 29% is very likely to be unrealistic and an under estimation.

(d) When the sample size is smaller in (c) compared to (b), the standard error of the sampling distribution of sample proportion is larger and, hence, a higher portion of the samples will have 35% or more who do not intend to work for pay at all.

7.22 (a) $P(0.89 < p < 0.91) = P(-0.4714 < Z < 0.4714) = 0.3626$
(b) $P(0.85 < p < 0.95) = P(-2.3570 < Z < 2.3570) = 0.9816$
(c) $P(p > 0.95) = P(Z > 2.3570) = 0.0092$
*Note*: The above answers are obtained using PHStat. They may be slightly different when Table E.2 is used.

7.24 Sample without replacement: Read from left to right in 3-digit sequences and continue unfinished sequences from end of row to beginning of next row.
Row 05: 338 505 855 551 438 855 077 186 579 488 767 833 170
Rows 05-06: 897
Row 06: 340 033 648 847 204 334 639 193 639 411 095 924
Rows 06-07: 707
Row 07: 054 329 776 100 871 007 255 980 646 886 823 920 461
Row 08: 893 829 380 900 796 959 453 410 181 277 660 908 887
Rows 08-09: 237
Row 09: 818 721 426 714 050 785 223 801 670 353 362 449
Rows 09-10: 406
Note: All sequences above 902 are discarded.

7.26 A simple random sample would be less practical for personal interviews because of travel costs (unless interviewees are paid to attend a central interviewing location).

7.28 Here all members of the population are equally likely to be selected and the sample selection mechanism is based on chance. But not every sample of size 2 has the same chance of being selected. For example the sample "B and C" is impossible.

7.30 (a) Row 16: 2323 6737 5131 8888 1718 0654 6832 4647 6510 4877
Row 17: 4579 4269 2615 1308 2455 7830 5550 5852 5514 7182
Row 18: 0989 3205 0514 2256 8514 4642 7567 8896 2977 8822
Row 19: 5438 2745 9891 4991 4523 6847 9276 8646 1628 3554
Row 20: 9475 0899 2337 0892 0048 8033 6945 9826 9403 6858
Row 21: 7029 7341 3553 1403 3340 4205 0823 4144 1048 2949
Row 22: 8515 7479 5432 9792 6575 5760 0408 8112 2507 3742
Row 23: 1110 0023 4012 8607 4697 9664 4894 3928 7072 5815
Row 24: 3687 1507 7530 5925 7143 1738 1688 5625 8533 5041
Row 25: 2391 3483 5763 3081 6090 5169 0546
Note: All sequences above 5000 are discarded. There were no repeating sequences.

(b)

| | | | | | | | | | |
|---|---|---|---|---|---|---|---|---|---|
| 089 | 189 | 289 | 389 | 489 | 589 | 689 | 789 | 889 | 989 |
| 1089 | 1189 | 1289 | 1389 | 1489 | 1589 | 1689 | 1789 | 1889 | 1989 |
| 2089 | 2189 | 2289 | 2389 | 2489 | 2589 | 2689 | 2789 | 2889 | 2989 |
| 3089 | 3189 | 3289 | 3389 | 3489 | 3589 | 3689 | 3789 | 3889 | 3989 |
| 4089 | 4189 | 4289 | 4389 | 4489 | 4589 | 4689 | 4789 | 4889 | 4989 |

(c) With the single exception of invoice #0989, the invoices selected in the simple random sample are not the same as those selected in the systematic sample. It would be highly unlikely that a random process would select the same units as a systematic process.

7.32 Before accepting the results of a survey of college students, you might want to know, for example:

Who funded the survey? Why was it conducted?
What was the population from which the sample was selected?
What sampling design was used?
What mode of response was used: a personal interview, a telephone interview, or a mail survey? Were interviewers trained? Were survey questions field-tested?
What questions were asked? Were they clear, accurate, unbiased, valid?
What operational definition of "vast majority" was used?
What was the response rate?
What was the sample size?

7.34 Before accepting the results of the survey on AOL subscribers, you might want to know, for example:

Who funded the study? Why was it conducted?
What was the population from which the sample was selected?
What sampling design was used?
What mode of response was used: a personal interview, a telephone interview, or a mail survey? Were interviewers trained? Were survey questions field-tested?
What other questions were asked? Were they clear, accurate, unbiased, and valid?
What was the response rate?

7.36 Before accepting the results of the Maritz poll, you might want to know, for example:

Who funded the study? Why was it conducted?
What was the population from which the sample was selected?
What sampling design was used?
What mode of response was used: a personal interview, a telephone interview, or a mail survey? Were interviewers trained? Were survey questions field-tested?
What operational definitions of "often or sometimes eating or drinking while driving" and "talking on cellphone" were used?
What other questions were asked? Were they clear, accurate, unbiased, and valid?
What was the response rate?

7.38 Before accepting the results of the survey conducted by Caravan, you might want to know, for example:

Who funded the study? Why was it conducted?
What was the population from which the sample was selected?
What was the sample size?
What sampling design was used?
What mode of response was used: a personal interview, a telephone interview, or a mail survey? Were interviewers trained? Were survey questions field-tested?
What operational definitions of "great food", "reasonable prices", "atmosphere", "quick service" and "don't know" were used?
What other questions were asked? Were they clear, accurate, unbiased, and valid?
What was the response rate?

7.40 The variation of the sample means becomes smaller as larger sample sizes are taken. This is due to the fact that an extreme observation will have a smaller effect on the mean in a larger sample than in a small sample. Thus, the sample means will tend to be closer to the population mean as the sample size increases.

7.42 The probability distribution is the distribution of a particular variable of interest, while the sampling distribution represents the distribution of a statistic.

7.44 A probability sample is one in which the individuals or items are selected based on known probabilities. A nonprobability sample is one in which the individuals or items are selected without regard to their probability of occurrence.

7.46 Sampling with replacement means that once a person or item is selected, it is returned to the frame where it has the same probability of being selected again. Sampling without replacement means that a person or item once selected is not returned to the frame and therefore cannot be selected again.

7.48 In a stratified sample, the *N* individuals or items in the population are first subdivided into separate subpopulations, or strata, according to some common characteristic. In a simple random sample, each individual item is selected randomly.

7.50 $\mu_{\bar{X}} = 0.753 \qquad \sigma_{\bar{X}} = \frac{\sigma_X}{\sqrt{n}} = \frac{0.004}{5} = 0.0008$

(a) $P(0.75 < \bar{X} < 0.753) = P(-3.75 < Z < 0) = 0.5 - 0.00009 = 0.4999$

(b) $P(0.74 < \bar{X} < 0.75) = P(-16.25 < Z < -3.75) = 0.00009$

(c) $P(\bar{X} > 0.76) = P(Z > 8.75) =$ virtually zero

(d) $P(\bar{X} < 0.74) = P(Z < -16.25) =$ virtually zero

(e) $P(\bar{X} < A) = P(Z < -1.48) = 0.07 \qquad X = 0.753 - 1.48(0.0008) = 0.7518$

7.52 $\mu_{\bar{X}} = 4.7 \qquad \sigma_{\bar{X}} = \frac{\sigma_X}{\sqrt{n}} = \frac{0.40}{5} = 0.08$

(a) $P(4.60 \le \bar{X}) = P(-1.25 < Z) = 1 - 0.1056 = 0.8944$

(b) $P(A < \bar{X} < B) = P(-1.04 < Z < 1.04) = 0.70$

$A = 4.70 - 1.04(0.08) = 4.6168$ ounces

$X = 4.70 + 1.04(0.08) = 4.7832$ ounces

(c) $P(\bar{X} > A) = P(Z > -0.74) = 0.77 \qquad A = 4.70 - 0.74(0.08) = 4.6408$

7.54 (a) $P(\bar{X} < 0) = P(Z < -2.3559) = 0.0092$

(b) $P(0 < \bar{X} < 6) = P(-2.3559 < Z < 2.3875) = 0.9823$

(c) $P(\bar{X} > 10) = P(Z > 5.5498) =$ virtually zero

7.56 Even though Internet polling is less expensive, faster and offers higher response rates than telephone surveys, it is a self-selection response method. Because respondents who choose to participate in the survey may not represent the view of the public, the data collected may not be appropriate for making inference about the general population.

7.58 (a) Given the low response rate (15.5%), the researchers should be especially concerned with nonresponse bias. The low response rate will also increase the sampling error.

(b) Researchers can follow up on the nonresponses by mail or telephone to encourage or remind those who have not returned the survey to complete it.

(c) The researchers can enlist the Chief of Police and the President of the Fraternal Order of Police to mobilize the supervisors of various units to convey to their subordinates the importance of completing the survey. Reminder memos can also be sent from the supervisors. Verbal reminders from the supervisors during weekly meetings will also serve the same purpose.

7.60 (a) Before accepting the results of this survey, you would like to know (i) what is the purpose of the survey, (ii) what sampling method is being used, (iii) what is the response rate, (iv) what is the frame used in the survey, and (v) how are the questions being phrased.

(b) The population will be all the working women which includes both those who do and do not take advantage of family-friendly schedules in the geographic region. The frame can be compiled from the list of the women who file income tax returns in the region. Since there are two natural strata in the population, those who take advantage of family-friendly schedules and those who do not, a stratified sampling method should be used to better represent the population.

7.68 $\sqrt{\frac{N-n}{N-1}} = \sqrt{\frac{400-100}{400-1}} = 0.8671$ $\qquad$ $\sqrt{\frac{N-n}{N-1}} = \sqrt{\frac{900-200}{900-1}} = 0.8824$

A sample of size 100 selected without replacement from a population a population of size 400 has a greater effect in reducing the standard error.

7.70 $\mu = 1.30$, $\sigma = 0.04$

Since $n/N = 16/500 > 0.05$ and the sample is selected without replacement, we need to perform the finite population correction.

$\mu_{\bar{X}} = \mu = 1.3 \qquad \sigma_{\bar{X}} = \frac{\sigma}{\sqrt{n}}\sqrt{\frac{N-n}{N-1}} = 0.0096$

$P(1.31 < \bar{X} < 1.33) = P(1.0417 < Z < 3.125) = 0.1479$

7.72 $\pi = .10$

Since $n/N = 400/5000 > 0.05$ and the sample is selected without replacement, we need to perform the finite population correction.

$\mu_p = .1 \qquad \sigma_p = \sqrt{\frac{\pi(1-\pi)}{n}}\sqrt{\frac{N-n}{N-1}} = 0.0144$

(a) $P(0.09 < p < 0.10) = P(-0.6944 < Z < 0) = 0.2563$

(b) $P(p < .08) = P(Z < -1.3889) = 0.0824$

# CHAPTER 8

## OBJECTIVES

- To be able to construct and interpret confidence interval estimates for the mean and the proportion
- To know how to determine the sample size necessary to develop a confidence interval for the mean and proportion

## OVERVIEW AND KEY CONCEPTS

### Why We Need Confidence Interval Estimates in Addition to Point Estimates

- Confidence interval estimates take into consideration variation in sample statistics from sample to sample.
- They provide information about closeness to unknown population parameters.
- The interval estimates are always stated in level of confidence, which is lower than 100%.

### Confidence Interval Estimate for the Mean when the Population Variance is Known

- **Assumptions:**
  - Population variance $\sigma^2$ is known.
  - Population is normally distributed or the sample size is large.
- **Point estimate for the population mean, $\mu$: $\bar{X}$**
- **Confidence interval estimate:**
  - $\bar{X} \pm Z_{\alpha/2}\frac{\sigma}{\sqrt{n}}$ where $Z_{\alpha/2}$ is the value corresponding to a cumulative area of $\left(1-\frac{\alpha}{2}\right)$ from a standardized normal distribution, i.e., the right-tail probability of $\alpha/2$.
- **Elements of confidence interval estimate**
  - **Level of confidence:** Measures the level of confidence in which the interval will contain the unknown population parameter.
  - **Precision (range):** Represents the closeness to the unknown parameter.
  - **Cost:** The cost required to obtain a sample of size *n*.
- **Factors affecting interval width (precision)**
  - **Data variation measured by $\sigma^2$:** The larger is the $\sigma^2$, the wider is the interval estimate.
  - **Sample size *n*:** The larger is the sample size, the narrower is the interval estimate.
  - **The level of confidence $100(1-\alpha)\%$:** The higher is the level of confidence, the wider is the interval estimate.

- **Interpretation of a $100(1-\alpha)\%$ confidence interval estimate:** If all possible samples of size *n* are taken and their sample means are computed, $100(1-\alpha)\%$ of the intervals contain the true population mean somewhere within the interval around their sample means and only $100(\alpha)\%$ of them do not.

## Confidence Interval Estimate for the Mean when the Population Variance is Unknown

- **Assumptions:**
  - Population variance $\sigma^2$ is unknown.
  - Population is normally distributed or the sample size is large.
- **Confidence interval estimate:**
  - $\bar{X} \pm t_{\alpha/2,n-1}\frac{S}{\sqrt{n}}$ where $t_{\alpha/2,n-1}$ is the value corresponding to a cumulative area of $\left(1-\frac{\alpha}{2}\right)$ from a Student's distribution with *n*-1 degrees of freedom, i.e., the right-tail probability of $\alpha/2$.

## Confidence Interval Estimate for the Proportion

- **Assumptions:**
  - Two categorical outcomes
  - Population follows Binomial distribution
  - Normal approximation can be used if $np \geq 5$ and $n(1-p) \geq 5$.
- **Point estimate for the population proportion of success, $\pi$:** $p = \frac{X}{n}$
- **Confidence interval estimate:**
  - $p \pm Z_{\alpha/2}\sqrt{\frac{p(1-p)}{n}}$

## Determining Sample Size

- **The sample size needed when estimating the population mean:**
  - $n = \frac{Z^2\sigma^2}{e^2}$ where *e* is the acceptable sampling error and $\sigma^2$ is estimated from past data, by an educated guess or by the data obtained from a pilot study.
- **The sample size needed when estimating the population proportion:**
  - $n = \frac{Z^2\pi(1-\pi)}{e^2}$ where *e* is the acceptable sampling error and $\pi$ is estimated from past information, by an educated guess or use 0.5.

# SOLUTIONS TO END OF SECTION AND CHAPTER REVIEW EVEN PROBLEMS

8.2 $\bar{X} \pm Z \cdot \frac{\sigma}{\sqrt{n}} = 125 \pm 2.58 \cdot \frac{24}{\sqrt{36}}$ $114.68 \leq \mu \leq 135.32$

8.4 Since the results of only one sample are used to indicate whether something has gone wrong in the production process, the manufacturer can never know with 100% certainty that the specific interval obtained from the sample includes the true population mean. In order to have 100% confidence, the entire population (sample size *N*) would have to be selected.

8.6 Approximately 5% of the intervals will not include the true population. Since the true population mean is not known, we do not know for certain whether it is contained in the interval (between 10.99408 and 11.00192 inches) that we have developed.

8.8 (a)

| | A | B |
|---|---|---|
| 1 | **Light Bulbs** | |
| 2 | | |
| 3 | **Population Standard Deviation** | **100** |
| 4 | **Sample Mean** | **350** |
| 5 | **Sample Size** | **64** |
| 6 | **Confidence Level** | **95%** |
| 7 | Standard Error of the Mean | 12.5 |
| 8 | Z Value | -1.95996108 |
| 9 | Interval Half Width | 24.49951353 |
| 10 | **Interval Lower Limit** | **325.5004865** |
| 11 | **Interval Upper Limit** | **374.4995135** |

$\bar{X} \pm Z \cdot \frac{\sigma}{\sqrt{n}} = 350 \pm 1.96 \cdot \frac{100}{\sqrt{64}}$ $325.5 \leq \mu \leq 374.50$

(b) No. The manufacturer cannot support a claim that the bulbs last an average 400 hours. Based on the data from the sample, a mean of 400 hours would represent a distance of 4 standard deviations above the sample mean of 350 hours.

(c) No. Since $\sigma$ is known and $n = 64$, from the Central Limit Theorem, we may assume that the sampling distribution of $\bar{X}$ is approximately normal.

(d) The confidence interval is narrower based on a process standard deviation of 80 hours rather than the original assumption of 100 hours.

(a) $\bar{X} \pm Z \cdot \frac{\sigma}{\sqrt{n}} = 350 \pm 1.96 \cdot \frac{80}{\sqrt{64}}$ $330.4 \leq \mu \leq 369.6$

(b) Based on the smaller standard deviation, a mean of 400 hours would represent a distance of 5 standard deviations above the sample mean of 350 hours. No, the manufacturer cannot support a claim that the bulbs have a mean life of 400 hours.

8.10 (a) $t_9 = 2.2622$
(b) $t_9 = 3.2498$
(c) $t_{31} = 2.0395$
(d) $t_{64} = 1.9977$
(e) $t_{15} = 1.7531$

8.12 $\bar{X} \pm t \cdot \frac{S}{\sqrt{n}} = 50 \pm 2.9467 \cdot \frac{15}{\sqrt{16}}$ $38.9499 \le \mu \le 61.0501$

8.14 Original data: $5.8571 \pm 2.4469 \cdot \frac{6.4660}{\sqrt{7}}$ $-0.1229 \le \mu \le 11.8371$

Altered data: $4.00 \pm 2.4469 \cdot \frac{2.1602}{\sqrt{7}}$ $2.0022 \le \mu \le 5.9978$

The presence of an outlier in the original data increases the value of the sample mean and greatly inflates the sample standard deviation.

8.16 (a) $\bar{X} \pm t \cdot \frac{S}{\sqrt{n}} = 32 \pm 2.0096 \cdot \frac{9}{\sqrt{50}}$ $29.44 \le \mu \le 34.56$

(b) The quality improvement team can be 95% confident that the population mean turnaround time is somewhere in between 29.44 hours and 34.56 hours.

(c) The project was a success because the initial turnaround time of 68 hours does not fall inside the 95% confidence interval.

8.18 (a) $\bar{X} \pm t \cdot \frac{S}{\sqrt{n}} = 23 \pm 2.0739 \cdot \frac{4.6024}{\sqrt{23}}$ $\$21.01 \le \mu \le \$24.99$

(b) You can be 95% confident that the mean bounced check fee for the population is somewhere between $21.01 and $24.99.

8.20 (a) $\bar{X} \pm t \cdot \frac{S}{\sqrt{n}} = 43.04 \pm 2.0096 \cdot \frac{41.9261}{\sqrt{50}}$ $31.12 \le \mu \le 54.96$

(b) The population distribution needs to be normally distribution.

8.20 cont. (c)

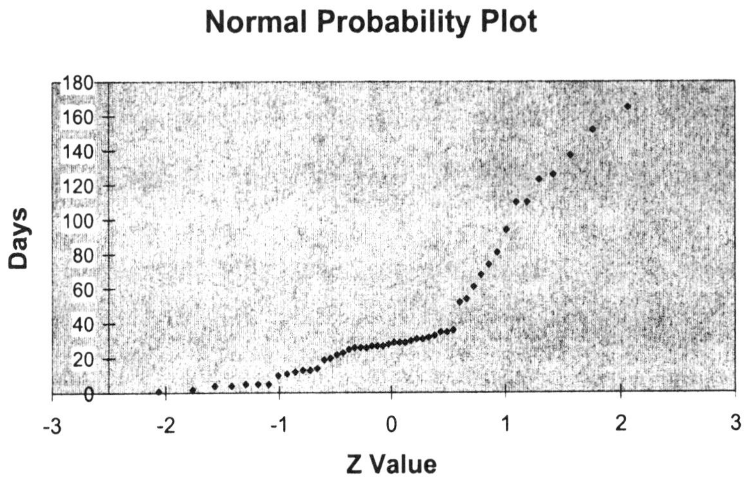


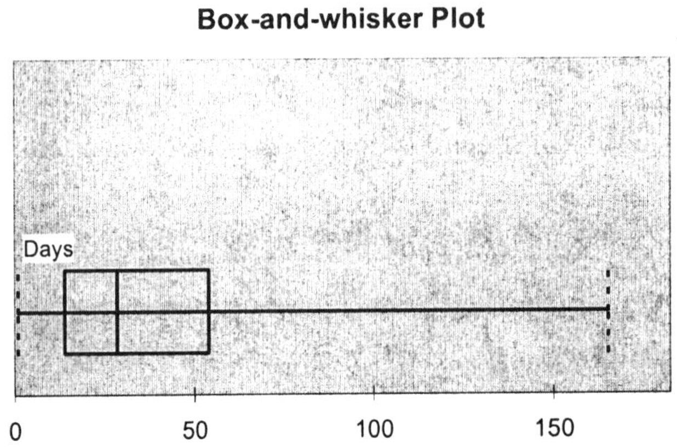


Both the normal probability plot and the box-and-whisker plot suggest that the distribution is skewed to the right.

(d) Even though the population distribution is not normally distributed, with a sample of 50, the $t$ distribution can still be used due to the Central Limit Theorem.

8.22 (a) $\bar{X} \pm t \cdot \frac{S}{\sqrt{n}} = 182.4 \pm 2.0930 \cdot \frac{44.2700}{\sqrt{20}}$ $\$161.68 \le \mu \le \$203.12$

(b) $\bar{X} \pm t \cdot \frac{S}{\sqrt{n}} = 45 \pm 2.0930 \cdot \frac{10.0263}{\sqrt{20}}$ $\$40.31 \le \mu \le \$49.69$

(c) The population distribution needs to be normally distributed.

8.22 (d)
cont.

Normal Probability Plot

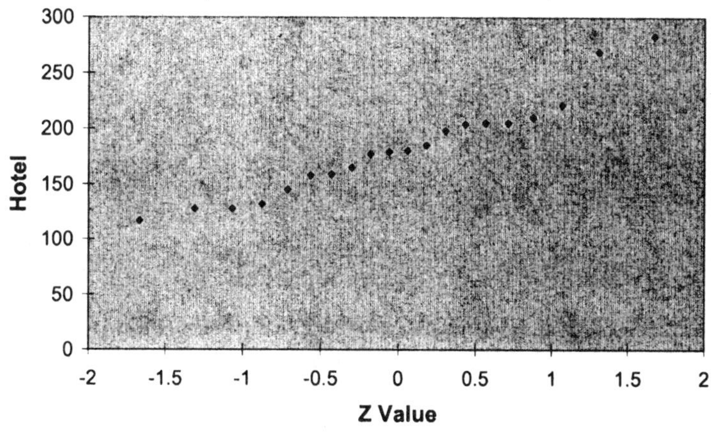


Box-and-whisker Plot

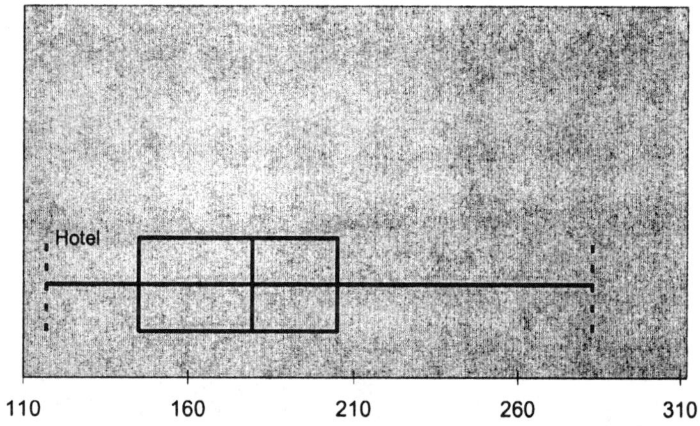


Both the normal probability plot and the box-and-whisker show that the population distribution for hotel cost is not normally distributed and is skewed to the right.

8.22 cont. (d)

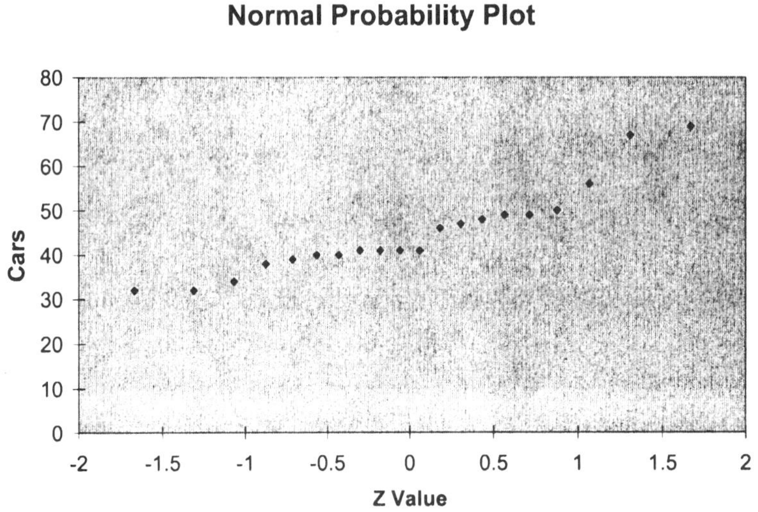


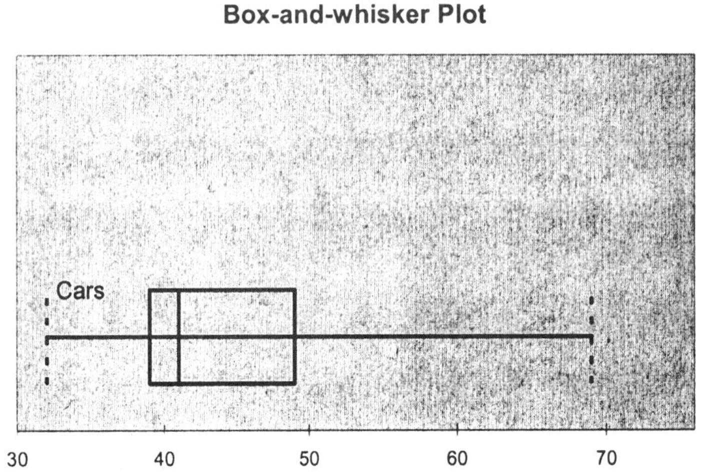


Both the normal probability plot and the box-and-whisker show that the population distribution for rental car cost is not normally distributed and is skewed to the right.

8.24 $p = \frac{X}{n} = \frac{50}{200} = 0.25 \quad p \pm Z \cdot \sqrt{\frac{p(1-p)}{n}} = 0.25 \pm 1.96\sqrt{\frac{0.25(0.75)}{200}}$

$0.19 \le \pi \le 0.31$

8.26 (a)

| | A | B |
|---|---|---|
| 1 | **Purchase Additional Telephone Line** | |
| 2 | | |
| 3 | **Sample Size** | **500** |
| 4 | **Number of Successes** | **135** |
| 5 | **Confidence Level** | **99%** |
| 6 | Sample Proportion | 0.27 |
| 7 | Z Value | -2.57583451 |
| 8 | Standard Error of the Proportion | 0.019854471 |
| 9 | Interval Half Width | 0.05114183 |
| 10 | **Interval Lower Limit** | **0.21885817** |
| 11 | **Interval Upper Limit** | **0.32114183** |

$p = \frac{X}{n} = \frac{135}{500} = 0.27 \quad p \pm Z \cdot \sqrt{\frac{p(1-p)}{n}} = 0.27 \pm 2.5758\sqrt{\frac{0.27(1-0.27)}{500}}$

$0.22 \le \pi \le 0.32$

(b) The manager in charge of promotional programs concerning residential customers can infer that the proportion of households that would purchase an additional telephone line if it were made available at a substantially reduced installation cost is between 0.22 and 0.32 with a 99% level of confidence.

8.28 (a) $p = 0.77 \quad p \pm Z \cdot \sqrt{\frac{p(1-p)}{n}} = 0.77 \pm 1.96\sqrt{\frac{0.77(0.23)}{1000}}$

$0.74 \le \pi \le 0.80$

(b) $p = 0.77 \quad p \pm Z \cdot \sqrt{\frac{p(1-p)}{n}} = 0.77 \pm 1.645\sqrt{\frac{0.77(0.23)}{1000}}$

$0.75 \le \pi \le 0.79$

(c) The 95% confidence interval is wider. The loss in precision reflected as a wider confidence interval is the price you have to pay to achieve a higher level of confidence.

8.30 (a) $p = \frac{X}{n} = 0.46 \quad p \pm Z \cdot \sqrt{\frac{p(1-p)}{n}} = 0.46 \pm 1.96\sqrt{\frac{0.46(1-0.46)}{500}}$

$0.4163 < \pi < 0.5037$

(b) $p = \frac{X}{n} = 0.10 \quad p \pm Z \cdot \sqrt{\frac{p(1-p)}{n}} = 0.10 \pm 1.96\sqrt{\frac{0.10(1-0.10)}{500}}$

$0.0737 < \pi < 0.1263$

8.32 (a) $p = \frac{X}{n} = \frac{450}{1000} = 0.45$

$$p \pm Z \cdot \sqrt{\frac{p(1-p)}{n}} = 0.45 \pm 1.96\sqrt{\frac{0.45(1-0.45)}{1000}}$$

$$0.4192 < \pi < 0.4808$$

(b) You are 95% confidence that the proportion of all working women in North America who believe that companies should hold positions for those on maternity leave for more than six months is between 0.4192 and 0.4808.

8.34 $n = \frac{Z^2\sigma^2}{e^2} = \frac{1.96^2 \cdot 15^2}{5^2} = 34.57$ Use $n = 35$

8.36 $n = \frac{Z^2\pi(1-\pi)}{e^2} = \frac{2.58^2(0.5)(0.5)}{(0.04)^2} = 1{,}040.06$ Use $n = 1{,}041$

8.38 (a) $n = \frac{Z^2\sigma^2}{e^2} = \frac{1.96^2 \cdot 400^2}{50^2} = 245.86$ Use $n = 246$

(b) $n = \frac{Z^2\sigma^2}{e^2} = \frac{1.96^2 \cdot 400^2}{25^2} = 983.41$ Use $n = 984$

8.40 $n = \frac{Z^2\sigma^2}{e^2} = \frac{1.96^2 \cdot (100)^2}{(20)^2} = 96.04$ Use $n = 97$

8.42 (a) $n = \frac{Z^2\sigma^2}{e^2} = \frac{2.58^2 \cdot 25^2}{5^2} = 166.41$ Use $n = 167$

(b) $n = \frac{Z^2\sigma^2}{e^2} = \frac{1.96^2 \cdot 25^2}{5^2} = 96.04$ Use $n = 97$

8.44 $n = \frac{Z^2\sigma^2}{e^2} = \frac{1.96^2 \cdot 20^2}{5^2} = 61.47$ Use $n = 62$

8.46 (a) $n = \frac{Z^2\pi(1-\pi)}{e^2} = \frac{1.96^2(0.45)(0.55)}{(0.02)^2} = 2376.8956$ Use $n = 2377$

(b) $n = \frac{Z^2\pi(1-\pi)}{e^2} = \frac{1.96^2(0.29)(0.71)}{(0.02)^2} = 1977.3851$ Use $n = 1978$

(c) The sample sizes differ because the estimated population proportions are different.

(d) Since purchasing groceries at wholesale clubs and purchasing groceries at convenience stores are not necessary mutually exclusive events, it is appropriate to use one sample and ask the respondents both questions. However, drawing two separate samples is also appropriate for the setup.

8.48 (a) $p = \frac{X}{n} = \frac{303}{326} = 0.9294$

$$p \pm Z \cdot \sqrt{\frac{p(1-p)}{n}} = 0.9294 \pm 1.96 \cdot \sqrt{\frac{0.9294(1-0.9294)}{326}}$$

$$0.9017 \le \pi \le 0.9572$$

(b) You are 95% confident that the population proportion of business men and women who have their presentations disturbed by cell phones is between 0.9017 and 0.9572.

(c) $n = \frac{Z^2\pi(1-\pi)}{e^2} = \frac{1.96^2(0.9294)(1-0.9294)}{(0.04)^2} = 157.5372$ Use $n = 158$

(d) $n = \frac{Z^2\pi(1-\pi)}{e^2} = \frac{2.5758^2(0.9294)(1-0.9294)}{(0.04)^2} = 272.0960$ Use $n = 273$

8.50 The only way to have 100% confidence is to obtain the parameter of interest, rather than a sample statistic. From another perspective, the range of the normal and $t$ distribution is infinite, so a $Z$ or $t$ value that contains 100% of the area cannot be obtained.

8.52 If the confidence level is increased, a greater area under the normal or $t$ distribution needs to be included. This leads to an increased value of $Z$ or $t$, and thus a wider interval.

8.54 In some applications such as auditing, interest is primarily on the total amount of a variable rather than the mean amount.

8.56 (a) The population from which this sample was drawn was the collection of all the people who visited the magazine's web site.

(b) The sample is not a random sample from this population. The sample consisted of only those who visited the magazine's web site and chose to fill out the survey.

(c) This is not a statistically valid study. There was selection bias since only those who visited the magazine's web site and chose to answer the survey were represented. There was possibly nonresponse bias as well. Visitors to the web site who chose to fill out the survey might not answer all questions and there was no way for the magazine to get back to them to follow-up on the nonresponses if this was an anonymous survey.

(d) To avoid the above potential pitfalls, the magazine could have drawn a random sample from the list of all subscribers to the magazine and offer them the option of filling out the survey over the Internet or on the survey form that is mailed to the subscribers. The magazine should also keep track of the subscribers who are invited to fill out the survey and follow up on the nonresponses after a specified period of time with mail or telephone to encourage them to participate in the survey.

The sample size needed is $n = \frac{Z^2 \cdot \pi \cdot (1-\pi)}{e^2} = \frac{1.96^2 \cdot (0.6195) \cdot (1-0.6195)}{(0.02)^2} = 2264$

8.58 (a) $p \pm Z \cdot \sqrt{\frac{p(1-p)}{n}} = 0.58 \pm 1.96 \cdot \sqrt{\frac{0.58(1-0.58)}{200}}$ $0.5116 < \pi < 0.6484$

(b) $p \pm Z \cdot \sqrt{\frac{p(1-p)}{n}} = 0.50 \pm 1.96 \cdot \sqrt{\frac{0.50(1-0.50)}{200}}$ $0.4307 < \pi < 0.5693$

(c) $p \pm Z \cdot \sqrt{\frac{p(1-p)}{n}} = 0.22 \pm 1.96 \cdot \sqrt{\frac{0.22(1-0.22)}{200}}$ $0.1626 < \pi < 0.2774$

(d) $p \pm Z \cdot \sqrt{\frac{p(1-p)}{n}} = 0.19 \pm 1.96 \cdot \sqrt{\frac{0.19(1-0.19)}{200}}$ $0.1356 < \pi < 0.2444$

(e) $n = \frac{Z^2 \cdot \pi \cdot (1-\pi)}{e^2} = \frac{1.96^2 \cdot (0.5) \cdot (0.5)}{(0.02)^2} = 2400.9 \cong 2401$

8.60 (a) $\bar{X} \pm t \cdot \frac{S}{\sqrt{n}} = 15.3 \pm 2.0227 \cdot \frac{3.8}{\sqrt{40}}$ $14.085 \le \mu \le 16.515$

(b) $p \pm Z \cdot \sqrt{\frac{p(1-p)}{n}} = 0.675 \pm 1.96 \cdot \sqrt{\frac{0.675(0.325)}{40}}$ $0.530 \le \pi \le 0.820$

(c) $n = \frac{Z^2 \cdot \sigma^2}{e^2} = \frac{1.96^2 \cdot 5^2}{2^2} = 24.01$ Use $n = 25$

(d) $n = \frac{Z^2 \cdot \pi \cdot (1-\pi)}{e^2} = \frac{1.96^2 \cdot (0.5) \cdot (0.5)}{(0.035)^2} = 784$ Use $n = 784$

(e) If a single sample were to be selected for both purposes, the larger of the two sample sizes ($n = 784$) should be used.

8.62 (a) $\bar{X} \pm t \cdot \frac{S}{\sqrt{n}} = 9.7 \pm 2.0639 \cdot \frac{4}{\sqrt{25}}$ $8.049 \le \mu \le 11.351$

(b) $p \pm Z \cdot \sqrt{\frac{p(1-p)}{n}} = 0.48 \pm 1.96 \cdot \sqrt{\frac{0.48(0.52)}{25}}$ $0.284 \le \pi \le 0.676$

(c) $n = \frac{Z^2 \cdot \sigma^2}{e^2} = \frac{1.96^2 \cdot 4.5^2}{1.5^2} = 34.57$ Use $n = 35$

(d) $n = \frac{Z^2 \cdot \pi \cdot (1-\pi)}{e^2} = \frac{1.645^2 \cdot (0.5) \cdot (0.5)}{(0.075)^2} = 120.268$ Use $n = 121$

(e) If a single sample were to be selected for both purposes, the larger of the two sample sizes ($n = 121$) should be used.

8.64 (a) $\bar{X} \pm t \cdot \frac{S}{\sqrt{n}} = \$28.52 \pm 1.9949 \cdot \frac{\$11.39}{\sqrt{70}}$ $\$25.80 \le \mu \le \$31.24$

(b) $p \pm Z \cdot \sqrt{\frac{p(1-p)}{n}} = 0.40 \pm 1.645 \cdot \sqrt{\frac{0.40(0.60)}{70}}$ $0.3037 \le \pi \le 0.4963$

(c) $n = \frac{Z^2 \cdot \sigma^2}{e^2} = \frac{1.96^2 \cdot 10^2}{2^2} = 96.04$ Use $n = 97$

(d) $n = \frac{Z^2 \cdot \pi \cdot (1-\pi)}{e^2} = \frac{1.645^2 \cdot (0.5) \cdot (0.5)}{(0.04)^2} = 422.82$ Use $n = 423$

(e) If a single sample were to be selected for both purposes, the larger of the two sample sizes ($n = 423$) should be used.

8.66 (a) $\bar{X} \pm t \cdot \frac{S}{\sqrt{n}} = \$38.54 \pm 2.0010 \cdot \frac{\$7.26}{\sqrt{60}}$ $\$36.66 \le \mu \le \$40.42$

(b) $p \pm Z \cdot \sqrt{\frac{p(1-p)}{n}} = 0.30 \pm 1.645 \cdot \sqrt{\frac{0.30(0.70)}{60}}$ $0.2027 \le \pi \le 0.3973$

(c) $n = \frac{Z^2 \cdot \sigma^2}{e^2} = \frac{1.96^2 \cdot 8^2}{1.5^2} = 109.27$ Use $n = 110$

(d) $n = \frac{Z^2 \cdot \pi \cdot (1-\pi)}{e^2} = \frac{1.645^2 \cdot (0.5) \cdot (0.5)}{(0.04)^2} = 422.82$ Use $n = 423$

(e) If a single sample were to be selected for both purposes, the larger of the two sample sizes ($n = 423$) should be used.

8.68 (a) $\bar{X} \pm t \cdot \frac{S}{\sqrt{n}} = 8.4209 \pm 2.0106 \cdot \frac{0.0461}{\sqrt{49}}$ $8.41 \le \mu \le 8.43$

(b) With 95% confidence, the population mean width of troughs is somewhere between 8.41 and 8.43 inches. Hence, the company's requirement of troughs being between 8.31 and 8.61 is being met with a 95% level of confidence.

8.70 (a) $\bar{X} \pm t \cdot \frac{S}{\sqrt{n}} = 0.2641 \pm 1.9741 \cdot \frac{0.1424}{\sqrt{170}}$ $0.2425 \le \mu \le 0.2856$

(b) $\bar{X} \pm t \cdot \frac{S}{\sqrt{n}} = 0.218 \pm 1.9772 \cdot \frac{0.1227}{\sqrt{140}}$ $0.1975 \le \mu \le 0.2385$

8.70 cont. (c)

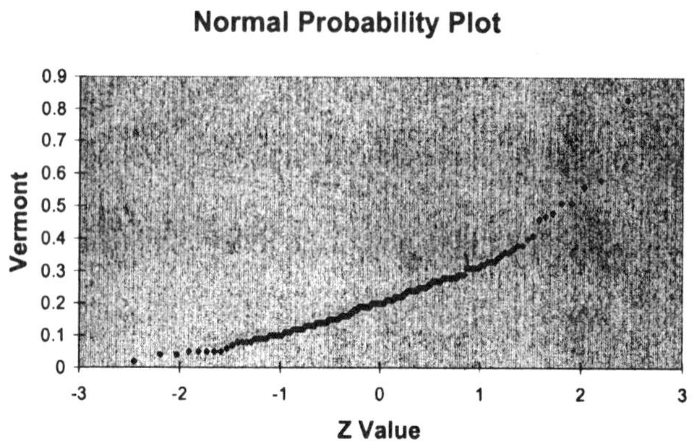


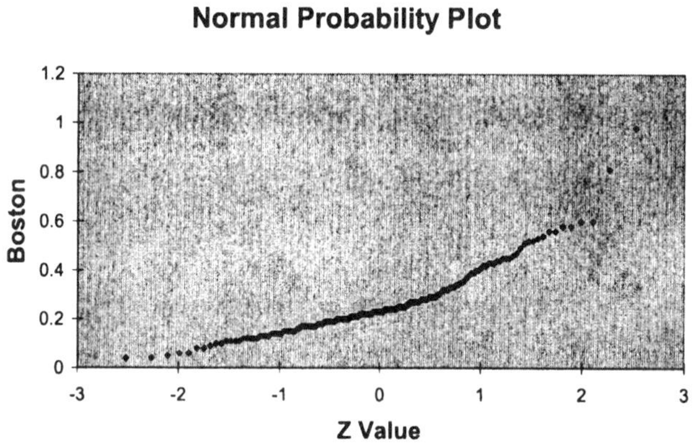


The amount of granule loss for both brands are skewed to the right.

(d) Since the two confidence intervals do not overlap, we can conclude that the mean granule loss of Boston shingles is higher than that of Vermont Shingles.

8.72 (a) NY, Food: $\bar{X} \pm t \cdot \frac{S}{\sqrt{n}} = 20.1 \pm 2.0096 \cdot \frac{2.0825}{\sqrt{50}}$ $19.51 \leq \mu \leq 20.69$

LI, Food: $\bar{X} \pm t \cdot \frac{S}{\sqrt{n}} = 20.54 \pm 2.0096 \cdot \frac{2.8586}{\sqrt{50}}$ $19.73 \leq \mu \leq 21.35$

NY, Décor: $\bar{X} \pm t \cdot \frac{S}{\sqrt{n}} = 17.12 \pm 2.0096 \cdot \frac{2.6927}{\sqrt{50}}$ $16.35 \leq \mu \leq 17.89$

LI, Décor: $\bar{X} \pm t \cdot \frac{S}{\sqrt{n}} = 17.64 \pm 2.0096 \cdot \frac{3.4862}{\sqrt{50}}$ $16.65 \leq \mu \leq 18.63$

NY, Services: $\bar{X} \pm t \cdot \frac{S}{\sqrt{n}} = 18.4 \pm 2.0096 \cdot \frac{2.3123}{\sqrt{50}}$ $17.74 \leq \mu \leq 19.06$

LI, Services: $\bar{X} \pm t \cdot \frac{S}{\sqrt{n}} = 19.04 \pm 2.0096 \cdot \frac{2.3730}{\sqrt{50}}$ $18.37 \leq \mu \leq 19.71$

NY, Price: $\bar{X} \pm t \cdot \frac{S}{\sqrt{n}} = 39.74 \pm 2.0096 \cdot \frac{9.6528}{\sqrt{50}}$ $37.00 \leq \mu \leq 42.48$

LI, Price: $\bar{X} \pm t \cdot \frac{S}{\sqrt{n}} = 33.7400 \pm 2.0096 \cdot \frac{7.7191}{\sqrt{50}}$ $31.55 \leq \mu \leq 35.93$

(b) With 95% confidence you can conclude the mean price per person in New York City is greater than the mean in Long Island. With 95% confidence you can conclude that there are no differences in the ratings for food, décor and service between the two cities.

# CHAPTER 9

## OBJECTIVES

- To understand the basic hypothesis testing procedure
- To be able to use hypothesis testing to test a mean, proportion, or variance
- To be aware of the assumptions of each hypothesis testing procedure, how to evaluate the assumptions, and what will be the consequences if the assumptions are seriously violated
- To understand how to avoid the pitfalls involved in hypothesis testing
- To be familiar with the ethical issues involved in hypothesis testing

## OVERVIEW AND KEY CONCEPTS

### Some Basic Concepts in Hypothesis Testing

- **Null hypothesis $(H_0)$:** The hypothesis that is always tested.
  - The null hypothesis always refers to a specified value of the population parameter, not a sample statistic.
  - The statement of the null hypothesis always contains an equal sign regarding the specified value of the population parameter.
- **Alternative hypothesis:** The opposite of the null hypothesis and represents the conclusion supported if the null hypothesis is rejected.
  - The statement of the alternative hypothesis never contains an equal sign regarding the specified value of the population parameter.
- **Critical value:** A value or values that separate the rejection region or regions from the remaining values.
- **Type I error:** A Type I error occurs if the null hypothesis is rejected when in fact it is true and should not be rejected.
- **Type II error:** A Type II error occurs if the null hypothesis is not rejected when in fact it is false and should be rejected.
- **Level of significance $(\alpha)$:** The probability of committing a Type I error.
- **The $\beta$ risk (the consumer's risk level):** The probability of committing a Type II error.
- **Factors that affect the $\beta$ risk:** Holding everything else constant,
  - $\beta$ increases when the difference between the hypothesized parameter and its true value decreases.
  - $\beta$ increases when $\alpha$ decreases.
  - $\beta$ increases when $\sigma$ increases.
  - $\beta$ increases when the sample size $n$ decreases.
- **The confidence coefficient $(1-\alpha)$:** The probability that the null hypothesis is not rejected when in fact it is true and should not be rejected.
- **The confidence level:** $100(1-\alpha)\%$
- **The power of a test $(1-\beta)$:** The probability of rejecting the null hypothesis when in fact it is false and should be rejected.

- **Risk in decision making:** There is a delicate balance between the probability of committing a Type I error and the probability of a Type II error.

**$H_0$: Innocent**

**E.g. Jury Trial**

| | The Truth | |
|---|---|---|
| **Verdict** | **Innocent** | **Guilty** |
| **Innocent** | Correct | Error |
| **Guilty** | Error | Correct |

[illegible]

| | The Truth | |
|---|---|---|
| **Decision** | **$H_0$ True** | **$H_0$ False** |
| **Do Not Reject $H_0$** | $1 - \alpha$ | Type II Error ($\beta$) |
| **Reject $H_0$** | Type I Error ($\alpha$) | Power ($1 - \beta$) |

  - Reducing the probability of Type I error will inevitably increase the probability of committing a Type II error holding everything else constant.
  - One should choose a smaller Type I error when the cost of rejecting the maintained hypothesis is high.
  - One should choose a larger Type I error when there is an interest in changing the status quo.
- ***p*-value (the observed level of significance):** The probability of obtaining a test statistic equal to or more extreme than the result obtained from the sample data, given the null hypothesis is true.
  - It is also the smallest level of significance at which the null hypothesis can be rejected.
  - Roughly speaking, it measures the amount of evidence against the null hypothesis. The smaller the $p$-value, the stronger is the evidence against the null hypothesis.
  - The statistical decision rule is to reject the null hypothesis if the $p$-value is less than the level of significance $(\alpha)$, and do not reject otherwise.

## The Six-Step Method in the Traditional Critical Value Approach to Hypothesis Testing

1. State the null hypothesis, $H_0$ and the alternative hypothesis, $H_1$.
2. Choose the level of significance, $\alpha$ and the sample size, $n$. The level of significance is specified according to the relative importance of the risks of committing Type I and Type II errors in the problem.
3. Determine the appropriate test statistic and sampling distribution.
4. Determine the critical values that divide the rejection and nonrejection regions.
5. Collect the data and compute the value of the test statistic.
6. Make the statistical decision and state the managerial conclusion. Compare the computed test statistic to the critical values. Reject $H_0$ when the computed test statistic falls in a rejection region; do not reject $H_0$ otherwise. The managerial conclusion is written in the context of the real-world problem.

## The Five-Step Method in the *p* Value Approach to Hypothesis Testing

1. State the null hypothesis, $H_0$ and the alternative hypothesis, $H_1$.
2. Choose the level of significance, $\alpha$ and the sample size, *n*. The level of significance is specified according to the relative importance of the risks of committing Type I and Type II errors in the problem.
3. Determine the appropriate test statistic and sampling distribution.
4. Collect the data, compute the value of the test statistic and obtain the *p*-value based on the computed test statistic.
5. Make the statistical decision and state the managerial conclusion. If the *p*-value is greater than or equal to $\alpha$, you do not reject the null hypothesis $H_0$. If the *p*-value is less than $\alpha$, you reject the null hypothesis. Remember the mantra, if the *p*-value is low, the $H_0$ must go. The managerial conclusion is written in the context of the real-world problem.

## *Z* Test for the Population Mean $(\mu)$ when $\sigma$ is Known

- **Assumptions:**
  - Population is normally distributed or large sample size.
  - $\sigma$ is known.
- **Test statistic:**
  - $Z = \dfrac{\bar{X} - \mu_{\bar{X}}}{\sigma_{\bar{X}}} = \dfrac{\bar{X} - \mu}{\sigma / \sqrt{n}}$
  - The alternative hypothesis can be one-tail with a right-tail rejection region, one-tail with a left-tail rejection region or two-tail with both right-tail and left-tail rejection regions.

## *t* Test for the Population Mean $(\mu)$ when $\sigma$ Is Unknown

- **Assumptions:**
  - Population is normally distributed or large sample size.
  - $\sigma$ is unknown.
- **Test statistic:**
  - $t = \dfrac{\bar{X} - \mu}{S / \sqrt{n}}$ with $(n - 1)$ degrees of freedom.
  - The alternative hypothesis can be one-tail with a right-tail rejection region, one-tail with a left-tail rejection region or two-tail with both right-tail and left-tail rejection regions.

## *Z* Test for the Population Proportion $(\pi)$

- **Assumptions:**
  - Population involves 2 categorical values.
  - Both *np* and $n(1\text{-}p)$ are at least 5.
- **Test statistic:**
  - $Z = \dfrac{p - \mu_p}{\sigma_p} = \dfrac{p - \pi}{\sqrt{\dfrac{\pi(1-\pi)}{n}}}$

- The alternative hypothesis can be one-tail with a right-tail rejection region, one-tail with a left-tail rejection region or two-tail with both right-tail and left-tail rejection regions.

## Potential Hypothesis-Testing Pitfalls

- To avoid potential hypothesis-testing pitfalls, you should:
  1. Consult with a person with substantial statistical training early in the process.
  2. Build in adequate controls from the beginning to avoid biases.
  3. Plan ahead by asking the following questions:
     - i. What is the goal of the survey, study, or experiment? How can you translate into a null hypothesis and an alternative hypothesis?
     - ii. Is the hypothesis test a two-tail test or one-tail test?
     - iii. Can you select a random sample from the underlying population of interest?
     - iv. What kinds of measurements will you collect from the sample? Are the sampled outcomes numerical or categorical?
     - v. At what significance level, or risk of committing a Type I error, should you conduct the hypothesis test?
     - vi. Is the intended sample size large enough to achieve the desired power of the test for the level of significance chosen?
     - vii. What statistical test procedure should you use and why?
     - viii. What conclusions and interpretations can you make from the results of the hypothesis test?

## Ethical Issues

- Ethical considerations arise when the hypothesis-testing process is manipulated.
  - **Data collection method should be randomized:** The data must be the outcome of a random sample from a population or from an experiment in which a randomization process was used. .Potential respondents should not be permitted to self-select for a study nor should they be purposely selected.
  - **Informed Consent from Human Respondents Being "Treated":** Any individual who is to be subjected to some "treatment" in an experiment should be made aware of the research endeavor and any potential behavioral or physical side effects. The subject should also provide informed consent with respect to participation.
  - **Type of Test—Two-Tail or One-Tail:** If prior information is available that leads you to test the null hypothesis against a specifically directed alternative, then a one-tail test is more powerful than a two-tail test. On the other hand, if you are interested only in differences from the null hypothesis, not in the direction of the difference, the two-tail test is the appropriate procedure to use.
  - **Choice of Level of Significance:** The level of significance should be selected before data collection occurs. It is also good practice to always report the *p*-value, not just the conclusions of the hypothesis test.
  - **Data Snooping:** It is unethical to perform a hypothesis test on a set of data, look at the results, and then decide on the level of significance or decide between a one-tail or two-tail test.
  - **Cleansing and Discarding of Data:** If a measurement is incomplete or grossly in error because of some equipment problem or unusual behavioral occurrence unrelated to the study, you can discard the value. In a well-designed experiment or study, you should decide, in advance, on all rules regarding the possible discarding of data.
  - **Reporting of Findings:** In conducting research, you should document both good and bad results. It is inappropriate to report the results of hypothesis tests that show

statistical significance but not those for which there is insufficient evidence in the findings.

- **Statistical Significance versus Practical Significance:** You need to make the distinction between the existence of a statistically significant result and its practical significance in the context within a field of application. Sometimes, due to a very large sample size, you will get a result that is statistically significant, but has little practical significance.

# SOLUTIONS TO END OF SECTION AND CHAPTER REVIEW EVEN PROBLEMS

9.2 $H_1$ is used to denote the alternative hypothesis.

9.4 $\beta$ is used to denote the risk or the chance of committing a Type II error.

9.6 $\alpha$ is the probability of making a Type I error – that is, the probability of incorrectly rejecting the null hypothesis when in reality the null hypothesis is true and should not be rejected.

9.8 The power of a test is the complement, which is (1 - $\beta$), of the probability $\beta$ of making a Type II error.

9.10 It is possible to not reject a false null hypothesis because the mean of a single sample can fall in the non-rejection region even though the hypothesized population mean is false.

9.12 Other things being equal, the closer the *hypothesized* mean is to the *actual* mean, the larger the risk of committing a Type II error will be.

9.14 Under the French judicial system, unlike ours in the United States, the null hypothesis assumes the defendant is guilty, the alternative hypothesis assumes the defendant is innocent. A Type I error would be not convicting a guilty person and a Type II error would be convicting an innocent person.

9.16 $H_0$: $\mu = 20$ minutes. 20 minutes is adequate travel time between classes.
$H_1$: $\mu \neq 20$ minutes. 20 minutes is not adequate travel time between classes.

9.18 $H_0$: $\mu = 1.00$. The mean amount of paint per can is one gallon.
$H_1$: $\mu \neq 1.00$. The mean amount of paint per can differs from one gallon.

9.20 Decision rule: Reject $H_0$ if $Z < -1.96$ or $Z > +1.96$.
Decision: Since $Z_{calc} = +2.21$ is greater than $Z_{crit} = +1.96$, reject $H_0$.

9.22 Decision rule: Reject $H_0$ if $Z < -2.58$ or $Z > +2.58$.

9.24 $p$-value = 2(1 – .9772) = 0.0456

9.26 $p$-value = 0.1676

9.28 (a) $H_0$: $\mu = 70$ pounds. The cloth has a mean breaking strength of 70 pounds.
$H_1$: $\mu \neq 70$ pounds. The cloth has a mean breaking strength that differs from 70 pounds.
Decision rule: Reject $H_0$ if $Z < -1.96$ or $Z > +1.96$.

Test statistic: $Z = \dfrac{\bar{X} - \mu}{\sigma / \sqrt{n}} = \dfrac{69.1 - 70}{3.5 / \sqrt{49}} = -1.80$

Decision: Since $Z_{calc} = -1.80$ is between the critical bounds of $\pm$ 1.96, do not reject $H_0$. There is not enough evidence to conclude that the cloth has a mean breaking strength that differs from 70 pounds.

(b) $p$-value = 2(0.0359) = 0.0718
Interpretation: The probability of getting a sample of 49 pieces that yield a mean strength that is farther away from the hypothesized population mean than this sample is 0.0718 or 7.18%.

(c) Decision rule: Reject $H_0$ if $Z < -1.96$ or $Z > +1.96$.

Test statistic: $Z = \dfrac{\bar{X} - \mu}{\sigma / \sqrt{n}} = \dfrac{69.1 - 70}{1.75 / \sqrt{49}} = -3.60$

Decision: Since $Z_{calc} = -3.60$ is less than the lower critical bound of $-1.96$, reject $H_0$. There is enough evidence to conclude that the cloth has a mean breaking strength that differs from 70 pounds.

(d) Decision rule: Reject $H_0$ if $Z < -1.96$ or $Z > +1.96$.

Test statistic: $Z = \dfrac{\bar{X} - \mu}{\sigma / \sqrt{n}} = \dfrac{69 - 70}{3.5 / \sqrt{49}} = -2.00$

Decision: Since $Z_{calc} = -2.00$ is less than the lower critical bound of $-1.96$, reject $H_0$. There is enough evidence to conclude that the cloth has a mean breaking strength that differs from 70 pounds.

9.30 (a) $H_0$: $\mu = 375$ hours. The mean life of the manufacturer's light bulbs is equal to 375 hours.
$H_1$: $\mu \neq 375$ hours. The mean life of the manufacturer's light bulbs differs from 375 hours.
Decision rule: Reject $H_0$ if $Z < -1.96$ or $Z > +1.96$.

Test statistic: $Z = \dfrac{\bar{X} - \mu}{\sigma / \sqrt{n}} = \dfrac{350 - 375}{100 / \sqrt{64}} = -2.00$

Decision: Since $Z_{calc} = -2.00$ is below the critical bound of $-1.96$, reject $H_0$. There is enough evidence to conclude that the mean life of the manufacturer's light bulbs differs from 375 hours.

(b) $p$-value = 2(0.0228) = 0.0456.
Interpretation: The probability of getting a sample of 64 light bulbs that will yield a mean life that is farther away from the hypothesized population mean than this sample is 0.0456.

(c) $\bar{X} \pm Z \cdot \dfrac{\sigma}{\sqrt{n}} = 350 \pm 1.96 \cdot \dfrac{100}{\sqrt{64}}$ $\quad 325.50 \le \mu \le 374.50$

(d) The results are the same. The confidence interval formed does not include the hypothesized value of 375 hours.

9.32

| | A | B |
|---|---|---|
| 1 | Salad Dressings | |
| 2 | | |
| 3 | Null Hypothesis μ= | 8 |
| 4 | Level of Significance | 0.05 |
| 5 | Population Standard Deviation | 0.15 |
| 6 | Sample Size | 50 |
| 7 | Sample Mean | 7.983 |
| 8 | Standard Error of the Mean | 0.021213203 |
| 9 | Z Test Statistic | -0.80138769 |
| 10 | | |
| 11 | Two-Tailed Test | |
| 12 | Lower Critical Value | -1.95996108 |
| 13 | Upper Critical Value | 1.959961082 |
| 14 | *p*-Value | 0.422907113 |
| 15 | Do not reject the null hypothesis | |

(a) $H_0: \mu = 8$ $\quad H_1: \mu \neq 8$

Decision rule: Reject $H_0$ if $Z < -1.96$ or $Z > 1.96$

Test statistic: $Z = \dfrac{7.983 - 8}{.15/\sqrt{50}} = -0.8$

Decision: Do not reject $H_0$. There is insufficient evidence to conclude that the amount of salad dressing placed in 8 oz bottle is significantly different from 8 oz.

(b) *p*-value = 0.4229. The probability of observing a $Z$ test statistic more extreme than −0.8 is 0.4229 if the population mean is indeed 8 oz.

(c) Decision rule: Reject $H_0$ if $Z < -1.96$ or $Z > +1.96$.

Test statistic: $Z = \dfrac{\overline{X} - \mu}{\sigma/\sqrt{n}} = \dfrac{7.983 - 8}{0.05/\sqrt{50}} = -2.40$

Decision: Since $Z_{calc} = -2.40$ is less than the lower critical bound of $-1.96$, reject $H_0$. There is enough evidence to conclude that the machine is filling bottles improperly.

(d) Decision rule: Reject $H_0$ if $Z < -1.96$ or $Z > +1.96$.

Test statistic: $Z = \dfrac{\overline{X} - \mu}{\sigma/\sqrt{n}} = \dfrac{7.952 - 8}{0.15/\sqrt{50}} = -2.26$

Decision: Since $Z_{calc} = -2.26$ is less than the lower critical bound of $-1.96$, reject $H_0$. There is enough evidence to conclude that the machine is filling bottles improperly.

9.34 $Z = 2.33$

9.36 $Z = -2.33$

9.38 *p*-value = 1 − 0.9772 = 0.0228

9.40 *p*-value = 0.0838

9.42 *p*-value = $P(Z < 1.38) = 0.9162$

9.44 $H_0$: $\mu \geq 2.8$ feet.
The mean length of steel bars produced is at least 2.8 feet and the production equipment does not need immediate adjustment.
$H_1$: $\mu < 2.8$ feet.
The mean length of steel bars produced is less than 2.8 feet and the production equipment does need immediate adjustment.

(a) Decision rule: If $Z < -1.645$, reject $H_0$.

Test statistic: $Z = \dfrac{\bar{X} - \mu}{\sigma/\sqrt{n}} = \dfrac{2.73 - 2.8}{0.2/\sqrt{25}} = -1.75$

Decision: Since $Z_{calc} = -1.75$ is less than $Z_{crit} = -1.645$, reject $H_0$. There is enough evidence to conclude the production equipment needs adjustment.

(b) Decision rule: If $p$-value $< 0.05$, reject $H_0$.

Test statistic: $Z = \dfrac{\bar{X} - \mu}{\sigma/\sqrt{n}} = \dfrac{2.73 - 2.8}{0.2/\sqrt{25}} = -1.75$

$p$-value $= 0.0401$
Decision: Since $p$ value $= 0.0401$ is less than $\alpha = 0.05$, reject $H_0$. There is enough evidence to conclude the production equipment needs adjustment.

(c) The probability of obtaining a sample whose mean is 2.73 feet or less when the null hypothesis is true is 0.0401.

(d) The conclusions are the same.

9.46 (a) $H_0$: $\mu \leq 5$
The mean number of trips that children take to the store is no more than 5.
$H_1$: $\mu > 5$
The mean number of trips that children take to the store is more than 5.

(b) A Type I error occurs when you conclude the mean number of trips that children take to the store is more than 5 when in fact the mean number is not more than five.
A Type II error occurs when you conclude the mean number of trips that children take to the store is not more than 5 when in fact the mean number is more than five.

(c) Decision rule: If $Z > 2.3263$ or when the $p$-value $< 0.01$, reject $H_0$.

Test statistic: $Z = \dfrac{\bar{X} - \mu}{\sigma/\sqrt{n}} = \dfrac{5.47 - 5}{1.6/\sqrt{100}} = 2.9375$

$p$-value $= 0.0017$
Decision: Since $Z_{calc} = 2.9375$ is greater than $Z_{crit} = 2.3263$ or the $p$-value of 0.0017 is less than 0.01, reject $H_0$. There is enough evidence to conclude the population mean number of trips to the store is greater than 5 per week.

(d) When the null hypothesis is true, the probability of obtaining a sample whose mean is 5.47 trips or more is 0.0017.

9.48 $t = \dfrac{\bar{X} - \mu}{S/\sqrt{n}} = \dfrac{56 - 50}{12/\sqrt{16}} = 2.00$

9.50 (a) For a two-tailed test with a 0.05 level of confidence, $t_{crit} = \pm 2.1315$.
(b) For an upper-tailed test with a 0.05 level of confidence, $t_{crit} = +1.7531$.

9.52 No, you should not use the $t$ test to test the null hypothesis that $\mu = 60$ on a population that is left-skewed because the sample size ($n = 16$) is less than 30. The $t$ test assumes that, if the underlying population is not normally distributed, the sample size is sufficiently large to enable the test statistic $t$ to be influenced by the Central Limit Theorem. If sample sizes are small ($n < 30$), the $t$ test should not be used because the sampling distribution does not meet the requirements of the Central Limit Theorem.

9.54 (a) $H_0$: $\mu \leq \$300$. The mean cost of textbooks per semester at a large university is no more than \$300.

$H_1$: $\mu > \$300$. The mean cost of textbooks per semester at a large university is more than \$300.

Decision rule: $d.f. = 99$. If $t > 1.2902$, reject $H_0$.

Test statistic: $t = \dfrac{\overline{X} - \mu}{S/\sqrt{n}} = \dfrac{\$315.40 - \$300.00}{\$43.20/\sqrt{100}} = 3.5648$

Decision: Since $t_{calc} = 3.5648$ is above the critical bound of $t = 1.2902$, reject $H_0$. There is enough evidence to conclude that the mean cost of textbooks per semester at a large university is more than \$300.

(b) $H_0$: $\mu \leq \$300$. The mean cost of textbooks per semester at a large university is no more than \$300.

$H_1$: $\mu > \$300$. The mean cost of textbooks per semester at a large university is more than \$300.

Decision rule: $d.f. = 99$. If $t > 1.6604$, reject $H_0$.

Test statistic: $t = \dfrac{\overline{X} - \mu}{S/\sqrt{n}} = \dfrac{\$315.40 - \$300.00}{\$75.00/\sqrt{100}} = 2.0533$

Decision: Since $t_{calc} = 2.0533$ is above the critical bound of $t = 1.6604$, reject $H_0$. There is enough evidence to conclude that the mean cost of textbooks per semester at a large university is more than \$300.

(c) $H_0$: $\mu \leq \$300$. The mean cost of textbooks per semester at a large university is no more than \$300.

$H_1$: $\mu > \$300$. The mean cost of textbooks per semester at a large university is more than \$300.

Decision rule: $d.f. = 99$. If $t > 1.2902$, reject $H_0$.

Test statistic: $t = \dfrac{\overline{X} - \mu}{S/\sqrt{n}} = \dfrac{\$305.11 - \$300.00}{\$43.20/\sqrt{100}} = 1.1829$

Decision: Since $t_{calc} = 1.1829$ is below the critical bound of $t = 1.2902$, do not reject $H_0$. There is not enough evidence to conclude that the mean cost of textbooks per semester at a large university is more than \$300.

9.56 $H_0$: $\mu \geq 3.7$ The mean waiting time is no less than 3.7 minutes.
$H_1$: $\mu < 3.7$ The mean waiting time is less than 3.7 minutes.
Decision rule: $d.f. = 63$. If $t < -1.6694$ or $p$-value $< 0.05$, reject $H_0$.

Test statistic: $t = \dfrac{\bar{X}-\mu}{S/\sqrt{n}} = \dfrac{3.57-3.7}{0.8/\sqrt{64}} = -1.3$

$p$-value = 0.0992

Decision: Since $t_{calc} = -1.3$ is $> t_{crit} = -1.6694$ and the $p$-value of 0.0992 is larger than 0.05, do not reject $H_0$. There is not enough evidence to conclude that the mean waiting time is less than 3.7 minutes.

9.58 (a) $H_0: \mu \leq 400$ The mean life of the batteries is not more than 400 hours.
$H_1: \mu > 400$ The mean life of the batteries is more than 400 hours.
Decision rule: Reject $H_0$ if $t > 1.7823$

Test statistic: $t = \dfrac{\bar{X}-\mu}{s/\sqrt{n}} = \dfrac{473.46\text{-}400}{210.77/\sqrt{13}} = 1.2567$

Decision: Since $t < 1.7823$, do not reject $H_0$. There is not enough evidence to conclude that the mean life of the batteries is more than 400 hours.

(b) $p$-value = 0.1164. If the population mean life is indeed no more than 400 hours, the probability of obtaining a sample of 13 batteries that result in a sample mean of 473.46 or more is 11.64%.

(c) Allowing for only 5% probability of making a Type I error, the manufacturer should not say in advertisements that these batteries should last more than 400 hours. They can make the claim that these batteries should last more than 400 hours only if they are willing to raise the level of significance to more than 0.1164.

(d) (a) $H_0: \mu \leq 400$ The mean life of the batteries is not more than 400 hours.
$H_1: \mu > 400$ The mean life of the batteries is more than 400 hours.
Decision rule: Reject $H_0$ if $t > 1.7823$

Test statistic: $t = \dfrac{\bar{X}-\mu}{s/\sqrt{n}} = \dfrac{550.38\text{-}400}{315.33/\sqrt{13}} = 1.7195$

Decision: Since $t < 1.7823$, do not reject $H_0$. There is not enough evidence to conclude that the mean life of the batteries is more than 400 hours.

(b) $p$-value = 0.0556. If the population mean life is indeed no more than 400 hours, the probability of obtaining a sample of 13 batteries that result in a sample mean of 550.38 or more is 5.56%.

(c) Allowing for only 5% probability of making a Type I error, the manufacturer should not say in advertisements that these batteries should last more than 400 hours. They can make the claim that these batteries should last more than 400 hours only if they are willing to raise the level of significance to more than 0.0556.

The extremely larger value of 1342 raises the sample mean and sample standard deviation and, hence, results in a higher measured t statistic of 1.7195. This is, however, still not enough to offset the lower hours in the remaining sample to the degree that the null hypothesis can be rejected.

9.60 (a) $H_0: \mu = 2$ $\quad H_1: \mu \neq 2$ $\quad d.f. = 49$

Decision rule: Reject $H_0$ if $|t| > 2.0096$

Test statistic: $t = \frac{\bar{X} - \mu}{S/\sqrt{n}} = \frac{2.0007-2}{0.0446/\sqrt{50}} = 0.1143$

Decision: Since $|t| < 2.0096$, do not reject $H_0$. There is not enough evidence to conclude that the mean amount of soft drink filled is different from 2.0 liters.

(b) $p$-value = 0.9095. If the population mean amount of soft drink filled is indeed 2.0 liters, the probability of observing a sample of 50 soft drinks that will result in a sample mean amount of fill more different from 2.0 liters is 0.9095.

(c)

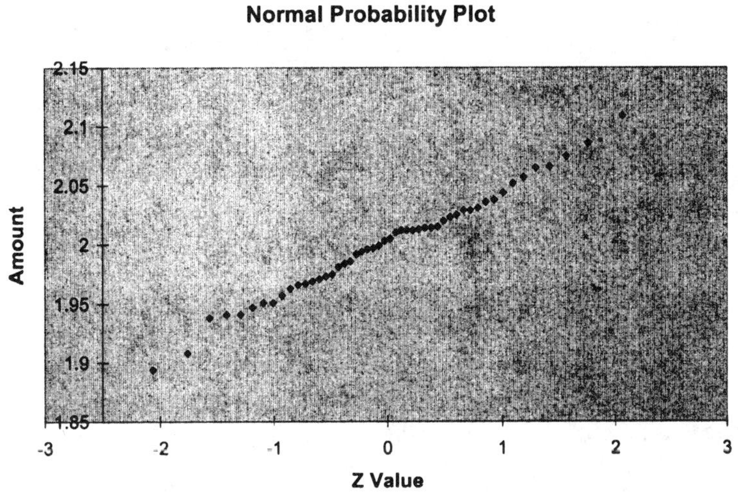


The normal probability plot suggests that the data are rather normally distributed. Hence, the results in (a) are valid in terms of the normality assumption.

(d)

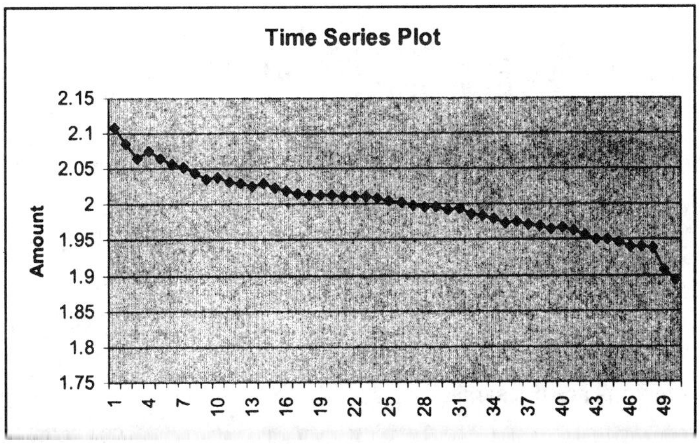


The time series plot of the data reveals that there is a downward trend in the amount of soft drink filled. This violates the assumption that data are drawn independently from a normal population distribution because the amount of fill in consecutive bottles appears to be closely related. As a result, the $t$ test in (a) becomes invalid.

9.62 (a) $H_0: \mu = 15.5$ $\quad H_1: \mu \neq 15.5$

Decision rule: Reject $H_0$ if $|t| > 2.6178$ $\quad d.f. = 119$

Test statistic: $t = \dfrac{\bar{X} - \mu}{S/\sqrt{n}} = \dfrac{14.9775 - 15.5}{1.007/\sqrt{120}} = -5.684$

Decision: Since $|t| > 2.6178$, reject $H_0$. There is enough evidence to conclude that the mean viscosity has changed from 15.5.

(b) The population distribution needs to be normal.

(c)

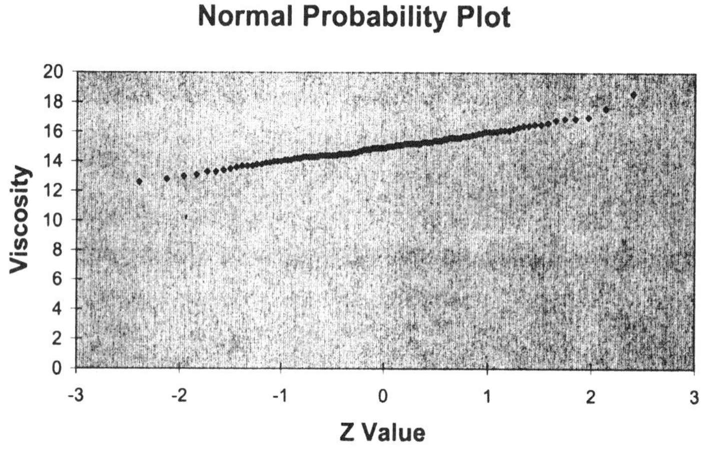


The normal probability plot indicates that the distribution is slightly skewed to the right. Even though the population distribution is probably not normally distributed, the result obtained in (a) should still be valid due to the Central Limit Theorem as a result of the relatively large sample size of 120.

9.64 (a) $H_0: \mu = 5.5$ $\quad H_1: \mu \neq 5.5$

Decision rule: Reject $H_0$ if $|t| > 2.680$ $\quad d.f. = 49$

Test statistic: $t = \dfrac{\bar{X} - \mu}{S/\sqrt{n}} = \dfrac{5.5014\text{-}5.5}{0.1058/\sqrt{50}} = 0.0935$

Decision: Since $|t| < 2.680$, do not reject $H_0$. There is not enough evidence to conclude that the mean amount of tea per bag is different than 5.5 grams.

(b) $\bar{X} \pm t \cdot \dfrac{s}{\sqrt{n}} = 5.5014 \pm 2.6800 \cdot \dfrac{0.1058}{\sqrt{50}}$ $\qquad 5.46 < \mu < 5.54$

With 99% confidence, you can conclude that the population mean amount of tea per bag is somewhere between 5.46 and 5.54 grams.

(c) The conclusions are the same.

9.66 $p = \dfrac{X}{n} = \dfrac{88}{400} = 0.22$

9.68 $H_0$: $\pi = 0.20$
$H_1$: $\pi \neq 0.20$
Decision rule: If $Z < -1.96$ or $Z > 1.96$, reject $H_0$.

Test statistic: $$Z = \frac{p - \pi}{\sqrt{\frac{\pi(1-\pi)}{n}}} = \frac{0.22 - 0.20}{\sqrt{\frac{0.20(0.80)}{400}}} = 1.00$$

Decision: Since $Z_{calc} = 1.00$ is between the critical bounds of $Z = \pm 1.96$, do not reject $H_0$.

9.70 $H_0$: $\pi \leq 0.43$ $H_1$: $\pi > 0.43$
Decision rule: If $Z > 1.645$ or $p$-value $< 0.05$, reject $H_0$.

Test statistic: $$Z = \frac{p - \pi}{\sqrt{\frac{\pi(1-\pi)}{n}}} = \frac{0.5 - 0.43}{\sqrt{\frac{0.43(1-0.43)}{362}}} = 2.6902$$

$p$-value = 0.0036
Decision: Since $Z_{calc} = 2.6902$ is above the critical bound of $Z = 1.645$ and the $p$-value of 0.0036 is less than 0.05, reject $H_0$. There is enough evidence to show that the proportion of employers that planned to hire new employees in 2004 is larger than the 2003 proportion of 0.43.

9.72 (a) $H_0$: $\pi = 0.50$
$H_1$: $\pi \neq 0.50$
Decision rule: If $Z < -1.96$ or $Z > 1.96$, reject $H_0$.

Test statistic: $$Z = \frac{p - \pi}{\sqrt{\frac{\pi(1-\pi)}{n}}} = \frac{0.5097 - 0.50}{\sqrt{\frac{0.50(0.50)}{1083}}} = 0.6381$$

Decision: Since $Z_{calc} = 0.6381$ is greater than the lower critical bound of $Z = -1.96$ and less than the upper critical bounds of $Z = 1.96$, do not reject $H_0$. You conclude that there is not enough evidence to show that the percentage of people who trust energy-efficiency ratings differs from 50%.

(b) $H_0$: $\pi = 0.50$
$H_1$: $\pi \neq 0.50$
Decision rule: If $p$-value $< 0.05$, reject $H_0$.

Test statistic: $$Z = \frac{p - \pi}{\sqrt{\frac{\pi(1-\pi)}{n}}} = \frac{0.5097 - 0.50}{\sqrt{\frac{0.50(0.50)}{1083}}} = 0.6381$$

$p$-value = 0.5234
Decision: Since the $p$-value of 0.5234 is greater than the 0.05 level of significance, do not reject $H_0$. You conclude that there is not enough evidence to show that the percentage of people who trust energy-efficiency ratings differs from 50%.
If the null hypothesis is true, the probability of obtaining a sample proportion further away from the hypothesized value of 0.50 is 0.5234.

9.74 (a) $p = 0.7112$

(b) $H_0$: $\pi \le 0.50$

$H_1$: $\pi > 0.50$

Decision rule: If $Z > 1.6449$, reject $H_0$.

Test statistic: $Z = \dfrac{p_s - p}{\sqrt{\dfrac{p(1-p)}{n}}} = \dfrac{0.7112 - 0.50}{\sqrt{\dfrac{0.50(0.50)}{187}}} = 5.7771$

Decision: Since $Z_{calc} = 5.7771 > 1.6449$, reject $H_0$. There is enough evidence to conclude that more than half of all successful women executives have children.

(c) $H_0$: $\pi \le 0.6667$

$H_1$: $\pi > 0.6667$

Decision rule: If $Z > 1.6449$, reject $H_0$.

Test statistic: $Z = \dfrac{p_s - p}{\sqrt{\dfrac{p(1-p)}{n}}} = \dfrac{0.7112 - 0.6667}{\sqrt{\dfrac{0.6667(0.3333)}{187}}} = 1.2927$

Decision: Since $Z_{calc} = 1.2927 < 1.6449$, do not reject $H_0$. There is not enough evidence to conclude that more than two-thirds of all successful women executives have children.

(d) The random sample assumption is not likely to be valid because the criteria used in defining "successful women executives" is very likely to be quite different than those used in defining the "most powerful women in business" who attended the summit.

9.76 A Type I error represents rejecting a true null hypothesis, while a Type II error represents not rejecting a false null hypothesis.

9.78 In a one-tailed test for a mean or proportion, the entire rejection region is contained in one tail of the distribution. In a two-tailed test, the rejection region is split into two equal parts, one in the lower tail of the distribution, and the other in the upper tail.

9.80 Assuming a two-tailed test is used, if the hypothesized value for the parameter does not fall into the confidence interval, then the null hypothesis can be rejected.

9.82 Some of the ethical issues that arise when dealing with hypothesis testing methodology include the data collection method, informed consent from human subjects being "treated," the type of test—two-tailed or one-tailed, the choice of level of significance $\alpha$, data snooping, the cleansing and discarding of data, and reporting of findings.

9.84 (a) La Quinta Motor Inns commits a Type I error when it purchases a site that is not profitable.

(b) Type II error occurs when La Quinta Motor Inns fails to purchase a profitable site. The cost to the Inns when a Type II error is committed is the loss on the amount of profit the site could have generated had the Inns decided to purchase the site.

(c) The executives at La Quinta Motor Inns are trying to avoid a Type I error by adopting a very stringent decision criterion. Only sites that are classified as capable of generating high profit will be purchased.

9.84 cont. (d) If the executives adopt a less stringent rejection criterion by buying sites that the computer model predicts will produce moderate or large profit, the probability of committing a Type I error will increase. On the other hand, the less stringent rejection criterion will lower the probability of committing a Type II error since now more potentially profitable sites will be purchased.

9.86 (a) $H_0$: $\mu = 10.0$ gallons. The mean gasoline purchase is equal to 10 gallons.
$H_1$: $\mu \neq 10.0$ gallons. The mean gasoline purchase differs from 10 gallons.
Decision rule: $d.f. = 59$. If $t < -2.0010$ or $t > 2.0010$, reject $H_0$.

Test statistic: $t = \dfrac{\bar{X} - \mu}{S/\sqrt{n}} = \dfrac{11.3 - 10.0}{3.1/\sqrt{60}} = 3.2483$

Decision: Since $t_{calc} = 3.2483$ is greater than the upper critical value of $t = 2.0010$, reject $H_0$. There is enough evidence to conclude that the mean gasoline purchase differs from 10 gallons.

(b) $p$-value = 0.0019.
*Note:* The-$p$ value was found using Excel.

(c) $H_0$: $\pi \geq 0.20$. At least 20% of the motorists purchase premium-grade gasoline.
$H_1$: $\pi < 0.20$. Less than 20% of the motorists purchase premium-grade gasoline.
Decision rule: If $Z < -1.645$, reject $H_0$.

Test statistic: $Z = \dfrac{p - \pi}{\sqrt{\dfrac{\pi(1-\pi)}{n}}} = \dfrac{0.1833 - 0.20}{\sqrt{\dfrac{0.20(0.80)}{60}}} = -0.32$

Decision: Since $Z_{calc} = -0.32$ is greater than the critical bound of $Z = -1.645$, do not reject $H_0$. There is not sufficient evidence to conclude that less than 20% of the motorists purchase premium-grade gasoline.

(d) $H_0$: $\mu = 10.0$ gallons. The mean gasoline purchase is equal to 10 gallons.
$H_1$: $\mu \neq 10.0$ gallons. The mean gasoline purchase differs from 10 gallons.
Decision rule: $d.f. = 59$. If $t < -2.0010$ or $t > 2.0010$, reject $H_0$.

Test statistic: $t = \dfrac{\bar{X} - \mu}{S/\sqrt{n}} = \dfrac{10.3 - 10.0}{3.1/\sqrt{60}} = 0.7496$

Decision: Since the test statistic of $t_{calc} = 0.7496$ is between the critical bounds of $t = \pm 2.0010$, do not reject $H_0$. There is not enough evidence to conclude that the mean gasoline purchase differs from 10 gallons.

(e) $H_0$: $\pi \geq 0.20$. At least 20% of the motorists purchase premium-grade gasoline.
$H_1$: $\pi < 0.20$. Less than 20% of the motorists purchase premium-grade gasoline.
Decision rule: If $Z < -1.645$, reject $H_0$.

Test statistic: $Z = \dfrac{p - \pi}{\sqrt{\dfrac{\pi(1-\pi)}{n}}} = \dfrac{0.1167 - 0.20}{\sqrt{\dfrac{0.20(0.80)}{60}}} = -1.61$

Decision: Since $Z_{calc} = -1.61$ is greater than the critical bound of $Z = -1.645$, do not reject $H_0$. There is not sufficient evidence to conclude that less than 20% of the motorists purchase premium-grade gasoline.

9.88 (a) $H_0$: $\mu \geq 5$ minutes. The mean waiting time at a bank branch in a commercial district of the city is at least 5 minutes during the 12:00 p.m. to 1 p.m. peak lunch period.
$H_1$: $\mu < 5$ minutes. The mean waiting time at a bank branch in a commercial district of the city is less than 5 minutes during the 12:00 p.m. to 1 p.m. peak lunch period.
Decision rule: $d.f. = 14$. If $t < -1.7613$, reject $H_0$.

Test statistic: $t = \dfrac{\bar{X} - \mu}{S/\sqrt{n}} = \dfrac{4.2866 - 5.0}{1.637985/\sqrt{15}} = -1.6867$

Decision: Since $t_{calc} = -1.6867$ is greater than the critical bound of $t = -1.7613$, do not reject $H_0$. There is not enough evidence to conclude that the mean waiting time at a bank branch in a commercial district of the city is less than 5 minutes during the 12:00 p.m. to 1 p.m. peak lunch period.

(b) To perform the $t$-test on the population mean, you must assume that the observed sequence in which the data were collected is random and that the data are approximately normally distributed.

(c) Normal probability plot:

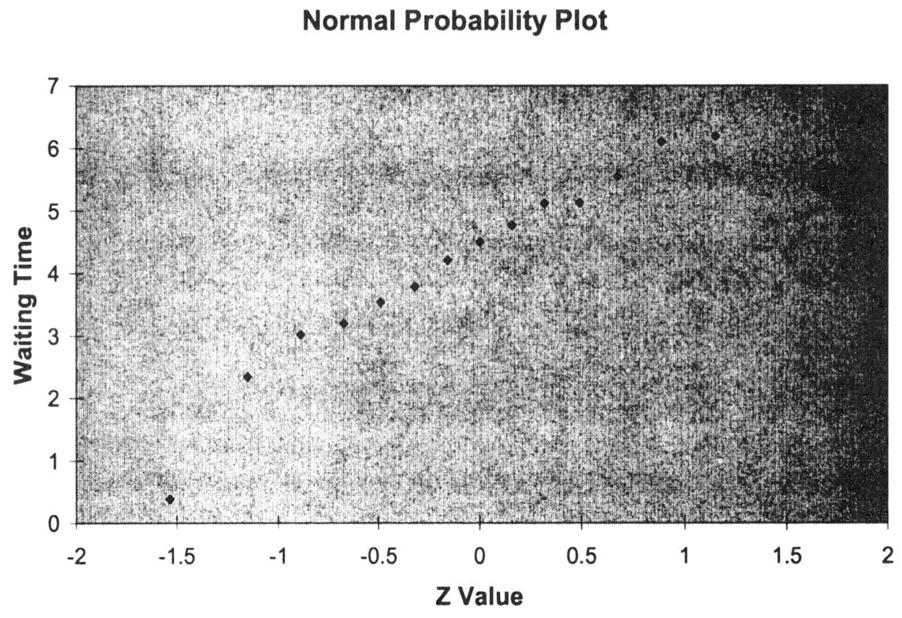


(c) With the exception of one extreme point, the data are approximately normally distributed.

(d) Based on the results of (a), the manager does not have enough evidence to make that statement.

9.90 (a) $H_0 : \mu \geq 0.35$ $H_1 : \mu < 0.35$

Decision rule: Reject $H_0$ if $t < -1.690$ $d.f. = 35$

Test statistic: $t = \dfrac{\bar{X} - \mu}{S/\sqrt{n}} = \dfrac{0.3167 - 0.35}{0.1357/\sqrt{36}} = -1.4735$

Decision: Since $t > -1.690$, do not reject $H_0$. There is not enough evidence to conclude that the mean moisture content is less than 0.35 pounds per 100 square feet.

9.90 cont. (b) $p$-value = 0.0748. If the population mean moisture content is in fact no less than 0.35 pounds per 100 square feet, the probability of observing a sample of 36 shingles that will result in a sample mean moisture content of 0.3167 pounds per 100 square feet or less is 7.48%.

(c) $H_0 : \mu \geq 0.35$ $\quad H_1 : \mu < 0.35$

Decision rule: Reject $H_0$ if $t < -1.6973$ $\quad d.f. = 30$

Test statistic: $t = \dfrac{\bar{X} - \mu}{S/\sqrt{n}} = \dfrac{0.2735 - 0.35}{0.1373/\sqrt{31}} = -3.1003$

Decision: Since $t < -1.6973$, reject $H_0$. There is enough evidence to conclude that the mean moisture content is less than 0.35 pounds per 100 square feet.

(d) $p$-value = 0.0021. If the population mean moisture content is in fact no less than 0.35 pounds per 100 square feet, the probability of observing a sample of 31 shingles that will result in a sample mean moisture content of 0.2735 pounds per 100 square feet or less is 0.21%.

(e) In order for the $t$ test to be valid, the data are assumed to be independently drawn from a population that is normally distributed. Since the sample sizes are 36 and 31, respectively, which are considered quite large, the $t$ distribution will provide a good approximation to the sampling distribution of the mean as long as the population distribution is not very skewed.

(f)

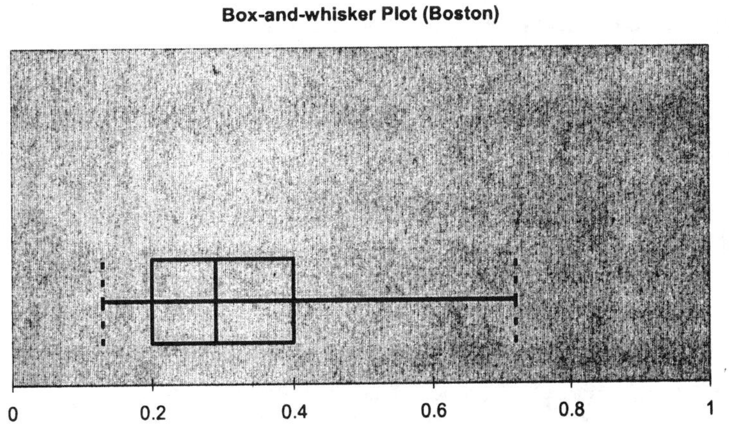


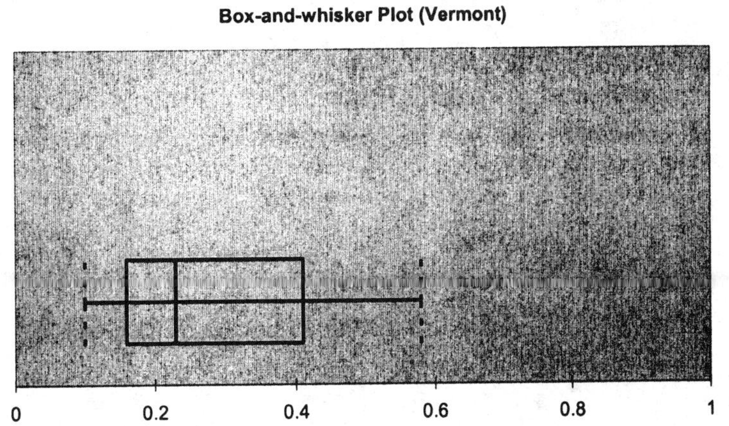

9.90 cont. (f) Both box-and-whisker plots suggest that the data are skewed slightly to the right, more so for the Boston shingles. To be more conservative, larger sample sizes should be used in both samples.

9.92 (a) $H_0: \mu = 0.5 \qquad H_1: \mu \neq 0.5$

Decision rule: Reject $H_0$ if $|t| > 1.9741$ $d.f. = 169$

Test statistic: $t = \dfrac{\bar{X} - \mu}{S/\sqrt{n}} = \dfrac{0.2641 - 0.5}{0.1424/\sqrt{170}} = -21.6059$

Decision: Since $t < -1.9741$, reject $H_0$. There is enough evidence to conclude that the mean granule loss is different from 0.5 grams.

(b) $p$-value is virtually zero. If the population mean granule loss is in fact 0.5 grams, the probability of observing a sample of 170 shingles that will yield a test statistic more extreme than –21.6059 is virtually zero.

(c) $H_0: \mu = 0.5 \qquad H_1: \mu \neq 0.5$

Decision rule: Reject $H_0$ if $|t| > 1.977$ $d.f. = 139$

Test statistic: $t = \dfrac{\bar{X} - \mu}{S/\sqrt{n}} = \dfrac{0.218 - 0.5}{0.1227/\sqrt{140}} = -27.1940$

Decision: Since $t < -1.977$, reject $H_0$. There is enough evidence to conclude that the mean granule loss is different from 0.5 grams.

(d) $p$-value is virtually zero. The probability of observing a sample of 140 shingles that will yield a test statistic more extreme than –27.1940 is virtually zero if the population mean granule loss is in fact 0.5 grams.

(e) In order for the $t$ test to be valid, the data are assumed to be independently drawn from a population that is normally distributed. Since the sample sizes are 170 and 140, respectively, which are considered large enough, the $t$ distribution will provide a good approximation to the sampling distribution of the mean even if the population is not normally distributed.

# CHAPTER 10

## OBJECTIVES

- To learn how to use hypothesis testing for comparing the difference between the means of two independent populations
- To be able to use hypothesis testing for comparing the difference between the means of two related populations
- To learn how to use hypothesis testing for comparing the difference between the means of two proportions
- To be able to use hypothesis testing for comparing the difference between the variances of two independent populations
- To learn hypothesis testing procedure to test the means of more than two populations

## OVERVIEW AND KEY CONCEPTS

### *Z* Test for Difference in Two Means $(\mu_1 - \mu_2)$

- **Assumptions:**
  - The two samples are randomly and independently drawn from normal distributions.
  - Population variances are known.
  - If the two populations are not normally distributed, large sample sizes are needed ($n_1 \geq 30$ and $n_2 \geq 30$).
- **Test statistic:**
  - $Z = \dfrac{(\bar{X}_1 - \bar{X}_2) - (\mu_1 - \mu_2)}{\sqrt{\dfrac{\sigma_1^2}{n_1} + \dfrac{\sigma_2^2}{n_2}}}$
  - The alternative hypothesis can be one-tail with a right-tail rejection region, one-tail with a left-tail rejection region or two-tail with both right-tail and left-tail rejection regions.

### Pooled-Variance *t* Test for Difference in Two Means $(\mu_1 - \mu_2)$

- **Assumptions:**
  - The two samples are randomly and independently drawn.
  - Both populations are normally distributed.
  - Population variances are unknown but assumed equal.
  - If the two populations are not normally distributed, large sample sizes are needed ($n_1 \geq 30$ and $n_2 \geq 30$).
- **Test statistic:**

- $t = \dfrac{(\bar{X}_1 - \bar{X}_2) - (\mu_1 - \mu_2)}{\sqrt{S_p^2\left(\dfrac{1}{n_1} + \dfrac{1}{n_2}\right)}}$ with $n_1 + n_2 - 2$ degrees of freedom

  where $S_p^2 = \dfrac{(n_1 - 1)S_1^2 + (n_2 - 1)S_2^2}{(n_1 - 1) + (n_2 - 1)}$
- The alternative hypothesis can be one-tail with a right-tail rejection region, one-tail with a left-tail rejection region or two-tail with both right-tail and left-tail rejection regions.

• **Confidence interval estimate:** Use the $100(1-\alpha)\%$ confidence interval for the difference in two means.
- $(\bar{X}_1 - \bar{X}_2) \pm t_{\alpha/2, n_1+n_2-2}\sqrt{S_p^2\left(\dfrac{1}{n_1} + \dfrac{1}{n_2}\right)}$

## Separate-Variance *t* Test for Difference in Two Means $(\mu_1 - \mu_2)$

• **Assumptions:**
- The two samples are randomly and independently drawn.
- Both populations are normally distributed.
- Both population variances are unknown and assumed not equal.
- If the two populations are not normally distributed, large sample sizes are needed.

• **Test statistic:**
- $t = \dfrac{(\bar{X}_1 - \bar{X}_2) - (\mu_1 - \mu_2)}{\sqrt{\dfrac{S_1^2}{n_1} + \dfrac{S_2^2}{n_2}}}$ with degrees of freedom $\nu$ taken to be the integer

  portion of $\nu = \dfrac{\left(\dfrac{S_1^2}{n_1} + \dfrac{S_2^2}{n_2}\right)^2}{\dfrac{\left(\dfrac{S_1^2}{n_1}\right)^2}{n_1 - 1} + \dfrac{\left(\dfrac{S_2^2}{n_2}\right)^2}{n_2 - 1}}$
- The alternative hypothesis can be one-tail with a right-tail rejection region, one-tail with a left-tail rejection region or two-tail with both right-tail and left-tail rejection regions.

## *Z* Test for the Mean Difference $(\mu_D)$ with Known Variance

• **Assumptions:**
- Both populations are normally distributed.
- Observations are matched or paired.
- Variance is known.
- The test is robust to the normal distribution assumption as long as the sample size is not too small and the population is not highly skewed.

• **Test statistic:**

- $Z = \dfrac{\bar{D} - \mu_D}{\dfrac{\sigma_D}{\sqrt{n}}}$ where $\bar{D} = \dfrac{\sum_{i=1}^{n} D_i}{n}$
- The alternative hypothesis can be one-tail with a right-tail rejection region, one-tail with a left-tail rejection region or two-tail with both right-tail and left-tail rejection regions.

## Paired *t* Test for the Mean Difference $(\mu_D)$ with Unknown Variance

- **Assumptions:**
  - Both populations are normally distributed.
  - Observations are matched or paired.
  - Variance is unknown.
  - The test is robust to the normal distribution assumption as long as the sample size is not too small and the population is not highly skewed.
- **Test statistic:**
  - $t = \dfrac{\bar{D} - \mu_D}{\dfrac{S_D}{\sqrt{n}}}$ with $n-1$ degrees of freedom

    where $\bar{D} = \dfrac{\sum_{i=1}^{n} D_i}{n}$ and $S_D = \sqrt{\dfrac{\sum_{i=1}^{n} (D_i - \bar{D})^2}{n-1}}$
  - The alternative hypothesis can be one-tail with a right-tail rejection region, one-tail with a left-tail rejection region or two-tail with both right-tail and left-tail rejection regions.
- **Confidence interval estimate:** Use the $100(1-\alpha)\%$ confidence interval for the mean difference.
  - $\bar{D} \pm t_{\alpha/2,n-1} \dfrac{S_D}{\sqrt{n}}$

## *Z* Test for Differences in Two Proportions $(\pi_1 - \pi_2)$

- **Assumptions:**
  - Samples are independently drawn.
  - Populations follow the binomial distribution.
  - Both sample sizes are large enough: $n_1 p_1 \geq 5$, $n_1(1-p_1) \geq 5$, $n_2 p_2 \geq 5$, $n_2(1-p_2) \geq 5$
- **Test statistic:**
  - $Z = \dfrac{(p_1 - p_2) - (\pi_1 - \pi_2)}{\sqrt{\bar{p}(1-\bar{p})\left(\dfrac{1}{n_1} + \dfrac{1}{n_2}\right)}}$ where $\bar{p} = \dfrac{X_1 + X_2}{n_1 + n_2}$ is the pooled estimate of the population proportion.

- The alternative hypothesis can be one-tail with a right-tail rejection region, one-tail with a left-tail rejection region or two-tail with both right-tail and left-tail rejection regions.

- **Confidence interval estimate:** Use the $100(1-\alpha)\%$ confidence interval for the difference in two proportions.
  - $(p_1 - p_2) \pm Z_{\alpha/2}\sqrt{\frac{p_1(1-p_1)}{n_1} + \frac{p_2(1-p_2)}{n_2}}$

## *F* Test for Difference in Two Variances $(\sigma_1^2 - \sigma_2^2)$

- **Assumptions:**
  - The two samples are randomly and independently drawn.
  - Both populations are normally distributed.
  - The test is not robust to violation of the normality assumption.
- **Test statistic:**
  - $F = \frac{S_1^2}{S_2^2}$ with $n_1 - 1$ numerator degrees of freedom and $n_2 - 1$ denominator degrees of freedom.
  - The upper-tail critical value has $n_1 - 1$ numerator degrees of freedom and $n_2 - 1$ denominator degrees of freedom.
  - The lower-tail critical value can be obtained using $F_L = \frac{1}{F_{U^*}}$ where $F_{U^*}$ is the upper-tail critical value with $n_2 - 1$ numerator degrees of freedom and $n_1 - 1$ denominator degrees of freedom.
  - The alternative hypothesis can be one-tail with a right-tail rejection region, one-tail with a left-tail rejection region or two-tail with both right-tail and left-tail rejection regions.

## General Experimental Setting

- Investigators have control over one or more independent variables called treatment variables or factors.
- Each treatment factor has two or more levels.
- Investigators observe the effects on the dependent variable, i.e., the response to the levels of the independent variable(s).
- **Experimental Design:** The plan used to test a hypothesis.

## The Completely Randomized Design

- The experimental units (subjects) are assigned randomly to treatments.
- The subjects are assumed to be homogenous.
- There is only one factor or independent variable with two or more treatment levels.
- The completely randomized design will be analyzed by one-way ANOVA.

## Some Important Identities in the Completely Randomized Design

- $SST = SSA + SSW$
- $SST = \sum_{j=1}^{c}\sum_{i=1}^{n_j}(X_{ij} - \bar{\bar{X}})^2$
- $SSA = \sum_{j=1}^{c} n_j(\bar{X}_j - \bar{\bar{X}})^2$
- $SSW = \sum_{j=1}^{c}\sum_{i=1}^{n_j}(X_{ij} - \bar{X}_j)^2$
- $MSA = \dfrac{SSA}{c-1}$
- $MSW = \dfrac{SSW}{n-c}$

  where $n$: the total number of observations in the sample
  
  $c$: the number of groups
  
  $n_j$: the number of observations in group $j$
  
  $X_{ij}$ : the $i^{th}$ observation in group $j$

  $\bar{\bar{X}} = \dfrac{\sum_{j=1}^{c}\sum_{i=1}^{n_j} X_{ij}}{c}$ : the overall or grand mean

  $\bar{X}_j$ : the sample mean of group $j$

## *F* Test for Differences in More than Two Means

- **Assumptions:**
  - Samples are randomly and independently drawn.
  - Populations are normally distributed. The $F$ test is robust to violation of this assumption.
  - Populations have equal variances. The $F$ test is less sensitive to violation of this assumption when samples are of equal size from each population.
- **The null and alternative hypotheses:**
  - $H_0 : \mu_1 = \mu_2 = \cdots = \mu_c$ There is no treatment effect
  - $H_1$ : Not all $\mu_j$ are the same. There is some treatment effect.
- **Test statistic:**
  - $F = \dfrac{MSA}{MSW}$ with $(c - 1)$ numerator degrees of freedom and $(n - c)$ denominator degrees of freedom
  - The $F$ test always has the rejection region in the right tail.

## One-way ANOVA Summary Table

| Source of Variation | Degrees of Freedom | Sum of Squares | Mean Squares (Variance) | F Statistic |
|---|---|---|---|---|
| Among (Factor) | $c-1$ | *SSA* | *MSA* = *SSA*/($c-1$) | *MSA*/*MSW* |
| Within (Error) | $n-c$ | *SSW* | *MSW* = *SSW*/($n-c$) | |
| Total | $n-1$ | *SST* = *SSA* + *SSW* | | |

## The Tukey-Kramer Procedure for the Completely Randomized Design

- A post hoc (a posteriori) procedure performed after rejection of the null hypothesis of equal means.
- Enables pair-wise comparison to see which pair of means is significantly different.
- **The Tukey-Kramer procedure:**
  1. Compute the absolute difference between any pair of sample means $\left|\bar{X}_j - \bar{X}_{j'}\right|$
  2. Compute the critical range for that pair of sample means using Critical Range $= Q_{U(c,n-c)}\sqrt{\frac{MSW}{2}\left(\frac{1}{n_j}+\frac{1}{n_{j'}}\right)}$ where $Q_{U(c,n-c)}$ is the upper-tail critical value from the Studentized range distribution with $c$ numerator degrees of freedom and $(n-c)$ denominator degrees of freedom, and $n_j$ and $n_{j'}$ are the two sample sizes for the pair of samples.
  3. The population means of a specific pair are declared significantly different if $\left|\bar{X}_j - \bar{X}_{j'}\right|$ is greater than the critical range.

## Levene's Test for Homogeneity of Variance

- Used to test the assumption of equal group variances required in the *F* test for difference in more than two means.
- **The null and alternative hypotheses:**
  - $H_0 : \sigma_1^2 = \sigma_2^2 = \cdots = \sigma_c^2$ All group variances are the same.
  - $H_1$ : Not all $\sigma_j^2$ are the same. Not all group variances are the same.
- **The Levene's test procedure:**
  - For each observation in each group, obtain the absolute value of the difference between each observation and the median of the group.
  - Carry out a one-way analysis of variance on these absolute differences.

# SOLUTIONS TO END OF SECTION AND CHAPTER REVIEW EVEN PROBLEMS

10.2 $H_0$: $\mu_1 = \mu_2$ $H_1$: $\mu_1 \neq \mu_2$

Decision rule: If $Z < -2.58$ or $Z > 2.58$, reject $H_0$.

$$\text{Test statistic: } Z = \frac{(\bar{X}_1 - \bar{X}_2) - (\mu_1 - \mu_2)}{\sqrt{\frac{\sigma_1^2}{n_1} + \frac{\sigma_2^2}{n_2}}} = \frac{(72-66)-0}{\sqrt{\frac{20^2}{40} + \frac{10^2}{50}}} = 1.73$$

Decision: Since $Z_{\text{calc}} = 1.73$ is between the critical bounds of $Z = \pm 2.58$, do not reject $H_0$. There is inadequate evidence to conclude the two population means are different.

10.4 (a)

$$S_p^2 = \frac{(n_1-1)\cdot S_1^2 + (n_2-1)\cdot S_2^2}{(n_1-1)+(n_2-1)} = \frac{(7)\cdot 4^2 + (14)\cdot 5^2}{7+14} = 22$$

$$t = \frac{(\bar{X}_1 - \bar{X}_2) - (\mu_1 - \mu_2)}{\sqrt{S_p^2\left(\frac{1}{n_1} + \frac{1}{n_2}\right)}} = \frac{(42-34)-0}{\sqrt{22\left(\frac{1}{8} + \frac{1}{15}\right)}} = 3.8959$$

(b) $d.f. = (n_1 - 1) + (n_2 - 1) = 7 + 14 = 21$

(c) Decision rule: $d.f. = 21$. If $t > 2.5177$, reject $H_0$.

(d) Decision: Since $t_{\text{calc}} = 3.8959$ is greater than the critical bound of $t = 2.5177$, reject $H_0$. There is enough evidence to conclude that the first population mean is larger than the second population mean.

10.6

$$(\bar{X}_1 - \bar{X}_2) \pm t\sqrt{S_p^2\left(\frac{1}{n_1} + \frac{1}{n_2}\right)} = (42-34) \pm 2.0796\sqrt{22\left(\frac{1}{8} + \frac{1}{15}\right)}$$

$$3.7296 \le \mu_1 - \mu_2 \le 12.2704$$

10.8 (a) $H_0$: $\mu_1 \le \mu_2$ where Populations: 1 = new machine, 2 = old machine

The mean breaking strength of parts produced by the new machine is not greater than the mean breaking strength of parts produced by the old machine.

$H_1$: $\mu_1 > \mu_2$

The mean breaking strength of parts produced by the new machine is greater than the mean breaking strength of parts produced by the old machine.

Decision rule: If $Z > 2.33$, reject $H_0$.

$$\text{Test statistic: } Z = \frac{(\bar{X}_1 - \bar{X}_2) - (\mu_1 - \mu_2)}{\sqrt{\frac{\sigma_1^2}{n_1} + \frac{\sigma_2^2}{n_2}}} = \frac{(72-65)-0}{\sqrt{\frac{9^2}{100} + \frac{10^2}{100}}} = 5.20$$

Decision: Since $Z_{\text{calc}} = 5.20$ is greater than the critical bound of 2.33, reject $H_0$. There is enough evidence to conclude that the mean breaking strength of parts produced by the new machine is greater than the mean breaking strength of parts produced by the old machine.

(b) $p$-value = virtually zero. The probability of obtaining samples whose means differ by 7 or more units of strength when the null hypothesis is true is virtually zero.

10.10 $H_0$: $\mu_1 = \mu_2$ $H_1$: $\mu_1 \neq \mu_2$

(a) **Age 8:**

PHStat output:

| Data | |
|---|---|
| **Hypothesized Difference** | **0** |
| **Level of Significance** | **0.05** |
| **Population 1 Sample** | |
| **Sample Size** | **27** |
| **Sample Mean** | **0.89** |
| **Sample Standard Deviation** | **0.98** |
| **Population 2 Sample** | |
| **Sample Size** | **22** |
| **Sample Mean** | **0.86** |
| **Sample Standard Deviation** | **1.07** |
| | |
| Intermediate Calculations | |
| Population 1 Sample Degrees of Freedom | 26 |
| Population 2 Sample Degrees of Freedom | 21 |
| Total Degrees of Freedom | 47 |
| Pooled Variance | 1.042836 |
| Difference in Sample Means | 0.03 |
| *t*-Test Statistic | 0.102284 |
| | |
| **Two-Tailed Test** | |
| **Lower Critical Value** | **-2.01174** |
| **Upper Critical Value** | **2.011739** |
| ***p*-Value** | **0.918966** |
| **Do not reject the null hypothesis** | |

Test statistic: $t = \dfrac{(\bar{X}_1 - \bar{X}_2) - (\mu_1 - \mu_2)}{\sqrt{\dfrac{S_1^2}{n_1} + \dfrac{S_2^2}{n_2}}} = 0.1023$

Decision: Since $t_{calc} = 0.1023$ is between the critical bounds of $\pm$ 2.0117, do not reject $H_0$. There is no evidence of a difference in two means for the Age 8 group.

10.10 (a) cont.

**Age 12:**

PHStat output:

| Data | |
|---|---|
| **Hypothesized Difference** | **0** |
| **Level of Significance** | **0.05** |
| **Population 1 Sample** | |
| **Sample Size** | **39** |
| **Sample Mean** | **0.88** |
| **Sample Standard Deviation** | **1.01** |
| **Population 2 Sample** | |
| **Sample Size** | **41** |
| **Sample Mean** | **0.09** |
| **Sample Standard Deviation** | **1.08** |
| | |
| Intermediate Calculations | |
| Population 1 Sample Degrees of Freedom | 38 |
| Population 2 Sample Degrees of Freedom | 40 |
| Total Degrees of Freedom | 78 |
| Pooled Variance | 1.095126 |
| Difference in Sample Means | 0.79 |
| *t*-Test Statistic | 3.375004 |
| | |
| **Two-Tailed Test** | |
| **Lower Critical Value** | **-1.99085** |
| **Upper Critical Value** | **1.990848** |
| ***p*-Value** | **0.001153** |
| **Reject the null hypothesis** | |

Test statistic: $t = \dfrac{(\bar{X}_1 - \bar{X}_2) - (\mu_1 - \mu_2)}{\sqrt{\dfrac{S_1^2}{n_1} + \dfrac{S_2^2}{n_2}}} = 3.375$

Decision: Since $t_{calc} = 3.375$ is greater than the upper critical bounds of 1.9908, reject $H_0$. There is evidence of a difference in two means for the Age 12 group.

10.10 (a) cont.

**Age 16:**

PHStat output:

| Data | |
|---|---|
| **Hypothesized Difference** | **0** |
| **Level of Significance** | **0.05** |
| **Population 1 Sample** | |
| **Sample Size** | **35** |
| **Sample Mean** | **0.41** |
| **Sample Standard Deviation** | **0.81** |
| **Population 2 Sample** | |
| **Sample Size** | **33** |
| **Sample Mean** | **-0.29** |
| **Sample Standard Deviation** | **0.92** |
| | |
| Intermediate Calculations | |
| Population 1 Sample Degrees of Freedom | 34 |
| Population 2 Sample Degrees of Freedom | 32 |
| Total Degrees of Freedom | 66 |
| Pooled Variance | 0.748367 |
| Difference in Sample Means | 0.7 |
| *t*-Test Statistic | 3.334858 |
| | |
| **Two-Tailed Test** | |
| **Lower Critical Value** | **-1.99656** |
| **Upper Critical Value** | **1.996564** |
| ***p*-Value** | **0.001403** |
| **Reject the null hypothesis** | |

Decision: Since $t_{calc} = 3.3349$ is greater than the upper critical bounds of 1.9966, reject $H_0$. There is evidence of a difference in two means for the Age 16 group.

(b) The test results show that children in the United States begin to develop preferences for brand name products as early as Age 12.

10.12 (a) $H_0$: $\mu_1 = \mu_2$ where Populations: 1 = Males, 2 = Females

Mean computer anxiety experienced by males and females is the same.

$H_1$: $\mu_1 \neq \mu_2$

Mean computer anxiety experienced by males and females is different.

Decision rule: $d.f. = 170$. If $t < -1.974$ or $t > 1.974$, reject $H_0$.

Test statistic:

$$S_p^{\,2} = \frac{(n_1 - 1)\cdot S_1^{\,2} + (n_2 - 1)\cdot S_2^{\,2}}{(n_1 - 1) + (n_2 - 1)} = \frac{(99)\cdot 13.35^2 + (71)\cdot 9.42^2}{99 + 71} = 140.8489$$

$$t = \frac{(\bar{X}_1 - \bar{X}_2) - (\mu_1 - \mu_2)}{\sqrt{S_p^{\,2}\left(\frac{1}{n_1} + \frac{1}{n_2}\right)}} = \frac{(40.26 - 36.85) - 0}{\sqrt{140.8489\left(\frac{1}{100} + \frac{1}{72}\right)}} = 1.859$$

Decision: Since $t_{calc} = 1.859$ is between the lower and upper critical bound of $-1.974$ and 1.974, do not reject $H_0$. There is not enough evidence to conclude that the mean computer anxiety experienced by males and females is different.

(b) Using PHStat, the $p$-value = 0.0648. The probability of obtaining a sample that yields a $t$ test statistic less than $-1.859$ or greater than 1.859 is 0.0648 if the mean computer anxiety experienced by males and females is the same.

(c) In order to use the pooled-variance $t$ test, you need to assume that the populations are normally distributed with equal variances.

10.14 (a) $H_0 : \mu_1 = \mu_2$ Mean waiting times of Bank 1 and Bank 2 are the same.

$H_1 : \mu_1 \neq \mu_2$ Mean waiting times of Bank 1 and Bank 2 are different.

PHStat output:

| t Test for Differences in Two Means | |
|---|---|
| **Data** | |
| Hypothesized Difference | 0 |
| Level of Significance | 0.05 |
| **Population 1 Sample** | |
| Sample Size | 15 |
| Sample Mean | 4.286667 |
| Sample Standard Deviation | 1.637985 |
| **Population 2 Sample** | |
| Sample Size | 15 |
| Sample Mean | 7.114667 |
| Sample Standard Deviation | 2.082189 |
| Intermediate Calculations | |
| Population 1 Sample Degrees of Freedom | 14 |
| Population 2 Sample Degrees of Freedom | 14 |
| Total Degrees of Freedom | 28 |
| Pooled Variance | 3.509254 |
| Difference in Sample Means | -2.828 |
| $t$-Test Statistic | -4.13431 |
| **Two-Tailed Test** | |
| Lower Critical Value | -2.04841 |
| Upper Critical Value | 2.048409 |
| $p$-Value | 0.000293 |
| Reject the null hypothesis | |

10.14 cont.

(a) Since the $p$-value of 0.000293 is less than the 5% level of significance, reject the null hypothesis. There is enough evidence to conclude that the mean waiting time is different in the two banks.

(b) $p$-value = 0.000293. The probability of obtaining a sample that will yield a $t$ test statistic more extreme than –4.13431 is 0.000293 if, in fact, the mean waiting times of Bank 1 and Bank 2 are the same.

(c) We need to assume that the two populations are normally distributed.

(d) $$\left(\bar{X}_1 - \bar{X}_2\right) \pm t\sqrt{S_p^2\left(\frac{1}{n_1}+\frac{1}{n_2}\right)} = (4.2867 - 7.1147) \pm 2.0484\sqrt{3.5093\left(\frac{1}{15}+\frac{1}{15}\right)}$$

$$-4.2292 \le \mu_1 - \mu_2 \le -1.4268$$

You are 95% confident that the difference in mean waiting time between Bank 1 and Bank 2 is between –4.2292 and –1.4268 minutes.

10.16 (a) $H_0 : \mu_1 = \mu_2$ Mean times to clear problems at Office I and Office II are the same.

$H_1 : \mu_1 \neq \mu_2$ Mean times to clear problems at Office I and Office II are different.

PHStat output:

| t Test for Differences in Two Means | |
|---|---|
| Data | |
| Hypothesized Difference | 0 |
| Level of Significance | 0.05 |
| Population 1 Sample | |
| Sample Size | 20 |
| Sample Mean | 2.214 |
| Sample Standard Deviation | 1.718039 |
| Population 2 Sample | |
| Sample Size | 20 |
| Sample Mean | 2.0115 |
| Sample Standard Deviation | 1.891706 |
| Two-Tailed Test | |
| Lower Critical Value | -2.02439 |
| Upper Critical Value | 2.024394 |
| p-Value | 0.725009 |
| Do not reject the null hypothesis | |

Since the $p$-value of 0.725 is greater than the 5% level of significance, do not reject the null hypothesis. There is not enough evidence to conclude that the mean time to clear problems in the two offices is different.

(b) $p$-value = 0.725. The probability of obtaining a sample that will yield a $t$ test statistic more extreme than 0.3544 is 0.725 if, in fact, the mean waiting times between Office 1 and Office 2 are the same.

(c) We need to assume that the two populations are normally distributed.

(d) $$\left(\bar{X}_1 - \bar{X}_2\right) \pm t\sqrt{S_p^2\left(\frac{1}{n_1}+\frac{1}{n_2}\right)} = (2.214 - 2.0115) \pm 2.0244\sqrt{3.2651\left(\frac{1}{20}+\frac{1}{20}\right)}$$

$$-0.9543 \le \mu_1 - \mu_2 \le 1.3593$$

You are 95% confident that the difference between the population means in the two offices is between –0.9543 and 1.3593 minutes.

10.18 (a) $H_0$: $\mu_1 = \mu_2$ $H_1$: $\mu_1 \neq \mu_2$

Excel output:

t-Test: Two-Sample Assuming Equal variances

| | *Untreated* | *Treated* |
|---|---|---|
| Mean | 165.0948 | 155.7314 |
| Variance | 41.6934168 | 62.4141 |
| Observations | 20 | 20 |
| Pooled Variance | 52.05375826 | |
| Hypothesized Mean Difference | 0 | |
| df | 38 | |
| t Stat | 4.104023608 | |
| P(T<=t) one-tail | 0.000103572 | |
| t Critical one-tail | 1.685953066 | |
| P(T<=t) two-tail | 0.000207144 | |
| t Critical two-tail | 2.024394234 | |

Decision: Since $t_{\text{calc}} = 4.104$ is greater than the upper critical bound of 2.024, reject $H_0$. There is evidence that the mean surface hardness of untreated steel plates is different than the mean surface hardness of treated steel plates.

(b) $p$-value = 0.0002. The probability of obtaining two samples with a mean difference of 9.3634 or more is 0.02% if there is evidence that the mean surface hardness of untreated steel plates is different than the mean surface hardness of treated steel plates.

(c) Since both sample sizes are smaller than 30, you need to assume that the populations of hardness of both untreated and treated steel plates are normally distributed.

(d)

$$\left(\bar{X}_1 - \bar{X}_2\right) + t\sqrt{S_p^2\left(\frac{1}{n_1} + \frac{1}{n_2}\right)}$$

$$= \left(165.0948 - 155.7314\right) + 2.0244\sqrt{52.0538\left(\frac{1}{20} + \frac{1}{20}\right)}$$

$$4.7447 \le \mu_1 - \mu_2 \le 13.9821$$

You are 95% confident that the difference in the mean surface hardness between untreated and treated steel plates is between 4.7447 and 13.9821.

10.20 (a) $H_0$: $\mu_1 = \mu_2$ where Populations: 1 = computer-assisted, individual based; 2 = team-based

Mean assembly times in seconds are the same between employees trained in a computer-assisted, individual-based program and those trained in a team-based program.

$H_1$: $\mu_1 \neq \mu_2$

Mean assembly times in seconds are different between employees trained in a computer-assisted, individual-based program and those trained in a team-based program.

Decision rule: $d.f. = 40$. If $t < -2.0211$ or $t > 2.0211$, reject $H_0$.

Test statistic:

$$S_p^2 = \frac{(n_1-1)\cdot S_1^2 + (n_2-1)\cdot S_2^2}{(n_1-1)+(n_2-1)} = \frac{(20)\cdot 1.9333^2 + (20)\cdot 4.5767^2}{20+20} = 12.3417$$

$$t = \frac{(\bar{X}_1 - \bar{X}_2) - (\mu_1 - \mu_2)}{\sqrt{S_p^2\left(\frac{1}{n_1}+\frac{1}{n_2}\right)}} = \frac{(17.5571 - 19.8905) - 0}{\sqrt{12.3417\left(\frac{1}{21}+\frac{1}{21}\right)}} = -2.1522$$

Decision: Since $t_{\text{calc}} = -2.1522$ is below the lower critical bound of $-2.0211$, reject $H_0$. There is enough evidence to conclude that the mean assembly times in seconds are different between employees trained in a computer-assisted, individual-based program and those trained in a team-based program.

(b) You must assume that each of the two independent populations is normally distributed.

(c) (a) $H_0$: $\mu_1 = \mu_2$ where Populations: 1 = computer-assisted, individual based; 2 = team-based

Mean assembly times in seconds are the same between employees trained in a computer-assisted, individual-based program and those trained in a team-based program.

$H_1$: $\mu_1 \neq \mu_2$

Mean assembly times in seconds are different between employees trained in a computer-assisted, individual-based program and those trained in a team-based program.

Decision rule: $d.f. = 26$. If $p$-value $< 0.05$, reject $H_0$.

Excel output:

t-Test: Two-Sample Assuming Unequal Variances

| | *Computer-Assisted Program* | *Team-based Program* |
|---|---|---|
| Mean | 17.55714286 | 19.89047619 |
| Variance | 3.737571429 | 20.94590476 |
| Observations | 21 | 21 |
| Hypothesized Mean Difference | 0 | |
| df | 27 | |
| t Stat | -2.152203195 | |
| P(T<=t) one-tail | 0.020240852 | |
| t Critical one-tail | 1.703288035 | |
| P(T<=t) two-tail | 0.040481703 | |
| t Critical two-tail | 2.051829142 | |

10.20 cont. (c) (a) Since $p$-value = 0.041 < 0.05, reject $H_0$. There is enough evidence to conclude that the mean assembly times in seconds are different between employees trained in a computer-assisted, individual-based program and those trained in a team-based program.

(d) The results in (a) and (c) are the same.

(e) Assuming equal variances:

$$\left(\bar{X}_1 - \bar{X}_2\right) + t\sqrt{S_p^2\left(\frac{1}{n_1}+\frac{1}{n_2}\right)} = (17.557 - 19.891) + 2.0211\sqrt{12.3417\left(\frac{1}{21}+\frac{1}{21}\right)}$$

$$-4.52 \le \mu_1 - \mu_2 \le -0.14$$

You are 95% confident that the difference between the population means of the two training methods is between –4.52 and –0.14.

10.22 $d.f. = n - 1 = 20 - 1 = 19$, where $n$ = number of pairs of data

10.24 (a) Define the difference in hotel rates as the rate in March 2004 minus the rate in June 2002.

$H_0: \mu_D = 0$ vs. $H_1: \mu_D \neq 0$

Excel output:

t-Test: Paired Two Sample for Means

| | *Hotel 2004* | *Hotel 2002* |
|---|---|---|
| Mean | 102.0394444 | 180.7222 |
| Variance | 718.6064173 | 2473.271 |
| Observations | 18 | 18 |
| Pearson Correlation | 0.310844429 | |
| Hypothesized Mean Difference | 0 | |
| df | 17 | |
| t Stat | -6.867169607 | |
| P(T<=t) one-tail | 1.36589E-06 | |
| t Critical one-tail | 1.739606432 | |
| P(T<=t) two-tail | 2.73178E-06 | |
| t Critical two-tail | 2.109818524 | |

Test statistic: $t = \dfrac{\bar{D} - \mu_D}{\dfrac{S_D}{\sqrt{n}}} = -6.8672$

Decision: Since $t = -6.8672$ is less than the lower critical value of –2.1098, reject $H_0$. There is enough evidence to conclude that there is a difference in the mean daily hotel rates in June 2002 and March 2004.

(b) You must assume that the distribution of the differences between the daily hotel rate in June 2002 and March 2004 is approximately normal.

(c) $p$-value is virtually zero. The probability of obtaining a mean difference in daily hotel rates that gives rise to a test statistic that deviates from 0 by 6.8672 or more in either direction is virtually zero if there is no difference in the mean daily hotel rate in June 2002 and March 2004.

10.24 (d) $\bar{D} \pm t\frac{S_D}{\sqrt{n}} = -78.68 \pm 2.1098\frac{48.6114}{\sqrt{18}}$ $-102.86 \le \mu_D \le -54.51$

cont. You are 95% confident that the mean difference in hotel rate between March 2004 and June 2002 is somewhere between –\$102.86 and –\$54.51.

10.26 (a) $H_0$: $\mu_D = 0$ There is no difference in the mean price of textbooks between the local bookstore and Amazon.com.

$H_1$: $\mu_D \ne 0$ There is a difference in the mean price of textbooks between the local bookstore and Amazon.com.

Decision rule: *d.f.* = 14. If $t < -2.9768$ or $t > 2.9768$, reject $H_0$.

Test statistic: $t = \frac{\bar{D} - \mu_{\bar{D}}}{S_{\bar{D}} / \sqrt{n}} = \frac{3.5307 - 0}{13.8493 / \sqrt{15}} = 0.9874$

Decision: Since $t_{calc} = 0.9874$ is between the critical bounds of $-2.9768$ and 2.9768, do not reject $H_0$. There is not enough evidence to conclude that there is a difference in the mean price of textbooks between the local bookstore and Amazon.com.

(b) You must assume that the distribution of the differences between the mean price of textbooks between on-campus and off-campus stores is approximately normal.

(c) $\bar{D} \pm t\frac{S_D}{\sqrt{n}} = 3.5307 \pm 2.9768\frac{13.8493}{\sqrt{15}}$ $-7.1141 \le \mu_D \le 14.1755$

You are 99% confident that the mean difference between the prices is between –7.1141 and 14.1755.

(d) The results in (a) and (c) are the same. The hypothesized value of 0 for the difference in the mean price of textbooks between the local bookstore and Amazon.com is inside the 99% confidence interval.

10.28 (a) Define the difference in bone marrow microvessel density as the density before the transplant minus the density after the transplant and assume that the difference in density is normally distributed.

$$H_0: \mu_D \le 0 \quad \text{vs.} \quad H_1: \mu_D > 0$$

Excel output:

t-Test: Paired Two Sample for Means

| | *Before* | *After* |
|---|---|---|
| Mean | 312.1429 | 226 |
| Variance | 15513.14 | 4971 |
| Observations | 7 | 7 |
| Pearson Correlation | 0.295069 | |
| Hypothesized Mean Difference | 0 | |
| df | 6 | |
| t Stat | 1.842455 | |
| P(T<=t) one-tail | 0.057493 | |
| t Critical one-tail | 1.943181 | |
| P(T<=t) two-tail | 0.114986 | |
| t Critical two-tail | 2.446914 | |

10.28 (a) Test statistic: $t = \dfrac{\bar{D} - \mu_D}{\dfrac{S_D}{\sqrt{n}}} = 1.8425$

cont. Decision: Since $t = 1.8425$ is less than the critical value of 1.943, do not reject $H_0$. There is not enough evidence to conclude that the mean bone marrow microvessel density is higher before the stem cell transplant than after the stem cell transplant.

(b) $p$-value = 0.0575. The probability of obtaining a mean difference in density that gives rise to a test statistic that deviates from 0 by 1.8425 or more is 5.75% if the mean density is not higher before the stem cell transplant than after the stem cell transplant.

(c) $\bar{D} \pm t\dfrac{S_D}{\sqrt{n}} = 86.1429 \pm 2.4469\dfrac{123.7005}{\sqrt{7}}$ $\quad -28.26 \le \mu_D \le 200.55$

You are 95% confident that the mean difference in bone marrow microvessel density before and after the stem cell transplant is somewhere between -28.26 and 200.55.

10.30 (a) $H_0$: $\mu_D \ge 0$ vs. $H_1$: $\mu_D < 0$

Decision rule: $d.f. = 39$. If $t < -2.4258$, reject $H_0$.

Test statistic: $t = \dfrac{\bar{D} - \mu_{\bar{D}}}{S_{\bar{D}}/\sqrt{n}} = -9.372$

Decision: Since $t_{calc} = -9.372$ is less than the critical bound of -2.4258, reject $H_0$. There is enough evidence to conclude that the mean strength is less at two days than at seven days.

(b) You must assume that the distribution of the differences between the mean strength of the concrete is approximately normal.

(c) $p$-value is virtually 0. The probability of obtaining a mean difference that gives rise to a test statistic that is -9.372 or less when the null hypothesis is true is virtually 0.

10.32 (a) $p_1 = \dfrac{X_1}{n_1} = \dfrac{45}{100} = 0.45,\ p_2 = \dfrac{X_2}{n_2} = \dfrac{25}{50} = 0.50,$

and $\bar{p} = \dfrac{X_1 + X_2}{n_1 + n_2} = \dfrac{45 + 25}{100 + 50} = 0.467$

$H_0$: $\pi_1 = \pi_2$ vs. $H_1$: $\pi_1 \ne \pi_2$

Decision rule: If $Z < -2.58$ or $Z > 2.58$, reject $H_0$.

Test statistic: $Z = \dfrac{(p_1 - p_2) - (\pi_1 - \pi_2)}{\sqrt{\bar{p}\cdot(1-\bar{p})\left(\dfrac{1}{n_1} + \dfrac{1}{n_2}\right)}} = \dfrac{(0.45 - 0.50) - 0}{\sqrt{0.467\cdot 0.533\left(\dfrac{1}{100} + \dfrac{1}{50}\right)}} = -0.58$

Decision: Since $Z_{calc} = -0.58$ is between the critical bound of $Z = \pm 2.58$, do not reject $H_0$. There is insufficient evidence to conclude that the two population proportions differ.

(b) $(p_1 - p_2) \pm Z\sqrt{\left(\dfrac{p_1(1-p_1)}{n_1} + \dfrac{p_2(1-p_2)}{n_2}\right)} = -0.05 \pm 2.5758\sqrt{\left(\dfrac{.45(.55)}{100} + \dfrac{.5(.5)}{50}\right)}$

$-0.2727 \le \pi_1 - \pi_2 \le 0.1727$

10.34 (a) $H_0$: $\pi_1 = \pi_2$ $H_1$: $\pi_1 \neq \pi_2$ where Populations: 1 = ages 2 to 7, 2 = ages 8 to 18

Decision rule: If $Z < -1.96$ or $Z > 1.96$, reject $H_0$.

Test statistic:

$$Z = \frac{(p_1 - p_2) - (\pi_1 - \pi_2)}{\sqrt{\bar{p}\cdot(1-\bar{p})\left(\frac{1}{n_1}+\frac{1}{n_2}\right)}} = \frac{(0.2596 - 0.5099) - 0}{\sqrt{0.4235\cdot(1-0.4235)\left(\frac{1}{1090}+\frac{1}{2065}\right)}} = -13.53$$

Decision: Since $Z_{calc} = -13.53$ is less than the lower critical bound of $Z = -1.96$, reject $H_0$. There is sufficient evidence to conclude that a significant difference exists in the proportion of children between the ages of 2 and 7, and between the age of 8 and 18 who use a computer each day.

(b) $p$-value is virtually 0. The probability of obtaining a difference in two sample proportions of $-0.2503$ or more is virtually 0 when the null hypothesis is true.

(c) $(p_1 - p_2) \pm Z\sqrt{\left(\frac{p_1(1-p_1)}{n_1} + \frac{p_2(1-p_2)}{n_2}\right)}$ $\qquad -0.2841 \le \pi_1 - \pi_2 \le -0.2165$

You are 95% confident that the difference between the population proportion of 2- to 7-year-old children and 8- to 18-year-old children who use a computer each day is between $-0.2841$ and $-0.2165$.

10.36 (a) $H_0$: $\pi_1 \ge \pi_2$ $H_1$: $\pi_1 < \pi_2$ where Populations: 1 = 2002, 2 = 2003

Decision rule: If $Z < -1.645$, reject $H_0$.

Test statistic:

$$Z = \frac{(p_1 - p_2) - (\pi_1 - \pi_2)}{\sqrt{\bar{p}\cdot(1-\bar{p})\left(\frac{1}{n_1}+\frac{1}{n_2}\right)}} = \frac{(0.25 - 0.4102) - 0}{\sqrt{0.3450\cdot(1-0.3450)\left(\frac{1}{500}+\frac{1}{729}\right)}} = -5.8019$$

Decision: Since $Z_{calc} = -5.8019$ is less than the critical bound of $-1.645$, reject $H_0$. There is sufficient evidence to conclude that the proportion of adults online who use the Internet to gather data about products/services was higher in December 2003 than in 2000.

(b) Using Excel, the $p$-value is virtually zero. The probability of obtaining a difference in two sample proportions of $-0.16$ or smaller is virtually zero when the null hypothesis is true.

10.38 (a) $H_0$: $\pi_1 \le \pi_2$ $H_1$: $\pi_1 > \pi_2$ Population 1 = white workers, 2 = black workers

Decision rule: If $Z > 1.645$, reject $H_0$.

Test statistic:

$$\bar{p} = \frac{X_1 + X_2}{n_1 + n_2} = \frac{29+126}{56+407} = 0.3348$$

$$Z = \frac{(p_1 - p_2) - (\pi_1 - \pi_2)}{\sqrt{\bar{p}\cdot(1-\bar{p})\left(\frac{1}{n_1}+\frac{1}{n_2}\right)}} = \frac{(0.5179 - 0.3096) - 0}{\sqrt{0.3348\cdot(1-0.3348)\left(\frac{1}{56}+\frac{1}{407}\right)}} = 3.0965$$

Decision: Since $Z_{calc} = 3.0965$ is greater than the critical bound of 1.645, reject $H_0$. There is sufficient evidence to conclude that white workers are more likely to claim bias than black workers.

(b) Using Excel, the $p$-value is 0.00098. The probability of obtaining a difference in two sample proportions of 0.20828 or larger is 0.00098 when the null hypothesis is true.

10.40 (a) $F_U = 2.20$, $F_L = \frac{1}{2.33} = 0.43$

(b) $F_U = 2.57$, $F_L = \frac{1}{2.76} = 0.36$

(c) $F_U = 3.09$, $F_L = \frac{1}{3.37} = 0.30$

(d) $F_U = 3.50$, $F_L = \frac{1}{3.88} = 0.26$

10.42 (a) $F_L = \frac{1}{2.33} = 0.429$

(b) $F_L = \frac{1}{2.76} = 0.362$

(c) $F_L = \frac{1}{3.37} = 0.297$

(d) $F_L = \frac{1}{3.88} = 0.258$

10.44 The degrees of freedom for the numerator is 24 and for the denominator is 24.

10.46 Since $F_{calc} = 0.826$ is between the critical bounds of $F_L = 0.441$ and $F_U = 2.27$, do not reject $H_0$. There is not enough evidence to conclude that the two population variances are different.

10.48 (a) $H_0$: $\sigma_1^2 = \sigma_2^2$ The population variances are the same.

$H_1$: $\sigma_1^2 \ne \sigma_2^2$ The population variances are different.

Decision rule: If $F > 3.18$ or $F < 0.3378$, reject $H_0$.

Test statistic: $F = \frac{S_1^2}{S_2^2} = \frac{47.3}{36.4} = 1.2995$

Decision: Since $F_{calc} = 1.2995$ is between the critical bounds of $F_U = 3.18$ and $F_L = 0.3378$, do not reject $H_0$. There is not enough evidence to conclude that the two population variances are different.

10.48 cont. (b) $H_0$: $\sigma_1^2 \le \sigma_2^2$ The variance for population 1 is less than or equal to the variance for population 2.
$H_1$: $\sigma_1^2 > \sigma_2^2$ The variance for population 1 is greater than the variance for population 2.
Decision rule: If $F > 2.62$, reject $H_0$.

Test statistic: $F = \frac{S_1^2}{S_2^2} = \frac{47.3}{36.4} = 1.2995$

Decision: Since $F_{calc} = 1.2995$ is less than the critical bound of $F_U = 2.62$, do not reject $H_0$. There is not enough evidence to conclude that the variance for population 1 is greater than the variance for population 2.

(c) $H_0$: $\sigma_1^2 \ge \sigma_2^2$ The variance for population 1 is greater than or equal to the variance for population 2.
$H_1$: $\sigma_1^2 < \sigma_2^2$ The variance for population 1 is less than the variance for population 2.
Decision rule: If $F < 0.4032$, reject $H_0$.

Test statistic: $F = \frac{S_1^2}{S_2^2} = \frac{47.3}{36.4} = 1.2995$

Decision: Since $F_{calc} = 1.2995$ is greater than the critical bound of $F_L = 0.4032$, do not reject $H_0$. There is not enough evidence to conclude that the variance for population 1 is less than the variance for population 2.

10.50 (a) $H_0$: $\sigma_1^2 = \sigma_2^2$ The population variances are the same.
$H_1$: $\sigma_1^2 \ne \sigma_2^2$ The population variances are different.
Decision rule: If $F < 0.653$ or $F > 1.556$, reject $H_0$.

Test statistic: $F = \frac{S_1^2}{S_2^2} = \frac{13.35^2}{9.42^2} = 2.008$

Decision: Since $F_{calc} = 2.008$ is greater than $F_U = 1.556$, reject $H_0$. There is enough evidence to conclude that the two population variances are different.

(b) $p$-value = 0.0022. The probability of obtaining a sample that yields a test statistic more extreme than 2.008 is 0.0022 if the null hypothesis that there is no difference in the two population variances is true.

(c) The test assumes that the two populations are both normally distributed.

(d) Based on (a) and (b), a separate-variance $t$ test should be used.

10.52 (a) $H_0$: $\sigma_1^2 = \sigma_2^2$ The population variances are the same.
$H_1$: $\sigma_1^2 \ne \sigma_2^2$ The population variances are different.
Decision rule: If $F < 0.3958$ or $F > 2.5264$, reject $H_0$.

Test statistic: $F = \frac{S_1^2}{S_2^2} = \frac{1.718^2}{1.8917^2} = 0.8248$

Decision: Since $F_{calc} = 0.8248$ is between $F_L = 0.3958$ and $F_U = 2.5264$, do not reject $H_0$. There is not enough evidence to conclude that the two population variances are different.

(b) $p$-value = 0.6789. The probability of obtaining a sample that yields a test statistic more extreme than 0.8248 is 0.6789 if the null hypothesis that there is no difference in the two population variances is true.

10.52 cont. (c) The test assumes that the two populations are both normally distributed.

Normal Probability Plot (Office I)

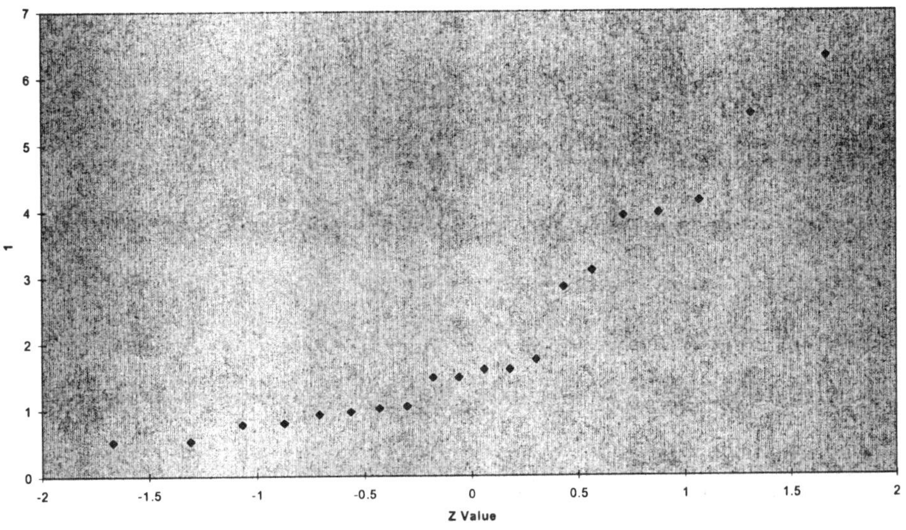


Normal Probability Plot (Office II)

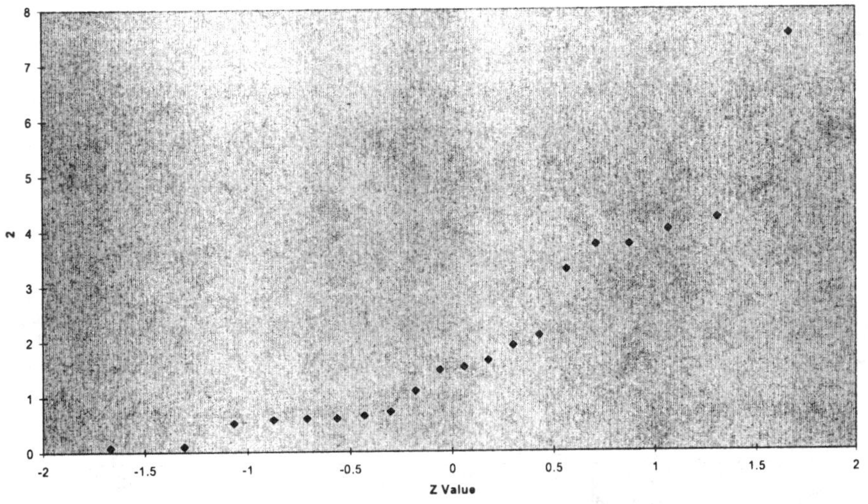


Both the normal probability plots and the box-and-whisker plots suggest that the time to clear problems in both offices does not appear to be normally distributed. Hence, the $F$ test for the difference in variances, which is sensitive to departure from the normality assumption, should not be used to test the equality of two variances. The box-and-whisker plot and the summary statistics suggest that the two samples appear to have about the same amount of dispersion with the exception of a somewhat larger range in Office I. Since the pooled-variance $t$ test is robust to departure from the normality assumption, it can be used to test for the difference in the means.

(d) Based on the results of (a), it is appropriate to use the pooled-variance $t$-test to compare the means of the two offices.

10.54 $H_0$: $\sigma_1^2 \le \sigma_2^2$ where Populations: 1 = Line A 2 = Line B
$H_1$: $\sigma_1^2 > \sigma_2^2$
Decision rule: If $F > 2.5437$, reject $H_0$.
Test statistic: $F = \frac{S_1^2}{S_2^2} = \frac{0.012^2}{0.005^2} = 5.76$
Decision: Since $F_{calc} = 5.76$ is above the critical bound of $F_U = 2.5437$, reject $H_0$. There is enough evidence to conclude that the variance in Line A is larger than the variance in Line B.

10.56 (a) $SSW = SST - SSA = 210 - 60 = 150$
(b) $MSA = \frac{SSA}{c-1} = \frac{60}{5-1} = 15$
(c) $MSW = \frac{SSW}{n-c} = \frac{150}{35-5} = 5$
(d) $F = \frac{MSA}{MSW} = \frac{15}{5} = 3$

10.58 (a) $df\,A = c - 1 = 3 - 1 = 2$
(b) $df\,W = n - c = 21 - 3 = 18$
(c) $df\,T = n - 1 = 21 - 1 = 20$

10.60 (a) Decision rule: If $F > 2.95$, reject $H_0$.
(b) Since $F_{cal} = 4$ is greater than the critical bound of 2.95, reject $H_0$.
(c) There are $c = 4$ degrees of freedom in the numerator and $n - c = 32 - 4 = 28$ degrees of freedom in the denominator. The table does not have 28 degrees of freedom in the denominator so use the next larger critical value, $Q_U = 3.90$.
(d) To perform the Tukey-Kramer procedure, the critical range is

$$Q_U\sqrt{\frac{MSW}{2}\left(\frac{1}{n_j}+\frac{1}{n_{j'}}\right)} = 3.90\sqrt{\frac{20}{2}\left(\frac{1}{8}+\frac{1}{8}\right)} = 6.166.$$

10.62 (a) $H_0: \mu_1 = \mu_2 = \mu_3$ where 1 = Experts, 2 = Readers, 3 = Darts
$H_1$: Not all $\mu_j$ are equal where $j$ = 1, 2, 3
Decision Rule: If $p$-value < 0.05, reject $H_0$.

| | Sum of Squares | df | Mean Square | F | *p*-value |
|---|---|---|---|---|---|
| Between Groups | 9195.435 | 2 | 4597.718 | 10.994 | .004 |
| Within Groups | 3763.928 | 9 | 418.214 | | |
| Total | 12959.363 | 11 | | | |

Since $p$-value = 0.004 < 0.05, reject the null hypothesis. There is enough evidence to conclude that there is a significant difference in the mean returns for the three categories.

10.62 cont. (b) To determine which of the means are significantly different from one another, you use the Tukey-Kramer procedure to establish the critical range: $Q_{U(c,\, n-c)} = Q_{U(3,\, 9)} =$ 3.95

| Tukey Kramer Multiple Comparisons | | | | | | | | |
|---|---|---|---|---|---|---|---|---|
| | Sample | Sample | | | Absolute | Std. Error | Critical | |
| Group | Mean | Size | | Comparison | Difference | of Difference | Range | |
| 1 | 6.475 | 4 | | Group 1 to Group 2 | 48.975 | 10.2251 | 40.389 | **Means are different** |
| 2 | -42.5 | 4 | | Group 1 to Group 3 | 16.125 | 10.2251 | 40.389 | **Means are not different** |
| 3 | 22.6 | 4 | | Group 2 to Group 3 | 65.1 | 10.2251 | 40.389 | **Means are different** |
| Other Data | | | | | | | | |
| Level of significance | 0.05 | | | Denominator d.f. | 9 | | | |
| Numerator d.f. | 3 | | | MSW | 418.214 | | | |
| Denominator d.f. | 9 | | | Q Statistic | 3.95 | | | |

At 5% level of significance, the Tukey Kramer multiple comparison test shows that there is enough evidence to conclude that Experts and Readers, and Readers and Darts differ in mean return.

(c) The data collected are the returns of the selected stocks by the 3 categories not the amount of drops compared to the previous returns of the stocks. Even if mean returns are concerned, the experts have the sample mean return of 6.475% while the readers have a sample mean return of –42.5%, and the stocks chosen using the darts have a sample mean return of 22.6%. However, these differences in sample means do not lead to the conclusion of significant differences between the Expert and Darts in population means according to the result of the Tukey-Kramer multiple comparison procedure in part (b).

(d) $H_0$: $\sigma_1^2 = \sigma_2^2 = \sigma_3^2$ $H_1$: At least one variance is different.

Minitab output for Levene's test for homogeneity of variance:

Test of Homogeneity of Variances

```
Levene's Test (any continuous distribution)

Test Statistic: 0.101
P-Value       : 0.905
```

Since the $p$-value = 0.905 > 0.05, do not reject $H_0$. There is not enough evidence to conclude there is a significant difference in the variation in the return for the three categories.

10.64 (a) $H_0$: $\mu_A = \mu_B = \mu_C = \mu_D$ $H_1$: At least one mean is different.

$$MSA = \frac{SSA}{c-1} = \frac{1986.475}{3} = 662.1583$$

$$MSW = \frac{SSW}{n-c} = \frac{495.5}{36} = 13.7639$$

$$F = \frac{MSA}{MSW} = \frac{662.1583}{13.76389} = 48.1084$$

$$F_{\alpha,c-1,n-c} = F_{0.05,3,36} = 2.8663$$

ANOVA

| *Source of Variation* | *SS* | *df* | *MS* | *F* | *P-value* | *F crit* |
|---|---|---|---|---|---|---|
| Between Groups | 1986.475 | 3 | 662.1583 | 48.10838 | 1.12E-12 | 2.866265 |
| Within Groups | 495.5 | 36 | 13.76389 | | | |
| | | | | | | |
| Total | 2481.975 | 39 | | | | |

Since the *p*-value is essentially zero and $F = 48.1084 > 2.8663$, you can reject $H_0$. There is sufficient evidence to conclude there is a difference in the mean strength of the four brands of trash bags.

(b)

| **Tukey Kramer Multiple Comparisons** | | | | | | | |
|---|---|---|---|---|---|---|---|
| | | | | | | | |
| **Group** | **Sample Mean** | **Sample Size** | **Comparison** | Absolute Difference | Std. Error of Difference | Critical Range | **Results** |
| 1 | 35.4 | 10 | **Group 1 to Group 2** | 0.9 | 1.17319601 | 4.446 | **Means are not different** |
| 2 | 36.3 | 10 | **Group 1 to Group 3** | 0.5 | 1.17319601 | 4.446 | **Means are not different** |
| 3 | 34.9 | 10 | **Group 1 to Group 4** | 16.1 | 1.17319601 | 4.446 | **Means are different** |
| 4 | 19.3 | 10 | **Group 2 to Group 3** | 1.4 | 1.17319601 | 4.446 | **Means are not different** |
| | | | **Group 2 to Group 4** | 17 | 1.17319601 | 4.446 | **Means are different** |
| Other Data | | | **Group 3 to Group 4** | 15.6 | 1.17319601 | 4.446 | **Means are different** |
| Level of significance | 0.05 | | | | | | |
| Numerator d.f. | 4 | | | | | | |
| Denominator d.f. | 36 | | | | | | |
| MSW | 13.76389 | | | | | | |
| Q Statistic | 3.79 | | | | | | |

$Q_u = 3.79$

$$\text{Critical range} = Q_u\sqrt{\frac{MSW}{2}\left(\frac{1}{n_j}+\frac{1}{n_{j'}}\right)} = 3.79\sqrt{\frac{13.7639}{2}\left(\frac{1}{10}+\frac{1}{10}\right)} = 4.446$$

From the Tukey-Kramer procedure, there is a difference in mean strength between Kroger and Tuffstuff, Glad and Tuffstuff, and Hefty and Tuffstuff.

10.64 (c) $H_0: \sigma_A^2 = \sigma_B^2 = \sigma_C^2 = \sigma_D^2$ $H_1$: At least one variance is different.

cont.

| | Data | | | |
|---|---|---|---|---|
| | KROGER | GLAD | HEFTY | TUFFSTUFF |
| | 34 | 32 | 33 | 26 |
| | 30 | 42 | 34 | 18 |
| | 40 | 34 | 32 | 20 |
| | 38 | 36 | 40 | 15 |
| | 36 | 32 | 40 | 20 |
| | 30 | 40 | 34 | 20 |
| | 30 | 36 | 36 | 17 |
| | 42 | 43 | 34 | 18 |
| | 36 | 30 | 32 | 19 |
| | 38 | 38 | 34 | 20 |
| **Median** | 36 | 36 | 34 | 19.5 |
| | | | | |
| | Absolute Difference from the Median | | | |
| | KROGER | GLAD | HEFTY | TUFFSTUFF |
| | 2 | 4 | 1 | 6.5 |
| | 6 | 6 | 0 | 1.5 |
| | 4 | 2 | 2 | 0.5 |
| | 2 | 0 | 6 | 4.5 |
| | 0 | 4 | 6 | 0.5 |
| | 6 | 4 | 0 | 0.5 |
| | 6 | 0 | 2 | 2.5 |
| | 6 | 7 | 0 | 1.5 |
| | 0 | 6 | 2 | 0.5 |
| | 2 | 2 | 0 | 0.5 |

ANOVA output for Levene's test for homogeneity of variance:

ANOVA

| *Source of Variation* | *SS* | *df* | *MS* | *F* | *P-value* | *F crit* |
|---|---|---|---|---|---|---|
| Between Groups | 24.075 | 3 | 8.025 | 1.457619 | 0.242358 | 2.866265 |
| Within Groups | 198.2 | 36 | 5.505556 | | | |
| | | | | | | |
| Total | 222.275 | 39 | | | | |

$$MSA = \frac{SSA}{c-1} = \frac{24.075}{3} = 8.025$$

$$MSW = \frac{SSW}{n-c} = \frac{198.2}{36} = 5.5056$$

$$F = \frac{MSA}{MSW} = \frac{8.025}{5.5056} = 1.4576$$

$$F_{\alpha,c-1,n-c} = F_{0.05,3,36} = 2.8663$$

Since the $p$-value = 0.2423 > 0.05 and $F$ = 1.458 < 2.866, do not reject $H_0$. There is not sufficient evidence to conclude that the variances in strength among the four brands of trash bags are different.

(d) From the results obtained in (a) and (b), Tuffstuff has the lowest mean strength and should be avoided.

10.66 (a) $H_0$: $\mu_A = \mu_B = \mu_C = \mu_D = \mu_E$ $H_1$: At least one mean is different.

ANOVA

| *Source of Variation* | *SS* | *df* | *MS* | *F* | *P-value* | *F crit* |
|---|---|---|---|---|---|---|
| Between Groups | 377.8667 | 4 | 94.46667 | 12.56206 | 9.74E-06 | 2.758711 |
| Within Groups | 188 | 25 | 7.52 | | | |
| | | | | | | |
| Total | 565.8667 | 29 | | | | |

Since the $p$-value is essentially zero, reject $H_0$. There is evidence of a difference in the mean rating of the five advertisements.

(b)

| **Tukey Kramer Multiple Comparisons** | | | | | | | |
|---|---|---|---|---|---|---|---|
| | | | | | | | |
| **Group** | **Sample Mean** | **Sample Size** | **Comparison** | Absolute Difference | Std. Error of Difference | Critical Range | **Results** |
| 1 | 18 | 6 | **Group 1 to Group 2** | 0.333333 | 1.11952371 | 4.668 | **Means are not different** |
| 2 | 17.66667 | 6 | **Group 1 to Group 3** | 6.666667 | 1.11952371 | 4.668 | **Means are different** |
| 3 | 11.33333 | 6 | **Group 1 to Group 4** | 9 | 1.11952371 | 4.668 | **Means are different** |
| 4 | 9 | 6 | **Group 1 to Group 5** | 2.666667 | 1.11952371 | 4.668 | **Means are not different** |
| 5 | 15.33333 | 6 | **Group 2 to Group 3** | 6.333333 | 1.11952371 | 4.668 | **Means are different** |
| | | | **Group 2 to Group 4** | 8.666667 | 1.11952371 | 4.668 | **Means are different** |
| Other Data | | | **Group 2 to Group 5** | 2.333333 | 1.11952371 | 4.668 | **Means are not different** |
| Level of significance | 0.05 | | **Group 3 to Group 4** | 2.333333 | 1.11952371 | 4.668 | **Means are not different** |
| Numerator d.f. | 5 | | **Group 3 to Group 5** | 4 | 1.11952371 | 4.668 | **Means are not different** |
| Denominator d.f. | 25 | | **Group 4 to Group 5** | 6.333333 | 1.11952371 | 4.668 | **Means are different** |
| MSW | 7.52 | | | | | | |
| Q Statistic | 4.17 | | | | | | |

There is a difference in the mean rating between advertisement A and C, between A and D, between B and C, between B and D and between D and E.

(c) $H_0$: $\sigma_A^2 = \sigma_B^2 = \sigma_C^2 = \sigma_D^2 = \sigma_E^2$ $H_1$: At least one variance is different.

ANOVA output for Levene's test for homogeneity of variance:

ANOVA

| *Source of Variation* | *SS* | *df* | *MS* | *F* | *P-value* | *F crit* |
|---|---|---|---|---|---|---|
| Between Groups | 14.13333 | 4 | 3.533333 | 1.927273 | 0.137107 | 2.758711 |
| Within Groups | 45.83333 | 25 | 1.833333 | | | |
| | | | | | | |
| Total | 59.96667 | 29 | | | | |

Since the $p$-value = 0.137 > 0.05, do not reject $H_0$. There is not enough evidence to conclude there is a difference in the variation in rating among the five advertisements.

10.66 cont. (d) There is no significant difference between advertisement A and B, and they have the highest mean rating among the five and should be used. There is no significant difference between advertisement C and D, and they are among the lowest in mean rating and should be avoided.

10.68 (a) To test at the 0.05 level of significance whether there is any evidence of a difference in the mean distance traveled by the golf balls differing in design, you conduct an $F$ test:

$H_0$: $\mu_1 = \mu_2 = \mu_3 = \mu_4$ $H_1$: At least one mean is different.

Decision rule: *df*: 3, 36. If $F > 2.866$, reject $H_0$.

ANOVA

| *Source of Variation* | *SS* | *df* | *MS* | *F* | *P-value* | *F crit* |
|---|---|---|---|---|---|---|
| Between Groups | 2990.99 | 3 | 996.9966 | 53.02982 | 2.73E-13 | 2.866265 |
| Within Groups | 676.8244 | 36 | 18.80068 | | | |
| Total | 3667.814 | 39 | | | | |

Since $F_{calc} = 53.03$ is greater than the critical bound of $F = 2.866$, reject $H_0$. There is enough evidence to conclude that there is significant difference in the mean distance traveled by the golf balls differing in design.

Note: The critical bound of $F$ is obtained using Excel. The critical bound of $F$ using the Table in the text with 3 numerator and 30 denominator degrees of freedom is 2.92.

(b) To determine which of the means are significantly different from one another, you use the Tukey-Kramer procedure to establish the critical range:

$Q_{U(c,\,n-c)} = Q_{U(4,\,36)}$. You use $Q_{U(4,\,40)} = 3.79$

critical range $= Q_{U(c,n-c)} \cdot \sqrt{\frac{MSW}{2} \cdot \left(\frac{1}{n_j} + \frac{1}{n_{j'}}\right)} = 3.79 \cdot \sqrt{\frac{18.8007}{2} \cdot \left(\frac{1}{10} + \frac{1}{10}\right)} =$ 5.1967

| **Tukey Kramer Multiple Comparisons** | | | | | |
|---|---|---|---|---|---|
| | **Sample** | **Sample** | | Absolute | |
| **Group** | **Mean** | **Size** | **Comparison** | Difference | **Results** |
| 1 | 206.614 | 10 | **Group 1 to Group 2** | 11.902 | **Means are different** |
| 2 | 218.516 | 10 | **Group 1 to Group 3** | 19.974 | **Means are different** |
| 3 | 226.588 | 10 | **Group 1 to Group 4** | 22.008 | **Means are different** |
| 4 | 228.622 | 10 | **Group 2 to Group 3** | 8.072 | **Means are different** |
| | | | **Group 2 to Group 4** | 10.106 | **Means are different** |
| **MSW** | 18.800677 | | **Group 3 to Group 4** | 2.034 | **Means are not different** |

At 5% level of significance, there is enough evidence to conclude that mean traveling distances between all pairs of designs are different with the only exception of the pair between design 3 and design 4.

10.68 cont. (c) The assumptions needed in (a) are (i) samples are randomly and independently drawn, (ii) populations are normally distributed, and (iii) populations have equal variances.

(d) To test at the 0.05 level of significance whether the variation within the groups is similar for all groups, you conduct a Levene's test for homogeneity of variance:

$H_0$: $\sigma_1^2 = \sigma_2^2 = \sigma_3^2 = \sigma_4^2$ $\quad$ $H_1$: At least one variance is different.

ANOVA

| *Source of Variation* | *SS* | *df* | *MS* | *F* | *P-value* | *F crit* |
|---|---|---|---|---|---|---|
| Between Groups | 40.63675 | 3 | 13.54558 | 2.093228 | 0.118276 | 2.866265 |
| Within Groups | 232.9613 | 36 | 6.471147 | | | |
| Total | 273.598 | 39 | | | | |

Since $p$-value = 0.1183 > 0.05, do not reject the null hypothesis. There is not enough evidence to conclude that there is any difference in the variation of the distance traveled by the golf balls differing in design.

(e) In order to produce golf balls with the farthest traveling distance, either design 3 or 4 can be used.

10.70 The pooled-variance $t$-test should be used when the populations are approximately normally distributed and the variances of the two populations are equal.

10.72 With independent populations, the outcomes in one population do not depend on the outcomes in the second population. With two related populations, either repeated measurements are obtained on the same set of items or individuals, or items or individuals are paired or matched according to some characteristic.

10.74 They are two different ways of investigating the concern of whether there is significant difference between the means of two independent populations. If the hypothesized value of 0 for the difference in two population means is not in the confidence interval, then, assuming a two-tailed test is used, the null hypothesis of no difference in the two population means can be rejected.

10.76 The major assumptions of ANOVA are randomness and independence, normality, and homogeneity of variance.

10.78 When the ANOVA has indicated that at least one of the groups has a different population mean than the others, you should use multiple comparison procedures for evaluating pairwise combinations of the group means. In such cases, the Tukey-Kramer procedure should be used to compare all pairs of means.

10.80 (a) $H_0 : \sigma_1^2 \geq \sigma_2^2$ Population: 1 = Internet 2 = brick-and-mortar market

Price variance on the Internet is not less than the price variance in the brick-and-mortar market.

$H_1 : \sigma_1^2 < \sigma_2^2$

Price variance on the Internet is less than the price variance in the brick-and-mortar market

(b) Type I error: Rejecting the null hypothesis that price variance on the Internet is not less than the price variance in the brick-and-mortar market when the price variance on the Internet is indeed not less than the price variance in the brick-and-mortar market.

Type II error: Failing to reject the null hypothesis that price variance on the Internet is not less than the price variance in the brick-and-mortar market when the price variance on the Internet is indeed less than the price variance in the brick-and-mortar market.

(c) An $F$ test for differences in two variances can be used.

(d) You need to assume that the two populations are both normally distributed.

(e) (a) $H_0 : \mu_1 \geq \mu_2$ Population: 1 = electronic market 2 = physical market

Mean price in electronic markets is not less than the mean price in physical markets.

$H_1 : \mu_1 < \mu_2$

Mean price in electronic markets is less than the mean price in physical markets.

(b) Type I error: Rejecting the null hypothesis that the mean price in electronic markets is not less than the mean price in physical markets when the mean price in electronic markets is indeed not less than the mean price in physical markets.

Type II error: Failing to reject the null hypothesis that mean price in electronic markets is not less than the mean price in physical markets when the mean price in electronic markets is indeed less than the mean price in physical markets.

(c) A paired-sample $t$ test for the mean difference can be used.

(d) You must assume that the distribution of the differences between the mean price in electronic markets and physical markets is approximately normal.

10.82 (a) The researchers could ask the teenagers, after viewing each ad, to rate the dangers of smoking using a scale from 0 to 10 with 10 representing the most dangerous.

(b) $H_0 : \mu_T \geq \mu_S$ The mean rating on the dangers of smoking for ads produced by Philip Morris is not less than the mean rating on the dangers of smoking for ads produced by the state.

$H_1 : \mu_T < \mu_S$ The mean rating on the dangers of smoking for ads produced by Philip Morris is less than the mean rating on the dangers of smoking for ads produced by the state.

10.82 cont. (c) Type I error is the error made by concluding that ads produced by the state are more effective than those produced by Philip Morris while it is not true. The risk of Type I error here is that teenagers can miss the opportunity from the better ads produced by Philip Morris to recognize the true dangers of smoking and the additional expenses the state will have to incur to produce and run the ads. Type II error is the error made by concluding that ads produced by Philip Morris are no less effective than those produced by the state while ads produced by the state are in fact more effective. The risk of Type II error here is that more teenagers will miss the opportunity to recognize the true dangers of smoking from the ads produced by the state.

(d) Since both ads are shown to the same group of teenagers, a paired-sample t test for the mean difference is most appropriate.

(e) Statistically reliable here means the conclusions drawn from the test are reliable because all the assumptions needed for the test to be valid are fulfilled.

10.84 (a) $H_0$: $\mu_{II} \le \$80$ The mean monthly electric bill is no more than \$80 for single-family homes in county II during the summer season.

$H_1$: $\mu_{II} > \$80$ The mean monthly electric bill is more than \$80 for single-family homes in county II during the summer season.

Decision rule: $d.f. = 20$. If $t > 2.528$, reject $H_0$.

Test statistic: $t = \dfrac{\bar{X} - \mu}{S/\sqrt{n}} = \dfrac{\$98 - \$80}{\$18/\sqrt{21}} = 4.5826$

Decision: Since $t_{\text{calc}} = 4.5826$ is above the critical bound of 2.528, reject $H_0$. There is sufficient evidence to conclude that the mean monthly electric bill is more than \$80 for single-family homes in county II during the summer season.

(b) $H_0$: $\sigma_I^2 = \sigma_{II}^2$ The population variances for monthly electric bills in county I and II are the same.

$H_1$: $\sigma_I^2 \ne \sigma_{II}^2$ The population variances for monthly electric bills in county I and II are not the same.

Decision rule: If $F < 0.3265$ or $F > 3.2220$, reject $H_0$.

Test statistic: $F = \dfrac{S_I^2}{S_{II}^2} = \dfrac{30^2}{18^2} = 2.78$

Decision: Since $F_{\text{calc}} = 2.78$ is between the two critical bounds, do not reject $H_0$. There is not enough evidence to conclude that County I and II have different population variances for monthly electric bills.

(c) $H_0$: $\mu_I \le \mu_{II}$ The mean monthly electric bill is not higher in County I than in County II.

$H_1$: $\mu_I > \mu_{II}$ The mean monthly electric bill is higher in County I than in County II.

Based on the results in (b) the pooled-variance *t*-test should be used here.

Decision: If *p*-value < 0.01, reject $H_0$.

10.84 cont. (c) PHStat output:

| t Test for Differences in Two Means | |
|---|---|
| **Data** | |
| **Hypothesized Difference** | **0** |
| **Level of Significance** | **0.01** |
| **Population 1 Sample** | |
| **Sample Size** | **25** |
| **Sample Mean** | **115** |
| **Sample Standard Deviation** | **30** |
| **Population 2 Sample** | |
| **Sample Size** | **21** |
| **Sample Mean** | **98** |
| **Sample Standard Deviation** | **18** |
| Intermediate Calculations | |
| Population 1 Sample Degrees of Freedom | 24 |
| Population 2 Sample Degrees of Freedom | 20 |
| Total Degrees of Freedom | 44 |
| Pooled Variance | 638.1818 |
| Difference in Sample Means | 17 |
| *t*-Test Statistic | 2.273408 |
| **Upper-Tail Test** | |
| **Upper Critical Value** | **2.414135** |
| ***p*-Value** | **0.013968** |
| **Do not reject the null hypothesis** | |

Since $p$-value = 0.0140 > 0.01, do not reject $H_0$. There is not enough evidence to conclude that the mean monthly bill is higher in county I than in county II.

(d)

$$\left(\bar{X}_1 - \bar{X}_2\right) + t\sqrt{S_p^2\left(\frac{1}{n_1}+\frac{1}{n_2}\right)} = (115-98) + 2.6923\sqrt{638.18\left(\frac{1}{25}+\frac{1}{21}\right)}$$

$$-3.1323 \le \mu_1 - \mu_2 \le 37.1323$$

You are 99% confident that the difference between the mean monthly bill in county I and county II is between –$3.13 and $37.13.

10.86 (a) $H_0$: $\mu \le 10$ minutes. Introductory computer students required no more than a mean of 10 minutes to write and run a program in Visual Basic.

$H_1$: $\mu > 10$ minutes. Introductory computer students required more than a mean of 10 minutes to write and run a program in Visual Basic.

Decision rule: $d.f. = 8$. If $t > 1.8595$, reject $H_0$.

Test statistic: $t = \dfrac{\bar{X}-\mu}{S/\sqrt{n}} = \dfrac{12-10}{1.8028/\sqrt{9}} = 3.3282$

Decision: Since $t_{calc} = 3.3282$ is greater than the critical bound of 1.8595, reject $H_0$. There is enough evidence to conclude that the introductory computer students required more than a mean of 10 minutes to write and run a program in Visual Basic.

10.86 cont. (b) $H_0$: $\mu \le 10$ minutes. Introductory computer students required no more than a mean of 10 minutes to write and run a program in Visual Basic.
$H_1$: $\mu > 10$ minutes. Introductory computer students required more than a mean of 10 minutes to write and run a program in Visual Basic.
Decision rule: $d.f. = 8$. If $t > 1.8595$, reject $H_0$.
Test statistic: $t = \dfrac{\bar{X} - \mu}{S/\sqrt{n}} = \dfrac{16 - 10}{13.2004/\sqrt{9}} = 1.3636$
Decision: Since $t_{calc} = 1.3636$ is less than the critical bound of 1.8595, do not reject $H_0$. There is not enough evidence to conclude that the introductory computer students required more than a mean of 10 minutes to write and run a program in Visual Basic.

(c) Although the mean time necessary to complete the assignment increased from 12 to 16 minutes as a result of the increase in one data value, the standard deviation went from 1.8 to 13.2, which in turn brought the $t$-value down because of the increased denominator.

(d) $H_0$: $\sigma_{IC}^2 = \sigma_{CS}^2$ The population variances are the same for Introduction to Computers students and computer majors.
$H_1$: $\sigma_{IC}^2 \ne \sigma_{CS}^2$ The population variances are different for Introduction to Computers students and computer majors.
Decision rule: If $F < 0.2328$ or $F > 3.8549$, reject $H_0$.
Test statistic: $F = \dfrac{S_{IC}^2}{S_{CS}^2} = \dfrac{1.8028^2}{2.0^2} = 0.8125$
Decision: Since $F_{calc} = 0.8125$ is between the critical bounds of 0.2328 and 3.8549, do not reject $H_0$. There is not enough evidence to conclude that the population variances are different for the Introduction to Computers students and computer majors. Hence, the pooled-variance $t$ test is a valid test to see whether computer majors can write a Visual Basic program (on average) in less time than introductory students, assuming that the distributions of the time needed to write a Visual Basic program for both the Introduction to Computers students and the computer majors are approximately normal.
$H_0$: $\mu_{IC} \le \mu_{CS}$ The mean amount of time needed by Introduction to Computers students is not greater than the mean amount of time needed by computer majors.
$H_1$: $\mu_{IC} > \mu_{CS}$ The mean amount of time needed by Introduction to Computers students is greater than the mean amount of time needed by computer majors.
Decision rule: $d.f. = 18$. If $t > 1.7341$, reject $H_0$.
Test statistic:

$$S_p^2 = \frac{(n_{IC}-1)\cdot S_{IC}^2 + (n_{CS}-1)\cdot S_{CS}^2}{(n_{IC}-1)+(n_{CS}-1)} = \frac{9\cdot 1.8028^2 + 11\cdot 2.0^2}{4+5} = 3.6667$$

$$t = \frac{(\bar{X}_{IC} - \bar{X}_{CS}) - (\mu_{IC} - \mu_{CS})}{\sqrt{S_p^2\left(\frac{1}{n_{IC}} + \frac{1}{n_{CS}}\right)}} = \frac{12.0 - 8.5}{\sqrt{3.6667\left(\frac{1}{9} + \frac{1}{11}\right)}} = 4.0666$$

Decision: Since $t_{calc} = 4.0666$ is greater than 1.7341, reject $H_0$. There is enough evidence to support a conclusion that the mean time is higher for Introduction to Computers students than for computer majors.

10.86 cont. (e) $p$-value = 0.000362. If the true population mean amount of time needed for Introduction to Computer students to write a Visual Basic program is indeed no more than 10 minutes, the probability for observing a sample mean greater than the 12 minutes in the current sample is 0.0362%, which means it will be a quite unlikely event. Hence, at a 95% level of confidence, you can conclude that the population mean amount of time needed for Introduction to Computer students to write a Visual Basic program is more than 10 minutes.

As illustrated in part (d) in which there is not enough evidence to conclude that the population variances are different for the Introduction to Computers students and computer majors, the pooled-variance $t$ test performed is a valid test to determine whether computer majors can write a Visual Basic program in less time than in introductory students, assuming that the distributions of the time needed to write a Visual Basic program for both the Introduction to Computers students and the computer majors are approximately normal.

10.88 (a) $H_0: \mu_1 \le \mu_2$ where Populations: 1 = men and 2 = women

$H_1: \mu_1 > \mu_2$

Decision rule: $df = 113$. If $t > 2.3598$, reject $H_0$.

Test statistic: $t = \dfrac{\bar{D} - \mu_{\bar{D}}}{S_{\bar{D}} / \sqrt{n}} = 7.8735$

Decision: Since $t_{calc} = 7.8735$ is greater than the critical bound of 2.3598, reject $H_0$. There is enough evidence to conclude that the mean salary for men is greater than the mean salary for women.

**Excel output:**

t-Test: Paired Two Sample for Means

| | *Male* | *Female* |
|---|---|---|
| Mean | 88683.23684 | 74575.17544 |
| Variance | 3834187011 | 2243135437 |
| Observations | 114 | 114 |
| Pearson Correlation | 0.973734531 | |
| Hypothesized Mean Difference | 0 | |
| df | 113 | |
| t Stat | 7.87346338 | |
| P(T<=t) one-tail | 1.14975E-12 | |
| t Critical one-tail | 2.359802238 | |
| P(T<=t) two-tail | 2.29949E-12 | |
| t Critical two-tail | 2.620035957 | |

(b) From the Excel output, the $p$-value is essentially zero.

10.88 (c)
cont.

F-Test Two-Sample for Variances

| | Male | Female |
|---|---|---|
| Mean | 88683.23684 | 74575.17544 |
| Variance | 3834187011 | 2243135437 |
| Observations | 114 | 114 |
| df | 113 | 113 |
| F | 1.709298042 | |
| P(F<=f) one-tail | 0.002354401 | |
| F Critical one-tail | 1.553353002 | |

$H_0$: $\sigma_1^2 = \sigma_2^2$ The population variances are the same.
$H_1$: $\sigma_1^2 \neq \sigma_2^2$ The population variances are different.
Decision rule: If $F < 0.614$ or $F > 1.629$, reject $H_0$.

Test statistic: $F = \frac{S_1^2}{S_2^2} = \frac{3,834,187,011}{2,243,135,437} = 1.709$

Decision: Since $F_{calc} = 1.709$ is greater than the upper critical bound of $F_U = 1.629$, reject $H_0$. There is enough evidence to conclude that the two population variances are different.

10.90

| | Manufacturer A | Manufacturer B |
|---|---|---|
| **Minimum** | 684 | 819 |
| **First Quartile** | 852 | 943 |
| **Median** | 916.5 | 1015.5 |
| **Third Quartile** | 972 | 1096 |
| **Interquartile Range** | 120 | 153 |
| **Maximum** | 1093 | 1230 |
| **Range** | 409 | 411 |
| **Mean** | 909.65 | 1018.35 |
| **Median** | 916.5 | 1015.5 |
| **Mode** | 926 | 1077 |
| **Standard Deviation** | 94.3052 | 96.9014 |
| **Sample Variance** | 8893.4641 | 9389.8744 |
| **Count** | 40 | 40 |

Box-and-whisker Plot

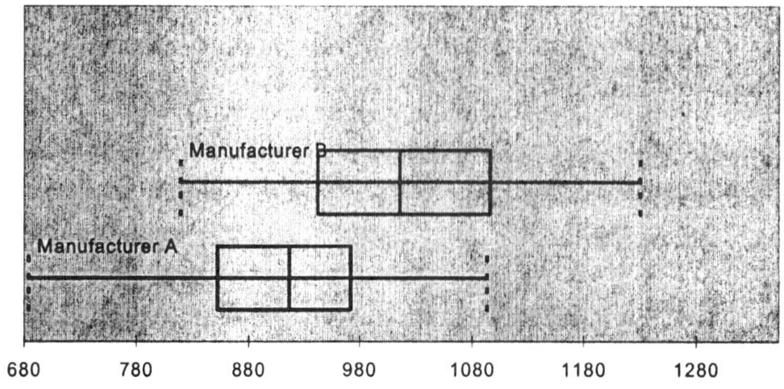

10.90 cont. From the box-and-whisker plot and the summary statistics, both data seem to have come from rather symmetrical distributions that are quite normally distributed.

The following *F* test for any evidence of difference between two population variances suggests that there is insufficient evidence to conclude that the two population variances are significantly different at 5% level of significance.

PHStat output:

| **F Test for Differences in Two Variances** | |
|---|---|
| **Level of Significance** | **0.05** |
| **Population 1 Sample** | |
| **Sample Size** | **40** |
| **Sample Standard Deviation** | **94.30516** |
| **Population 2 Sample** | |
| **Sample Size** | **40** |
| **Sample Standard Deviation** | **96.90136** |
| *F*-Test Statistic | 0.947133 |
| Population 1 Sample Degrees of Freedom | 39 |
| Population 2 Sample Degrees of Freedom | 39 |
| **Two-Tailed Test** | |
| **Lower Critical Value** | **0.5289** |
| **Upper Critical Value** | **1.890719** |
| ***p*-Value** | **0.866186** |
| **Do not reject the null hypothesis** | |

Since both data are drawn from independent populations, the most appropriate test for any difference in the life of the bulbs between the two manufacturers is the pooled-variance *t* test.

| **Pooled Variance t Test for Differences in Two Means** | |
|---|---|
| **Data** | |
| **Hypothesized Difference** | **0** |
| **Level of Significance** | **0.05** |
| **Population 1 Sample** | |
| **Sample Size** | **40** |
| **Sample Mean** | **909.65** |
| **Sample Standard Deviation** | **94.3052** |
| **Population 2 Sample** | |
| **Sample Size** | **40** |
| **Sample Mean** | **1018.35** |
| **Sample Standard Deviation** | **96.9014** |
| Intermediate Calculations | |
| Population 1 Sample Degrees of Freedom | 39 |
| Population 2 Sample Degrees of Freedom | 39 |
| Total Degrees of Freedom | 78 |
| Pooled Variance | 9141.676 |
| Difference in Sample Means | -108.7 |
| *t*-Test Statistic | -5.08431 |
| **Two-Tailed Test** | |
| **Lower Critical Value** | **-1.99085** |
| **Upper Critical Value** | **1.990848** |
| ***p*-Value** | **2.47E-06** |
| **Reject the null hypothesis** | |

10.90 cont. Since the $p$-value is virtually zero, at the 5% level of significance, there is sufficient evidence to reject the null hypothesis of no difference in the mean life of the bulbs between the two manufacturers. You can conclude that there is significant difference in the mean life of the bulbs between the two manufacturers.

Based on the above analyses, you can conclude that there is significant difference in the life of the bulbs between the two manufacturers.

10.92 From Problem 3.77, you saw that the distribution of all the variables was skewed. The $F$ test for the difference in variances, which is sensitive to departure from the normal distribution assumption, will not be appropriate. You also saw that the variances of all the variables between SUV and non-SUV are also quite different. Hence, you perform a separate-variance $t$ tests on the difference of means.

**MPG:**

$H_0 : \mu_1 = \mu_2$ vs. $H_1 : \mu_1 \neq \mu_2$

t-Test: Two-Sample Assuming Unequal Variances

| | *MPG* | *MPG* |
|---|---|---|
| Mean | 22.15556 | 16.48387 |
| Variance | 18.73958 | 7.258065 |
| Observations | 90 | 31 |
| Hypothesized Mean Difference | 0 | |
| df | 85 | |
| t Stat | 8.527657 | |
| P(T<=t) one-tail | 2.44E-13 | |
| t Critical one-tail | 1.662979 | |
| P(T<=t) two-tail | 4.88E-13 | |
| t Critical two-tail | 1.988269 | |

Since the $p$-value is essentially zero, reject $H_0$. There is sufficient evidence to conclude that the mean MPGs are different between SUVs and non-SUVs.

**Length:**

$H_0 : \mu_1 = \mu_2$ vs. $H_1 : \mu_1 \neq \mu_2$

t-Test: Two-Sample Assuming Unequal Variances

| | *Length* | *Length* |
|---|---|---|
| Mean | 187.9778 | 184.9032 |
| Variance | 161.4377 | 209.557 |
| Observations | 90 | 31 |
| Hypothesized Mean Difference | 0 | |
| df | 47 | |
| t Stat | 1.05125 | |
| P(T<=t) one-tail | 0.14926 | |
| t Critical one-tail | 1.677927 | |
| P(T<=t) two-tail | 0.298519 | |
| t Critical two-tail | 2.011739 | |

Since the $p$-value $= 0.2985$ is greater than the 5% level of significance, do not reject $H_0$. There is not sufficient evidence to conclude that the mean length is different between SUVs and non-SUVs.

10.92 cont. **Width:**

$H_0: \mu_1 = \mu_2$ vs. $H_1: \mu_1 \neq \mu_2$

t-Test: Two-Sample Assuming Unequal Variances

| | *Width* | *Width* |
|---|---|---|
| Mean | 71 | 72.32258 |
| Variance | 9.865169 | 11.09247 |
| Observations | 90 | 31 |
| Hypothesized Mean Difference | 0 | |
| df | 50 | |
| t Stat | -1.93447 | |
| P(T<=t) one-tail | 0.029362 | |
| t Critical one-tail | 1.675905 | |
| P(T<=t) two-tail | 0.058724 | |
| t Critical two-tail | 2.00856 | |

Since the $p$-value = 0.0587 is greater than the 5% level of significance, do not reject $H_0$. There is not sufficient evidence to conclude that the mean width is different between SUVs and non-SUVs.

**Weight:**

$H_0: \mu_1 = \mu_2$ vs. $H_1: \mu_1 \neq \mu_2$

t-Test: Two-Sample Assuming Unequal Variances

| | *Weight* | *Weight* |
|---|---|---|
| Mean | 3391.722 | 4267.419 |
| Variance | 232210.8 | 783086.5 |
| Observations | 90 | 31 |
| Hypothesized Mean Difference | 0 | |
| df | 36 | |
| t Stat | -5.24822 | |
| P(T<=t) one-tail | 3.51E-06 | |
| t Critical one-tail | 1.688297 | |
| P(T<=t) two-tail | 7.02E-06 | |
| t Critical two-tail | 2.028091 | |

Since the $p$-value is essentially zero, reject $H_0$. There is sufficient evidence to conclude that the mean weight is different between SUVs and non-SUVs.

**Luggage Capacity:**

$H_0: \mu_1 = \mu_2$ vs. $H_1: \mu_1 \neq \mu_2$

t-Test: Two-Sample Assuming Unequal Variances

| | *Cargo Volume* | *Cargo Volume* |
|---|---|---|
| Mean | 22.39444 | 42.35484 |
| Variance | 323.7837 | 183.7532 |
| Observations | 90 | 31 |
| Hypothesized Mean Difference | 0 | |
| df | 69 | |
| t Stat | -6.46746 | |
| P(T<=t) one-tail | 6.05E-09 | |
| t Critical one-tail | 1.667238 | |
| P(T<=t) two-tail | 1.21E-08 | |
| t Critical two-tail | 1.994945 | |

10.92 cont. Since the $p$-value is essentially zero, reject $H_0$. There is sufficient evidence to conclude that the mean luggage capacity is different between SUVs and non-SUVs.

**Turning Circle:**

$H_0: \mu_1 = \mu_2$ vs. $H_1: \mu_1 \neq \mu_2$

t-Test: Two-Sample Assuming Unequal Variances

| | *Turning Circle* | *Turning Circle* |
|---|---|---|
| Mean | 39.7 | 40.58065 |
| Variance | 6.324719 | 11.31828 |
| Observations | 90 | 31 |
| Hypothesized Mean Difference | 0 | |
| df | 42 | |
| t Stat | -1.33465 | |
| P(T<=t) one-tail | 0.094591 | |
| t Critical one-tail | 1.681951 | |
| P(T<=t) two-tail | 0.189182 | |
| t Critical two-tail | 2.018082 | |

Since the $p$-value = 0.1892 is greater than the 5% level of significance, do not reject $H_0$. There is not sufficient evidence to conclude that the mean turning circle requirement is different between SUVs and non-SUVs.

10.94

**Prices:**

| | USA_Price | Imported_Price |
|---|---|---|
| **Minimum** | 2.36 | 4.63 |
| **First Quartile** | 3.71 | 5.41 |
| **Median** | 4.065 | 5.68 |
| **Third Quartile** | 6.12 | 6.39 |
| **Maximum** | 7.79 | 7.8 |
| **Mean** | 4.7133 | 5.8627 |
| **Median** | 4.065 | 5.68 |
| **Mode** | 4.02 | #N/A |
| **Standard Deviation** | 1.4753 | 0.9030 |
| **Sample Variance** | 2.1766 | 0.8154 |
| **Range** | 5.43 | 3.17 |
| **Count** | 54 | 15 |
| **Interquartile Range** | 2.41 | 0.98 |
| **1.33 (Std. Dev.)** | 1.9622 | 1.2010 |
| **6 (Std. Dev)** | 8.8518 | 5.418 |

10.94
cont.

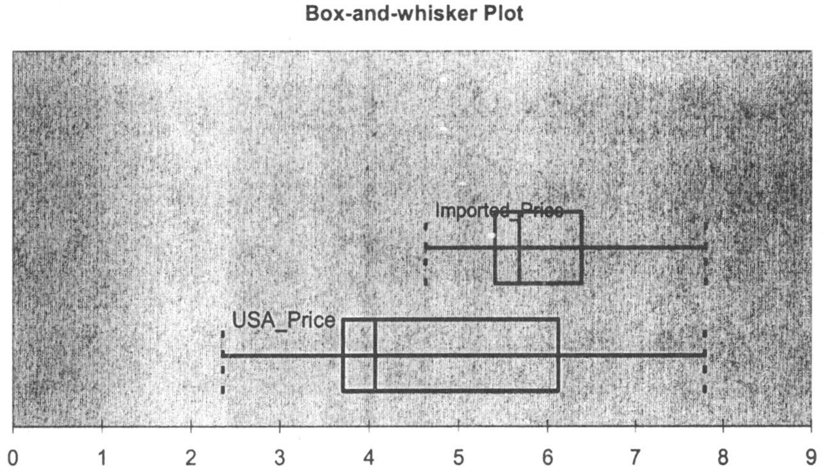
Box-and-whisker Plot
Imported_Price
USA_Price
0
1
2
3
4
5
6
7
8
9

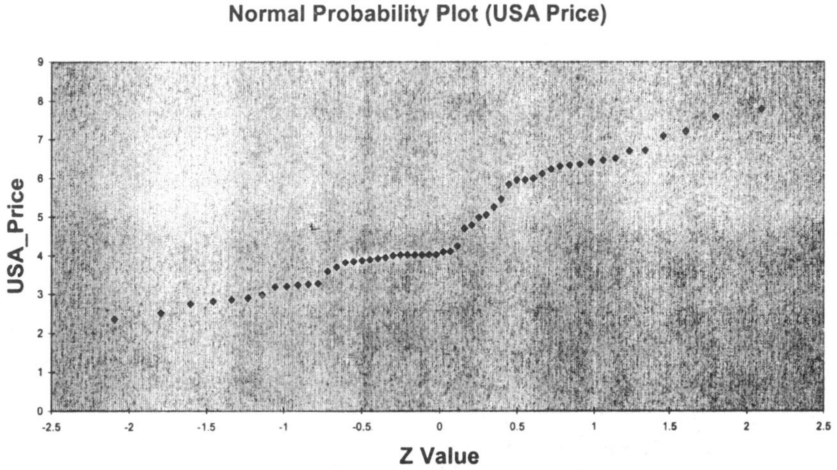
Normal Probability Plot (USA Price)
USA_Price
Z Value

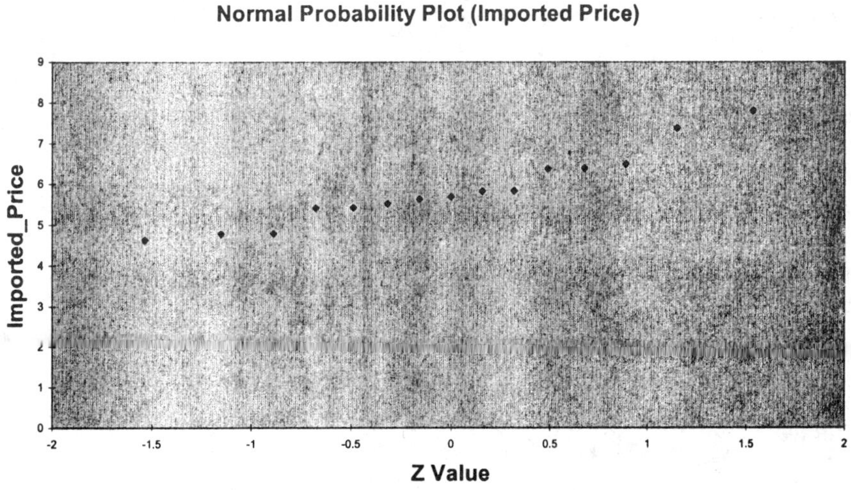
Normal Probability Plot (Imported Price)
Imported_Price
Z Value

10.94 cont. The box-and-whisker plot, normal probability plot and summary statistics all suggest that the distributions of price of beers brewed in the U.S. and those imported are both skewed to the right. Since both distributions are quite far from being symmetrical, the normality assumption of the population distributions is violated for the price data set so the *F* test for difference in two variances is not appropriate here. Also the two sample variances suggest that the dispersions in the two populations are quite different. The sample size for beers brewed in the U.S. is quite large at 54 but the sample size for imported beers is only 15. Strictly speaking, neither the pooled-variance *t* test nor the separate-variance *t* test for difference in the means is appropriate for the analysis of this data set. Nevertheless, the test result for the separate-variance *t* test is reported next.

$H_0: \mu_I = \mu_{II}$ Mean prices of domestic and imported beers are the same.

$H_1: \mu_I \neq \mu_{II}$ Mean prices of domestic and imported beers are different.

Excel output:

t-Test: Two-Sample Assuming Unequal Variances

| | *U.S.* | *Imported* |
|---|---|---|
| Mean | 4.713333 | 5.862667 |
| Variance | 2.176626 | 0.815392 |
| Observations | 54 | 15 |
| Hypothesized Mean Difference | 0 | |
| df | 37 | |
| t Stat | -3.73547 | |
| P(T<=t) one-tail | 0.000315 | |
| t Critical one-tail | 1.687094 | |
| P(T<=t) two-tail | 0.00063 | |
| t Critical two-tail | 2.02619 | |

Since the *p*-value of 0.00063 is less than the 5% level of significance, there is sufficient evidence to conclude that the mean prices are different between domestic and imported beers.

**Calories:**

| | *U.S.* | *Imported* |
|---|---|---|
| Mean | 143.3889 | 138.6 |
| Standard Error | 4.173844 | 7.129282 |
| Median | 148 | 148 |
| Mode | 143 | 148 |
| Standard Deviation | 30.67137 | 27.61159 |
| Sample Variance | 940.7327 | 762.4 |
| Kurtosis | 1.650411 | 1.632721 |
| Skewness | -1.2957 | -1.67381 |
| Range | 143 | 89 |
| Minimum | 58 | 71 |
| Maximum | 201 | 160 |
| Sum | 7743 | 2079 |
| Count | 54 | 15 |
| First Quartile | 142 | 140 |
| Third Quartile | 160 | 155 |

10.94
cont.

Normal Probability Plot of Calorie

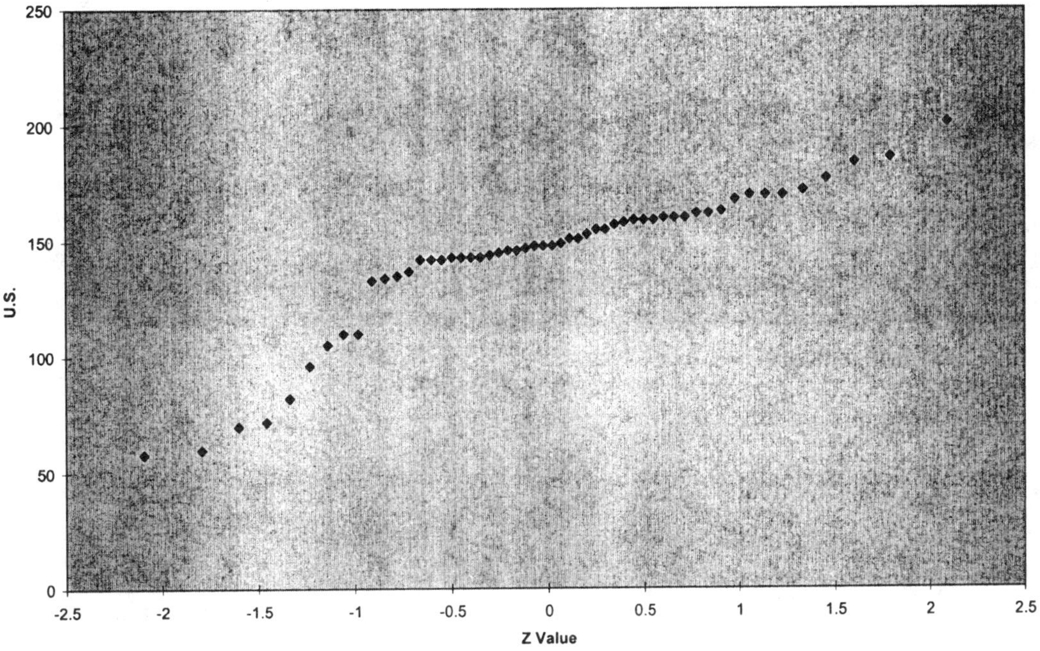


Normal Probability Plot of Calorie

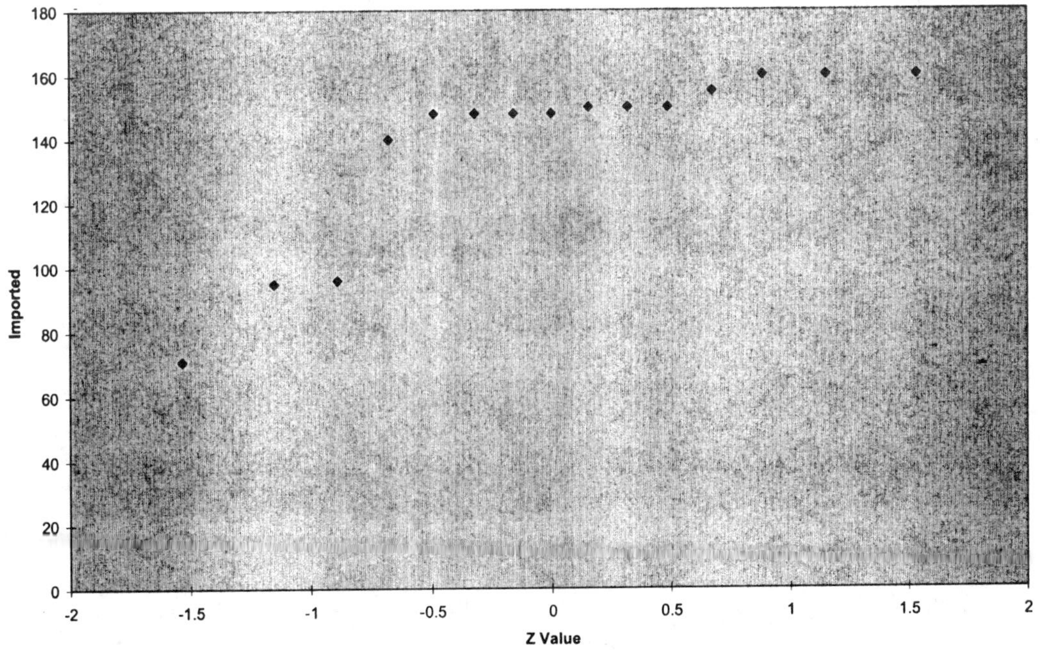

10.94
cont.

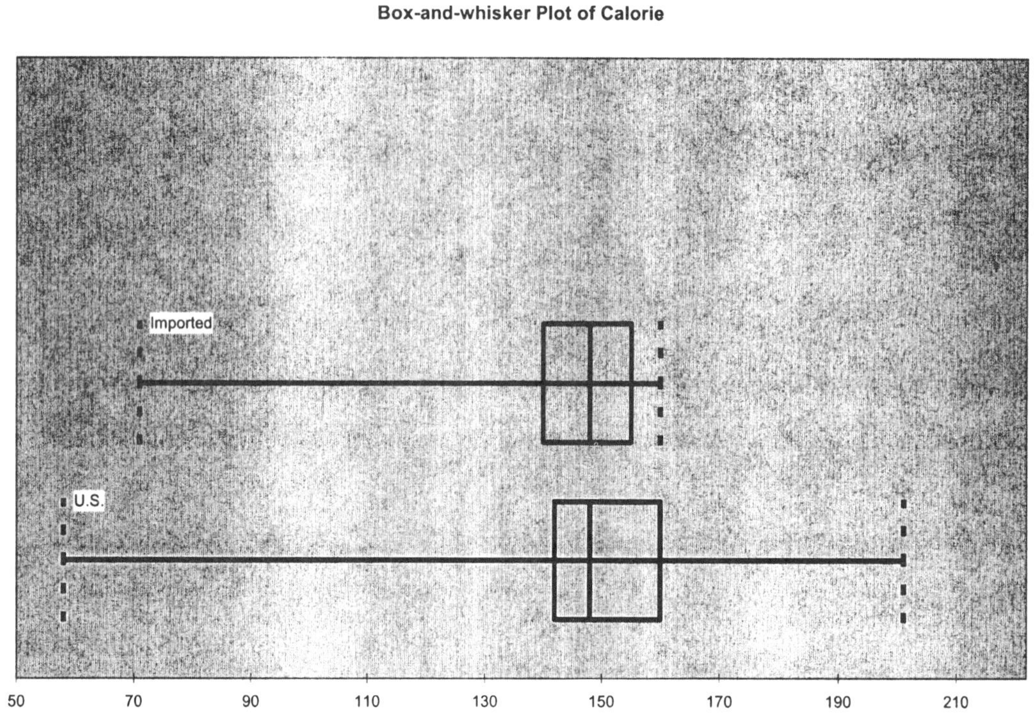


The normal probability plots, box-and-whisker plots and summary statistics all suggest that the distributions of calories of beers brewed in the U.S. and those imported are both skewed to the left. Since both distributions are quite far from being symmetrical, the normality assumption of the population distributions is violated for the calorie data set so the *F* test for difference in two variances is not appropriate here. The two sample variances, however, suggest that the dispersions in the two populations are not very different. The pooled-variance *t* test is appropriate for the analysis of this data set.

$H_0 : \mu_I = \mu_{II}$ Mean calories of domestic and imported beers are the same.

$H_1 : \mu_I \neq \mu_{II}$ Mean calories of domestic and imported beers are different.

10.94 cont. Excel output:

| t Test for Differences in Two Means | |
|---|---|
| **Data** | |
| **Hypothesized Difference** | **0** |
| **Level of Significance** | **0.05** |
| **Population 1 Sample** | |
| **Sample Size** | **54** |
| **Sample Mean** | **143.3889** |
| **Sample Standard Deviation** | **30.67137** |
| **Population 2 Sample** | |
| **Sample Size** | **15** |
| **Sample Mean** | **138.6** |
| **Sample Standard Deviation** | **27.61159** |
| Intermediate Calculations | |
| Population 1 Sample Degrees of Freedom | 53 |
| Population 2 Sample Degrees of Freedom | 14 |
| Total Degrees of Freedom | 67 |
| Pooled Variance | 903.4693 |
| Difference in Sample Means | 4.7889 |
| *t*-Test Statistic | 0.54588 |
| **Two-Tailed Test** | |
| **Lower Critical Value** | **-1.99601** |
| **Upper Critical Value** | **1.996009** |
| ***p*-Value** | **0.586962** |
| **Do not reject the null hypothesis** | |

Since the $p$-value of 0.587 is greater than the 5% level of significance, do not reject the null hypothesis. There is insufficient evidence to conclude that there is any difference in mean calories between domestic beers and imported beers.

**Alcohol content:**

| | *U.S.* | *Imported* |
|---|---|---|
| Mean | 4.5 | 4.133333 |
| Standard Error | 0.208586 | 0.450256 |
| Median | 4.9 | 4.9 |
| Mode | 4.9 | 5 |
| Standard Deviation | 1.532786 | 1.743833 |
| Sample Variance | 2.349434 | 3.040952 |
| Kurtosis | 4.782198 | 3.274632 |
| Skewness | -2.35183 | -2.07045 |
| Range | 6 | 5.6 |
| Minimum | 0 | 0 |
| Maximum | 6 | 5.6 |
| Sum | 243 | 62 |
| Count | 54 | 15 |
| First Quartile | 4.5 | 4.1 |
| Third Quartile | 5.3 | 5 |

10.94
cont.

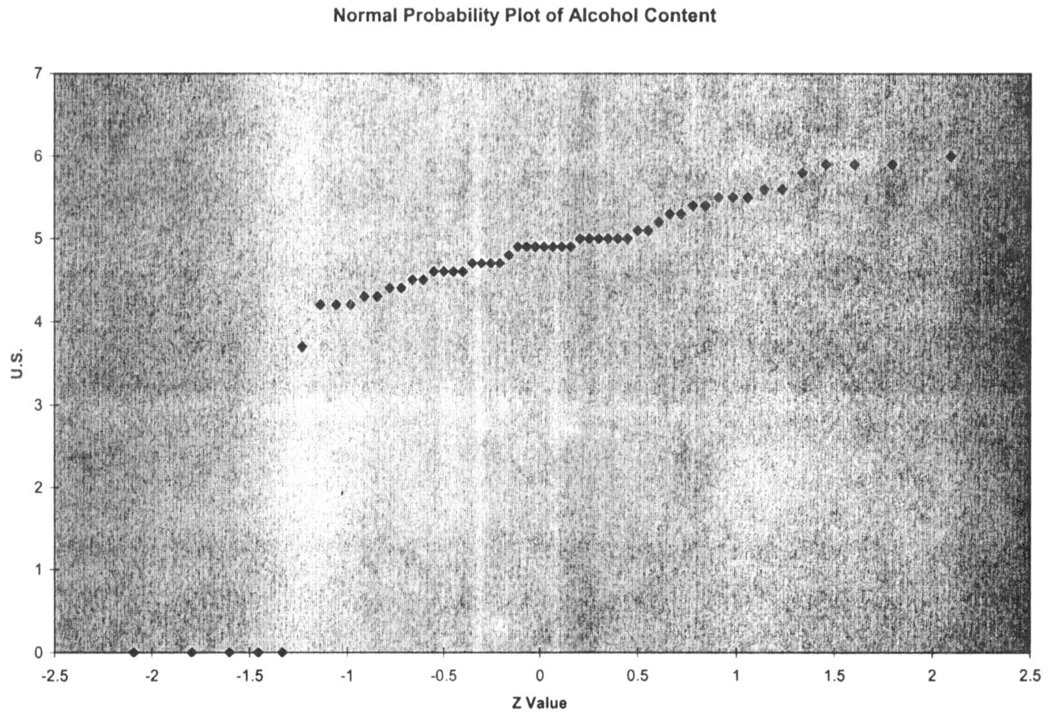
Normal Probability Plot of Alcohol Content
U.S.
Z Value
7
6
5
4
3
2
1
0
-2.5
-2
-1.5
-1
-0.5
0
0.5
1
1.5
2
2.5

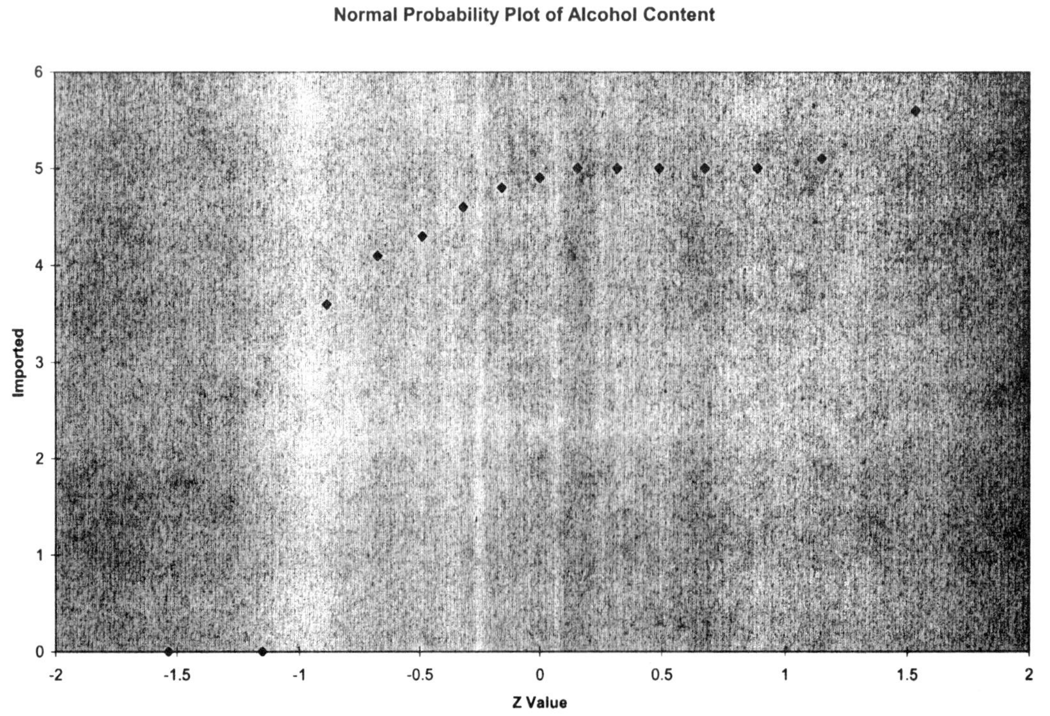
Normal Probability Plot of Alcohol Content
Imported
Z Value
6
5
4
3
2
1
0
-2
-1.5
-1
-0.5
0
0.5
1
1.5
2

10.94
cont.

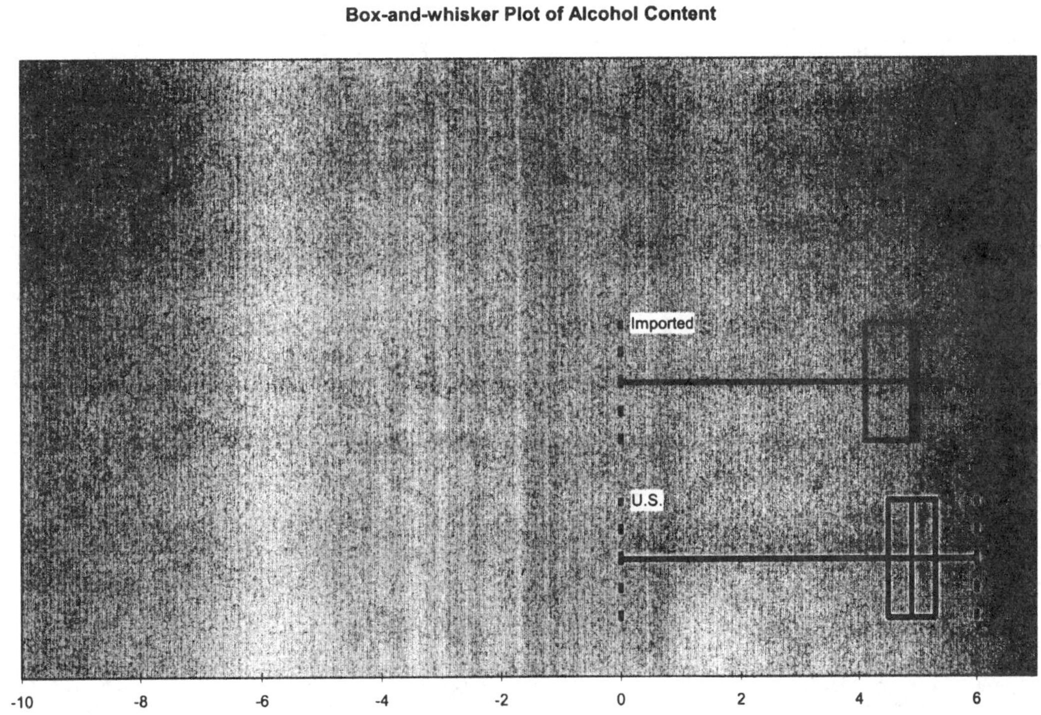


The normal probability plots, box-and-whisker plots and summary statistics all suggest that the distributions of alcohol content of beers brewed in the U.S. and those imported are both skewed to the left. Since both distributions are quite far from being symmetrical, the normality assumption of the population distributions is violated for the alcohol content data set so the $F$ test for difference in two variances is not appropriate here. The two sample variances, however, suggest that the dispersions in the two populations are not very different. The pooled-variance $t$ test is appropriate for the analysis of this data set.

$H_0 : \mu_I = \mu_{II}$ Mean alcohol contents of domestic and imported beers are the same.

$H_1 : \mu_I \neq \mu_{II}$ Mean alcohol contents of domestic and imported beers are different.

10.94 cont. PHStat output:

| t Test for Differences in Two Means | |
|---|---|
| **Data** | |
| Hypothesized Difference | 0 |
| Level of Significance | 0.05 |
| **Population 1 Sample** | |
| Sample Size | 54 |
| Sample Mean | 4.5 |
| Sample Standard Deviation | 1.532786 |
| **Population 2 Sample** | |
| Sample Size | 15 |
| Sample Mean | 4.13333 |
| Sample Standard Deviation | 1.743833 |
| Intermediate Calculations | |
| Population 1 Sample Degrees of Freedom | 53 |
| Population 2 Sample Degrees of Freedom | 14 |
| Total Degrees of Freedom | 67 |
| Pooled Variance | 2.49393 |
| Difference in Sample Means | 0.36667 |
| *t*-Test Statistic | 0.79552 |
| **Two-Tailed Test** | |
| Lower Critical Value | -1.99601 |
| Upper Critical Value | 1.996009 |
| *p*-Value | 0.42912 |
| **Do not reject the null hypothesis** | |

Since the $p$-value of 0.429 is greater than the 5% level of significance, do not reject the null hypothesis. There is insufficient evidence to conclude that there is any difference in mean alcohol content between domestic beers and imported beers.

10.96 (a) $H_0: \sigma_1^2 = \sigma_2^2$ vs. $H_1: \sigma_1^2 \neq \sigma_2^2$

| F Test for Differences in Two Variances | |
|---|---|
| | |
| **Data** | |
| Level of Significance | 0.05 |
| **Population 1 Sample** | |
| Sample Size | 43 |
| Sample Standard Deviation | 8109.497 |
| **Population 2 Sample** | |
| Sample Size | 37 |
| Sample Standard Deviation | 4437.92 |
| | |
| Intermediate Calculations | |
| *F*-Test Statistic | 3.339096 |
| Population 1 Sample Degrees of Freedom | 42 |
| Population 2 Sample Degrees of Freedom | 36 |
| | |
| **Two-Tailed Test** | |
| Lower Critical Value | 0.532047 |
| Upper Critical Value | 1.909555 |
| *p*-Value | 0.000361 |
| **Reject the null hypothesis** | |

Since $p$-value = 0.000361 < 0.05, reject $H_0$. There is evidence of a difference

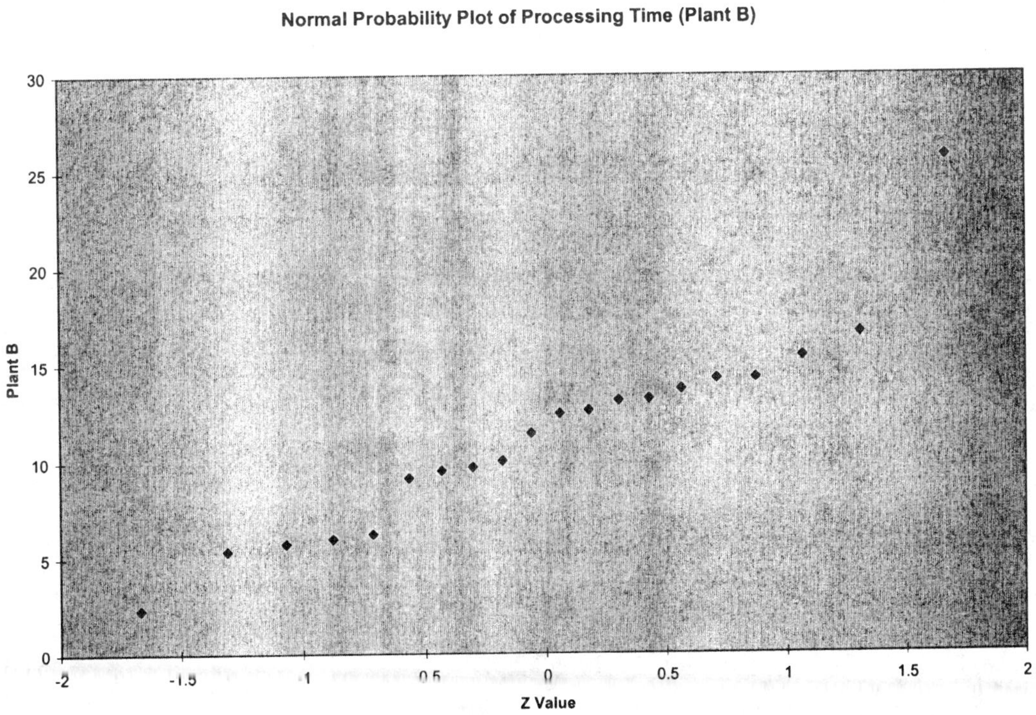


between the variances in the attendance at games with promotions and games without promotions.

10.96 cont. (b) Since the variances cannot assumed to be equal, a separate-variance *t* test for differences in two means should be used.

$H_0 : \mu_I = \mu_{II}$ Mean attendance at games with promotions and games without promotions are the same.

$H_1 : \mu_I \neq \mu_{II}$ Mean attendance at games with promotions and games without promotions are different.

t-Test: Two-Sample Assuming Unequal Variances

| | Y | N |
|---|---|---|
| Mean | 20748.93 | 13935.7 |
| Variance | 65763939 | 19695135 |
| Observations | 43 | 37 |
| Hypothesized Mean Difference | 0 | |
| df | 67 | |
| t Stat | 4.745049 | |
| P(T<=t) one-tail | 5.67E-06 | |
| t Critical one-tail | 1.667916 | |
| P(T<=t) two-tail | 1.13E-05 | |
| t Critical two-tail | 1.996009 | |

Since the *p*-value is essentially zero, reject $H_0$.

(c) There is evidence that there is a difference in the mean attendance at games with promotions and games without promotions at a 5% level of significance.

10.98

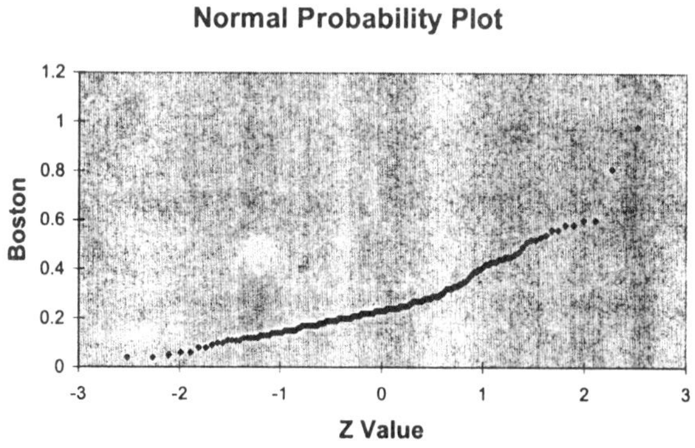


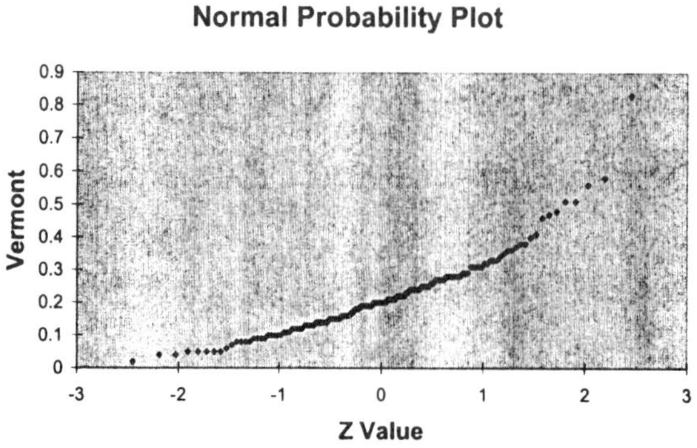

10.98 cont. The normal probability plots suggest that the two populations are not normally distributed so an $F$ test is inappropriate for testing the difference in two variances. The sample variances for Boston and Vermont shingles are 0.0203 and 0.015, respectively, which are not very different. It appears that a pooled-variance $t$ test is appropriate for testing the difference in means.

$H_0 : \mu_B = \mu_V$ Mean granule loss of Boston and Vermont shingles are the same.

$H_1 : \mu_B \neq \mu_V$ Mean granule loss of Boston and Vermont shingles are different.

t-Test: Two-Sample Assuming Equal Variances

| | Boston | Vermont |
|---|---|---|
| Mean | 0.264059 | 0.218 |
| Variance | 0.020273 | 0.015055 |
| Observations | 170 | 140 |
| Pooled Variance | 0.017918 | |
| Hypothesized Mean Difference | 0 | |
| df | 308 | |
| t Stat | 3.014921 | |
| P(T<=t) one-tail | 0.001392 | |
| t Critical one-tail | 1.649817 | |
| P(T<=t) two-tail | 0.002784 | |
| t Critical two-tail | 1.967696 | |

Since the $p$-value = 0.0028 is less than the 5% level of significance, reject $H_0$. There is sufficient evidence to conclude that there is a difference in the mean granule loss of Boston and Vermont shingles.

10.100 (a) To test the homogeneity of variance, you perform a Levene's Test.

$H_0$: $\sigma_1^2 = \sigma_2^2 = \sigma_3^2$ $H_1$: Not all $\sigma_j^2$ are the same

Excel output:

ANOVA

| *Source of Variation* | *SS* | *df* | *MS* | *F* | *P-value* | *F crit* |
|---|---|---|---|---|---|---|
| Between Groups | 0.07 | 2 | 0.035 | 0.07468 | 0.928383 | 3.682317 |
| Within Groups | 7.03 | 15 | 0.468667 | | | |
| | | | | | | |
| Total | 7.1 | 17 | | | | |

Since the $p$-value = 0.928 > 0.05, do not reject $H_0$. There is not enough evidence of a significant difference in the variances of the breaking strengths for the three air-jet pressures.

(b) $H_0$: $\mu_1 = \mu_2 = \mu_3$ $H_1$: At least one of the means differs.

Decision rule: If $F > 3.68$, reject $H_0$.

Minitab Output

One-Way Analysis of Variance

Analysis of Variance on Strength

| Source | DF | SS | MS | F | p |
|---|---|---|---|---|---|
| Pressure | 2 | 8.074 | 4.037 | 4.09 | 0.038 |
| Error | 15 | 14.815 | 0.988 | | |
| Total | 17 | 22.889 | | | |

Test statistic: $F = 4.09$

Decision: Since $F_{calc} = 4.09$ is greater than the critical bound of $F = 3.68$, reject $H_0$. There is enough evidence to conclude that the mean breaking strengths differ for the three air-jet pressures.

10.100 (c) $Q_{(c,n-c)} = Q_{U(3,\,15)} = 3.67$

cont. critical range = $Q_{U(c,\,n-c)}\sqrt{\frac{MSW}{2}\left(\frac{1}{n_j}+\frac{1}{n_{j'}}\right)} = 3.67\sqrt{\frac{0.988}{2}\left(\frac{1}{6}+\frac{1}{6}\right)} = 1.489$

The pair of means that differs at the 0.05 level is marked with * below.

$\left|\bar{X}_{30}-\bar{X}_{40}\right| = 1.30$ $\left|\bar{X}_{30}-\bar{X}_{50}\right| = 1.516*$ $\left|\bar{X}_{40}-\bar{X}_{50}\right| = 0.216$

Breaking strength scores under 30 psi are significantly higher than those under 50 psi.

(d) Other things being equal, use 30 psi.

10.104 It is reasonable to think that those mutual funds with fees will have to be compensated with higher mean return. Hence, you will like to find out if there is evidence that mutual funds with fees have a higher mean return than those without fees.

Populations: 1 = with fees, 2 = without fees

**2003 return:**

$H_0$: $\sigma_1^2 = \sigma_2^2$ The population variances are the same.

$H_1$: $\sigma_1^2 \neq \sigma_2^2$ The population variances are different.

PHStat output:

| | |
|---|---|
| **Data** | |
| **Level of Significance** | **0.05** |
| **Population 1 Sample** | |
| **Sample Size** | **97** |
| **Sample Standard Deviation** | **13.5483** |
| **Population 2 Sample** | |
| **Sample Size** | **24** |
| **Sample Standard Deviation** | **10.9817** |
| | |
| Intermediate Calculations | |
| *F*-Test Statistic | 1.522055 |
| Population 1 Sample Degrees of Freedom | 96 |
| Population 2 Sample Degrees of Freedom | 23 |
| | |
| **Two-Tailed Test** | |
| **Lower Critical Value** | **0.554225** |
| **Upper Critical Value** | **2.059167** |
| ***p*-Value** | **0.249905** |
| **Do not reject the null hypothesis** | |

Decision rule: If $F > 2.0592$ or $F < 0.5542$, reject $H_0$.

Test statistic: $F = \frac{S_1^2}{S_2^2} = \frac{13.5482^2}{10.9817^2} = 1.5221$

Decision: Since $F = 1.5221$ is between the critical bounds of $F_U = 2.0592$ and $F_L = 0.5542$, do not reject $H_0$. There is not enough evidence to conclude that the two population variances are different. Hence, the appropriate test for the difference in two means is the pooled-variance *t* test.

10.104 cont.

$H_0$: $\mu_1 \leq \mu_2$ $H_1$: $\mu_1 > \mu_2$

PHStat output:

| Data | |
|---|---|
| **Hypothesized Difference** | **0** |
| **Level of Significance** | **0.05** |
| **Population 1 Sample** | |
| **Sample Size** | **97** |
| **Sample Mean** | **42.60515** |
| **Sample Standard Deviation** | **13.5483** |
| **Population 2 Sample** | |
| **Sample Size** | **24** |
| **Sample Mean** | **42.6875** |
| **Sample Standard Deviation** | **10.9817** |
| | |
| Intermediate Calculations | |
| Population 1 Sample Degrees of Freedom | 96 |
| Population 2 Sample Degrees of Freedom | 23 |
| Total Degrees of Freedom | 119 |
| Pooled Variance | 171.3879 |
| Difference in Sample Means | -0.08235 |
| *t*-Test Statistic | -0.02759 |
| | |
| **Upper-Tail Test** | |
| **Upper Critical Value** | **1.657759** |
| ***p*-Value** | **0.510983** |
| **Do not reject the null hypothesis** | |

Decision: Since $t = -0.0276$ is less than the upper critical bound of 1.6578, do not reject $H_0$. There is insufficient evidence to conclude that the mean 2003 return is higher for mutual funds with fees than those without fees.

10.104 **3-year return:**

cont.

$H_0$: $\sigma_1^2 = \sigma_2^2$ The population variances are the same.

$H_1$: $\sigma_1^2 \neq \sigma_2^2$ The population variances are different.

PHStat output:

| Data | |
|---|---|
| **Level of Significance** | **0.05** |
| **Population 1 Sample** | |
| **Sample Size** | **97** |
| **Sample Standard Deviation** | **9.541635** |
| **Population 2 Sample** | |
| **Sample Size** | **24** |
| **Sample Standard Deviation** | **10.64768** |
| | |
| Intermediate Calculations | |
| *F*-Test Statistic | 0.803037 |
| Population 1 Sample Degrees of Freedom | 96 |
| Population 2 Sample Degrees of Freedom | 23 |
| | |
| **Two-Tailed Test** | |
| **Lower Critical Value** | **0.554225** |
| **Upper Critical Value** | **2.059167** |
| ***p*-Value** | **0.455238** |
| **Do not reject the null hypothesis** | |

Decision rule: If $F < 0.5542$ or $F > 2.0592$, reject $H_0$.

Test statistic: $F = \dfrac{S_1^2}{S_2^2} = \dfrac{9.5416^2}{10.6477^2} = 0.8030$

Decision: Since $F = 0.8030$ is between the critical bounds of $F_L = 0.5542$ and $F_U = 2.0592$, do not reject $H_0$. There is not enough evidence to conclude that the two population variances are different. Hence, the appropriate test for the difference in two means is the pooled-variance $t$ test.

10.104 cont.

$H_0$: $\mu_1 \le \mu_2$ $H_1$: $\mu_1 > \mu_2$

PHStat output:

| Data | |
|---|---|
| **Hypothesized Difference** | **0** |
| **Level of Significance** | **0.05** |
| **Population 1 Sample** | |
| **Sample Size** | **97** |
| **Sample Mean** | **7.596907** |
| **Sample Standard Deviation** | **9.541635** |
| **Population 2 Sample** | |
| **Sample Size** | **24** |
| **Sample Mean** | **8.354167** |
| **Sample Standard Deviation** | **10.64768** |
| | |
| Intermediate Calculations | |
| Population 1 Sample Degrees of Freedom | 96 |
| Population 2 Sample Degrees of Freedom | 23 |
| Total Degrees of Freedom | 119 |
| Pooled Variance | 95.35874 |
| Difference in Sample Means | -0.75726 |
| *t*-Test Statistic | -0.34014 |
| | |
| **Upper-Tail Test** | |
| **Upper Critical Value** | **1.657759** |
| ***p*-Value** | **0.632826** |
| **Do not reject the null hypothesis** | |

Decision: Since $t = -0.3401$ is less than the upper critical bound of 1.6578, do not reject $H_0$. There is insufficient evidence to conclude that the mean 3-year return is higher for mutual funds with fees than those without fees.

10.104 **5-year return:**
cont.

$H_0$: $\sigma_1^2 = \sigma_2^2$ The population variances are the same.
$H_1$: $\sigma_1^2 \neq \sigma_2^2$ The population variances are different.

PHStat output:

| Data | |
|---|---|
| **Level of Significance** | **0.05** |
| **Population 1 Sample** | |
| **Sample Size** | **97** |
| **Sample Standard Deviation** | **6.503054** |
| **Population 2 Sample** | |
| **Sample Size** | **24** |
| **Sample Standard Deviation** | **5.560471** |
| | |
| Intermediate Calculations | |
| *F*-Test Statistic | 1.367765 |
| Population 1 Sample Degrees of Freedom | 96 |
| Population 2 Sample Degrees of Freedom | 23 |
| | |
| **Two-Tailed Test** | |
| **Lower Critical Value** | **0.554225** |
| **Upper Critical Value** | **2.059167** |
| ***p*-Value** | **0.394741** |
| **Do not reject the null hypothesis** | |

Decision rule: If $F < 0.5542$ or $F > 2.0592$, reject $H_0$.

Test statistic: $F = \dfrac{S_1^2}{S_2^2} = 1.3678$

Decision: Since $F = 1.3678$ is between the critical bounds of $F_L = 0.5542$ and $F_U = 2.0592$, do not reject $H_0$. There is not enough evidence to conclude that the two population variances are different. Hence, the appropriate test for the difference in two means is the pooled-variance $t$ test.

10.104 cont. $H_0$: $\mu_1 \le \mu_2$ $H_1$: $\mu_1 > \mu_2$

PHStat output:

| Data | |
|---|---|
| Hypothesized Difference | 0 |
| Level of Significance | 0.05 |
| Population 1 Sample | |
| Sample Size | 97 |
| Sample Mean | 12.4134 |
| Sample Standard Deviation | 6.503054 |
| Population 2 Sample | |
| Sample Size | 24 |
| Sample Mean | 13.36667 |
| Sample Standard Deviation | 5.560471 |
| | |
| Intermediate Calculations | |
| Population 1 Sample Degrees of Freedom | 96 |
| Population 2 Sample Degrees of Freedom | 23 |
| Total Degrees of Freedom | 119 |
| Pooled Variance | 40.09198 |
| Difference in Sample Means | -0.95327 |
| *t*-Test Statistic | -0.66037 |
| | |
| Upper-Tail Test | |
| Upper Critical Value | 1.657759 |
| *p*-Value | 0.744853 |
| Do not reject the null hypothesis | |

Decision: Since $t = -0.6604$ is less than the upper critical bound of 1.6578, do not reject $H_0$. There is insufficient evidence to conclude that the mean 5-year return is higher for mutual funds with fees than those without fees.

Even though you may think that those mutual funds with fees will have a higher mean return than those without fees to compensate for the fees that investors will have to pay, the test results do not support this belief. There is not enough evidence to conclude that mutual funds with fees have a higher mean 2003 return, mean 3-year return or mean 5-year return compared to those without fees.

# CHAPTER 11

## OBJECTIVES

- To understand how to use and when to use the Chi-Square test for contingency tables
- To understand how to use the Marascuilo procedure for determining pairwise differences when evaluating more than two proportions

## OVERVIEW AND KEY CONCEPTS

### $\chi^2$ Test for Differences in Two Proportions (Independent Samples)

- **Assumptions:**
  - Independent samples
  - Large sample sizes: All expected frequencies $\geq$ 5.
- **Test statistic:**
  - $\chi^2 = \sum_{\text{All Cells}} \frac{(f_0 - f_e)^2}{f_e}$ with 1 degree of freedom

    where

    $f_o$ : observed frequency in a cell

    $f_e$ = [(row total)(column total)]/n : expected frequency in a cell
  - The rejection region is always in the right tail.

### $\chi^2$ Test for Differences among More Than Two Proportions

- **Assumptions:**
  - Independent samples
  - Large sample sizes: All expected frequencies $\geq$ 1.
- **Test statistic:**
  - $\chi^2 = \sum_{\text{All Cells}} \frac{(f_0 - f_e)^2}{f_e}$ with $(c-1)$ degree of freedom

    where

    $f_o$ : observed frequency in a cell

    $f_e$ = [(row total)(column total)]/n: expected frequency in a cell.
  - The rejection region is always in the right tail.

## Marasculio Procedure

- Enable one to make comparison between all pairs of groups.
- **The Marasculio multiple comparison procedure:**
  1. Compute the absolute differences $\left|p_j - p_{j'}\right|$ among all pairs of groups.
  2. The critical range for a pair where $j \neq j'$ is $\sqrt{\chi_U^2}\sqrt{\frac{p_j(1-p_j)}{n_j}+\frac{p_{j'}(1-p_{j'})}{n_{j'}}}$ where

     $\chi_U^2$ is the upper-tail critical value from a $\chi^2$ distribution with $(c-1)$ degrees of freedom.
  3. A specific pair is considered significantly different if $\left|p_j - p_{j'}\right|$ > critical range.

## $\chi^2$ Test of Independence

- **Assumptions:**
  - One sample is drawn with two factors; each factor has two or more levels (categories) of responses.
  - Large sample sizes: All expected frequencies $\geq 1$.
- **Test statistic:**
  - $\chi^2 = \sum_{\text{All Cells}} \frac{(f_0 - f_e)^2}{f_e}$ with $(r-1)(c-1)$ degree of freedom

    where

    $f_o$ : observed frequency in a cell

    $f_e$ = [(row total)(column total)]/n: expected frequency in a cell

    *r*: the number of rows in the contingency table.

    *c*: the number of columns in the contingency table.
  - The rejection region is always in the right tail.
  - The $\chi^2$ test does not show the nature of any relationship nor causality.

# SOLUTIONS TO END OF SECTION AND CHAPTER REVIEW EVEN PROBLEMS

11.2 (a) For $df = 1$ and $\alpha = 0.95$, $\chi^2 = 0.0039$.
(b) For $df = 1$ and $\alpha = 0.975$, $\chi^2 = 0.00098$.
(c) For $df = 1$ and $\alpha = 0.99$, $\chi^2 = 0.000157$.

11.4 (a)

| | | | | |
|---|---|---|---|---|
| Observed Freq | *Expected Freq* | Observed Freq | *Expected Freq* | Total Obs, Row 1 |
| 20 | 25 | 30 | 25 | 50 |
| chi-sq contrib= 1.00 | | chi-sq contrib= 1.00 | | |
| Observed Freq | *Expected Freq* | Observed Freq | *Expected Freq* | Total Obs, Row 2 |
| 30 | 25 | 20 | 25 | 50 |
| chi-sq contrib= 1.00 | | chi-sq contrib= 1.00 | | |
| Total Obs, Col 1 | | Total Obs, Col 2 | | GRAND TOTAL |
| 50 | | 50 | | 100 |

(b) Decision rule: If $\chi^2 > 3.841$, reject $H_0$.

Test statistic: $\chi^2 = \sum \frac{(f_0 - f_e)^2}{f_e} = 1.00 + 1.00 + 1.00 + 1.00 = 4$

Decision: Since $\chi^2_{calc} = 4$ is greater than the critical value of 3.841, it is significant at the 5% level of significance.

11.6 (a) $H_0$: $\pi_1 = \pi_2$ $H_1$: $\pi_1 \neq \pi_2$
Decision rule: $df = 1$. If $\chi^2 > 3.841$, reject $H_0$.
Test statistic: $\chi^2 = 1$
Decision: Since $\chi^2 = 1$ is less than the upper critical bound of 3.841, do not reject $H_0$. There is not enough evidence to conclude that there is a significant difference between males and females in the proportion who make gas mileage a priority.

(b) $H_0$: $\pi_1 = \pi_2$ $H_1$: $\pi_1 \neq \pi_2$
Decision rule: $df = 1$. If $\chi^2 > 3.841$, reject $H_0$.
Test statistic: $\chi^2 = 10$
Decision: Since $\chi^2 = 10$ is greater than the upper critical bound of 3.841, reject $H_0$. There is enough evidence to conclude that there is a significant difference between males and females in the proportion who make gas mileage a priority.

(c) The larger sample size in (b) increases the difference between the observed and expected frequencies and, hence, results in a larger test statistic value.

11.8 (a) $H_0$: $\pi_1 = \pi_2$ $H_1$: $\pi_1 \neq \pi_2$

PHStat output with computation:

| | | | | | | |
|---|---|---|---|---|---|---|
| **Observed Frequencies** | | | | | | |
| | **Column variable** | | | | **Calculations** | |
| **Row variable** | **African Americans** | **Whites** | **Total** | | **fo-fe** | |
| **Own Stocks** | **370** | **420** | **790** | | -25 | 25 |
| **Do Not Own Stocks** | **130** | **80** | **210** | | 25 | -25 |
| **Total** | **500** | **500** | **1000** | | | |
| Expected Frequencies | | | | | | |
| | Column variable | | | | | |
| Row variable | African Americans | Whites | Total | | **(fo-fe)^2/fe** | |
| Own Stocks | 395 | 395 | 790 | | 1.58227 | 1.58227 |
| Do Not Own Stocks | 105 | 105 | 210 | | 5.95238 | 5.95238 |
| Total | 500 | 500 | 1000 | | | |
| **Data** | | | | | | |
| **Level of Significance** | **0.05** | | | | | |
| Number of Rows | 2 | | | | | |
| Number of Columns | 2 | | | | | |
| Degrees of Freedom | 1 | | | | | |
| **Results** | | | | | | |
| **Critical Value** | **3.841455** | | | | | |
| **Chi-Square Test Statistic** | **15.06932** | | | | | |
| ***p*-Value** | **0.000104** | | | | | |
| **Reject the null hypothesis** | | | | | | |

Decision rule: $df = 1$. If $\chi^2 > 3.841$, reject $H_0$.

Test statistic: $\chi^2 = \sum_{\text{all cells}} \frac{(f_0 - f_e)^2}{f_e} = 15.0693$

Decision: Since $\chi^2_{\text{calc}} = 15.0693$ is greater than the upper critical bound of 3.841, reject $H_0$. There is enough evidence to conclude that there is a significant difference in the proportion of African American and whites who invest in stocks.

(b) $p$-value is 0.0001. The probability of obtaining a test statistic of 15.0693 or larger when the null hypothesis is true is 0.0001.

(c) The results of (a) and (b) are exactly the same as those of Problem 10.39. The $\chi^2_{calc}$ in (a) and the $Z_{calc}$ in Problem 10.39 (a) satisfy the relationship that $\chi^2_{calc} = 15.0693 = (Z_{calc})^2 = (-3.8819)^2$ and the $p$-value in Problem 10.39 (b) is exactly the same as the $p$-value obtained in (b).

11.10 (a) $H_0$: $\pi_1 = \pi_2$ $H_1$: $\pi_1 \neq \pi_2$

Decision rule: $df = 1$. If $\chi^2 > 3.841$, reject $H_0$.

Test statistic: $\chi^2 = 33.333$

Decision: Since $\chi^2_{calc} = 33.333$ is greater than the upper critical bound of 3.841, reject $H_0$. There is enough evidence to conclude that there is a significant difference between the proportion of males and females who place more importance on brand names today than a few years ago.

(b) $p$-value is virtually 0. The probability of obtaining a test statistic of 33.333 or larger when the null hypothesis is true is virtually 0.

11.12 (a) The expected frequencies in the first row are 20, 30, and 40.

The expected frequencies in the second row are 30, 45, and 60.

(b) $\chi^2 = 12.500$. The critical value with 2 degrees of freedom and $\alpha = 0.05$ is 5.991. The result is deemed significant.

(c) Pairs of proportions that differ at the 0.05 level are marked with * below:

| **Pairwise Comparisons** | **Critical Range** | $\lvert p_j - p_{j'} \rvert$ |
|---|---|---|
| A to B | 0.19582 | 0.2* |
| A to C | 0.1848 | 0.3* |
| B to C | 0.1848 | 0.1 |

There are two (2) pairs of proportions that differ significantly.

11.14 PHStat output:

| Observed Frequencies | | | | | | |
|---|---|---|---|---|---|---|
| | Column variable | | | | | |
| Row variable | Germany | France | UK | Greece | US | Total |
| Yes | 100 | 120 | 280 | 390 | 570 | 1460 |
| No | 900 | 880 | 720 | 610 | 430 | 3540 |
| Total | 1000 | 1000 | 1000 | 1000 | 1000 | 5000 |

| Expected Frequencies | | | | | | |
|---|---|---|---|---|---|---|
| | Column variable | | | | | |
| Row variable | Germany | France | UK | Greece | US | Total |
| Yes | 292 | 292 | 292 | 292 | 292 | 1460 |
| No | 708 | 708 | 708 | 708 | 708 | 3540 |
| Total | 1000 | 1000 | 1000 | 1000 | 1000 | 5000 |

| Data | |
|---|---|
| **Level of Significance** | **0.05** |
| Number of Rows | 2 |
| Number of Columns | 5 |
| Degrees of Freedom | 4 |

| Results | |
|---|---|
| **Critical Value** | **9.487728** |
| **Chi-Square Test Statistic** | **742.3961** |
| ***p*-Value** | **2.3E-159** |
| **Reject the null hypothesis** | |

(a) $H_0: \pi_1 = \pi_2 = \pi_3 = \pi_4 = \pi_5$ $\qquad H_1:$ Not all $\pi_j$ are equal.

where population 1 = Germany, 2 = France, 3 = UK, 4 = Greece, 5 = US

Test statistic: $\chi^2 = \sum_{\text{All cells}} \frac{(f_o - f_e)^2}{f_e} = 742.3961$

Decision: Since the calculated test statistic 742.3961 is greater than the critical value of 9.4877, you reject $H_0$ and conclude that there is a difference in the proportion of people who eat out at least once a week in the various countries.

(b) *p*-value is virtually zero. The probability of obtaining a data set which gives rise to a test statistic of 742.3961 or more is virtually zero if there is no difference in the proportion of people who eat out at least once a week in the various countries.

11.14 (c) cont.

Excel output of the Marascuilo procedure:

| Group | Sample Proportion | Sample Size | | |
|---|---|---|---|---|
| 1 | 0.10 | 1000 | | |
| 2 | 0.12 | 1000 | | |
| 3 | 0.28 | 1000 | | |
| 4 | 0.39 | 1000 | | |
| 5 | 0.57 | 1000 | | |
| | | | | |
| | | | | |
| Other Data | | | | |
| Level of significance | 0.05 | | | |
| d.f | 4 | | | |
| Sqrt(chi-square) | 3.0802 | | | |
| | | | | |
| Comparison | Absolute Difference | Std. Error of Difference | Critical Range | Results |
| Group 1 to Group 2 | 0.02 | 0.01399 | 0.04308 | Means are not different |
| Group 1 to Group 3 | 0.18 | 0.01708 | 0.05260 | Means are different |
| Group 1 to Group 4 | 0.29 | 0.01811 | 0.05578 | Means are different |
| Group 1 to Group 5 | 0.47 | 0.01831 | 0.05639 | Means are different |
| Group 2 to Group 3 | 0.16 | 0.01753 | 0.05399 | Means are different |
| Group 2 to Group 4 | 0.27 | 0.01853 | 0.05709 | Means are different |
| Group 2 to Group 5 | 0.45 | 0.01873 | 0.05768 | Means are different |
| Group 3 to Group 4 | 0.11 | 0.02096 | 0.06457 | Means are different |
| Group 3 to Group 5 | 0.29 | 0.02114 | 0.06510 | Means are different |
| Group 4 to Group 5 | 0.18 | 0.02198 | 0.06769 | Means are different |

At 5% level of significance, there is no significant difference between the proportions of Germany and France while there is significant difference between all the remaining pairs of countries.

11.16 (a) $H_0: \pi_1 = \pi_2 = \pi_3$  $H_1$: at least one proportion differs

where population 1 = under 35, 2 = 35-54, 3 = over 54

PHStat output:

| **Observed Frequencies** | | | | | | | |
|---|---|---|---|---|---|---|---|
| | **Column variable** | | | | **Calculations** | | |
| **Row variable** | **Under 35** | **35-54** | **Over 54** | **Total** | **fo-fe** | | |
| **Saturday** | **48** | **56** | **24** | **128** | 5.333 | 13.333 | -18.667 |
| **A Day other than Saturday** | **152** | **144** | **176** | **472** | -5.333 | -13.333 | 18.667 |
| **Total** | **200** | **200** | **200** | **600** | | | |
| | | | | | | | |
| Expected Frequencies | | | | | | | |
| | Column variable | | | | | | |
| Row variable | Under 35 | 35-54 | Over 54 | Total | **(fo-fe)^2/fe** | | |
| Saturday | 42.667 | 42.667 | 42.667 | 128 | 0.667 | 4.167 | 8.167 |
| A Day other than Saturday | 157.333 | 157.333 | 157.333 | 472 | 0.181 | 1.130 | 2.215 |
| Total | 200 | 200 | 200 | 600 | | | |

| **Data** | |
|---|---|
| **Level of Significance** | **0.05** |
| Number of Rows | 2 |
| Number of Columns | 3 |
| Degrees of Freedom | 2 |
| | |
| **Results** | |
| **Critical Value** | **5.9915** |
| **Chi-Square Test Statistic** | **16.5254** |
| ***p*-Value** | **0.0003** |
| **Reject the null hypothesis** | |

Decision rule: $df = (c-1) = (3-1) = 2$. If $\chi^2 > 5.9915$, reject $H_0$.

Test statistic: $\chi^2 = \sum_{\text{all cells}} \frac{(f_0 - f_e)^2}{f_e} = 16.5254$

Decision: Since $\chi^2_{calc} = 16.5254$ is greater than the upper critical bound of 5.9915, reject $H_0$. There is enough evidence to conclude that there is a significant relationship between age and major grocery shopping day.

(b) $p$-value = 0.0003. The probability of obtaining a sample that gives rise to a test statistic that is equal to or more than 16.5254 is 0.03% if the null hypothesis is true.

11.16 (c) cont.

| Pairwise Comparisons | Critical Range | $\lvert p_j - p_{j'} \rvert$ |
|---|---|---|
| 1 to 2 | 0.1073 | 0.04 |
| 2 to 3 | 0.0959 | 0.16* |
| 1 to 3 | 0.0929 | 0.12* |

There is a significance difference between the 35-54 and over 54 groups, and between the under 35 and over 54 groups.

(d) The stores can use this information to target their marketing on the specific group of shoppers on Saturday and the days other than Saturday.

11.18 (a) $H_0: \pi_1 = \pi_2 = \pi_3$ $H_1$: at least one proportion differs

where population 1 = insurance companies, 2 = pharmacies, 3 = medical researchers

Decision rule: $df = (c-1) = (3-1) = 2$. If $\chi^2 > 5.9915$, reject $H_0$.

Test statistic: $\chi^2 = 128.24$

Decision: Since $\chi^2_{calc} = 128.24$ is greater than the upper critical bound of 5.9915, reject $H_0$. There is enough evidence to show that there is a significant difference in the proportion of people who object to their medical records being shared.

(b)

| Pairwise Comparisons | Critical Range | $\lvert p_j - p_{j'} \rvert$ |
|---|---|---|
| 1 to 2 | 0.0483 | 0.23* |
| 2 to 3 | 0.0527 | 0.08* |
| 1 to 3 | 0.0470 | 0.15* |

There is a significance difference between any pair of the organizations.

11.20 (a) $H_0: \pi_1 = \pi_2 = \pi_3$ $H_1$: Not all $\pi_j$ are equal.

**Observed Frequencies:**

| | City | | | |
|---|---|---|---|---|
| **Minibar Charges Posted** | **Hong Kong** | **New York** | **Paris** | **Total** |
| **Yes** | 86 | 76 | 78 | 240 |
| **No** | 14 | 24 | 22 | 60 |
| **Total** | 100 | 100 | 100 | 300 |

**Expected Frequencies:**

| | City | | | |
|---|---|---|---|---|
| **Minibar Charges Posted** | **Hong Kong** | **New York** | **Paris** | **Total** |
| **Yes** | 80 | 80 | 80 | 240 |
| **No** | 20 | 20 | 20 | 60 |
| **Total** | 100 | 100 | 100 | 300 |

| | |
|---|---|
| **Level of Significance** | 0.05 |
| Number of Rows | 2 |
| Number of Columns | 3 |
| Degrees of Freedom | 2 |
| **Critical Value** | 5.991476 |
| **Chi-Square Test Statistic** | 3.499998 |
| ***p*-Value** | 0.173774 |
| **Do not reject the null hypothesis** | |

Test statistic: $$\chi^2 = \sum_{\text{All cells}} \frac{(f_o - f_e)^2}{f_e} = 3.50$$

11.20 cont. (a) Decision: Since the calculated test statistic of 3.50 is smaller than the critical value of 5.991, you do not reject the null hypothesis. There is not sufficient evidence to conclude that there is a difference in the proportion of hotels that correctly post minibar charges among the three cities.

(b) The $p$-value is 0.174. The probability of obtaining a sample that gives rise to a test statistic equal to or more extreme than 3.5 is 0.174 if the null hypothesis is true.

11.22 Since the null hypotheses are not rejected for all the 3 items, it is not necessary to perform the Marascuilo procedure.

11.24 $df = (r-1)(c-1) = (3-1)(4-1) = 6$

11.26 (a) $H_0$: There is no relationship between the quarter of the year and the numbers assigned.

$H_1$: There is a relationship between the quarter of the year and the numbers assigned.

Decision rule: If $\chi^2 > 12.592$, reject $H_0$.

**Lottery Fairness**

**Observed Frequencies:**

| | Quarter of Year | | | | |
|---|---|---|---|---|---|
| Number Set | Jan-Mar | Apr-June | Jul-Sept | Oct-Dec | Total |
| Low | 21 | 28 | 35 | 38 | 122 |
| Medium | 34 | 22 | 29 | 37 | 122 |
| High | 36 | 41 | 28 | 17 | 122 |
| Total | 91 | 91 | 92 | 92 | 366 |

**Expected Frequencies:**

| | Quarter of Year | | | | |
|---|---|---|---|---|---|
| Number Set | Jan-Mar | Apr-June | Jul-Sept | Oct-Dec | Total |
| Low | 30.333333 | 30.333333 | 30.666667 | 30.666667 | 122 |
| Medium | 30.333333 | 30.333333 | 30.666667 | 30.666667 | 122 |
| High | 30.333333 | 30.333333 | 30.666667 | 30.666667 | 122 |
| Total | 91 | 91 | 92 | 92 | 366 |

| | |
|---|---|
| **Level of Significance** | 0.05 |
| Number of Rows | 3 |
| Number of Columns | 4 |
| Degrees of Freedom | 6 |
| **Critical Value** | 12.5916 |
| **Chi-Square Test Statistic** | 20.6802 |
| ***p*-Value** | 0.00209 |
| **Reject the null hypothesis** | |

Test statistic: $\chi^2 = 20.680$

Decision: Since the $\chi^2_{\text{calc}} = 20.680$ is greater than the critical bound of 12.592, reject $H_0$. There is evidence of a relationship between the quarter of the year in which draftable-aged men were born and the numbers assigned as their draft eligibilities during the Vietnam War.

(b) It appears that the results of the lottery drawing are different from what would be expected if the lottery were random.

11.26 cont. (c) (a) $H_0$: There is no relationship between the quarter of the year in which draftable-aged men were born and the numbers assigned as their draft eligibilities during the Vietnam War.

$H_1$: There is a relationship between the quarter of the year in which draftable-aged men were born and the numbers assigned as their draft eligibilities.

Decision rule: If $\chi^2 > 12.592$, reject $H_0$.

Test statistic: $\chi^2 = 9.803$

Decision: Since $\chi^2_{calc} = 9.803$ is less than the critical bound of 12.592, do not reject $H_0$. There is not enough evidence to conclude there is any relationship between the quarter of the year in which draftable-aged men were born and the numbers assigned as their draft eligibilities during the Vietnam War.

(b) It appears that the results of the lottery drawing are consistent with what would be expected if the lottery were random.

11.28 (a) $H_0$: There is no relationship between the commuting time of company employees and the level of stress-related problems observed on the job.

$H_1$: There is a relationship between the commuting time of company employees and the level of stress-related problems observed on the job.

PHStat output:

| **Observed Frequencies** | | | | | | | |
|---|---|---|---|---|---|---|---|
| | **Stress** | | | | **Calculations** | | |
| **Commuting Time** | **High** | **Moderate** | **Low** | **Total** | **fo-fe** | | |
| **Under 15 min.** | 9 | 5 | 18 | 32 | -3.1379 | -0.2414 | 3.3793 |
| **15-45 min.** | 17 | 8 | 28 | 53 | -3.1034 | -0.6810 | 3.7845 |
| **Over 45 min.** | 18 | 6 | 7 | 31 | 6.2414 | 0.9224 | -7.1638 |
| **Total** | 44 | 19 | 53 | 116 | | | |
| **Expected Frequencies** | | | | | | | |
| | **Stress** | | | | | | |
| **Commuting Time** | **High** | **Moderate** | **Low** | **Total** | **(fo-fe)^2/fe** | | |
| **Under 15 min.** | 12.1379 | 5.2414 | 14.6207 | 32 | 0.8112 | 0.0111 | 0.7811 |
| **15-45 min.** | 20.1034 | 8.6810 | 24.2155 | 53 | 0.4791 | 0.0534 | 0.5915 |
| **Over 45 min.** | 11.7586 | 5.0776 | 14.1638 | 31 | 3.3129 | 0.1676 | 3.6233 |
| **Total** | 44 | 19 | 53 | 116 | | | |
| **Level of Significance** | **0.01** | | | | | | |
| Number of Rows | 3 | | | | | | |
| Number of Columns | 3 | | | | | | |
| Degrees of Freedom | 4 | | | | | | |
| **Results** | | | | | | | |
| **Critical Value** | **13.2767** | ***p*-Value** | **0.04337** | | | | |
| **Chi-Square Test Statistic** | **9.8311** | **Do not reject the null hypothesis** | | | | | |

11.28 cont. (a) Decision rule: If $\chi^2 > 13.277$, reject $H_0$.

Test statistic: $\chi^2 = \sum_{\text{all cells}} \frac{(f_0 - f_e)^2}{f_e} = 9.831$

Decision: Since $\chi^2_{\text{calc}} = 9.831$ is less than the critical bound of 13.277, do not reject $H_0$. There is not enough evidence to conclude there is any relationship between the commuting time of company employees and the level of stress-related problems observed on the job.

(b) Decision rule: If $\chi^2 > 9.488$, reject $H_0$.

Test statistic: $\chi^2 = 9.831$

Decision: Since the $\chi^2_{\text{calc}} = 9.831$ is greater than the critical bound of 9.488, reject $H_0$. There is enough evidence at the 0.05 level to conclude there is a relationship between the commuting time of company employees and the level of stress-related problems observed on the job.

11.30 $H_0$: There is no relationship between when the decision is made of what to have for dinner and the type of household.
$H_1$: There is a relationship between when the decision is made of what to have for dinner and the type of household.
Decision rule: $d.f. = 12$. If $\chi^2 > 21.026$, reject $H_0$. Test statistic: $\chi^2 = 129.520$
Decision: Since the $\chi^2_{\text{calc}} = 129.520$ is greater than the critical bound of 21.026, reject $H_0$. There is enough evidence to conclude there is a relationship between when the decision is made of what to have for dinner and the type of household.

11.32 The Chi-square test for the difference between two proportions can be used only when the alternative hypothesis is two-tailed.

11.34 (a) $H_0$: There is no relationship between a student's gender and his/her pizzeria selection.
$H_1$: There is a relationship between a student's gender and his/her pizzeria selection.
Decision rule: $d.f. = 1$. If $\chi^2 > 3.841$, reject $H_0$. Test statistic: $\chi^2 = 0.412$
Decision: Since the $\chi^2_{\text{calc}} = 0.412$ is smaller than the critical bound of 3.841, do not reject $H_0$. There is not enough evidence to conclude that there is a relationship between a student's gender and his/her pizzeria selection.

(b) Test statistic: $\chi^2 = 2.624$
Decision: Since the $\chi^2_{\text{calc}} = 2.624$ is less than the critical bound of 3.841, do not reject $H_0$. There is not enough evidence to conclude that there is a relationship between a student's gender and his/her pizzeria selection.

(c) $H_0$: There is no relationship between price and pizzeria selection.
$H_1$: There is a relationship between price and pizzeria selection.
Decision rule: $d.f. = 2$. If $\chi^2 > 5.991$, reject $H_0$. Test statistic: $\chi^2 = 4.956$
Decision: Since the $\chi^2_{\text{calc}} = 4.956$ is smaller than the critical bound of 5.991, do not reject $H_0$. There is not enough evidence to conclude that there is a relationship between price and pizzeria selection.

(d) $p$-value = 0.0839. The probability of obtaining a sample that gives a test statistic equal to or greater than 4.956 is 8.39% if the null hypothesis of no relationship between price and pizzeria selection is true.

11.34 cont. (e) Since there is no evidence that price and pizzeria selection are related, it is inappropriate to determine which prices are different in terms of pizzeria preference.

11.36 (a) $H_0: \pi_1 = \pi_2$ $H_1: \pi_1 \neq \pi_2$

where population 1 = boys, 2 = girls

Test statistic: $\chi^2 = \sum_{\text{All cells}} \frac{(f_o - f_e)^2}{f_e} = 3.3084$

Decision: Since the calculated test statistic 3.3084 is less than the critical value of 3.8415, you do not reject $H_0$; you conclude that there is not a significant difference between the proportion of boys and girls who worry about having enough money.

(b) $p$-value = 0.0689. The probability of obtaining a data set which gives rise to a test statistic larger than 3.3084 is 6.89% if there is no difference between the proportion of boys and girls who worry about having enough money.

11.38 (a) $H_0$: There is no relationship between type of user and the seriousness of concern over the first statement.

$H_1$: There is a relationship between type of user and the seriousness of concern over the first statement.

Decision rule: If $\chi^2 > 3.841$, reject $H_0$. Test statistic: $\chi^2 = 12.026$

Decision: Since the $\chi^2_{\text{calc}} = 12.026$ is greater than the critical bound of 3.841, reject $H_0$. There is enough evidence to conclude there is a relationship between type of user and the seriousness of concern over the first statement.

(b) The $p$-value = 0.000525. The probability of obtaining a sample that gives rise to a test statistic of 12.026 or larger is 0.000525 if there is in fact no relationship between type of user and the seriousness of concern over the first statement.

(c) $H_0$: There is no relationship between type of user and the seriousness of concern over the second statement.

$H_1$: There is a relationship between type of user and the seriousness of concern over the first statement.

Decision rule: If $\chi^2 > 3.841$, reject $H_0$. Test statistic: $\chi^2 = 7.297$

Decision: Since the $\chi^2_{\text{calc}} = 7.297$ is greater than the critical bound of 3.841, reject $H_0$. There is enough evidence to conclude there is a relationship between type of user and the seriousness of concern over the second statement.

(d) The $p$-value = 0.00691. The probability of obtaining a sample that gives rise to a test statistic of 7.297 or larger is 0.00691 if there is in fact no relationship between type of user and the seriousness of concern over the second statement.

11.40 (a) $H_0$: There is no relationship between the attitudes of employees toward the use of self-managed work teams and employee job classification.
$H_1$: There is a relationship between the attitudes of employees toward the use of self-managed work teams and employee job classification.
Decision rule: If $\chi^2 > 12.592$, reject $H_0$.
Test statistic: $\chi^2 = 11.895$
Decision: Since $\chi^2_{\text{calc}} = 11.895$ is less than the critical bound 12.592, do not reject $H_0$. There is not enough evidence to conclude that there is a relationship between the attitudes of employees toward the use of self-managed work teams and employee job classification.

(b) $H_0$: There is no relationship between the attitudes of employees toward vacation time without pay and employee job classification.
$H_1$: There is a relationship between the attitudes of employees toward vacation time without pay and employee job classification.
Decision rule: If $\chi^2 > 12.592$, reject $H_0$.
Test statistic: $\chi^2 = 3.294$
Decision: Since $\chi^2_{\text{calc}} = 3.294$ is less than the critical bound 12.592, do not reject $H_0$. There is not enough evidence to conclude that there is a relationship between the attitudes of employees toward vacation time without pay and employee job classification.

11.42 $H_0$: There is no relationship between type of incident and type of model.
$H_1$: There is a relationship between type of incident and type of model.

Test statistic: $$\chi^2 = \sum_{\text{All cells}} \frac{(f_o - f_e)^2}{f_e} = 160.38$$

Decision rule: If $\chi^2 > 5.991$, reject $H_0$.
Decision: Since $\chi^2_{\text{calc}} = 160.38$ is greater than the critical bound 5.991, reject $H_0$. There is enough evidence to conclude that there is a relationship between type of incident and type of model.

# CHAPTER 12

## OBJECTIVES

- To use regression analysis to predict the value of a dependent variable based on an independent variable
- To understand the meaning of the regression coefficient $b_0$ and $b_1$
- To be familiar with the assumptions of regression analysis, how to evaluate the assumptions, and what to do if the assumptions are violated
- To be able to make inferences about the slope and correlation coefficient
- To be able to estimate mean values and predict individual values

## OVERVIEW AND KEY CONCEPTS

### Purpose of Regression Analysis

- Regression analysis is used for predicting the values of a dependent (response) variable based on the value of at least one independent (explanatory) variable.

### The Simple Linear Regression Model

- The relationship between the dependent variable $(Y)$ and the explanatory variable $(X)$ is described by a linear function.
- The change of the explanatory variable causes the explained (dependent) variable to change.
- The value of the explained variable depends on the explanatory variable.
- The population linear regression: $Y_i = \beta_0 + \beta_1 X_i + \varepsilon_i$ where $\beta_0$ is the intercept and $\beta_1$ is the slope of the population regression line $\mu_{Y|X} = \beta_0 + \beta_1 X_i$ and $\varepsilon_i$ is called the error term.

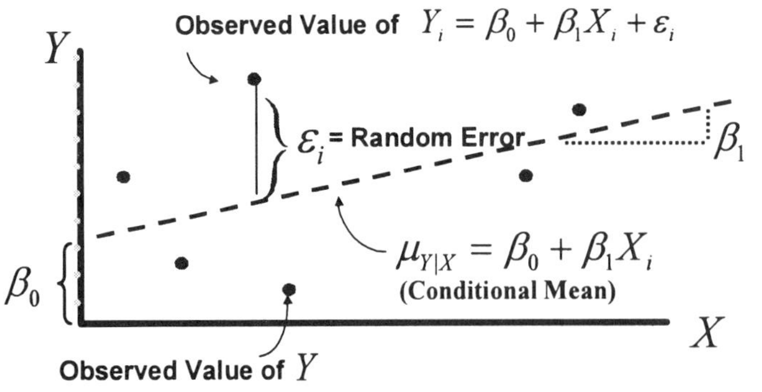


- The parameters $\beta_0$ and $\beta_1$ are unknown and need to be estimated.
- The least squares estimates for $\beta_0$ and $\beta_1$ are $b_0$ and $b_1$, respectively, obtained by minimizing the sum of squared residuals, $\sum_{i=1}^{n}\left(Y_i - (b_0 + b_1 X_i)\right)^2 = \sum_{i=1}^{n} e_i^2$.

- The sample linear regression: $Y_i = b_0 + b_1 X_i + e_i$ where $b_0$ is the intercept and $b_1$ is the slope of the simple linear regression equation $\hat{Y} = b_0 + b_1 X_i$ and $e_i$ is called the residual.
- The simple linear regression equation (sample regression line) $\hat{Y} = b_0 + b_1 X_i$ can be used to predict the value of the dependent variable for a given value of the independent variable $X$.

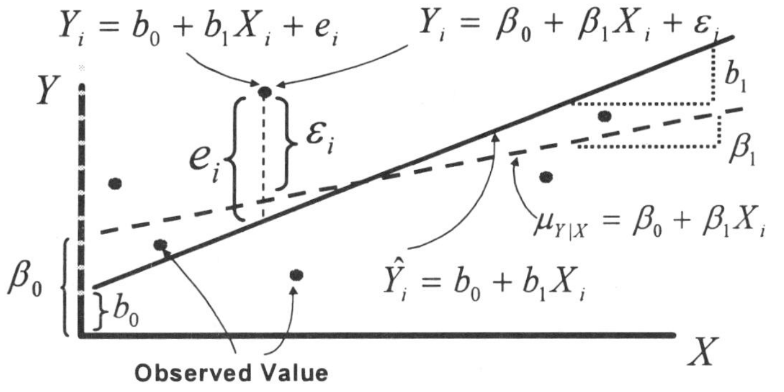


**Interpretations of $\beta_0$, $\beta_1$, $b_0$ and $b_1$**

- $\beta_0 = E(Y \mid X = 0) = \mu_{Y|X=0}$ is the average value of $Y$ when the value of $X$ is zero.
- $b_0 = \hat{E}(Y \mid X = 0) = \hat{Y}(X = 0)$ is the *estimated* average value of $Y$ when the value of $X$ is zero.
- $\beta_1 = \dfrac{\text{change in } E(Y \mid X)}{\text{change in } X} = \dfrac{\text{change in } \mu_{Y|X}}{\text{change in } X}$ measures the change in the average value of $Y$ as a result of a one-unit change in $X$.
- $b_1 = \dfrac{\text{change in } \hat{E}(Y \mid X)}{\text{change in } X} = \dfrac{\text{change in } \hat{Y}}{\text{change in } X}$ measures the ***estimated*** change in the average value of $Y$ as a result of a one-unit change in $X$.

**Some Important Identities in the Simple Linear Regression Model**

- $Y_i = \beta_0 + \beta_1 X_i + \varepsilon_i = \mu_{Y|X} + \varepsilon_i$. The value of the dependent variable is decomposed into the value on the population regression line and the error term.
- $Y_i = b_0 + b_1 X_i + e_i = \hat{Y}_i + e_i$. The value of the dependent variable is decomposed into the value on the sample regression line (fitted regression line) and the residual term.
- $\mu_{Y|X} = \beta_0 + \beta_1 X_i = E(Y \mid X)$ is the population regression line, which measures the average value of the dependent variable $Y$ for a particular value of the independent variable $X$. Hence, it is also sometimes called the conditional mean regression line.
- $\hat{Y}_i = b_0 + b_1 X_i$ is the sample regression line (simple linear regression equation), which measures the ***estimated*** average value of the dependent variable $Y$ for a particular value of the independent variable $X$. It also provides prediction for the value of $Y$ for a given value of $X$.
- $\varepsilon_i = Y_i - \mu_{Y|X} = Y_i - (\beta_0 + \beta_1 X_i)$ is the error.
- $e_i = Y_i - \hat{Y}_i = Y_i - (b_0 + b_1 X_i)$ is the residual.

- $SST = \sum_{i=1}^{n}(Y_i - \bar{Y})^2$ is the total sum of squares.
- $SSR = \sum_{i=1}^{n}(\hat{Y}_i - \bar{Y})^2$ is the regression (explained) sum of squares.
- $SSE = \sum_{i=1}^{n}(Y_i - \hat{Y}_i)^2 = \sum_{i=1}^{n} e_i^2$ is the error (residual) sum of squares.
- $MSR = \frac{SSR}{k} = \frac{SSR}{1}$ where $k$ is the number of the independent variable, which is 1 in the simple linear regression model.
- $MSE = \frac{SSE}{n-k-1} = \frac{SSE}{n-2}$
- The coefficient of determination
  - $r^2 = \frac{SSR}{SST} = \frac{\text{Regression Sum of Squares}}{\text{Total Sum of Squares}}$
  - The coefficient of determination measures the proportion of variation in $Y$ that is explained by the independent variable $X$ in the regression model.
- Standard error of estimate
  - $S_{YX} = \sqrt{\frac{SSE}{n-2}} = \sqrt{\frac{\sum_{i=1}^{n}(Y - \hat{Y}_i)^2}{n-2}}$
  - The standard error of estimate is the standard deviation of the variation of observations around the sample regression line $\hat{Y}_i = b_0 + b_1 X_i$.

## The ANOVA Table for the Simple Linear Regression Model as Presented in Excel

| ANOVA | | | | | |
|---|---|---|---|---|---|
| | **df** | **SS** | **MS** | **F** | **Significance F** |
| **Regression** | *k* | *SSR* | *MSR=SSR/k* | *MSR/MSE* | *p*-value of the F Test |
| **Residuals** | *n-k-1* | *SSE* | *MSE=SSE/(n-k-1)* | | |
| **Total** | *n-1* | *SST* | | | |

## Assumptions Needed for the Simple Linear Regression Model

- Normality of error: The errors around the population regression line are normally distributed at each $X$ value. This also implies that the dependent variable is normally distributed at each value of the independent variable.
- Homoscedasticity: The variance (amount of variation) of the errors around the population regression line is the same at each $X$ value.
- Independence of errors: The errors around the population regression line are independent for each value of $X$.

## Residual Analysis

- Residual analysis is used to evaluate whether the regression model that has been fitted to the data is an appropriate model.
- **Residual analysis for linearity:**

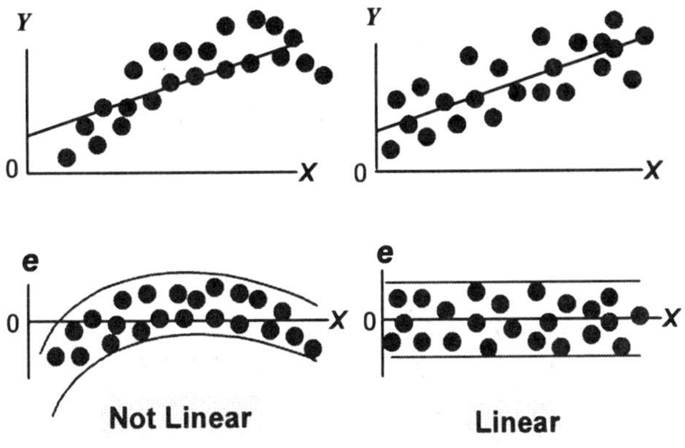


- **Residual analysis for homoscedasticity:**

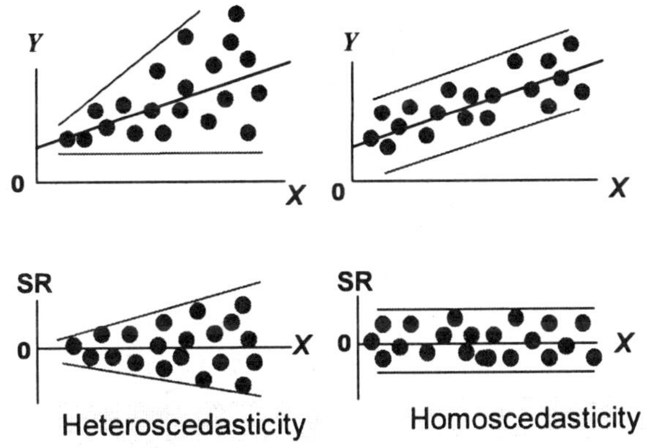


- **Residual analysis for independence:**

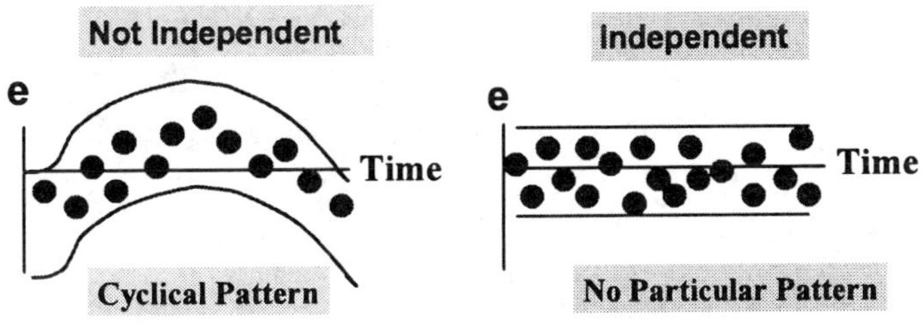


**Residual Is Plotted Against Time to Detect Any Autocorrelation**

- **Residual analysis for independence using Durbin-Watson statistic:**
    1. $H_0$: No autocorrelation (error terms are independent)

       $H_1$: There is autocorrelation (error terms are not independent)
    2. Compute the Durbin-Watson statistic $D = \dfrac{\sum_{i=2}^{n}(e_i - e_{i-1})^2}{\sum_{i=1}^{n} e_i^2}$
    3. Obtain the critical values $d_L$ and $d_U$ from a table.
    4. Compare the Durbin-Watson statistic with the critical values.

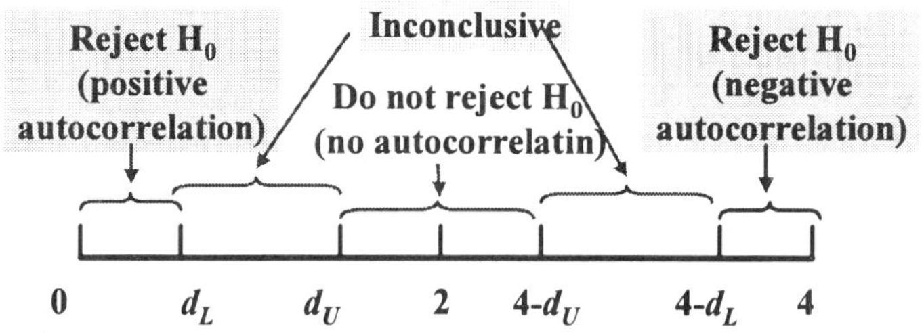


    5. Make a statistical decision.
    6. Draw a conclusion.

## *t* Test for the Slope Parameter $\beta_1$

- $H_0 : \beta_1 = 0$ (*Y* does not depend on *X*)

  $H_1 : \beta_1 \neq 0$ (*Y* depends linearly on *X*)
- **Test statistic:**
    - $t = \dfrac{b_1 - \beta_1}{S_{b_1}}$ with $(n-2)$ degrees of freedom, where $S_{b_1} = \dfrac{S_{YX}}{\sqrt{\sum_{i=1}^{n}(X_i - \bar{X})^2}}$
    - The *t* test can also be a one-tail test for a one-tail alternative.
- **Confidence interval estimate:** Use the $100(1-\alpha)\%$ confidence interval for the slope parameter $\beta_1$.
    - $b_1 \pm t_{\alpha/2,n-2} S_{b_1}$

### $F$ Test for the Slope Parameter $\beta_1$

- $H_0 : \beta_1 = 0$ ($Y$ does not depend on $X$)

  $H_1 : \beta_1 \neq 0$ ($Y$ depends linearly on $X$)
- **Test statistic:**
  - $F = \dfrac{\dfrac{SSR}{1}}{\dfrac{SSE}{(n-2)}}$ with 1 numerator degrees of freedom and $(n-2)$ denominator degrees of freedom.
  - The $F$ test always has a right-tail rejection region and can only be used for the two-tail alternative.

### The Relationship between the $t$ Test and $F$ Test for the Slope Parameter $\beta_1$

- For $H_0 : \beta_1 = 0$ vs $H_1 : \beta_1 \neq 0$, $t^2 = F$ and the $p$-value of the $t$ test is identical to the $p$-value of the $F$ test.

### Correlation Analysis

- Correlation analysis is concerned with the strength of any linear relationship between 2 quantitative variables.
- There is no causal effect implied in a correlation analysis.
- The population correlation coefficient $\rho$ is used to measure the strength of the linear relationship between the variables while the sample correlation coefficient $r$ provides an estimate of the strength.
- **Features of $\rho$ and $r$:**
  - They are unit free.
  - Their values range between $-1$ and $1$.
  - The close is the value to $-1$, the stronger is the negative linear relationship.
  - The close is the value to $+1$, the stronger is the positive linear relationship.
  - The close is the value to 0, the weaker is any linear relationship.

### $t$ Test for a Linear Relationship

- **Hypotheses:**
  - $H_0 : \rho = 0$ (There is no linear relationship)
  - $H_1 : \rho \neq 0$ (There is some linear relationship)
- **Test statistic:**
  - $t = \dfrac{r-\rho}{\sqrt{\dfrac{1-r^2}{n-2}}}$ with $(n-2)$ degrees of freedom, where

    $$r = \sqrt{r^2} = \frac{\sum_{i=1}^{n}(X_i - \bar{X})(Y_i - \bar{Y})}{\sqrt{\sum_{i=1}^{n}(X_i - \bar{X})^2 \sum_{i=1}^{n}(Y_i - \bar{Y})^2}}.$$
  - The $t$ test can be a one-tail test for a one-tail alternative.

## Confidence Interval Estimate for the Mean of $Y$ $(\mu_{Y|X})$

- The point estimate for $\mu_{Y|X=X_i}$ is $\hat{Y}_i$
- The confidence interval estimate for $\mu_{Y|X}$ is $\hat{Y}_i \pm t_{\alpha/2,n-2} S_{YX} \sqrt{\frac{1}{n} + \frac{(X_i - \bar{X})^2}{\sum_{i=1}^{n}(X_i - \bar{X})^2}}$

## Prediction Interval for an Individual Response $Y$

- The point prediction for an individual response $Y_i$ at a particular $X_i$, denoted as $Y_{X=X_i}$ is $\hat{Y}_i = b_0 + b_1 X_i$
- The prediction interval for an individual response $Y_i$ is $\hat{Y}_i \pm t_{\alpha/2,n-2} S_{YX} \sqrt{1 + \frac{1}{n} + \frac{(X_i - \bar{X})^2}{\sum_{i=1}^{n}(X_i - \bar{X})^2}}$

## Common Pitfalls in Regression Analysis

- Lacking an awareness of the assumptions underlying least-squares regression
- Not knowing how to evaluate the assumptions
- Not knowing what the alternatives to least-squares regression are if a particular assumption is violated
- Using a regression model without knowledge of the subject matter
- Extrapolating outside the relevant range
- Concluding that a significant relationship identified in an observational study is due to a cause-and-effect relationship

## Strategy for Avoiding the Pitfalls in Regression

- Always start with a scatter plot to observe the possible relationship between $X$ and $Y$
- Check the assumptions of the regression after the regression model has been fit, before moving on to using the results of the model
- Plot the residuals versus the independent variable to determine whether the model fit to the data is appropriate and check visually for violations of the homoscedasticity assumption
- Use a histogram, stem-and-leaf display, box-and-whisker plot, or normal probability plot of the residuals to graphically evaluate whether the normality assumption has been seriously violated
- If the evaluations indicate violations in the assumptions, use alternative methods to least-squares regression or alternative least-squares models (quadratic or multiple regression) depending on what the evaluation has indicated
- If the evaluations do not indicate violations in the assumptions, then the inferential aspects of the regression analysis can be undertaken, tests for the significance of the regression coefficients can be done, and confidence and prediction intervals can be developed
- Avoid making predictions and forecasts outside the relevant range of the independent variable

- Always note that the relationships identified in observational studies may or may not be due to a cause-and-effect relationship, and remember that while causation implies correlation, correlation does not imply causation

# SOLUTIONS TO END OF SECTION AND CHAPTER REVIEW EVEN PROBLEMS

12.2 (a) yes, (b) no, (c) no, (d) yes

12.4 (a)

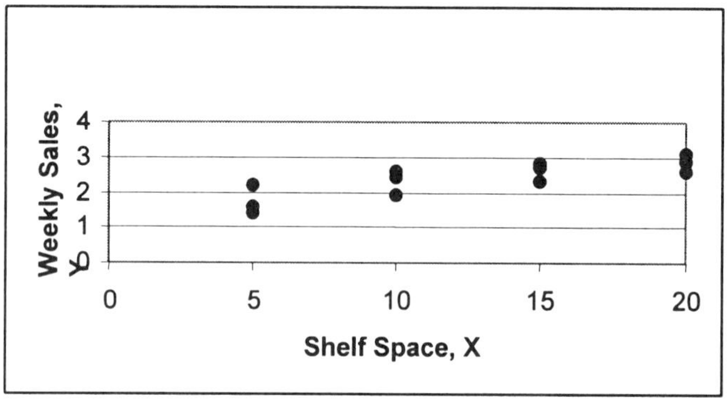


(b) For each increase in shelf space of an additional foot, there is an expected increase in weekly sales of an estimated 0.074 hundreds of dollars, or $7.40.

(c) $\hat{Y} = 1.45 + 0.074X = 1.45 + 0.074(8) = 2.042$, or $204.20

12.6 (a)

Scatter Diagram

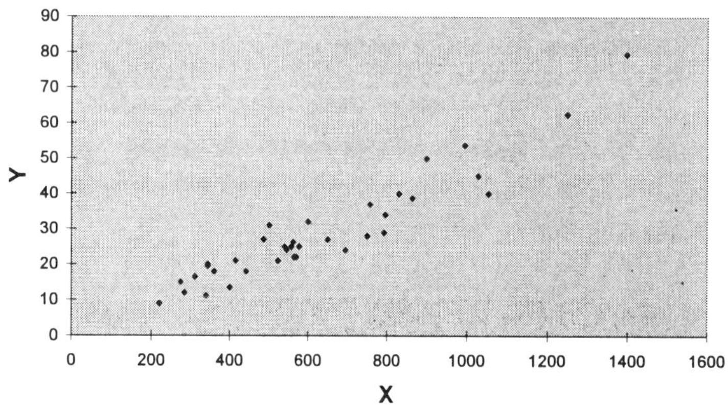


(b) Partial Excel output:

| | Coefficients | Standard Error | t Stat | P-value |
|---|---|---|---|---|
| Intercept | -2.3697 | 2.0733 | -1.1430 | 0.2610 |
| Feet | 0.0501 | 0.0030 | 16.5223 | 0.0000 |

(c) The estimated mean amount of labor will increase by 0.05 hour for each additional cubic foot moved.

(d) $\hat{Y} = -2.3697 + 0.0501(500) = 22.6705$

12.8 (a)

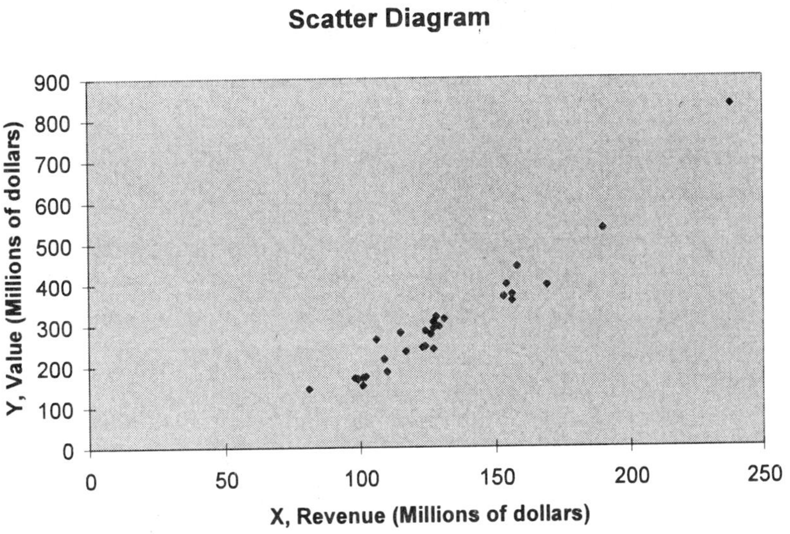


(b) $b_0 = -246.2599$, $b_1 = 4.1897$

(c) For each additional million dollars increase in revenue, the mean annual value will increase by an estimated 4.1897 million dollars. Since revenue cannot be 0, the $Y$ intercept has no practical interpretation. Also, since the $Y$ intercept is outside the range of the observed values of the $X$ variable, its interpretation should be made cautiously.

(d) $\hat{Y} = -246.2599 + 4.1897(150) = 382.2005$ million dollars.

12.10 (a)

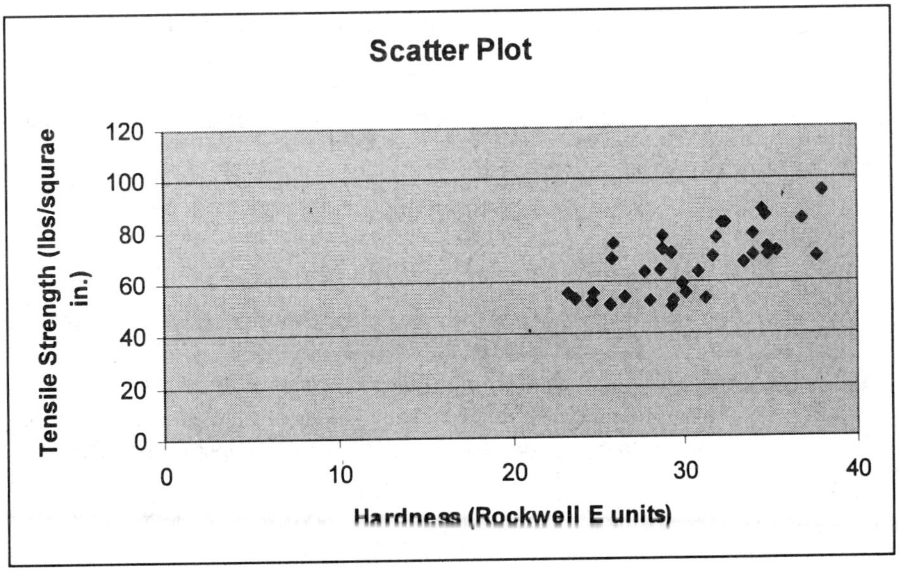

12.10 cont.

(b) $\hat{Y} = 6.0483 + 2.0191X$

(c) For each increase of one additional Rockwell E unit in hardness, the estimated mean tensile strength will increase by 2.0191 thousand pounds per square inch.

(d) $\hat{Y} = 6.0483 + 2.0191(30) = 66.620$ thousand pounds per square inch.

12.12 $SST = 40$ and $r^2 = 0.90$. So, 90% of the variation in the dependent variable can be explained by the variation in the independent variable.

12.14 $r^2 = 0.75$. So, 75% of the variation in the dependent variable can be explained by the variation in the independent variable.

12.16 (a) $r^2 = \frac{SSR}{SST} = \frac{2.0535}{3.0025} = 0.684$. So, 68.4% of the variation in the dependent variable can be explained by the variation in the independent variable.

(b) $S_{YX} = \sqrt{\frac{SSE}{n-2}} = \sqrt{\frac{\sum_{i=1}^{n}\left(Y_i - \hat{Y}_i\right)^2}{n-2}} = \sqrt{\frac{0.949}{10}} = 0.308$

(c) Based on (a) and (b), the model should be very useful for predicting sales.

12.18 (a) $r^2 = 0.8892$. So, 88.92% of the variation in the dependent variable can be explained by the variation in the independent variable.

(b) $S_{YX} = 5.0314$

(c) Based on (a) and (b), the model should be very useful for predicting labor hours.

12.20 (a) $r^2 = 0.9424$. So, 94.24% of the variation in value of a baseball franchise can be explained by the variation in its annual revenue.

(b) $S_{YX} = 33.7876$

(c) Based on (a) and (b), the model should be very useful for predicting the value of a baseball franchise.

12.22 (a) $r^2 = 0.4613$. So, 46.13% of the variation in the dependent variable can be explained by the variation in the independent variable.

(b) $S_{YX} = 9.0616$

(c) Based on (a) and (b), the model is only marginally useful for predicting tensile strength.

12.24 A residual analysis of the data indicates a pattern, with sizeable clusters of consecutive residuals that are either all positive or all negative. If the data is cross-sectional, this pattern indicates a violation of the assumption of linearity and a quadratic model should be investigated. If the data is time-series, the pattern indicates a violation of the assumption of independence of errors.

12.26 (a)

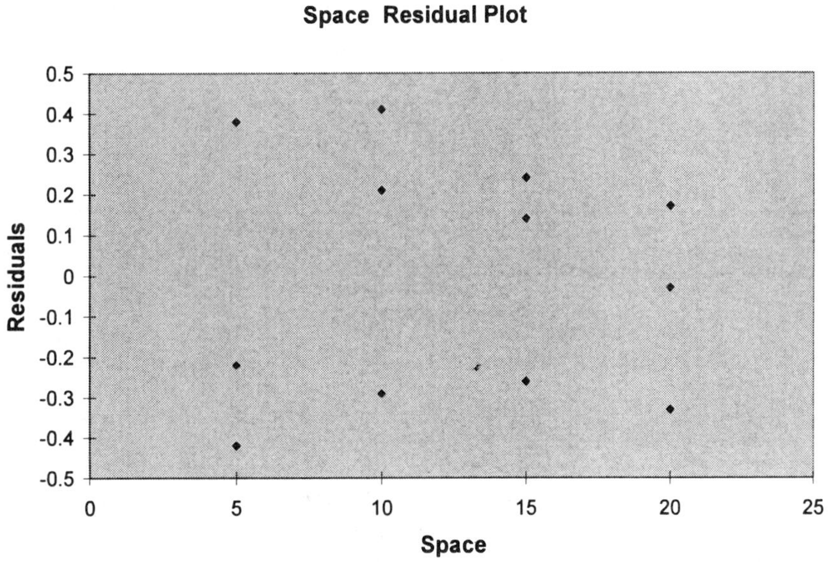


Based on the residual plot, there does not appear to be a pattern in the residual plot.

(b)

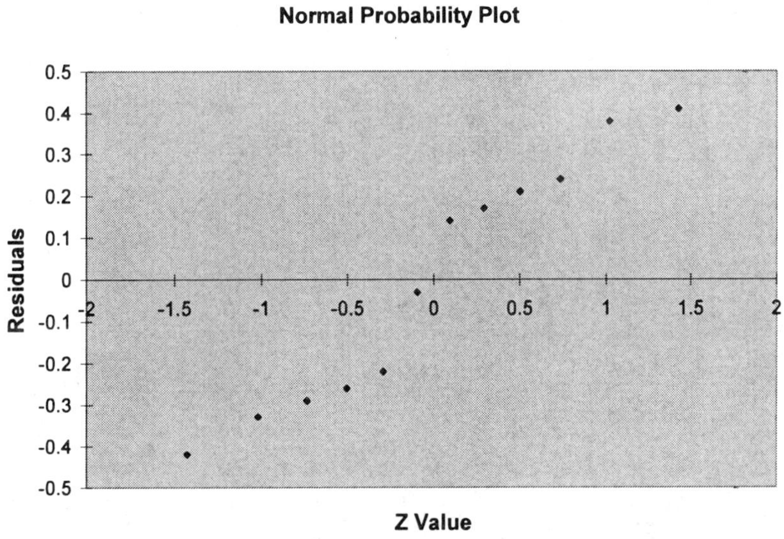


Based on the residual plot, there is not apparent heteroscedasticity effect. The normal probability plot of the residuals indicates a departure from the normality assumption.

12.28 (a)

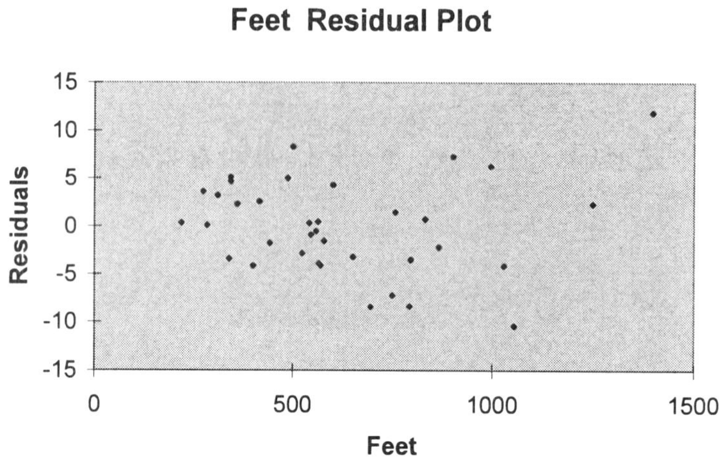


Based on the residual plot, there appears to be a nonlinear pattern in the residuals. A quadratic model should be investigated.

(b)

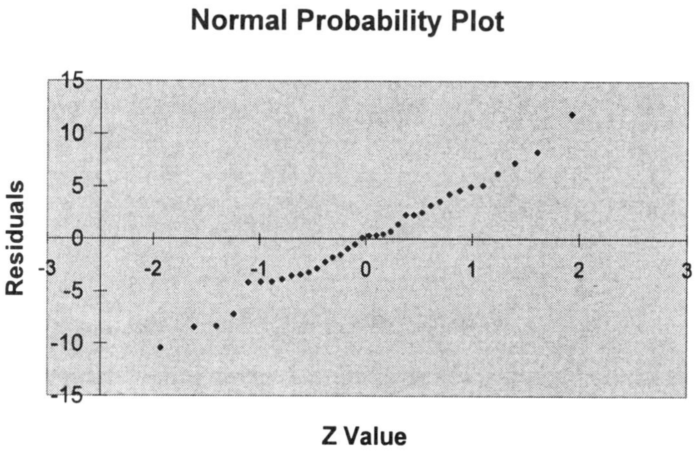


The assumptions of normality and equal variance do not appear to be seriously violated.

12.30 (a)

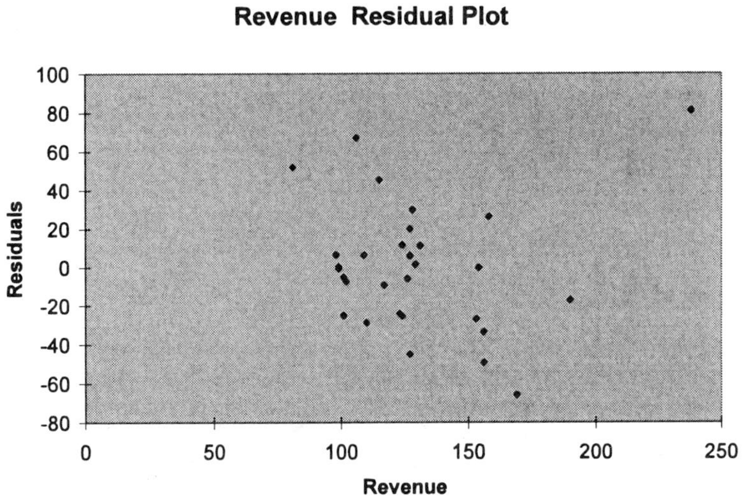


Based on the residual plot, there appears to be a nonlinear pattern in the residuals. A quadratic model should be investigated.

(b)

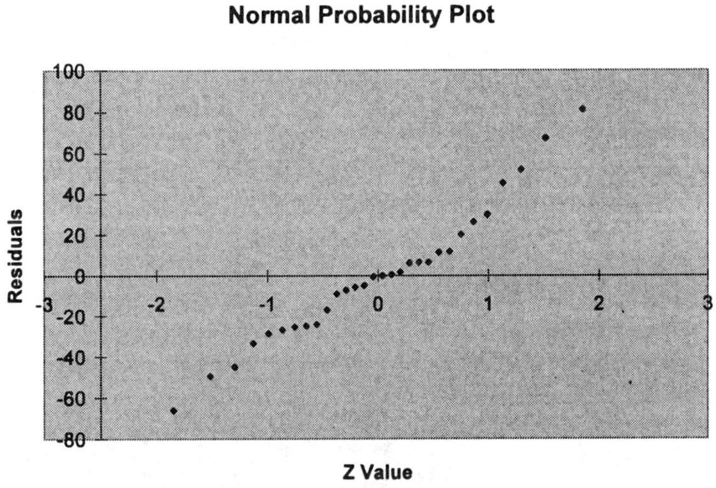


The normal probability plot of the residuals does not reveal significant departure from the normality assumption. The assumption of equal variance does not appear to be seriously violated.

12.32 (a)

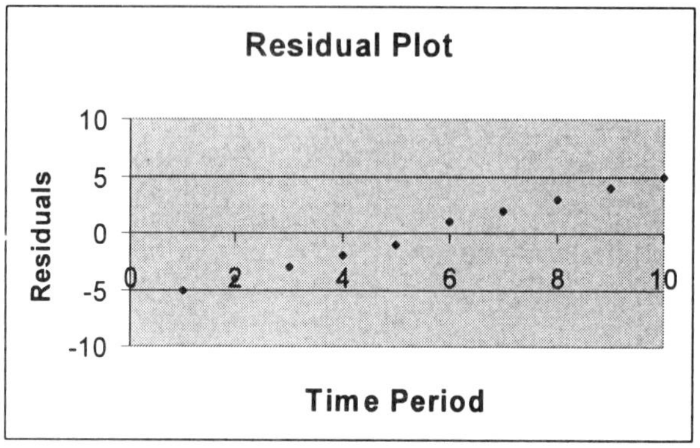


An increasing linear relationship exists.

(b) There appears to be strong positive autocorrelation among the residuals.

12.34 (a) No, it is not necessary to compute the Durbin-Watson statistic since the data have been collected for a single period for a set of stores.

(b) If a single store was studied over a period of time and the amount of shelf space varied over time, computation of the Durbin-Watson statistic would be necessary.

12.36 (a) $b_1 = \dfrac{SSXY}{SSX} = \dfrac{201399.05}{12495626} = 0.0161$

$b_0 = \bar{Y} - b_1\bar{X} = 71.2621 - 0.0161(4393) = 0.458$

(b) $\hat{Y} = 0.458 + 0.0161X = 0.458 + 0.0161(4500) =$ 72.908 or \$72,908

(c)

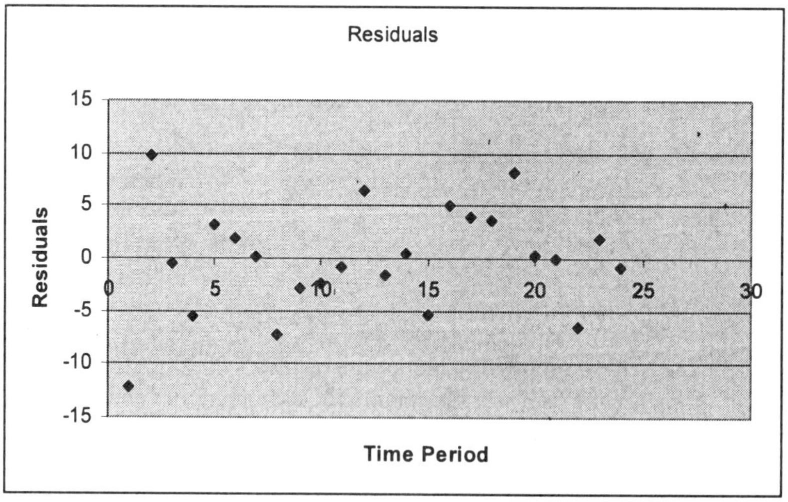


(d) $D = \dfrac{\sum_{i=2}^{n}(e_i - e_{i-1})^2}{\sum_{i=1}^{n} e_i^2} = \dfrac{1243.2244}{599.0683} = 2.08 > 1.45$. There is no evidence of positive autocorrelation among the residuals.

(e) Based on a residual analysis, the model appears to be adequate.

12.38 (a) $b_0 = -2.535$, $b_1 = 0.060728$

(b) $\hat{Y} = -2.535 + 0.060728X = -2.535 + 0.060728(83) = 2.5054$ or \$2505.40

(c)

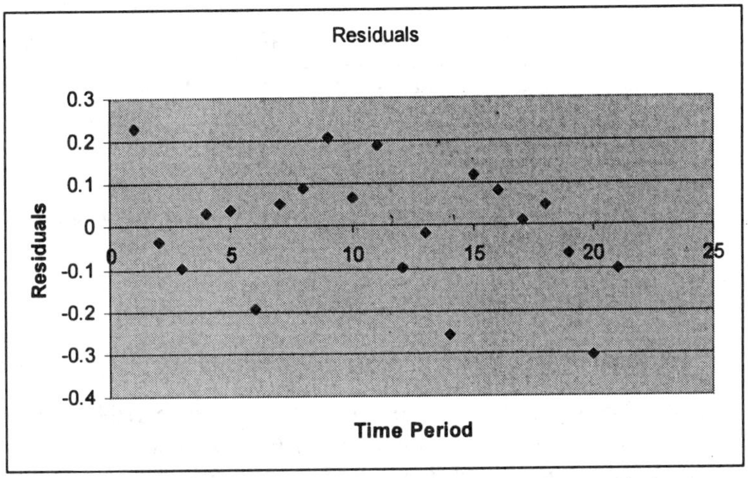


(d) $D = 1.64 > 1.42$. There is no evidence of positive autocorrelation among the residuals.

(e) The plot of the residuals versus time period shows some clustering of positive and negative residuals for intervals in the domain, suggesting a nonlinear model might be better. Otherwise, the model appears to be adequate.

12.40 (a) $H_0: \beta_1 = 0 \quad H_1: \beta_1 \neq 0$

Test statistic: $t = (b_1 - 0)/s_{b_1} = 4.5/1.5 = 3.00$

(b) With n = 18, df = 18 – 2 =16, $t_{16} = \pm 2.1199$.

(c) Reject $H_0$. There is evidence that the fitted linear regression model is useful.

(d) $b_1 - t_{16}s_{b_1} \leq \beta_1 \leq b_1 + t_{16}s_{b_1}$

$4.5 - 2.1199(1.5) \leq \beta_1 \leq 4.5 + 2.1199(1.5)$

$1.32 \leq \beta_1 \leq 7.68$

12.42 (a) $H_0: \beta_1 = 0 \quad H_1: \beta_1 \neq 0$

$t = \frac{b_1 - \beta_1}{S_{b_1}} = \frac{0.074}{0.0159} = 4.65 > t_{10} = 2.2281$ with 10 degrees of freedom for $\alpha = 0.05$. Reject $H_0$. There is enough evidence to conclude that the fitted linear regression model is useful.

(b) $b_1 \pm t_{n-2}S_{b_1} = 0.074 \pm 2.2281(0.0159)$ $\quad 0.0386 \leq \beta_1 \leq 0.1094$

12.44 (a) $t = 16.5223 > t_{34} = 2.0322$ for $\alpha = 0.05$. Reject $H_0$. There is evidence that the fitted linear regression model is useful.

(b) $0.0439 \leq \beta_1 \leq 0.0562$

12.46 (a) $H_0 : \beta_1 = 0$ $H_1 : \beta_1 \neq 0$

PHStat output:

| | Coefficients | Standard Error | t Stat | P-value | Lower 95% | Upper 95% |
|---|---|---|---|---|---|---|
| Intercept | -246.2599 | 26.0405 | -9.4568 | 0.0000 | -299.6015 | -192.9183 |
| Revenue | 4.1897 | 0.1957 | 21.4075 | 0.0000 | 3.7888 | 4.5906 |

Since the $p$-value is essentially zero, reject $H_0$ at 5% level of significance. There is evidence of a linear relationship between annual revenue sales and franchise value.

(b) $3.7888 \leq \beta_1 \leq 4.5906$

12.48 (a) $p$-value = 7.26497E-06 < 0.05. Reject $H_0$. There is evidence that the fitted linear regression model is useful.

(b) $1.2463 \leq \beta_1 \leq 2.7918$

12.50 (a) $(\% \text{ daily change in ULPIX}) = b_0 + 2.00(\% \text{ daily change in S\&P 500 Index})$

(b) If the S&P gains 30% in a year, the ULPIX is expected to gain an estimated 60%.

(c) If the S&P loses 35% in a year, the ULPIX is expected to lose an estimated 70%.

(d) Since the leverage funds have higher volatility and, hence, higher risk than the market, risk averse investors should stay away from these funds. Risk takers, on the other hand, will benefit from the higher potential gain from these funds.

12.52 (a) $r = -0.4014$.

(b) $t = -1.8071$, $p$-value = 0.089 > 0.05. Do not reject $H_0$. At the 0.05 level of significance, there is no linear relationship between the turnover rate of pre-boarding screeners and the security violations detected.

(c) There is not sufficient evidence to conclude that there is a linear relationship between the turnover rate of pre-boarding screeners and the security violations detected.

12.54 (a) $r = 0.4838$

(b) $t = 2.5926$, $p$-value = 0.0166 < 0.05. Reject $H_0$. At the 0.05 level of significance, there is a linear relationship between the cold-cranking amps and the price.

(c) The higher the price of a battery is, the higher is its cold-cranking amps.

(d) Yes, the expectation that batteries with higher cranking amps to have a higher price is borne out by the data.

12.56 (a) When $X = 4$, $\hat{Y} = 5 + 3X = 5 + 3(4) = 17$

$$h = \frac{1}{n} + \frac{(X_i - \bar{X})^2}{\sum_{i=1}^{n}(X_i - \bar{X})^2} = \frac{1}{20} + \frac{(4-2)^2}{20} = 0.25$$

95% confidence interval: $\hat{Y} \pm t_{18} s_{YX} \sqrt{h} = 17 \pm 2.1009 \cdot 1 \cdot \sqrt{0.25}$

$$15.95 \leq \mu_{Y|X=4} \leq 18.05$$

(b) 95% prediction interval: $\hat{Y} \pm t_{18} s_{YX} \sqrt{1+h} = 17 \pm 2.1009 \cdot 1 \cdot \sqrt{1.25}$

$$14.651 \leq Y_{X=4} \leq 19.349$$

(c) The intervals in this problem are wider because the value of $X$ is farther from $\bar{X}$.

12.58 (a) $\hat{Y}_i \pm t_{n-2} S_{YX} \sqrt{h_i} = 2.042 \pm 2.2281(0.3081)\sqrt{0.1373}$

$$1.7876 \le \mu_{Y|X=8} \le 2.2964$$

(b) $\hat{Y}_i \pm t_{n-2} S_{YX} \sqrt{1+h_i} = 2.042 \pm 2.2281(0.3081)\sqrt{1+0.1373}$

$$1.3100 \le Y_{X=8} \le 2.7740$$

(c) Part (b) provides an interval prediction for the individual response given a specific value of the independent variable, and part (a) provides an interval estimate for the mean value given a specific value of the independent variable. Since there is much more variation in predicting an individual value than in estimating a mean value, a prediction interval is wider than a confidence interval estimate holding everything else fixed.

12.60 (a) $20.7990 \le \mu_{Y|X=500} \le 24.5419$

(b) $12.2755 \le Y_{X=500} \le 33.0654$

(c) Part (b) provides an interval prediction for the individual response given a specific value of the independent variable, and part (a) provides an interval estimate for the mean value given a specific value of the independent variable. Since there is much more variation in predicting an individual value than in estimating a mean value, a prediction interval is wider than a confidence interval estimate holding everything else fixed.

12.62 (a) $367.0757 \le \mu_{Y|X=150} \le 397.3254$

(b) $311.3562 \le Y_{X=150} \le 453.0448$

(c) Part (b) provides an interval prediction for the individual response given a specific value of the independent variable, and part (a) provides an interval estimate for the mean value given a specific value of the independent variable. Since there is much more variation in predicting an individual value than in estimating a mean value, a prediction interval is wider than a confidence interval estimate holding everything else fixed.

12.64 The slope of the line, $b_1$, represents the estimated expected change in $Y$ per unit change in $X$. It represents the estimated mean amount that $Y$ changes (either positively or negatively) for a particular unit change in $X$. The $Y$ intercept $b_0$ represents the estimated mean value of $Y$ when $X$ equals 0.

12.66 The unexplained variation or error sum of squares (SSE) will be equal to zero only when the regression line fits the data perfectly and the coefficient of determination equals 1.

12.68 Unless a residual analysis is undertaken, you will not know whether the model fit is appropriate for the data. In addition, residual analysis can be used to check whether the assumptions of regression have been seriously violated.

12.70 The normality of error assumption can be evaluated by obtaining a histogram, box-and-whisker plot, and/or normal probability plot of the residuals. The homoscedasticity assumption can be evaluated by plotting the residuals on the vertical axis and the X variable on the horizontal axis. The independence of errors assumption can be evaluated by plotting the residuals on the vertical axis and the time order variable on the horizontal axis. This assumption can also be evaluated by computing the Durbin-Watson statistic.

12.72 The confidence interval for the mean response estimates the mean response for a given X value. The prediction interval estimates the value for a single item or individual.

12.74 (a) $b_0 = 24.84$, $b_1 = 0.14$

(b) 24.84 is the portion of estimated mean delivery time that is not affected by the number of cases delivered. For each additional case, the estimated mean delivery time increases by 0.14 minutes.

(c) $\hat{Y} = 24.84 + 0.14X = 24.84 + 0.14(150) = 45.84$

(d) No, 500 cases is outside the relevant range of the data used to fit the regression equation.

(e) $r^2 = 0.972$. So, 97.2% of the variation in delivery time can be explained by the variation in the number of cases.

(f) Based on a visual inspection of the graphs of the distribution of residuals and the residuals versus the number of cases, there is no pattern. The model appears to be adequate.

(g) $t = 24.88 > t_{18} = 2.1009$ with 18 degrees of freedom for $\alpha = 0.05$. Reject $H_0$. There is evidence that the fitted linear regression model is useful.

(h) $44.88 \le \mu_{Y|X=150} \le 46.80$

(i) $41.56 \le Y_{X=150} \le 50.12$

(j) $0.1282 \le \beta_1 \le 0.1518$

12.76 (a)

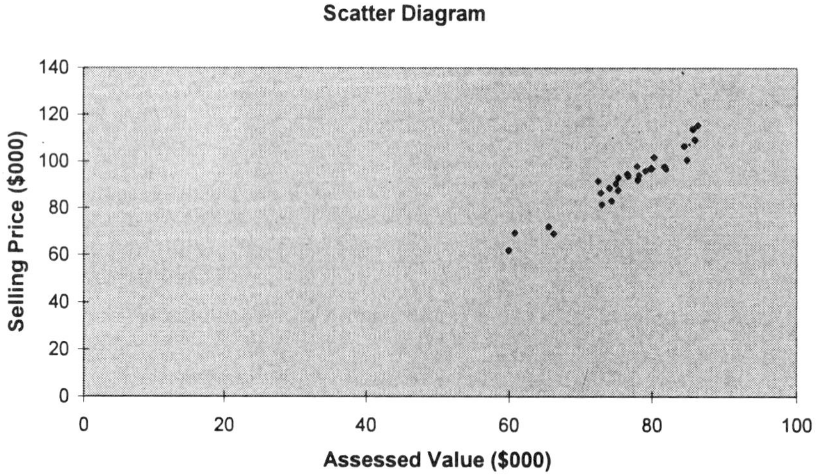


$b_0 = -44.172$, $b_1 = 1.78171$

12.76 cont. (b) Since the assessed value of a home cannot be zero, the intercept has no practical interpretation. −44.172 is the portion of estimated mean selling price that is not affected by the assessed value. For each additional dollar in assessed value, the estimated mean selling price increases by \$1.78.

(c) $\hat{Y} = -44.172 + 1.78171X = -44.172 + 1.78171(70) = 80.458$ or \$80,458

(d) $r^2 = 0.926$. 92.6% of the variation in selling price can be explained by the variation in the assessed value.

(e) Based on a visual inspection of the graphs of the distribution of residuals and the residuals versus the assessed value, there is no pattern. The model appears to be adequate.

(f) $t = 18.66 > t_{28} = 2.0484$ with 28 degrees of freedom for $\alpha = 0.05$. Reject $H_0$. There is evidence that the fitted linear regression model is useful.

(g) $78.707 \le \mu_{Y|X=70} \le 82.388$

(h) $73.195 \le Y_{X=70} \le 87.900$

(i) $1.5862 \le \beta_1 \le 1.9772$

12.78 (a)

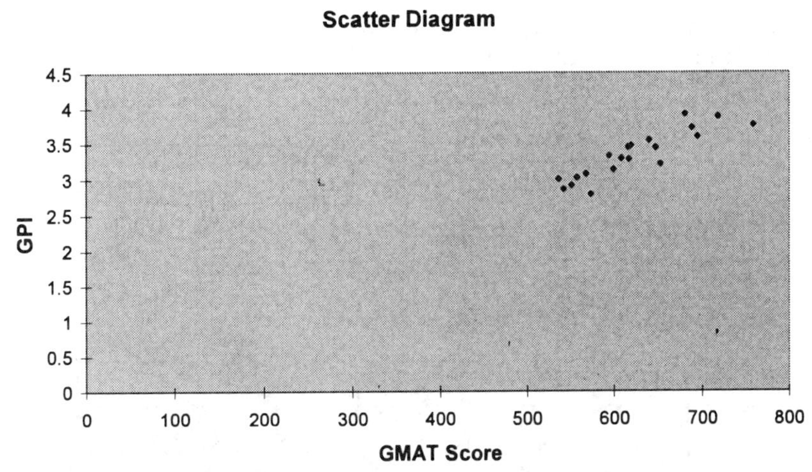


$b_0 = 0.30$, $b_1 = 0.00487$

(b) 0.30 is the portion of estimated mean GPI index that is not affected by the GMAT score. The mean GPI index of a student with a zero GMAT score is estimated to be 0.30. For each additional point on the GMAT score, the estimated mean GPI will increase by 0.00487.

(c) $\hat{Y} = 0.30 + 0.00487X = 0.30 + 0.00487(600) = 3.222$

(d) $r^2 = 0.7978$. 79.78% of the variation in the GPI can be explained by the variation in the GMAT score.

(e) Based on a visual inspection of the graphs of the distribution of residuals and the residuals versus the GMAT score, there is no pattern. The model appears to be adequate.

(f) $t = 8.428 > t_{18} = 2.1009$ with 18 degrees of freedom for $\alpha = 0.05$. Reject $H_0$. There is evidence that the fitted linear regression model is useful.

(g) $3.144 \le \mu_{Y|X=600} \le 3.301$

12.78 (h) $2.886 \le Y_{X=600} \le 3.559$

cont. (i) $0.00366 \le \beta_1 \le 0.00608$

12.80 (a)

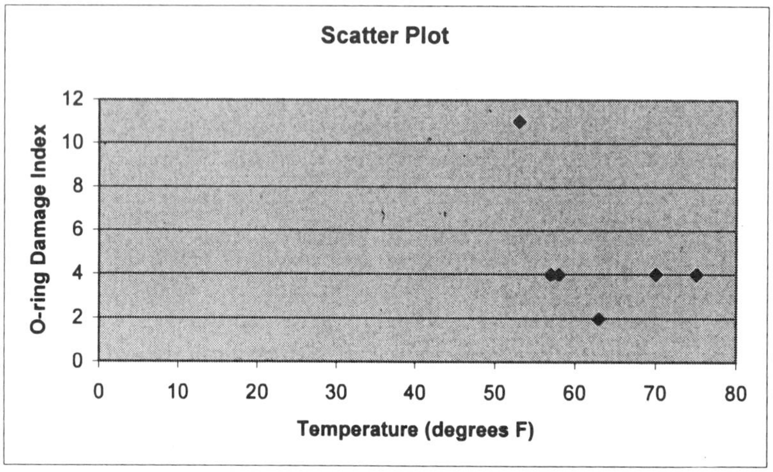


There is not any clear relationship between atmospheric temperature and O-ring damage from the scatter plot.

(b),(f)

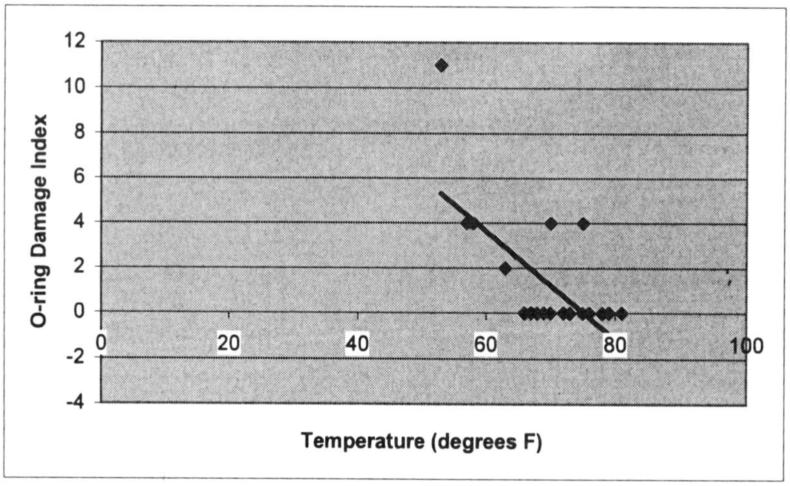


(c) In (b), there are 16 observations with an O-ring damage index of 0 for a variety of temperatures. If one concentrates on these observations with no O-ring damage, there is obviously no relationship between O-ring damage index and temperature. If all observations are used, the observations with no O-ring damage will bias the estimated relationship. If the intention is to investigate the relationship between the degrees of O-ring damage and atmospheric temperature, it makes sense to focus only on the flights in which there was O-ring damage.

(d) Prediction should not be made for an atmospheric temperature of 31 $^0$F because it is outside the range of the temperature variable in the data. Such prediction will involve extrapolation, which assumes that any relationship between two variables will continue to hold outside the domain of the temperature variable.

12.80 cont.

(e) $\hat{Y} = 18.036 - 0.240X$

(g) A nonlinear model is more appropriate for these data.

(h)

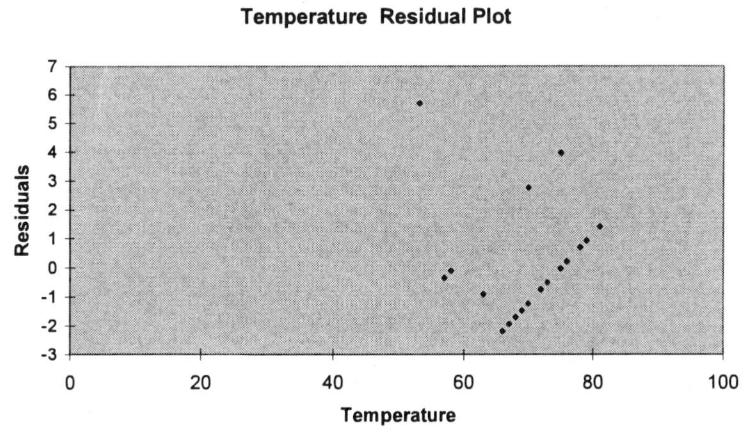


The string of negative residuals and positive residuals that lie on a straight line with a positive slope in the lower-right corner of the plot is a strong indication that a nonlinear model should be used if all 23 observations are to be used in the fit.

12.82

(a) $\hat{Y} = -2629.222 + 82.4717X$

$b_0 = -2629.222$, $b_1 = 82.4717$

(b) For each increase of one centimeter in circumference, the estimated mean weight of a pumpkin will increase by 82.4717 grams.

(c) $\hat{Y} = -2629.222 + 82.4717(60) = 2319.080$ grams.

(d) There appears to be a positive relationship between weight and circumference of a pumpkin. It is a good idea for the farmer to sell pumpkins by circumference instead of weight for circumference is a good predictor of weight, and it is much easier to measure the circumference of a pumpkin than its weight.

(e) $r^2 = 0.9373$. 93.73% of the variation in pumpkin weight can be explained by the variation in circumference.

(f)

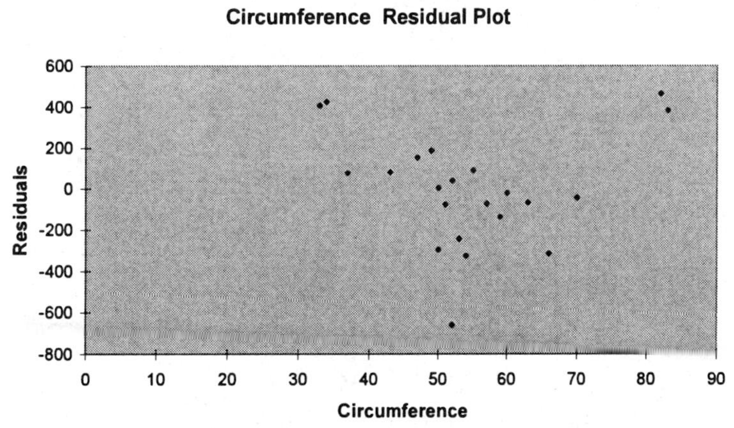


There appears to be a nonlinear relationship between circumference and weight.

12.82 cont. (g) $p$-value is virtually 0. Reject $H_0$. There is sufficient evidence to conclude that there is a linear relationship between the circumference and the weight of a pumpkin.

(h) $72.7875 < \beta_1 < 92.1559$

(i) $2186.9589 < \mu_{Y|X=60} < 2451.2020$

(j) $1726.5508 < Y_{X=60} < 2911.6101$

12.84 (a)

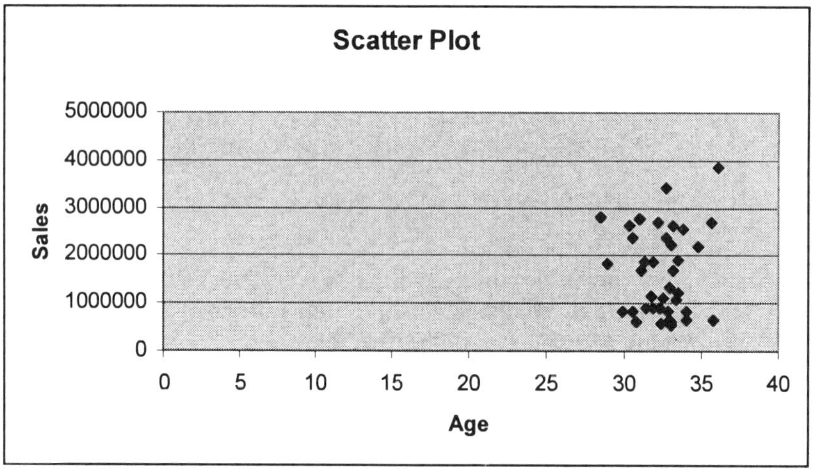


There appears to be a positive linear relationship between median age of customer base and the latest one-month sales total.

(b) $\hat{Y} = 931626.16 + 21782.76X$

$b_0 = 931626.16$, $b_1 = 21782.76$

(c) Since median age of customer base cannot be 0, $b_0$ just captures the portion of the latest one-month sales total that varies with factors other than median age.

$b_1 = 21782.76$ means that as the median age of customer base increases by one year, the estimated mean latest one-month sales total will increase by $21782.76.

(d) $r^2 = 0.0017$. Only 0.17% of the total variation in the franchise's latest one-month sales total can be explained by using the median age of customer base.

(e)

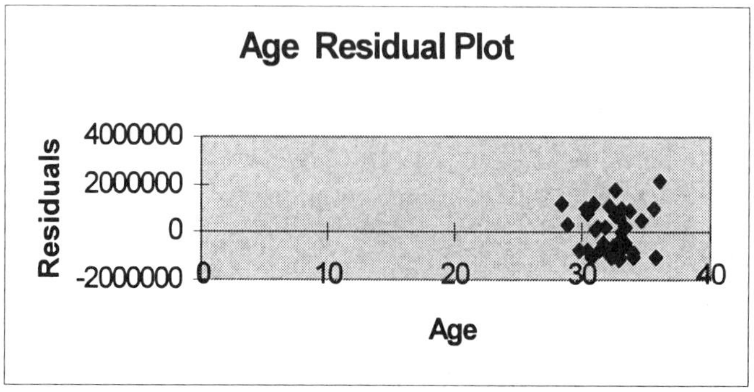


The residuals are very evenly spread out across different range of median age.

12.84 (f) $H_0 : \rho = 0 \qquad H_1 : \rho \neq 0$

cont. Test statistic: $t = \dfrac{r}{\sqrt{\dfrac{1-r^2}{n-2}}} = 0.2482$

Decision rule: Reject $H_0$ when $|t|$>2.0289.

Decision: Since $t$ = 0.2482 is less than the upper critical bound 2.4926, do not reject $H_0$. There is not enough evidence to conclude that there is a linear relationship between one-month sales total and median age of customer base.

(g) $b_1 \pm t_{n-2} S_{b_1} = 21782.76354 \pm 2.0281(87749.63)$

$$-156181.50 \leq \beta_1 \leq 199747.02$$

You are 95% confident that the slope is somewhere between –156181.50 and 199747.02.

12.86 (a)

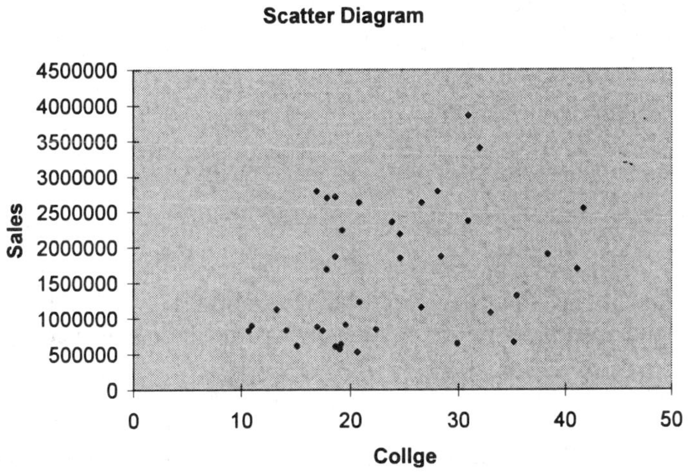


There is a positive linear relationship between total sales and percentage of customer base with a college diploma.

(b) $\hat{Y} = 789847.38 + 35854.15X$

$b_0 = 789847.38$, $b_1 = 35854.15$

(c) $b_1 = 35854.15$ means that as the percent of customer base with a college diploma increases by one, the estimated mean latest one-month sales total will increase by \$35854.15. $b_0 = 789847.38$ means that the estimated mean latest one-month sales total is \$789847.38 when the percent of customer based with a college diploma is 0. Since the Y intercept is outside the range of the observed values of the X variable, its interpretation should be made cautiously.

(d) $r^2 = 0.1036$. 10.36% of the total variation in the franchise's latest one-month sales total can be explained by the percentage of customer base with a college diploma.

12.86 cont. (e)

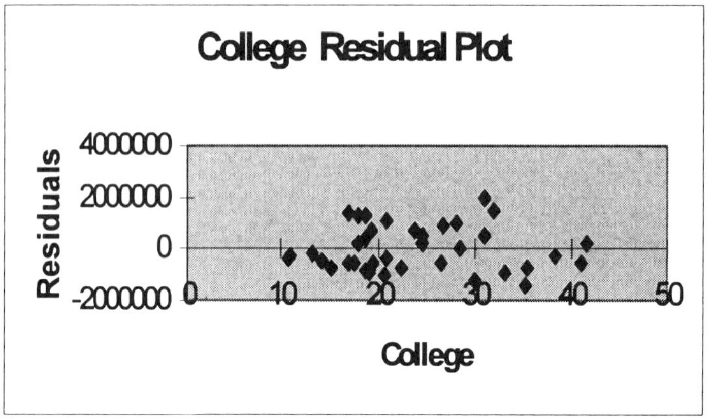


The residuals are quite evenly spread out around zero even though there might be a slight tendency for the variance to increase as the percentage of customer base with a college diploma increases.

(f) $H_0: \rho = 0$ $\qquad H_1: \rho \neq 0$

Test statistic: $t = \dfrac{r}{\sqrt{\dfrac{1-r^2}{n-2}}} = 2.0392$

Decision rule: Reject $H_0$ when $|t|$>2.0289.

Decision: Since $t$ = 2.0392 is greater than the upper critical bound 2.4926, reject $H_0$. There is enough evidence to conclude that there is a linear relationship between one-month sales total and percentage of customer base with a college diploma.

(g) $b_1 \pm t_{n-2} S_{b_1} = 35854.15 \pm 2.0281(17582.269)$

$$195.75 \leq \beta_1 \leq 71512.60$$

You are 95% confident that the slope is somewhere between 195.75 and 71512.60.

12.88 (a) $\hat{Y} = -13.6561 + 0.8932X$

$b_0 = -13.6561$, $b_1 = 0.8932$

(b) Since no restaurant will receive a summated rating of 0, it is not meaningful to interpret $b_0$. For each additional unit of increase in summated rating, the estimated mean price per person will increase by $0.8932.

(c) $\hat{Y} = -13.6561 + 0.8932(50) = \$31.01$

(d) $r^2$ = 0.4246. 42.46% of the variation in price per person can be explained by the variation in summated rating.

12.88 (e)
cont.

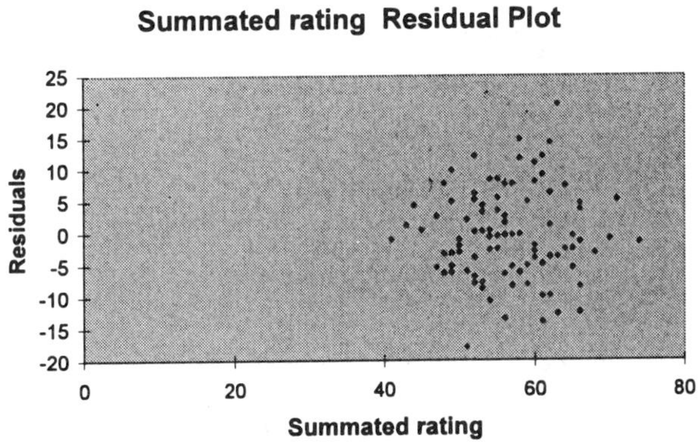


Based on a visual inspection of the residual plot of summated rating, there may be a violation of the homoscedasticity assumption.

(f) *p*-value is virtually 0. Reject $H_0$. There is very strong evidence to conclude that there is a linear relationship between price per person and summated rating.

(g) $\$29.07 \le \mu_{Y|X=50} \le \$32.94$

(h) $\$16.95 \le Y_{X=50} \le \$45.06$

(i) $0.6848 \le \beta_1 \le 1.1017$

(j) The linear regression model appears to have provided an adequate fit and shown a significant linear relationship between price per person and summated rating. Since 42.46% of the variation in price per person can be explained by the variation in summated rating, price per person is moderately useful in predicting the price.

12.90 (a)

| | MSFT | FORD | GM | IAL |
|---|---|---|---|---|
| MSFT | 1 | 0.167371 | 0.156788 | -0.23227 |
| FORD | | 1 | 0.866746 | 0.696919 |
| GM | | | 1 | 0.628925 |
| IAL | | | | 1 |

(b) There is a strongly positive linear relationship between the stock price of Ford and GM, a moderately strong positive linear relationship between the stock price of Ford and IAL and between GM and IAL, a very weak positive linear relationship between the stock price of Ford and Microsoft, and between GM and Microsoft, and a rather weak negative linear relationship between Microsoft and IAL.

(c) It is not a good idea to have all the stocks in an individual's portfolio be strongly, positively correlated among each other because the portfolio risk can be reduced when a pair of stock prices is negatively related in a two-stock portfolio.

# CHAPTER 13

## OBJECTIVES

- To learn how to develop a multiple regression model
- To know how to interpret the regression coefficients
- To learn how to determine which independent variables to include in the regression model
- To be able to use categorical variable in regression models
- To be able to use quadratic terms in a regression model

## OVERVIEW AND KEY CONCEPTS

### The Multiple Regression Model

- The multiple regression model describes the relationship between one dependent variable and 2 or more independent variables in a linear function.

**Population Y-intercept** **Population slopes** **Random Error**

$$Y_i = \beta_0 + \beta_1 X_{1i} + \beta_2 X_{2i} + \cdots + \beta_k X_{ki} + \varepsilon_i$$

$$Y_i = b_0 + b_1 X_{1i} + b_2 X_{2i} + \cdots + b_k X_{ki} + e_i$$

**Dependent (response) variable** **Independent (explanatory) variables** **Residual**

### The Simple Linear Regression and Multiple Regression Compared

- Coefficients in a simple regression pick up the impact of that variable plus the impacts of other variables that are correlated with it and the dependent variable.
- Coefficients in a multiple regression net out the impacts of other variables in the equation. Hence, they are called *net regression coefficients*.

### Interpretation of the Estimated Coefficients

- **The *Y* intercept $(b_0)$:** The estimated average value of $Y_i$ when all $X_i = 0$.
- **Slope $(b_i)$:** Estimated that the average value of *Y* changes by $b_i$ for each one-unit increase in $X_i$ holding constant the effect of all other independent variables.

### Predicting the Dependent Variable Y

- Use the estimated sample regression equation (multiple linear regression equation): $\hat{Y}_i = b_0 + b_1 X_{1i} + \cdots + b_k X_{ki}$

## The Venn Diagram and Explanatory Power of the Multiple Regression Model

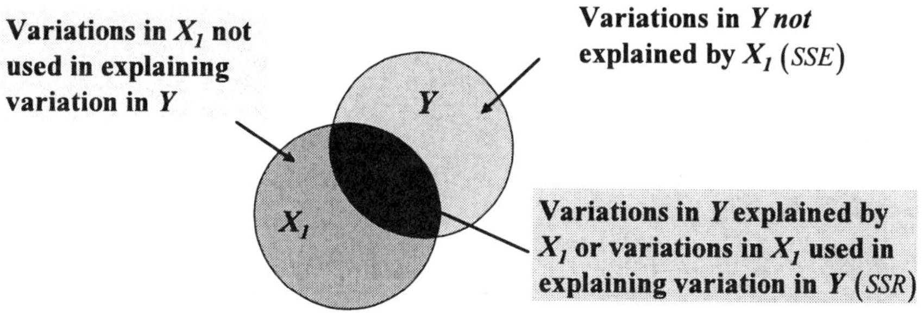


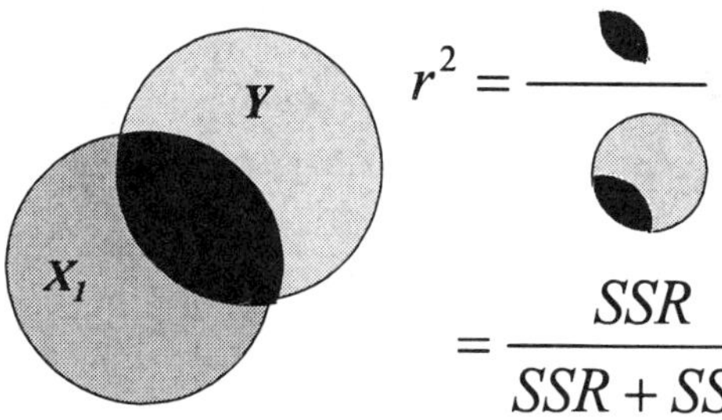


$$= \frac{SSR}{SSR + SSE}$$

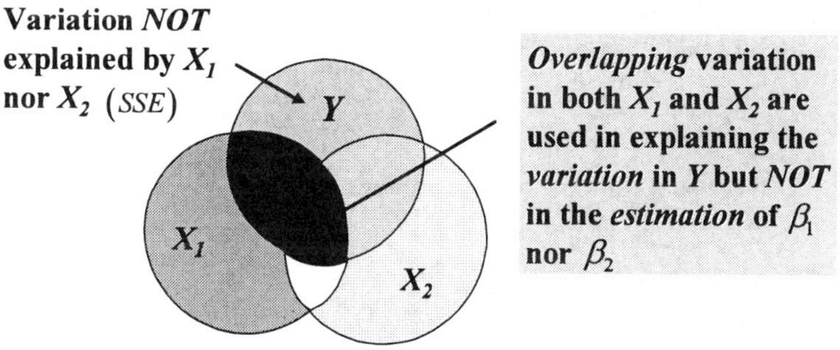

## Coefficient of Multiple Determination

- Coefficient of multiple determination measures the proportion of total variation in $Y$ explained by all $X$ variables taken together.
- $r^2_{Y\bullet 12\cdots k} = \dfrac{SSR}{SST} = \dfrac{\text{Explained Variation}}{\text{Total Variation}}$
- It never decreases when an additional $X$ variable is added to the model, which is a disadvantage when comparing among models.

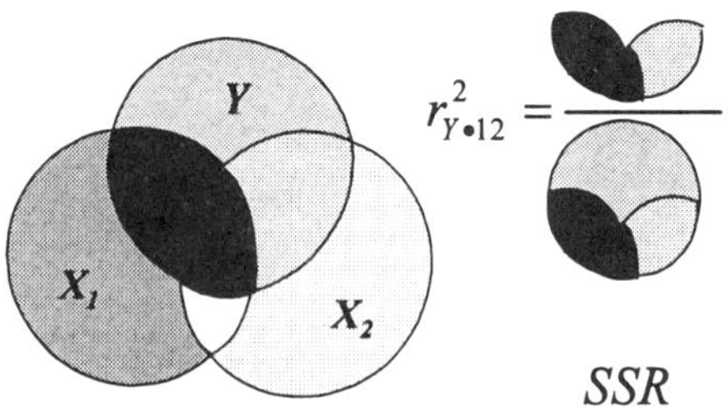


$$= \frac{SSR}{SSR + SSE}$$

## Adjusted Coefficient of Multiple Determination

- It measures the proportion of variation in $Y$ explained by all $X$ variables adjusted for the number of $X$ variables used.
- $r^2_{adj} = 1 - \left[ \left(1 - r^2_{Y\bullet 12\cdots k}\right) \dfrac{n-1}{n-k-1} \right]$
- It penalizes excessive use of independent variables.
- It is smaller than $r^2_{Y\bullet 12\cdots k}$.
- It is useful in comparing among models.
- It can have a negative value.
- Its value can decrease when an additional explanatory variable is added to the existing model.

## Interpretation of Coefficient of Multiple Determination

- $r^2_{Y\bullet 12\cdots k}$ measures the proportion of total variation in $Y$ that can be explained by all $X$ variables.
- $r^2_{adj}$ measures the proportion of total variation in $Y$ that can be explained by all $X$ variables after adjusting for the number of independent variables and sample size.

## *F* Test for the Significance of the Entire Multiple Regression Model

- **The hypotheses:**
  - $H_0: \beta_1 = \beta_2 = \cdots = \beta_k = 0$ (There is no linear relationship)
  - $H_1:$ At least one $\beta_i \neq 0$ (At least one independent variable affects *Y*)
- **Test statistic:**
  - $F = \frac{MSR}{MSE} = \frac{SSR(\text{all})/k}{SSE(\text{all})/(n-k-1)}$ with *k* numerator degrees of freedom and $(n-k-1)$ denominator degrees of freedom.
  - The rejection region is always in the right tail.

## *t* Test for the Significance of Individual Variables

- **The hypotheses:**
  - $H_0: \beta_i = 0$ ($X_i$ does not affect $Y$)
  - $H_1: \beta_i \neq 0$ ($X_i$ affects *Y*)
- **Test statistic:**
  - $t = \frac{b_j - \beta_j}{S_{b_j}}$ with $(n-k-1)$ degrees of freedom.
  - The *t* test can also be a one-tail test for a one-tail alternative.
- Confidence interval estimate for $\beta_j$: Use the $100(1-\alpha)\%$ confidence interval for $\beta_j$.
  - $b_j \pm t_{\alpha/2,n-k-1} S_{b_j}$

## Dummy-Variable Model and Interactions

- Dummy variables are used to represent categorical explanatory variables with two or more levels.
- A dummy variable is always coded as 0 and 1.
- The number of dummy variables needed is equal to the number of levels minus 1.
- **Interpretation of the estimated slope coefficient of a dummy variable:** The slope coefficient of a dummy variable measures the estimated average incremental effect of the presence of the characteristic captured by the dummy variable holding constant the effect of all other independent variables.
- In the dummy-variable model, it is assumed that the slope of the dependent variable *Y* with an independent variable *X* is the same for each of the two levels of the dummy variable.

## The Quadratic Regression Model

- In a quadratic regression model, the relationship between the dependent variable and one or more independent variable is a quadratic polynomial function.
- The quadratic regression model is useful when the residual plot reveals nonlinear relationship.
- The quadratic regression model:
  - $Y_i = \beta_0 + \beta_1 X_{1i} + \beta_2 X_{1i}^2 + \varepsilon_i$
  - The quadratic relationship can be between $Y$ and more than one $X$ variable as well.
- **Testing for the overall significance of the quadratic regression model:**
  - The test for the overall significance of the quadratic regression model is exactly the same as testing for the overall significance of any multiple regression model.
  - **Test statistic:** $F = \dfrac{MSR}{MSE}$.
- **Testing for quadratic effect:**
  - **The hypotheses:** $H_0 : \beta_2 = 0$ (no quadratic effect) vs. $H_1 : \beta_2 \neq 0$ (the quadratic term is needed)
  - **Test statistic:** $t = \dfrac{b_2 - \beta_2}{S_{b_2}}$.
  - This is a two-tail test with a left tail and a right-tail rejection region.

# SOLUTIONS TO END OF SECTION AND CHAPTER REVIEW EVEN PROBLEMS

13.2 (a) Holding constant the effect of $X_2$, for each increase of one unit in $X_1$, the response variable $Y$ is estimated to increase an average of 2 units. Holding constant the effect of $X_1$, for each increase of one unit in $X_2$, the response variable $Y$ is estimated to increase an average of 7 units.

(b) The $Y$-intercept 50 is the estimate of the mean value of $Y$ if $X_1$ and $X_2$ are both 0.

13.4 (a) $\hat{Y} = -2.72825 + 0.047114X_1 + 0.011947X_2$ where

$X_1$ = sales (in thousands of dollars),

$X_2$ = the number of orders received.

(b) For a given number of orders, each increase of $1,000 in sales is estimated to result in a mean increase in distribution cost of $47.114. For a given amount of sales, each increase of one order is estimated to result in a mean increase in distribution cost of $11.95.

(c) The interpretation of $b_0$ has no practical meaning here because it would have been the estimated mean distribution cost when there were no sales and no orders.

(d) $\hat{Y}_i = -2.72825 + 0.047114(400) + 0.011947(4500) = 69.878$ or $69,878

(e) $\$66,419.93 \le \mu_{Y|X} \le \$73,337.01$

(f) $\$59,380.61 \le Y_X \le \$80,376.33$

13.6 (a) $\hat{Y} = 156.4 + 13.081X_1 + 16.795X_2$ where

$X_1$ = radio advertising (in thousands of dollars),

$X_2$ = newspaper advertising (in thousands of dollars).

(b) For a given amount of newspaper advertising, each increase of $1000 in radio advertising is estimated to result in a mean increase in sales of $13,081. For a given amount of radio advertising, each increase of $1000 in newspaper advertising is estimated to result in the mean increase in sales of $16,795.

(c) When there is no money spent on radio advertising and newspaper advertising, the estimated mean amount of sales is $156,430.44.

(d) $\hat{Y}_i = 156.4 + 13.081(20) + 16.795(20) = 753.95$ or $753,950

(e) $\$623,038.31 \le \mu_{Y|X} \le \$884,860.93$

(f) $\$396,522.63 \le Y_X \le \$1,111,376.60$

13.8 (a) $\hat{Y} = 400.8057 + 456.4485X_1 - 2.4708X_2$ where $X_1$ = Land, $X_2$ = Age

(b) For a given age, each increase by one acre in land area is estimated to result in a mean increase in appraised value of $456.45 thousands. For a given acreage, each increase of one year in age is estimated to result in the mean decrease in appraised value of $2.47 thousands.

(c) The interpretation of $b_0$ has no practical meaning here because it would have meant the estimated mean appraised value of a new house that has no land area.

13.8 cont.

(d) $\hat{Y} = 400.8057 + 456.4485(0.25) - 2.4708(45) =$ \$403.73 thousands.

(e) $372.7370 \le \mu_{Y|X} \le 434.7243$

(f) $235.1964 \le Y_X \le 572.2649$

13.10

(a) $MSR = SSR/k = 30/2 = 15$
$MSE = SSE/(n-k-1) = 120/10 = 12$

(b) $F = MSR/MSE = 15/12 = 1.25$

(c) $F = 1.25 < F_{U(2,13-2-1)} = 4.103$. Do not reject $H_0$. There is not sufficient evidence of a significant linear relationship.

(d) $r^2 = \dfrac{SSR}{SST} = \dfrac{30}{150} = 0.2$. So, 20% of the variation in the dependent variable ($Y$) can be explained by the variation in the independent variable ($X$).

(e) $r^2_{adj} = 1 - \left[ \left(1 - r^2_{Y.12}\right) \dfrac{n-1}{n-k-1} \right] = 0.04$

13.12

(a) $F = 97.69 > F_{U(2,15-2-1)} = 3.89$. Reject $H_0$. There is evidence of a significant linear relationship with at least one of the independent variables.

(b) $p$-value = virtually zero. The probability of obtaining an $F$ test statistic of 97.69 or larger is virtually zero if $H_0$ is true.

(c) $r^2 = SSR/SST = 12.6102/13.38473 = 0.9421$. So, 94.21% of the variation in the long-term ability to absorb shock can be explained by variation in forefoot absorbing capability and variation in midsole impact.

(d) $r^2_{adj} = 1 - \left[ (1 - r^2_{Y.12}) \dfrac{n-1}{n-k-1} \right] = 1 - \left[ (1 - 0.9421) \dfrac{15-1}{15-2-1} \right] = 0.93245$

13.14

(a) $MSR = SSR/k = 3368.087/2 = 1684.04$
$MSE = SSE/(n-k-1) = 477.043/21 = 22.72$
$F = MSR/MSE = 1684/22.7 = 74.13$
$F = 74.13 > F_{U(2,24-2-1)} = 3.467$. Reject $H_0$. There is evidence of a significant linear relationship.

(b) $p$-value = virtually zero. The probability of obtaining an $F$ test statistic of 74.13 or larger is virtually zero if $H_0$ is true.

(c) $r^2 = SSR/SST = 3368.087/3845.13 = 0.8759$. So, 87.59% of the variation in distribution cost can be explained by variation in sales and variation in number of orders.

(d) $r^2_{adj} = 1 - \left[ (1 - r^2_{Y.12}) \dfrac{n-1}{n-k-1} \right] = 1 - \left[ (1 - 0.8759) \dfrac{24-1}{24-2-1} \right] = 0.8641$

13.16 (a) $MSR = SSR/k = 2,028,033/2 = 1,014,016$

$MSE = SSE/(n-k-1) = 479,759.9/19 = 25,251$

$F = MSR/MSE = 1,014,016/25,251 = 40.16$

$F = 40.16 > F_{U(2,22-2-1)} = 3.522$. Reject $H_0$. There is evidence of a significant linear relationship.

(b) $p$-value < 0.001. The probability of obtaining an $F$ test statistic of 40.16 or larger is less than 0.001 if $H_0$ is true.

(c) $r^2 = SSR/SST = 2,028,033/2,507,793 = 0.8087$. So, 80.87% of the variation in sales can be explained by variation in radio advertising and variation in newspaper advertising.

(d) $$r^2_{adj} = 1 - \left[(1 - r^2_{Y.12})\frac{n-1}{n-k-1}\right] = 1 - \left[(1-0.8087)\frac{22-1}{22-2-1}\right] = 0.7886$$

13.18 (a) Based upon a residual analysis the model appears adequate.

(b) There is no evidence of a pattern in the residuals versus time.

(c) $$D = \frac{\sum_{i=2}^{n}(e_i - e_{i-1})^2}{\sum_{i=1}^{n} e_i^2} = \frac{1077.0956}{477.0430} = 2.26$$

(d) D = 2.26 > 1.55. There is no evidence of positive autocorrelation in the residuals.

13.20 There appears to be a quadratic relationship in the plot of the residuals against both radio and newspaper advertising. Thus, quadratic terms for each of these explanatory models should be considered for inclusion in the model.

13.22

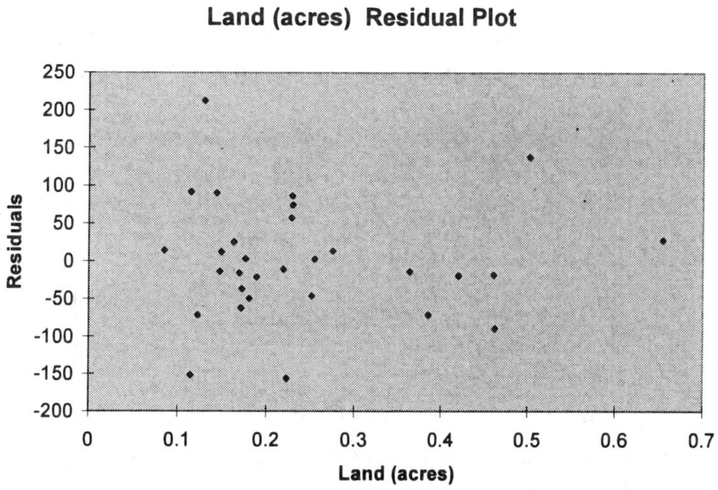

13.22
cont.

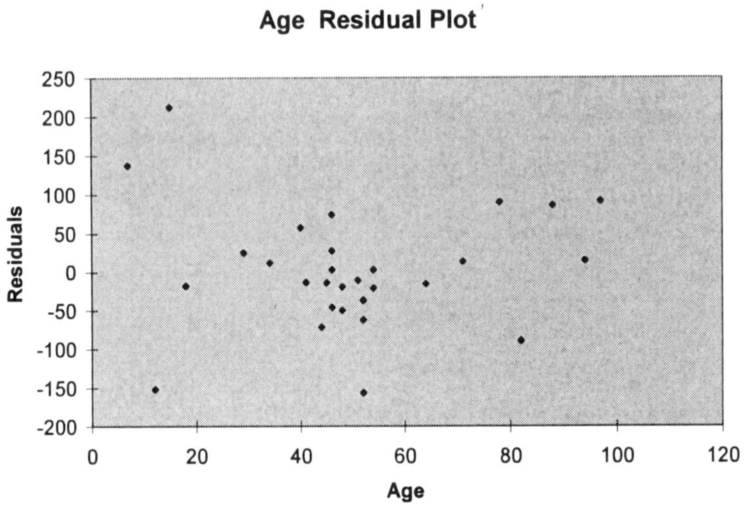


There is no particular pattern in the residual plots and the model appears to be adequate.

13.24 (a) The slope of $X_2$ in terms of the $t$ statistic is 3.75 which is larger than the slope of $X_1$ in terms of the $t$ statistic which is 3.33.

(b) 95% confidence interval on $\beta_1$: $b_1 \pm t_{n-k-1}s_{b_1}$, $4 \pm 2.1098(1.2)$

$$1.46824 \le \beta_1 \le 6.53176$$

(c) For $X_1$: $t = b_1 / s_{b_1} = 4/1.2 = 3.33 > t_{17} = 2.1098$ with 17 degrees of freedom for $\alpha = 0.05$. Reject $H_0$. There is evidence that the variable $X_1$ contributes to a model already containing $X_2$.
For $X_2$: $t = b_2 / s_{b_2} = 3/0.8 = 3.75 > t_{17} = 2.1098$ with 17 degrees of freedom for $\alpha = 0.05$. Reject $H_0$. There is evidence that the variable $X_2$ contributes to a model already containing $X_1$.
Both variables $X_1$ and $X_2$ should be included in the model.

13.26 (a) 95% confidence interval on $\beta_1$: $b_1 \pm t_{n-k-1}s_{b_1}$, $0.0471 \pm 2.0796(0.0203)$

$$0.00488 \le \beta_1 \le 0.08932$$

(b) For $X_1$: $t = b_1 / s_{b_1} = 0.0471/0.0203 = 2.32 > t_{21} = 2.0796$ with 21 degrees of freedom for $\alpha = 0.05$. Reject $H_0$. There is evidence that the variable $X_1$ contributes to a model already containing $X_2$.
For $X_2$: $t = b_2 / s_{b_2} = 0.01195/0.00225 = 5.31 > t_{21} = 2.0796$ with 21 degrees of freedom for $\alpha = 0.05$. Reject $H_0$. There is evidence that the variable $X_2$ contributes to a model already containing $X_1$.
Both variables $X_1$ and $X_2$ should be included in the model.

13.28 (a) 95% confidence interval on $\beta_1$: $b_1 \pm t_{n-k-1} s_{b_1}$, $13.0807 \pm 2.093(1.7594)$

$9.398 \le \beta_1 \le 16.763$

(b) For $X_1$: $t = b_1 / s_{b_1} = 13.0807/1.7594 = 7.43 > t_{19} = 2.093$ with 19 degrees of freedom for $\alpha = 0.05$. Reject $H_0$. There is evidence that the variable $X_1$ contributes to a model already containing $X_2$.

For $X_2$: $t = b_2 / s_{b_2} = 16.7953/2.9634 = 5.67 > t_{19} = 2.093$ with 19 degrees of freedom for $\alpha = 0.05$. Reject $H_0$. There is evidence that the variable $X_2$ contributes to a model already containing $X_1$.

Both variables $X_1$ and $X_2$ should be included in the model.

13.30 (a) $227.5865 \le \beta_1 \le 685.3104$

(b) For $X_1$: $t = b_1 / s_{b_1} = 456.4485/111.5405 = 4.0922$ and $p$-value = 0.0003. Since $p$-value < 0.05, reject $H_0$. There is evidence that the variable $X_1$ contributes to a model already containing $X_2$.

For $X_2$: $t = b_2 / s_{b_2} = -2.4708/0.6808 = -3.6295$ and $p$-value = 0.0012. Since $p$-value < 0.05, reject $H_0$. There is evidence that the variable $X_2$ contributes to a model already containing $X_1$.

Both variables $X_1$ and $X_2$ should be included in the model.

13.32 (a) $\hat{Y} = 43.737 + 9.219X_1 + 12.697X_2$, where $X_1$ = number of rooms and $X_2$ = neighborhood (east = 0).

(b) Holding constant the effect of neighborhood, for each additional room, the selling price is estimated to increase by a mean of 9.219 thousands of dollars, or \$9219. For a given number of rooms, a west neighborhood is estimated to increase average selling price over an east neighborhood by 12.697 thousands of dollars, or \$12,697.

(c) $\hat{Y} = 43.737 + 9.219(9) + 12.697(0) = 126.71$ or \$126,710

$109.5600 \le Y_{X=X_i} \le 143.8551$ $\quad$ $121.4714 \le \mu_{Y|X=X_i} \le 131.9437$

(d) Based on a residual analysis, the model appears adequate.

(e) $F = 55.39 > F_{2,17} = 3.5915$. Reject $H_0$. There is evidence of a relationship between selling price and the two dependent variables.

(f) For $X_1$: $t = 8.95 > t_{17} = 2.1098$. Reject $H_0$. Number of rooms makes a significant contribution and should be included in the model.

For $X_2$: $t = 3.59 > t_{17} = 2.1098$. Reject $H_0$. Neighborhood makes a significant contribution and should be included in the model.

Based on these results, the regression model with the two independent variables should be used.

(g) $7.0466 \le \beta_1 \le 11.3913$, $5.2377 \le \beta_2 \le 20.1557$

(h) $r^2 = 0.867$. 86.7% of the variation in selling price can be explained by variation in number of rooms and variation in neighborhood.

(i) $r^2_{adj} = 0.851$

(j) The slope of selling price with number of rooms is the same regardless of whether the house is located in an east or west neighborhood.

13.32 cont. (k) $\hat{Y} = 53.95 + 8.032X_1 - 5.90X_2 + 2.089X_1X_2$.
For $X_1 X_2$: the $p$-value is 0.330. Do not reject $H_0$. There is no evidence that the interaction term makes a contribution to the model.

(l) The two-variable model in (a) should be used.

13.34 (a) $\hat{Y} = 8.0100 + 0.0052X_1 - 2.1052X_2$, where $X_1$ = depth (in feet) and $X_2$ = type of drilling (wet = 0, dry = 1).

(b) Holding constant the effect of type of drilling, for each foot increase in depth of the hole, the additional drilling time is estimated to increase by a mean of 0.0052 minutes. For a given depth, a dry drilling is estimated to reduce mean additional drilling time over wet drilling by 2.1052 minutes.

(c) Dry drilling: $\hat{Y} = 8.0101 + 0.0052(100) - 2.1052 = 6.4276$ minutes.

$6.2096 \le \mu_{Y|X=X_i} \le 6.6457$, $\quad 4.92304 \le Y_{X=X_i} \le 7.9322$

(d)

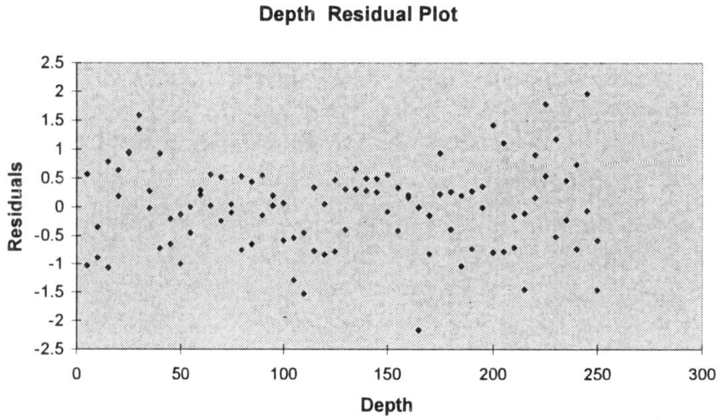


Based on a residual analysis, the model appears adequate.

(e) $F = 111.109$ with 2 and 97 degrees of freedom, $F_{2,97} = 3.09$ using Excel. $p$-value is virtually 0. Reject $H_0$ at 5% level of significance. There is evidence of a relationship between additional drilling time and the two dependent variables.

(f) For $X_1$: $t = 5.0289 > t_{97} = 1.9847$. Reject $H_0$. Depth of the hole makes a significant contribution and should be included in the model.
For $X_2$: $t = -14.0331 < t_{97} = -1.9847$. Reject $H_0$. Type of drilling makes a significant contribution and should be included in the model.
Based on these results, the regression model with the two independent variables should be used.

(g) $0.0032 \le \beta_1 \le 0.0073$, $-2.4029 \le \beta_2 \le -1.8075$

(h) $r^2 = 0.6961$. 69.61% of the variation in additional drilling time can be explained by the depth of the hole and variation in type of drilling.

(i) $r^2_{adj} = 0.6899$

(j) The slope of additional drilling time with depth of the hole is the same regardless of whether it is a dry drilling hole or a wet drilling hole.

13.34 cont. (k) $\hat{Y} = 7.9120 + 0.0060X_1 - 1.9091X_2 - 0.0015X_1X_2$.

For $X_1X_2$: the $p$-value is $0.4624 > 0.05$. Do not reject $H_0$. There is not evidence that the interaction term makes a contribution to the model.

(l) The two-variable model in (a) should be used.

13.36 (a) $\hat{Y} = 31.5594 + 0.0296X_1 + 0.0041X_2 + 1.7159\times10^{-5}X_3$.

where $X_1$ = sales, $X_2$ = orders, $X_3 = X_1 X_2$

For $X_1X_2$: the $p$-value is $0.3249 > 0.05$. Do not reject $H_0$. There is not enough evidence that the interaction term makes a contribution to the model.

(b) Since there is not enough evidence of any interaction effect between sales and orders, the model in problem 13.4 should be used.

13.38 (a) $\hat{Y} = -1293.3105 + 43.6600X_1 + 56.9335X_2 - 0.8430X_3$.

where $X_1$ = radio advertisement, $X_2$ = newspaper advertisement, $X_3 = X_1 X_2$

For $X_1X_2$: the $p$-value is $0.0018 < 0.05$. Reject $H_0$. There is enough evidence that the interaction term makes a contribution to the model.

(b) Since there is enough evidence of an interaction effect between radio and newspaper advertisement, the model in this problem should be used.

13.40 (a) $\hat{Y} = 250.4237 + 0.0127X_1 - 1.4785X_2 + 0.004X_3$.

where $X_1$ = staff present, $X_2$ = remote hours, $X_3 = X_1 X_2$

For $X_1X_2$: the $p$-value is $0.2353 > 0.05$. Do not reject $H_0$. There is not enough evidence that the interaction term makes a contribution to the model.

(b) Since there is not enough evidence of an interaction effect between total staff present and remote hours, the model in problem 13.7 should be used.

13.42 (a)

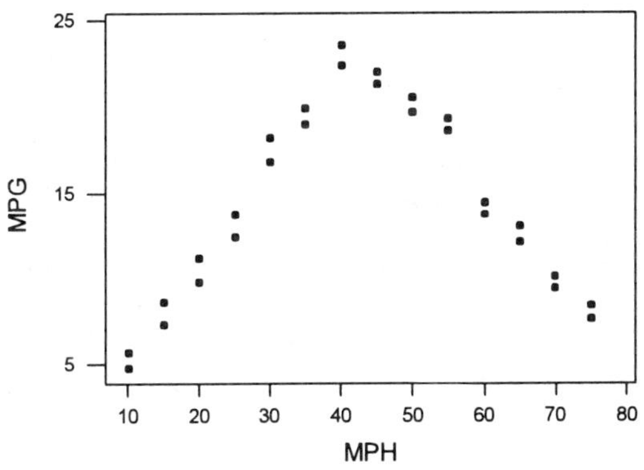


(b) $\hat{Y} = -7.556 + 1.2717X_1 - 0.0145X_1^2$

13.42 (c) $\hat{Y} = -7.556 + 1.2717(55) - 0.0145(55^2) = 18.52$

cont. (d) Based on residual analysis, there are patterns in the residuals vs. highway speed, vs. the quadratic variable (speed squared), and vs. the fitted values.

(e) $F = 141.46 > F_{2,25} = 3.39$. Reject $H_0$. The overall model is significant. The $p$-value $< 0.001$.

(f) The $p$-value $< 0.001$. $t = -16.63 < -t_{25} = -2.0595$. Reject $H_0$. The quadratic effect is significant. Therefore, the quadratic model is a better fit than the linear regression model.

(g) $r^2 = 0.919$. 91.9% of the variation in miles per gallon can be explained by the quadratic relationship between miles per gallon and highway speed.

(h) $r^2_{adj} = 0.912$

13.44 (a)

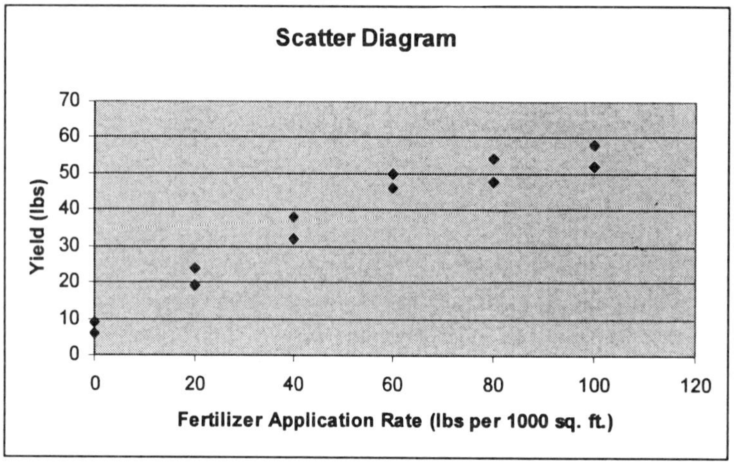


(b) $\hat{Y} = 6.643 + 0.895X_1 - 0.0041X_1^2$

(c) $\hat{Y} = 6.643 + 0.895(70) - 0.0041(70^2) = 49.17$

13.44 (d)
cont.

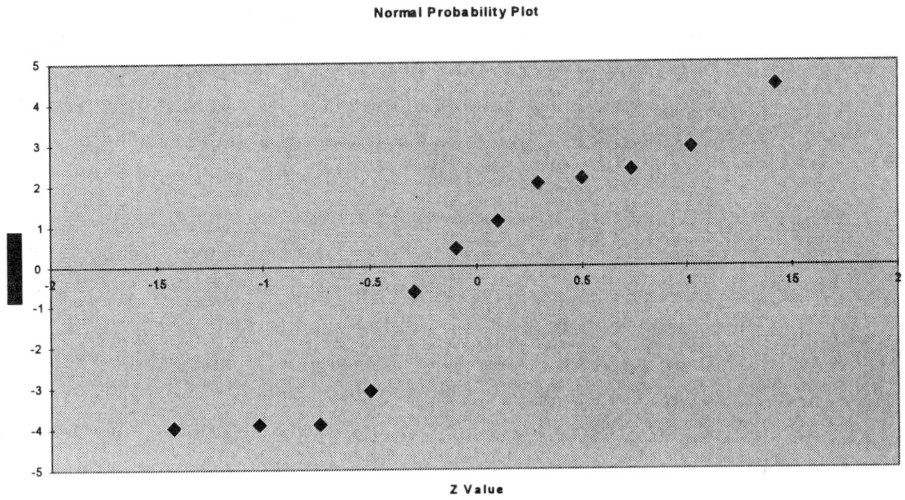


A residual analysis indicates no strong patterns. However, the distribution of residuals appears to deviate from a normal distribution according to the normal probability plot.

(e) $F = 157.32 > F_{2,9} = 4.26$. Reject $H_0$. The overall model is significant.

(f) The $p$-value < 0.001 indicates that the probability of having an $F$-test statistic of at least 157.32 when $\beta_1 = 0$ and $\beta_2 = 0$ is less than 0.001.

(g) $t = -4.27 < -t_9 = -2.2622$. Reject $H_0$. The quadratic effect is significant.

(h) The $p$-value = 0.002 indicates that the probability of having a $t$-test statistic with an absolute value of at least 4.27 is equal to 0.002 when $\beta_2 = 0$.

(i) $r^2 = 0.972$. So, 97.2% of the variation in yield can be explained by the quadratic relationship between yield and fertilizer application rate.

(j) $r^2_{adj} = 0.966$

13.46 In the case of the simple linear regression model, the slope $b_1$ represents the change in the estimated mean of $Y$ per unit change in $X$ and does not take into account any other variables. In the multiple linear regression model, the slope $b_1$ represents the change in the estimated mean of $Y$ per unit change in $X_1$, taking into account the effect of all the other independent variables.

13.48 You test whether the interaction of the dummy variable and each of the independent variables in the model make a significant contribution to the regression model.

13.50 It is assumed that the slope of the dependent variable $Y$ with an independent variable $X$ is the same for each of the two levels of the dummy variable.

13.52 (a) $\hat{Y} = -44.988 + 1.7506X_1 + 0.368X_2$, where $X_1$ = assessed value (in thousands of dollars) and $X_2$ = time period (in months).

(b) Holding constant the effects of time period, for each additional thousand dollars in assessed value the selling price of the house is estimated to increase on the average by 1.7506 thousands of dollars, or $1,750.60. Holding constant the effects of assessed value, for each additional month the selling price of the house is estimated to increase on the average by 0.368 thousands of dollars, or $368.

(c) $\hat{Y} = -44.988 + 1.7506(70) + 0.368(12) = 81.969$ or $81,969

(d) All four residual plots indicate that the fitted model appears to be adequate.

(e) $F = 223.46 > F_{U(2,27)} = 3.35$ with 2 and 27 degrees of freedom. Reject $H_0$. At least one of the independent variables is linearly related to the dependent variable.

(f) The $p$-value is less than 0.001. This means that the probability of obtaining an $F$ test statistic of 223.46 or greater if there were not relationship between the dependent variable and independent variables is less than 0.001.

(g) $r^2 = 0.943$. So, 94.3% of the variation in selling price can be explained by the variation in assessed value and the variation in time period.

(h) $r^2_{adj} = 0.939$

(i) For $X_1$: $t = 20.41 > t_{27} = 2.0518$ with 27 degrees of freedom. Reject $H_0$. There is enough evidence that $X_1$ significantly contributes to a model already containing $X_2$. For $X_2$: $t = 2.873 > t_{27} = 2.0518$ with 27 degrees of freedom. Reject $H_0$. There is enough evidence that $X_2$ significantly contributes to a model already containing $X_1$. Therefore, each independent variable makes a significant contribution in the presence of the other variable, and both variables should be included in the model.

(j) For $X_1$, the $p$-value is less than 0.001. This means the probability of obtaining a $t$-test statistic which differs from zero by 20.41 or more (positively or negatively) when $\beta_1 = 0$ is less than 0.001. For $X_2$, the $p$-value is 0.008. This means the probability of obtaining a $t$-test statistic which differs from zero by 2.873 or more (positively or negatively) when $\beta_2 = 0$ is 0.008.

(k) $1.575 \le \beta_1 \le 1.927$. This is a net regression coefficient. That is, taking into account the time period, this coefficient measures the expected increase in selling price for each additional thousand dollars in assessed value. In Problem 12.76, the coefficient did not take into account (and hold constant) the effects of the time period.

13.54 (a) $\hat{Y} = 63.7751 + 10.7252X_1 - 0.2843X_2$, where $X_1$ = size (in thousands of square feet) and $X_2$ = age (in years).

(b) Holding constant the effects of age, for each additional thousand square feet the assessed value of the house is estimated to increase by a mean of 10.7252 thousands of dollars, or $10,725.20. Holding constant the effects of size, for each year of age the assessed value of the house is estimated to decrease by a mean of 0.2843 thousands of dollars, or $284.30.

(c) $\hat{Y} = 63.7751 + 10.7252(1.75) - 0.2843(10) = 79.702$ or $79,702

(d) The residual plot against age indicates a potential pattern that may require the addition of nonlinear terms. One value appears to be an outlier in all four plots.

(e) $F = 28.58 > F_{U(2,12)} = 3.89$ with 2 and 12 degrees of freedom. Reject $H_0$. At least one of the independent variables is linearly related to the dependent variable.

13.54 cont. (f) The $p$-value is less than 0.001. This means that the probability of obtaining an $F$ test statistic of 28.58 or greater if there were not relationship between the dependent variable and independent variables is less than 0.001.

(g) $r^2 = 0.8265$. 82.65% of the variation in assessed value can be explained by the variation in size and the variation in age.

(h) $r^2_{adj} = 0.7976$

(i) For $X_1$: $t = 3.558 > t_{12} = 2.1788$ with 12 degrees of freedom. Reject $H_0$. There is evidence that $X_1$ significantly contributes to a model already containing $X_2$. For $X_2$: $t = -3.400 < -t_{12} = -2.1788$ with 12 degrees of freedom. Reject $H_0$. There is evidence that $X_2$ significantly contributes to a model already containing $X_1$. Therefore, each independent variable makes a significant contribution in the presence of the other variable, and both variables should be included in the model.

(j) For $X_1$, the $p$-value is 0.004. This means the probability of obtaining a $t$-test statistic which differs from zero by 3.558 or more (positively or negatively) when $\beta_1 = 0$ is 0.004. For $X_2$, the $p$-value is 0.005. This means the probability of obtaining a $t$-test statistic which differs from zero by 3.4 or more (positively or negatively) when $\beta_2 = 0$ is 0.005.

(k) $4.158 \le \beta_1 \le 17.293$. This is a net regression coefficient. That is, taking into account the age of the house, this coefficient measures the expected increase in assessed value for each additional thousand square feet of size. In Problem 12.77, the coefficient did not take into account (and hold constant) the effects of age.

(l) $r^2_{Y1.2} = 0.5134$. For a given age of the house, 51.34% of the variation in assessed value can be explained by variation in size. $r^2_{Y2.1} = 0.4907$. For a given amount of size in square feet, 49.07% of the variation in assessed value can be explained by variation in age. Based on your answers to (a) through (k), you do not agree with the statement.

13.56 (a) $\hat{Y} = 40.8765 - 0.0121 \text{ length} - 0.0050 \text{ weight}$

(b) $b_1 = -0.0121$: Holding weight fixed, the estimated mean mileage of a car will decrease by 0.0121 miles per gallon as the length of the car increases by one inch. $b_2 = -.0050$: Holding length fixed, the estimate mean mileage of a car will decrease by .0050 miles per gallon as the weight of the car increases by one pound.

(c) 23.6603 miles per gallon.

(d)

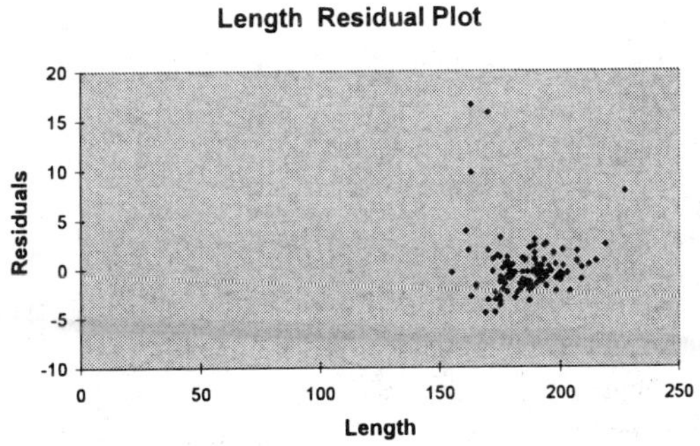

13.56 cont. (d) According to the residual plot of length, the homoscedasticity assumption seems to have been violated. From the residual plot of weight, there seems to be a quadratic relationship between mileage and weight.

(e) Yes, there is a significant relationship between gasoline mileage and the two explanatory variables at the 0.05 level of significance because the $p$-value of the $F$ test is essentially zero.

(f) The $p$-value is essentially zero. It is almost impossible to have observed data which will give rise to an $F$ test statistic equal to or more extreme than 92.9287 if there is really no significant relationship between gasoline mileage and the two explanatory variables.

(g) 61.17% of the total variation in gasoline mileage can be explained by length and

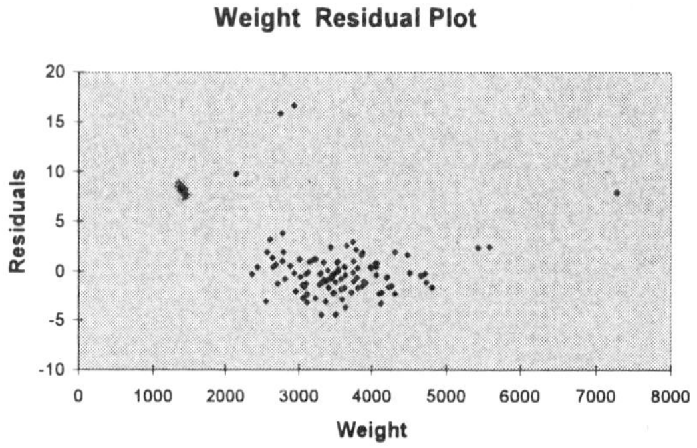


weight of a car.

(h) $r^2_{adj} = 0.6051$

(i) PHStat output:

| | Coefficients | Standard Error | t Stat | P-value |
|---|---|---|---|---|
| Intercept | 40.87650495 | 4.059910501 | 10.06832661 | 1.3805E-17 |
| Length | -0.012071414 | 0.02632727 | -0.458513689 | 0.647426793 |
| Weight | -0.004954095 | 0.000483677 | -10.24256569 | 5.32269E-18 |

At 0.05 level of significance, only weight makes a significant contribution to the regression model. The model should include only weight as the explanatory variable.

(j) The $p$-value for length is 0.6474. The probability of observing a data set which yields a $t$-test statistic for length equal to or more extreme than –0.4585 is 64.74%. The $p$-value for weight is essentially zero. The probability of observing a data set which yields a $t$ test statistic for weight more extreme than –10.2426 is essentially zero.

(k) $-0.0059 \le \beta_2 \le -0.0040$

13.58 (a) $\hat{Y} = 152.0316 - 2.4587X_1 - 15.8687X_2$, where $X_1$ = league dummy (0 = American, 1 = National) and $X_2$ = ERA.

(b) Holding constant the effect of ERA, the estimated mean number of wins for a team in the American league is 2.4587 above that of the National league. Holding constant the effect of league, for each unit increase in ERA, the estimated mean number of wins is estimated to decrease by 15.8687.

(c) $\hat{Y} = 152.0316 - 2.4587(0) - 15.8687(4.5) \cong 81$ wins.

13.58 (d)
cont.

E.R.A. Residual Plot

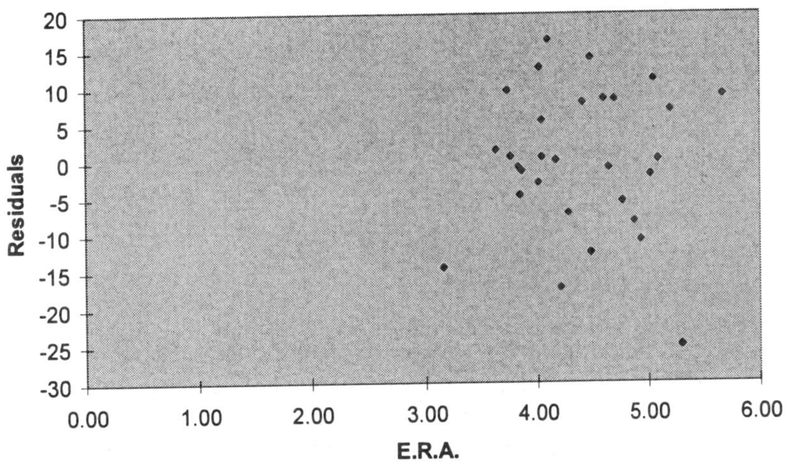


Based on the residual analysis, the model appears adequate.

(e) $F = 11.4784$ with 2 and 27 degrees of freedom.
$p$-value = 0.00025< 0.05. Reject $H_0$. There is evidence of a relationship between number of wins and the two dependent variables.

(f) For $X_1$: $t = -0.6447$. $p$-value = 0.5246 > 0.05. Do not reject $H_0$. Which league the team is in does not make a significant contribution and should not be included in the model.
For $X_2$: $t = -4.7763$. $p$-value is virtually zero < 0.05. Reject $H_0$. ERA makes a significant contribution and should be included in the model.
The model should include ERA but not the league dummy.

(g) $-10.2842 \le \beta_1 \le 5.3668$, $-22.6856 \le \beta_2 \le -9.0518$

(h) $r^2 = 0.4595$. 45.95% of the variation in number of wins can be explained by variation in type of league and variation in ERA.

(i) $r^2_{adj} = 0.4195$

(j) The slope of number of wins with ERA is the same regardless of whether the team is in the American or National league.

(k) $\hat{Y} = 162.6777 - 21.8842X_1 - 18.2211X_2 + 4.4027X_1X_2$.
For $X_1 X_2$: the $p$-value is 0.5189. Do not reject $H_0$. There is no evidence that the interaction term makes a contribution to the model.

(l) The two-variable model in (a) should be used.

# CHAPTER 14

## OBJECTIVES

- To understand the basic themes of quality management and Deming's 14 points
- To understand the basic aspects of the Six Sigma Management approach
- To be able to construct various control charts
- To know which control chart to use for a particular type of data

## OVERVIEW AND KEY CONCEPTS

### Themes of Quality Management

1. The primary focus is on process improvement.
2. Most of the variation in a process is due to the system and not the individual.
3. Teamwork is an integral part of a quality management organization.
4. Customer satisfaction is a primary organizational goal.
5. Organizational transformation must occur in order to implement quality management.
6. Fear must be removed from organizations.
7. Higher quality costs less not more but it requires an investment in training.

### Deming's 14 Points for Management

1. Create constancy of purpose for improvement of product and service.

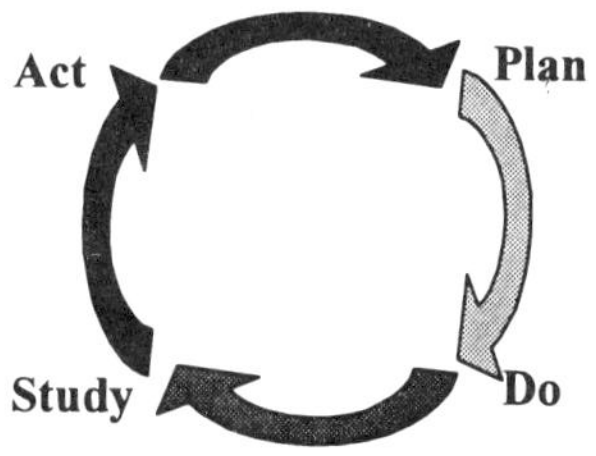


**The Shewhart-Deming Cycle Focuses on Constant Improvement**

2. Adopt the new philosophy.
3. Cease dependence on inspection to achieve quality.
4. End the practice of awarding business on the basis of price tag alone. Instead, minimize total cost by working with a single supplier.
5. Improve constantly and forever every process for planning, production and service.
6. Institute training on the job.
7. Adopt and institute leadership.
8. Drive out fear.
9. Break down barriers between staff areas.
10. Eliminate slogans, exhortations, and targets for the workforce.
11. Eliminate numerical quotas for the workforce and numerical goals for management.
12. Remove barriers that rob people of pride of workmanship. Eliminate the annual rating or merit system.
13. Institute a vigorous program of education and self-improvement for everyone.
14. Put everyone in the company to work to accomplish the transformation.

## Six Sigma Management

- A method for breaking processes into a series of steps in order to eliminate defects and produce near perfect results.
- Has a clear focus on obtaining bottom-line results in a relatively short three to six-month period of time.
- **The Six Sigma DMAIC model:**
  - **Define:** The problem to be solved needs to be defined along with the costs, benefits of the project, and the impact on the customer.
  - **Measure:** Operational definitions for each Critical-To-Quality (CTQ) characteristic must be developed. In addition, the measurement procedure must be verified so that it is consistent over repeated measurements.
  - **Analyze:** The root causes of why defects can occur need to be determined along with the variables in the process that cause these defects to occur. Data are collected to determine the underlying value for each process variable often using control charts.
  - **Improve:** The importance of each process variable on the CTQ characteristic is studied using designed experiments. The objective is to determine the best level for each variable that can be maintained in the long term.
  - **Control:** The objective is to maintain the gains that have been made with a revised process in the long term by avoiding potential problems that can occur when a process is changed.
- Its implementation requires a data-oriented approach using statistical tools such as control charts and designed experiments.
- Involves training everyone in the company in the DMAIC model.

## Control Charts

- The **control chart** is a means of monitoring variation in the characteristic of a product or services by focusing on the time dimension in which the process produces products or services and studying the nature of the variability in the process.
- **Special (assignable) causes of variation:** Large fluctuations or patterns in the data that are not inherent to a process. They are often caused by changes in the process that represents either problems to be fixed or opportunities to exploit.
- **Chance (common) causes of variation:** The inherent variability that exists in a process. These consist of the numerous small causes of variability that operate randomly or by chance.
- An **out-of-control process** contains both common causes of variation and assignable causes of variation. Because assignable causes of variation are not part of the process design, an out-of-control process is unpredictable.
- An **in-control process** contains only common causes of variation. Because theses causes of variation are inherent to the process, an in-control process is predictable. An in-control-process is sometimes said to be in a **state of statistical control**.
- **Control limits:**
  - Statistical measure of interest $\pm$ 3 standard deviations

- **Identifying pattern in control charts:**

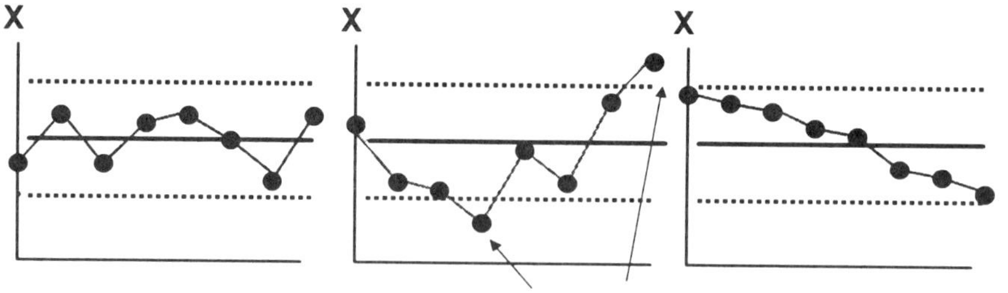


Common Cause Variation: No Points Outside Control Limits

Special Cause Variation: 2 Points Outside Control Limits

Downward Pattern: No Points Outside Control Limits but Trend Exists

  - A trend exists if there are 8 consecutive points above (or below) the centerline or 8 consecutive points that are increasing (or decreasing).
- **The first type of control error:** The belief that observed value represents special cause when in fact it is due to common cause.
- **The second type of control error:** Treating special cause variation as if it is common cause variation.
- When a process is out-of-control, the assignable causes of variation must be identified. If the assignable causes of variation are detrimental to the quality of the product or service, a plan to eliminate this source of variation must be implemented. If an assignable cause of variation increases quality, the process should be change so that it is incorporated into the process design and becomes a common cause source of variation and the process is improved.
- When a process is in control, it must be determined whether the amount of common cause variation in the process is small enough to satisfy the customers of the products or services. If it is small enough to consistently satisfy the customers, the control charts can be used to monitor the process on a continuous basis to make sure that it does not go out-of-control. If it is too large, the process should be altered.

## Control Chart for the Proportion of Nonconforming Item (the *p* Chart)

- It is an attribute chart, which is used when sampled items are classified according to whether they conform or do not conform to operationally defined requirement.
- When used with unequal sample sizes over time, the unequal sample sizes should not differ by more than 25% from average sample size.

- $LCL_p = \max\left(0, \bar{p} - 3\sqrt{\frac{\bar{p}(1-\bar{p})}{\bar{n}}}\right)$, $UCL_p = \bar{p} + 3\sqrt{\frac{\bar{p}(1-\bar{p})}{\bar{n}}}$

  where

  $X_i =$ number of nonforming items in sample $i$

  $n_i =$ sample size for sample $i$

  $p_i = X_i / n_i =$ proportion of nonconforming items in sample $i$

  $$\bar{n} = \frac{\sum_{i=1}^{k} n_i}{k}$$

  $$\bar{p} = \frac{\sum_{i=1}^{k} X_i}{\sum_{i=1}^{k} n_i}$$

  $k =$ number of samples

### Morals of the Red Bead Example

- Variation is an inherent part of any process.
- The system is primarily responsible for worker performance.
- Only management can change the system.
- Some workers will always be above average and some will be below.

### The $c$ Chart

- It is an attribute chart and a control chart for the number of nonconformities (or occurrences) in a unit (called an area of opportunity).
- $LCL_c = \bar{c} - 3\sqrt{\bar{c}}$ , $UCL_c = \bar{c} + 3\sqrt{\bar{c}}$

  where

  $$\bar{c} = \frac{\sum_{i=1}^{k} c_i}{k}$$

  $\bar{c} =$ average number of occurrences

  $k =$ number of units sampled

  $c_i =$ number of occurrences in unit $i$

### Control Chart for the Range $(R)$ and Mean $(\bar{X})$

- They are variable control charts.
- They are more sensitive in detecting special-cause variation than the $p$ chart.
- They are typically used in pairs
- The $R$ chart monitors the variation in the process while the $\bar{X}$ chart monitors the process average.
- The $R$ chart should be examined first because if it indicates the process is out-of-control, the interpretation of the $\bar{X}$ chart will be misleading.

- **Control chart for the range ($R$ chart):**
  - $LCL_R = D_3\bar{R}$, $UCL_R = D_4\bar{R}$

    where

    $$\bar{R} = \frac{\sum_{i=1}^{k} R_i}{k}$$

    $D_3$ and $D_4$ are to obtained from a table.
- **Control chart for the mean ($\bar{X}$ chart):**
  - $LCL_{\bar{X}} = \bar{\bar{X}} - A_2\bar{R}$, $UCL_{\bar{X}} = \bar{\bar{X}} + A_2\bar{R}$

    where

    $$\bar{\bar{X}} = \frac{\sum_{i=1}^{k} \bar{X}_i}{k}$$

    $$\bar{R} = \frac{\sum_{i=1}^{k} R_i}{k}$$

    $\bar{X} =$ the sample mean of $n$ observations at time $i$

    $R_i =$ the range of $n$ observations at time $i$

    $k =$ number of subgroups

    and $A_2$ is to be obtained from a table.

## SOLUTIONS TO END OF SECTION AND CHAPTER REVIEW EVEN PROBLEMS

14.2 (a) Proportion of nonconformances largest on Day 4, smallest on Day 3.

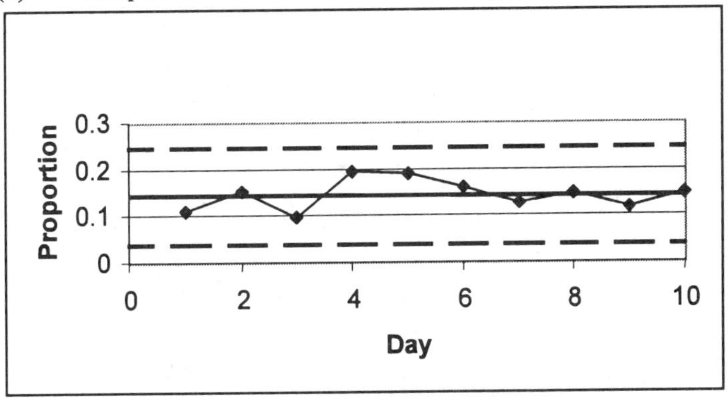


(b) $\bar{n} = 1036/10 = 103.6,\ \bar{p} = 148/1036 = 0.142857,$

$$LCL = \bar{p} - 3\sqrt{\frac{\bar{p}(1-\bar{p})}{\bar{n}}} = 0.142857 - 3\sqrt{\frac{0.142857(1-0.142857)}{103.6}} = 0.039719$$

$$UCL = \bar{p} + 3\sqrt{\frac{\bar{p}(1-\bar{p})}{\bar{n}}} = 0.142857 + 3\sqrt{\frac{0.142857(1-0.142857)}{103.6}} = 0.245995$$

(c) Proportions are within control limits, so there does not appear to be any special causes of variation.

14.4 (a) $n = 500,\ \bar{p} = 761/16000 = 0.0476$

$$LCL = \bar{p} - 3\sqrt{\frac{\bar{p}(1-\bar{p})}{n}} = 0.0476 - 3\sqrt{\frac{0.0476(1-0.0476)}{500}} = 0.0190 > 0$$

$$UCL = \bar{p} + 3\sqrt{\frac{\bar{p}(1-\bar{p})}{n}} = 0.0476 + 3\sqrt{\frac{0.0476(1-0.0476)}{500}} = 0.0761$$

14.4 (a)
cont.

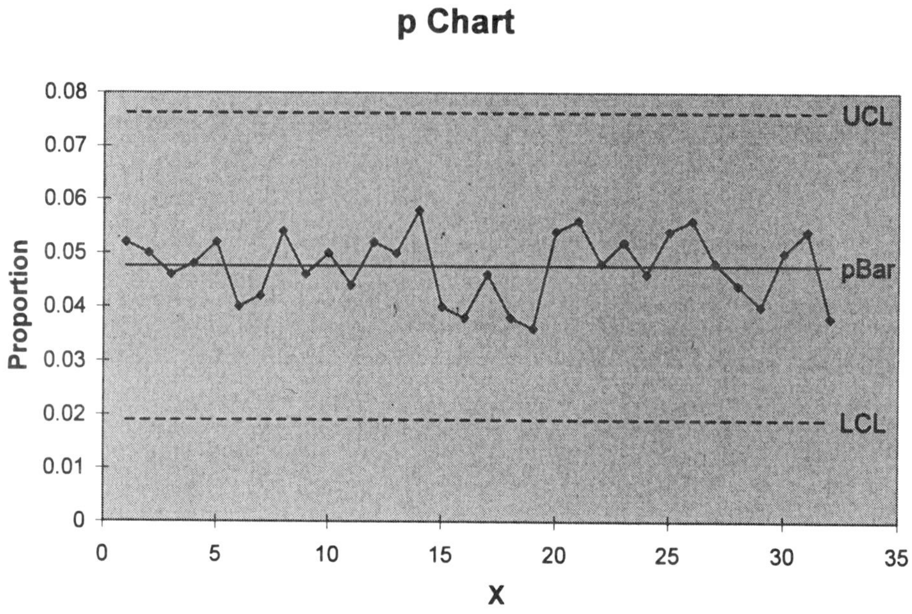


(b) Since the individual points are distributed around $\bar{p}$ without any pattern and all the points are within the control limits, the process is in a state of statistical control.

14.6 (a) $\bar{n} = 113345/22 = 5152.0455$, $\bar{p} = 1460/113345 = 0.01288$,

$$LCL = \bar{p} - 3\sqrt{\frac{\bar{p}(1-\bar{p})}{\bar{n}}} = 0.01288 - 3\sqrt{\frac{0.01288(1-0.01288)}{5152.0455}} = 0.00817$$

$$UCL = \bar{p} + 3\sqrt{\frac{\bar{p}(1-\bar{p})}{\bar{n}}} = 0.01288 - 3\sqrt{\frac{0.01288(1-0.01288)}{5152.0455}} = 0.01759$$

14.6 cont. (a)

**PHStat output:**

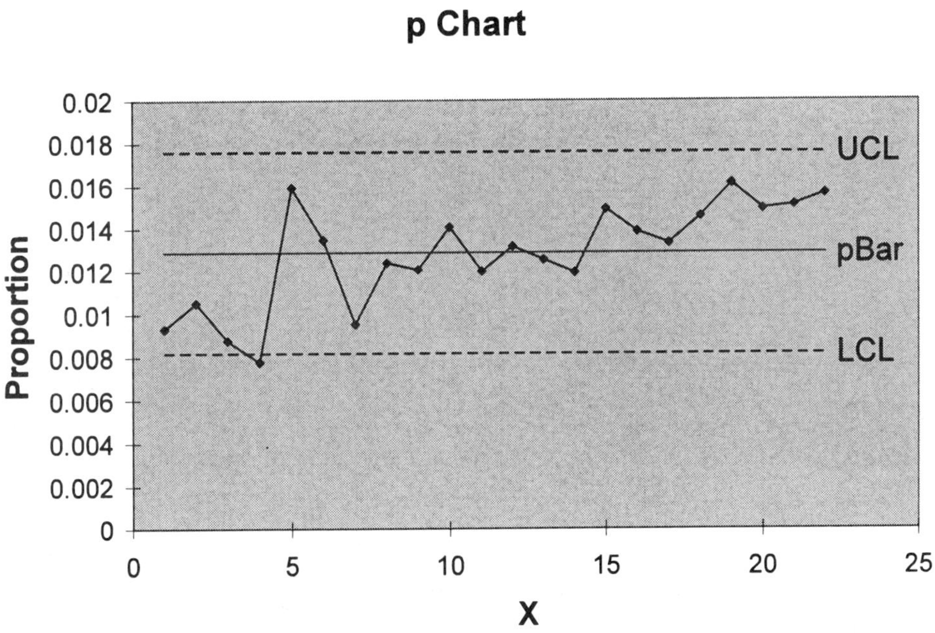


The proportion of unacceptable cans is below the LCL on Day 4. There is evidence of a pattern over time, since the last eight points are all above the mean and most of the earlier points are below the mean. Thus, the special causes that might be contributing to this pattern should be investigated before any change in the system of operation is contemplated.

(b) Once special causes have been eliminated and the process is stable, Deming's fourteen points should be implemented to improve the system. They might also look at day 4 to see if they could identify and exploit the special cause that led to such a low proportion of defects on that day.

14.8 (a)

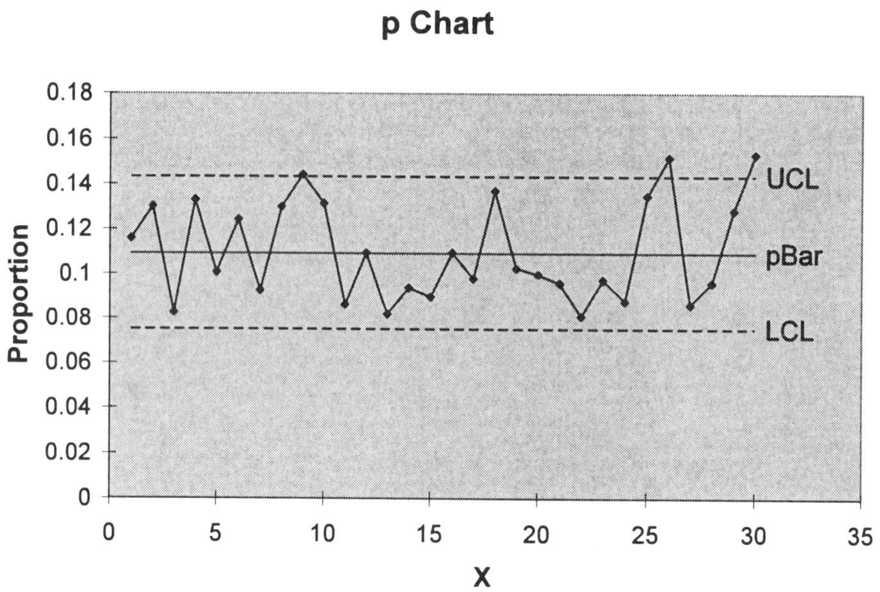


$\bar{p} = 0.1091$, $LCL = 0.0751$, $UCL = 0.1431$. Points 9, 26, and 30 are above the $UCL$.

(b) First, the reasons for the special cause variation would need to be determined and local corrective action taken. Once special causes have been eliminated and the process is stable, Deming's fourteen points should be implemented to improve the system.

14.12 (a) $\bar{R} = \dfrac{\sum_{i=1}^{k} R_i}{k} = \dfrac{66.8}{20} = 3.34$, $\bar{\bar{X}} = \dfrac{\sum_{i=1}^{k} \bar{X}_i}{k} = \dfrac{118.325}{20} = 5.916.$

$R$ chart:

$UCL = D_4\bar{R} = 2.282(3.34) = 7.6219$

$LCL$ does not exist.

$\bar{X}$ chart:

$UCL = \bar{\bar{X}} + A_2\bar{R} = 5.9163 + 0.729(3.34) = 8.3511$

$LCL = \bar{\bar{X}} - A_2\bar{R} = 5.9163 - 0.729(3.34) = 3.4814$

14.12 (a)
cont.

**PHStat R Chart output:**

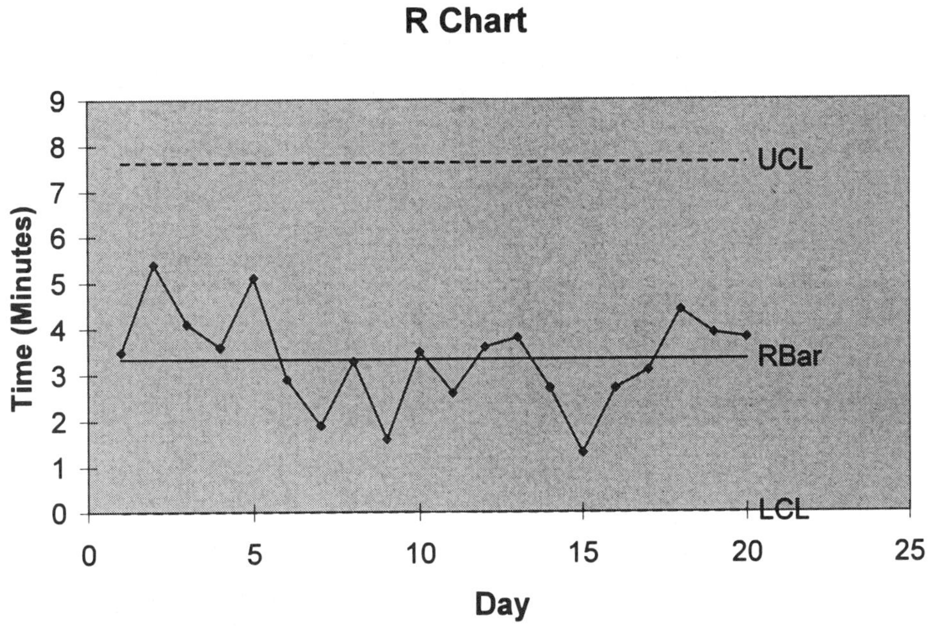


**PHStat $\bar{X}$ Chart output:**

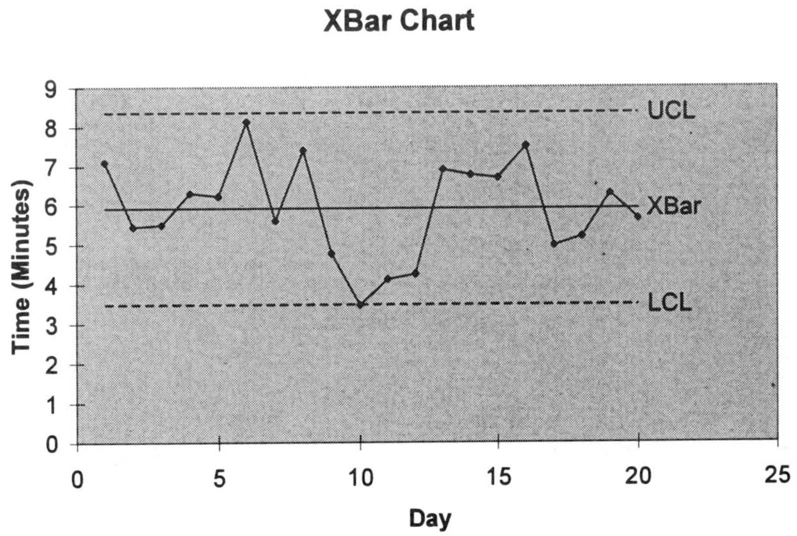


(b) The $\bar{X}$ of sample 10 is slightly below the *LCL*. The process is out-of-control.

14.14 (a) $\bar{R} = 0.8794$, $R$ chart: $UCL = 2.0068$; $LCL$ does not exist

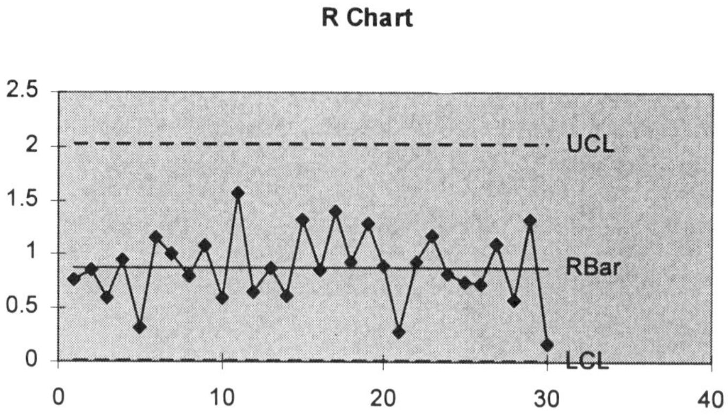


(b) $\bar{\bar{X}} = 20.1065$, $\bar{X}$ chart: $UCL = 20.7476$; $LCL = 19.4654$

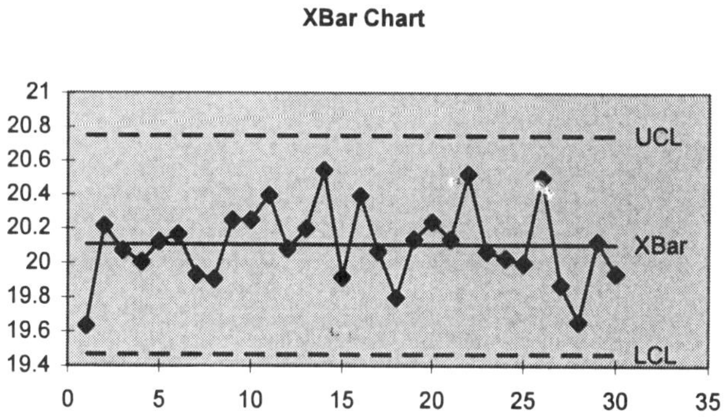


(c) The process appears to be in control since there are no points outside the lower and upper control limits of both the R-chart and Xbar-chart, and there is no pattern in the results over time.

14.16 (a)

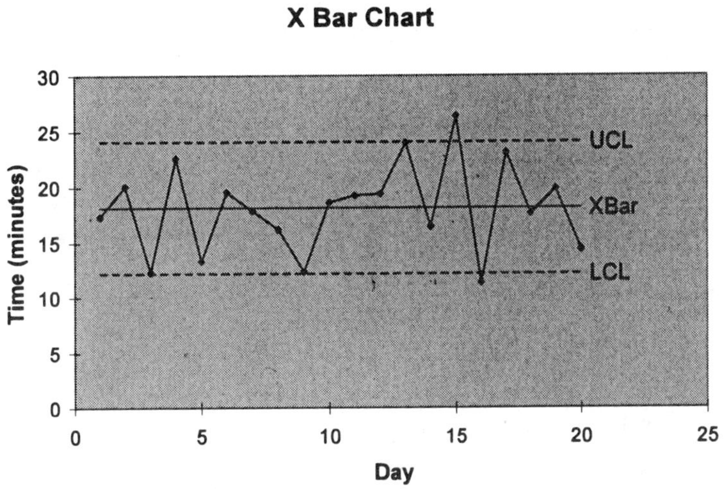


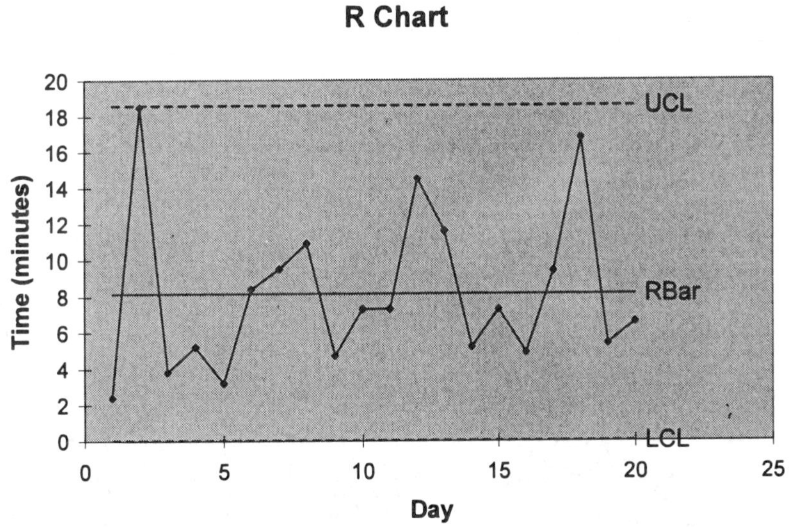


$\overline{R} = 8.145$, $\overline{\overline{X}} = 18.12$.

$R$ chart: $LCL = D_3\,\overline{R} = 0\,(8.145) = 0$. $LCL$ does not exist.

$UCL = D_4\,\overline{R} = (2.282)\,(8.145) = 18.58689$.

For $\overline{X}$ chart: $LCL = \overline{\overline{X}} - A_2\,\overline{R} = 18.12 - (0.729)\,(8.145) = 12.1823$

$UCL = \overline{\overline{X}} + A_2\,\overline{R} = 18.12 + (0.729)\,(8.145) = 24.0577$

(b) There are no sample ranges outside the control limits and there does not appear to be a pattern in the range chart. The sample mean on Day 15 is above the $UCL$ and the sample mean on Day 16 is below the $LCL$, which is an indication there is evidence of special cause variation in the sample means.

14.18 (a) $\bar{R} = 0.3022$, $R$ chart: $UCL = 0.6389$; $LCL$ does not exist

$\bar{\bar{X}} = 90.1317$, $\bar{X}$ chart: $UCL = 90.3060$; $LCL = 89.9573$

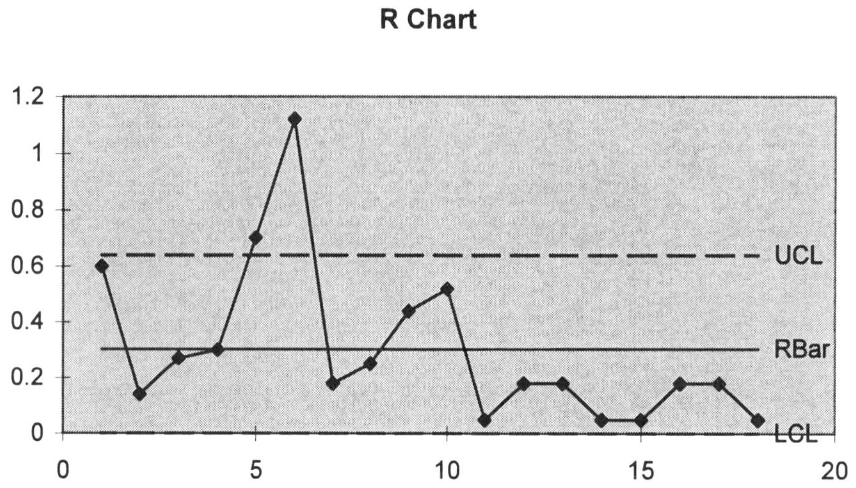


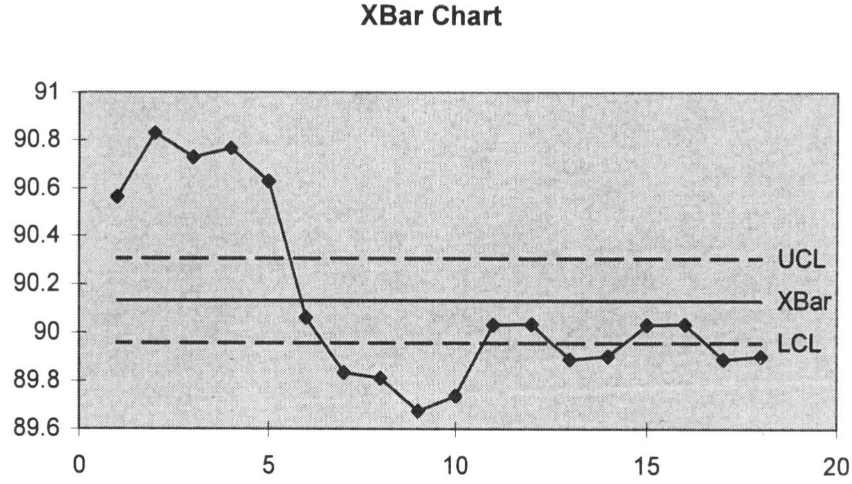


(b) The R-chart is out-of-control because the 5th and 6th data points fall above the upper control limit. There is also a downward trend in the right tail of the R-chart, which signifies that special causes of variation must be identified and corrected. Even though the X-bar chart also appears to be out-of-control because a majority of the data point fall above or below the control limit, any interpretation will be misleading because the R-chart has indicated the presence of out-of-control conditions. There is also a downward trend in the control chart. Special causes of variation should be investigated and eliminated.

14.20 Find the reasons for the special causes and take corrective action to prevent their occurrence in the future or exploit them if they improve the process.

14.22 Attribute control charts are used for categorical data such as the proportion of nonconformances. Variables control charts are used for numerical variables and are based on statistics such as the mean and standard deviation.

14.24 From the red bead experiment you learned that variation is an inherent part of any process, that workers work within a system over which they have little control, that it is the system that primarily determines their performance, and that only management can change the system.

14.26 (a)

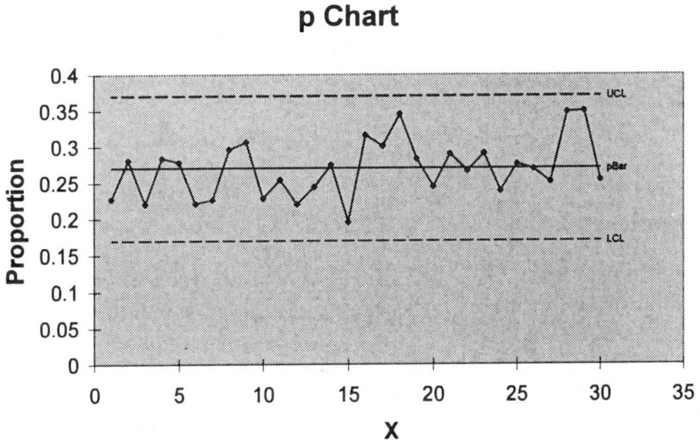


(b) Yes, RudyBird's market share is in control before the start of the in-store promotion since all sample proportions fall within the control limits.

(c)

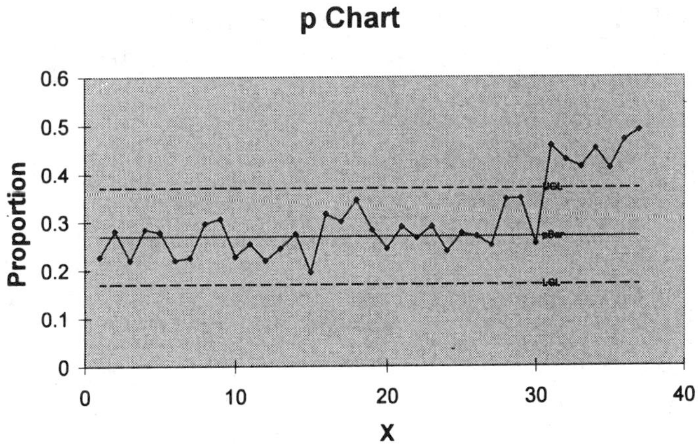


After including the data for days 31-37, there is an apparent upward trend in the p chart during the promotion period and all the market share proportions in that period are above the upper control limit. The process became out-of-control. This assignable-cause variation can be attributed to the in-store promotion. The promotion was successful in increasing the market share of RudyBird.

14.28 (a)

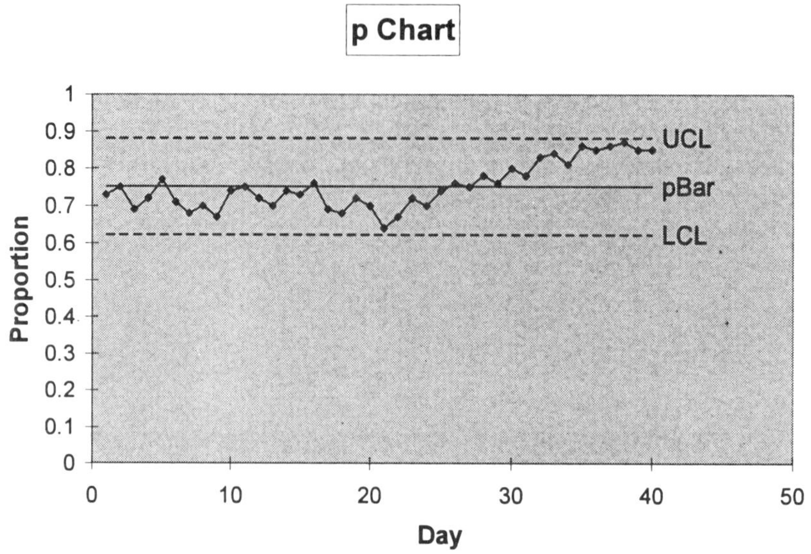


$\bar{p} = 0.75175$, $LCL = 0.62215$, $UCL = 0.88135$. Although none of the points are outside either the $LCL$ or $UCL$, there is a clear pattern over time with lower values occurring in the first half of the sequence and higher values occurring toward the end of the sequence.

(b) This would explain the pattern in the results over time.

(c) The control chart would have been developed using the first 20 days and then, using those limits, the additional proportion could have been plotted.

14.30 (a) $\bar{p} = 0.1198$, $LCL = 0.0205$, $UCL = 0.2191$.

(b) The process is out of statistical control. The proportion of trades that are undesirable is below the $LCL$ on Day 24 and are above the $UCL$ on Day 4.

(c) Special causes of variation should be investigated and eliminated. Next, process knowledge should be improved to decrease the proportion of trades that are undesirable.